# SECRETLY WILD
## BOOK SEVEN OF THE ALASKA OFF GRID SURVIVAL SERIES

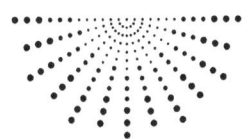

## MILES MARTIN

**Secretly Wild**
*By Miles Martin*

Book Seven of The Alaska Off Grid Survival Series
©2021 Miles Martin
Artwork, Photos, Original Poetry ©2021 by Miles Martin - All rights reserved

This Book may not be re-sold or given away to others. All rights reserved, including the rights to reproduce this Book.

No part of this text may be reproduced, transmitted, downloaded, scanned, or copied in any form or means, whether electronic or mechanical, without the express written permission of the publisher.

Any distribution of this Book without the permission of the publisher is illegal and punishable by law. Please purchase only authorized editions of this book and do not take part in or encourage piracy of copyrighted materials.

Published by:
Alaska Dreams Publishing
www.alaskadp.com
2nd ADP Edition December 2021
PRINT PAPERBACK ISBN: 978-1-956303-10-0
PRINT HARDCOVER ISBN: 978-1-956303-11-7
*This book was previously published by Miles of Alaska*

Visit www.milesofalaska.com to find a bio of Miles, additional photos, stories, how-to videos, handmade artwork, and raw materials for sale.

My Einstein look. You see, I am so brainy there is not enough room so my hair gets pushed out.

# CONTENTS

| | |
|---|---|
| *Preface* | 7 |
| *Introduction* | 9 |
| Chapter 1 | 13 |
| *Trip to prison, State general population, Almost die, Blood everywhere* | |
| Chapter 2 | 41 |
| *Federal prison, Prisoner stories, Horticulture class* | |
| Chapter 3 | 71 |
| *Reading old classic book, Doing ok, Halfway through my time* | |
| Chapter 4 | 102 |
| *Green hotdogs, Christmas in prison, Corruption* | |
| Chapter 5 | 131 |
| *Write son, Spaceship planned to mars, Out of prison* | |
| Chapter 6 | 162 |
| *Tucson trip Mom, Social Security, Computer tapped, My books on Amazon* | |
| Chapter 7 | 192 |
| *Two die in jail, River trip, Subsistence in the news* | |
| Photo Section | 225 |
| Chapter 8 | 246 |
| *A partner not working out, Move a shed* | |
| Chapter 9 | 281 |
| *Authentic Indian Art, True public sentiment, Probation issues, Reality TV is interested* | |
| Chapter 10 | 308 |
| *Teasing Miles, they understand teasing!* | |
| Chapter 11 | 341 |
| *Fishing waste, Land dispute, Government issues* | |
| Chapter 12 | 375 |
| *City money, Politics, Shady dealings* | |
| Chapter 13 | 397 |
| *River trip mammoth tusks, Greenpeace issues, Corruption* | |
| *About The Alaska Off Grid Survival Series* | 429 |
| *Magazine and News Stories* | 432 |
| *Other Titles Available From Alaska Dreams Publishing* | 434 |
| *Notes* | 435 |

# PREFACE

I color outside the lines. *Is that a good way to put it?* I started out at twenty-two going out into the wilds of Alaska to be alone and free as a Mountain man- trapper. The Viet Nam War had something to do with that. My first years and couple of books had to do with dealing with bears, and other high adventure in the wilds. While struggling to be a hero, on the cutting edge of new discoveries, I feel more like a square peg in a round world. Many of my childhood goals/dreams, alter as I mature, and get older. I can't forget, society admires me, put me in a four full pages of the New York Times! I was featured in GEO in Europe, been in Alaska magazine five times, and on the cover of more than one magazine. I'm apparently very good at what I do. But what exactly does that mean? Good at what? Especially as I enter book seven, Secretly Wild, on my way to prison as a felon.

My ongoing story should be of interest to those who think of homesteading, being off the grid, believe in freedom, self-sufficiency and high adventure. I live the reality of those dreams.

Thanks to my wife Iris for helping with editing, and being part of the story!

"Miles! I didn't know you were married!" Yes. Well, I suppose it depends on who is asking. We have been together…

"How long has it been now, Honey?" Five to six years. "You know how I am with numbers!" More important is the relationship, not the piece of paper. Anyhow, *it takes me five years to remember your name, ten to figure we might be friends. Twenty years and I guess we know each other and can talk about trust.* Yes, I have a dozen people I have known over twenty years and trust. There are 100,000 others who know me by name. I nod and smile.

## PREFACE

"Miles, that was Sam from the fair, who collects your knives." Iris reminds me who just waved and said hi. *Ah yes.* Sometimes after I begin chatting, the blanks get filled in. Data starts loading.

# INTRODUCTION

It is not absolutely necessary you read the previous six books in this series. However, reading this book as an introduction is like watching the next to the last episode of a good TV series as a first. There is an ongoing theme that grows throughout the series, showing how I got here from there. (You can find a summary of all the books in the back.)

This book is the 7$^{th}$ in the series. I began book one in 1972 at twenty-one years, beginning my 'life of survival' series. My first book, 'Going Wild,' is about wild adventures in the Alaskan wilderness. I almost die several times. Part of the definition of 'romantic' is lack of understanding, not having all the facts. Reality and time change romance. As we follow my story, I get sled dogs, cut trapline, and make a living trapping for a lot of years. I build a houseboat to live on, even in winter. There are a lot of adventures on the river acquiring a total of four homesteads. I'm not only off the grid, but off the map. No ID, job, address, or bank account. As time passes my dreams and goals adjust to new information, changing laws, and environment.

Running parallel, and on a crash course with my freedom, are gas/oil explorations in my area, gun rights, native land issues, Federal Government takeover of previous state jurisdiction, subsistence life definition changes, economic and social changes. Kennedy, who was president when I began my dream, was about physical fitness as a requirement and priority in school. Daniel Boone was a weekly TV show. Jeremiah Johnson was a number one movie.

Reality is, the real Jeremiah Johnson was nicknamed Liver Eating Johnson. He

## INTRODUCTION

killed Indians for fun and ate their liver. Life alone in the wilds tends to make people a little quirky.

I quote the news media often. Partly I am in a routine with Iris. We are reading the newspaper each morning. I selectively quote articles that are bias to my views. Not because I believe the news, and think this is the only truth. But because someone else besides me thinks of the same thing, and believes others want to hear it. I am partly forced, partly prefer to think I choose, to move to the village of Nenana, Alaska, where I give up trapping in favor of being an artist, writer, and seller of raw craft materials off the land. I end up with a web store, very successful, selling teeth, and claws. I am selling internationally, grossing an amount I prefer not to talk about. In the top five in search engines. Of interest because I begin with no money, education or connections. I started with $100 investment. *You too could follow your dream!* High profile gets me on the radar screen.

"The nail that sticks up gets hammered." I'm arrested for selling animal parts. In this book I am a convicted felon headed off to prison. I explain to my customers on my web site, "Imagine the problems Tarzan would have, trading his leopard skin loin cloth for pizza." I'm off to be punished, that society can be made safer with people like me locked up.

I keep a diary and record prison life. I assume my diary will be a record of how to be a better person. I discover even the prison cannot operate legally and stay in business. The stated goal is to re-introduce me into society as rehabilitated. I cannot vote, own a gun, or make over $500 without explaining myself. I've been castrated. Is society safer now? Paperwork stated, "In order to send a message to others!" What will that message be? The expected and stated message is doom and gloom, the war on crime continues, specific minority groups and legal activities are considered criminal. I'm determined not to spread that message.

A story of survival and hope continues. Not as openly. I do seem to have answers others around me are looking for, but cannot find. Even as a felon, I have no particular money problems, am happy, have choices, am respected, lots of free time, and have everything I want and need. Well, if not, try to accept how things are, look at the bright side. I focus on the pony, more than the piles of do-do and flies. That might be of interest to those who struggle with making ends meet, or those just interested in choices others have made and how that looks. We can better understand ourselves observing others. It's not necessarily easy. Much has to do with what we do with what has been handed to us.

# INTRODUCTION

Finding mammoth tusks is still part of my life.

# CHAPTER ONE

## TRIP TO PRISON, STATE GENERAL POPULATION, ALMOST DIE, BLOOD EVERYWHERE

"Miles, I looked up the times Alaska Air leaves Fairbanks. It looks like you leave for prison later this afternoon, at three, and should be there sometime tonight." Iris likes to look things up on the computer, so has information for me. She looked up the prison, 'Hotel Fed,' and showed me pictures. There is a farm, spacious grounds, with a glowing description of life for prisoners.

"Miles, each prisoner gets their own room. Only a few might have to share sometimes." *Because this is minimum security?* There is a library, educational courses offered, with food grown organically right off the farm - prisoners work at! We think I might even get lucky and be able to have a laptop computer if I am not on line! ☺ :) Why not! Work on my book! It may not be so hard to do the six months' time I got. I kind of believe all this, or want to, because educated people I know complain how well prisoners have it. How we need to change the system, and actually punish criminals!

"Prisoners get out of prison with a free education and degrees! Geez!" I agree this is wrong, to reward prisoners! I am personally disgusted with how much money gets spent on prisoners! For all the prisoners talk, they most likely deserve what they got. If it was not this crime, it would be some other deed they deserve to be hung for! Felons are bad people, and good riddance to them! Since I am headed for prison, maybe I can grin! *Your tax dollars at work! I can return a new man! Show me what a legal person looks like!* I'm nervous, but I trust the system. It is hard not to, because think of what the implications are if my government cannot be trusted! We had a disagreement. I am sad my side was never heard. I think I would have won.

But I understand. No one is going to fork over a million dollars to prove a mistake was made. I was out there at the legal edge. *I should have been more careful. Less open. Kept my mouth shut. I said things that made Fish and Wildlife angry. Not very bright of me.*

Iris drives me to the courthouse where I am to report for incarceration in the minimum security prison. This is a fifty mile drive from the village of Nenana, population 300. The two lane road is one of only two roads connecting the biggest cities—Fairbanks and Anchorage—a six hour drive apart. We think Fairbanks is big at 70,000 people. It is the hub for the whole interior of the state, serving a hundred smaller villages like Nenana. The rolling hills are beautiful. Tourists stop to take pictures of the vast open wilderness seen from the road pull outs. No roads, nothing human for as far as the eye can see. At least fifty miles. I comment, "It was nice of the judge to give me a couple of months to get the garden planted. You have the garden to eat from while I am gone." I feel lucky as well, my bank account was not shut down, and my transportation was not confiscated. The argument could be made, the money was illegally obtained and the transportation moved illegal items.

"Therefore, it belongs to us." That is how the law reads.

It is hard to know what to expect! Neither Iris or I know much about crime, criminals, the justice system. We do not know any criminals, have never been to jail, had a relative, friend, or acquaintance who was in jail or talked about it. We hear rumors, read articles, and get information in tidbits from others who know as little as we do. Jail is for 'them.' Bad people.

Or this is an unmentionable subject, like farting. We are of the protected, privileged race and class. We assume the internet information is accurate. *How can it not be, the pictures are there to see?* I only answer my unconscious with a non-committal, "Hmmm." This is 2013. I just filed for my first Social Security check, but am told I cannot collect it as a prisoner. I'm able to run my web business, as long as I am not selling animal parts. No more antlers, teeth, claws, bones, furs, which were all an important part of my business over the past forty years.

Iris does not know how to use the computer much beyond looking up things that interest her. She will not be able to work my web site. She can answer emails. If items sell, she has no way to remove them from the web site. She will do the best she can. I'll be in federal prison for six months. Minimum security, so supposedly not with the hardened psychopaths. Blue collar people, corporate crimes, tax frauds and such. A lot races through my mind of course.

We arrive at the courthouse, and make it through security. I am checked in. I pay the $7,000 fine with cash. *Is this a good idea? Does this make it look like I am more flush with money than looks good?* Iris assures me no one here cares. Just paying the fine, it's routine. This is good, to just get the fine out of the way while I can do so. *The Feds kept asking whenever they could slip it in, how much cash I have on hand. They had access to my bank account, Pay Pal, any financial records. But not my cash.* Yes, I follow my unconscious drift of this conversation. If I answer and lie, that becomes a crime. I'm not convinced I have to answer to, "We just need some basic information for our records, name please? Address?" Until, "Cash on hand?" *Yeah right!* I reply, "I'd need legal advice before I answered this question." True, because I do not know how 'cash' is defined. Does it involve any trade goods, credit owed me, bonds, gold, gemstones? I only answer what they already know or can easily find out. So here we are, at the pearly gate, and no one knows how much cash I have. Folks make fun of me for not trusting banks. *Am I the only one who looks at the banking system and says 'Ponzi scheme?'* I'm brought to reality with handcuffs coming out.

This was not expected. I'm minimum security, showed up on my own and all that. Iris is pretty upset seeing me carted off in cuffs. This is the last I see of her for a while. I say to the escorts, "So it looks like I'll be in Washington by tonight?" They both laugh harshly, "Yeah, sure!" I assume I am being escorted to the airport. Information is not forthcoming. I assume from the behavior, I'm a prisoner now. I deserve nothing. I'm ignored like I am not here. I am escorted to the state prison, the general population. I'm simply puzzled. *This is a federal issue. Why am I in a state facility? It has been my understanding the State and the Feds hate each other, and do not work together.* I learn fast, prisoners who ask questions do not do well. Shut up, do what you're told, keep your eyes down. I have not lived a life that required these skills. I've been King of the forest. I've never lowered my eyes, bowed to, nor feared anyone, or anything, not even God.

I'm handed my prison clothes and shoved in a room to change. There is blood on the walls, the door knob, the floor. After getting dressed I am shoved in a cell alone. There is blood here as well. On the walls, the floor, sink, and the door knob. The single steel sleeping cot has a blanket, no mattress. There is a water leak from the ceiling, dripping on the bed, so it would not be possible to sleep. I hear someone far off screaming, beating their head hard against the bars in the hope of ending the pain and terror. *That must be where all the blood comes from I'm seeing.* The screams, the single light bulb, small room, blood, wet bed, peeling paint, isolation, all have a psychological effect. I assume, designed to. Because I understand the whole purpose is to reduce me to putty and a blubbering idiot, I remain in control. A big part of control is knowledge. I feel sorry for the others not as strong as I am.

The routine is loose. I can see how it would be easy to forget what cell you put someone in and 'whoops!' No knowledge until the smell of a rotting dead body drew attention a month from now. Guessing it happens. Even, often. This is not in the least what I read about or pictured. I understand better why no one talks about it. *Obviously, I'm missing my flight to Washington.* The next day I am moved again. I am in general population. I begin a quiet, polite, "Excuse me, Sir, could you tell me..." and this is as far as I get. A loud laugh and holler.

"Hey! We have a prisoner who wants to know something!" Everyone, including prisoners, laugh heartily. "You know what happens to prisoners who have questions?" Guards gather around. I try to lighten up the situation.

"Do I get three guesses?" They laugh and walk away. Whatever it is that happens, I got out of it - *No more questions, just observe and try to learn.*

"I need my pills. I'm on blood pressure and diabetic medication. I was told that would get taken care of." The guard is not interested, even snorts with a, 'what planet are you from' tone. There is a nurse who is supposed to be available. She is amazingly overworked, not available. Bummer, but meanwhile I'm dizzy, blood pressure going out of sight, and this prison food is not exactly good for diabetics.

"Without my meds I could die."

Another snort, and, "Well don't do the fish flop on my watch!" The guard walks away. Another prisoner tells me how it works. You have to put in a request and fill out a form. This might take a couple days or more, if I live that long.

THREE DAYS later I see the nurse and explain. She is a little nervous and upset. I suspect not for the sake of my health, but the liability issue if I were to die and there was an inquiry as to why.

"Well, I was not told!"

"I had the meds I needed with me when I arrived. They were confiscated. I was told not to worry about it, you'd take care of me."

"Well, can you call someone, and have them bring the right meds to the prison?" I'm exasperated. We were already here with my meds! My wife is in Nenana, a long ways away. She may not have the meds, because she handed them all to me. The ones that got confiscated.

"She could maybe fill my prescription at the VA hospital."

"We can come up with something and work out the dosage." So after this, part of my prison routine is to report each morning to stand in the medical line for my pills. This might take an hour. But what else do I have to do. Out in the real world I have a saying, "The line forms behind me!" I do not stand in lines. I chose a place and a lifestyle to ensure there would be no lines. It was a lot to go through to get what I wanted. Now look, nothing but lines! I smile. It's a test, I zone out. My unconscious and I are buddies, so know how to do stuff like that. Poof! Time disappears. It never happened. It's an Einstein thing, making mass disappear. The mind is a wonderful thing. I do not need drugs to go on a trip.

Days go by. *When am I going into the minimum security prison?* Other prisoners are waiting as well. Talk is, sometimes if the sentence is short, like six months, a prisoner will spend that whole time here. It saves money. Who would know, and who would care? The only information that reaches the outside world is issued by the system, not the prisoners. Phone calls are monitored, mail is monitored. After a week, Iris gets word I'm still in Fairbanks. She assumed I have been a week in Washington. This is one reason I'd rather not look things up ahead of time, and outguess what is going on. I'd rather take it as it is dished out. I have access to a prison phone for the first time.

"So, I can come visit on visiting days? When are you going to the minimum security prison?"

"I have no idea. Maybe never, we are not told much. That's part of the punishment."

Iris tells me our friend Foil, who came to Alaska to visit, has helped by cutting firewood for her.

"Yea, I think he had a good time at the homestead!" I had dropped him off to stay a month at my remote cabin, for free, just help with boat gas cost. Iris had fed him, taken him the hundred miles round trip to town when he needed to go. Cutting wood for her is thoughtful. She now feels more secure going into winter alone without me. We figure out how to use the prison phone, which requires passwords, codes, and a method to be followed. I'm not good with numbers and directions. I miss our talks. I let her know, "Iris, I am keeping notes for my book. I have trouble getting paper and pencil. I have to write on the back of forms we fill out that are request sheets. Pencils are considered weapons and hard to get. I'm sure this is all hard to comprehend. All prisoners I talk to have the same issues with relatives and calls outside the prison. How do we answer, "So how are you doing?" Honestly explaining gets silence. On the back of a 'request for interview' form I begin my diary for day one.[1]

A US MARSHAL brings me to state prison. I am told all I need is my ID. I had brought my meds, name of my meds on separate sheet of paper, and reading glasses. I was told I'd be leaving for Washington tonight. I wonder how I am going to get my evening blood pressure meds.

I'm put in a cell. I am not told for how long. I measure it at 6 x 6 feet. Next day I am moved to a dorm type room in general prison population. About twelve of us to a room. I gather bits of information while listening to other prisoners.

I overhear on a phone, "Shut up, bitch, while I talk!" Pause, while there is a short reply followed by, "Well he pulled the gun on me, so I just took it and shot him." Another pause. "I know I have a temper, so be afraid, because I am going to get you and everyone else." Pause. "I already took care of that guy in the gym yesterday." This might be why he has cuts on him.

This is one of my twelve roommates. I'm in the phone line waiting for my turn. This can take hours.

Another guy is on the phone now talking drug deals. Three others are discussing the advantage of the latest drugs, their cost, and profit margins. A note over the phone says, "Your calls may be monitored."

I am guessing by looking around, it is possible to disappear here and not have it ever reach the outside world. Few here know what is going on. Even among the officials. Staff appears to be overworked, under paid and not very bright. People being shuffled around, paperwork not following them, is the norm.

Day three at 6:00 am. Still without meds. Feel dizzy, forgetful. Prisoners come and go. This appears to be a temporary holding cell for those the prison does not know what to do with yet. One roommate arrives with gang tattoos on his knuckles. Been in prison seventeen years. Tells me of all the people he has killed. It is difficult to know if he did this, or is bragging, making it up, or hallucinating. Many prisoners I meet seem to me to be more crazy than criminal. They need medical help, or belong in a nut house. It seems pointless to punish people who are insane. There is no library, no gym, no mail. I do spot a gym being used to house the overcrowding, with rows of cots and bodies. A hundred prisoners in one room. Nowhere else to put them. One open toilet.

8:00 am is med call.

"And you are?" I am not in any records. No one knows I am here, according to records. No record of being checked in. No record of having asked for my medication. All new staff, starting over fresh.

"Hello, I am now day three without my blood pressure medication. Do you think we could possibly get that for me?"

"It might be a week. We are pretty backlogged."

"I might be dead by then."

"That's possible. Next!"

I smile. When I am dead, they will know who I am. I am not afraid to die. Dying is the easy part, staying alive is the challenge.

---

THERE IS SOME GOOD NEWS. I remember one of the guards who asked randomly if there is anyone who wants a book to read! Few answer up. I am eager to have something to read, so speak up. A kind looking elderly bent over black man pushing a cart comes to my cell of twelve inmates.

"Whatcho like ter read?"

I'm in the mood for just a fast read, so say, "Louis L'Amour would do. I know he wrote a lot of western books, so maybe you can find one?" The old man tips his ball cap with a grin. He comes across as the only sane and human here. Everyone else, "Look at me, and be afraid!" The guard comes back with two books. One is called 'Silka.' Also, paper and pencil are handed to me.

It appears to me, we are not all equal here. Those who want to do their time and get out, get along, seem sane, can receive help. I'm guessing half the prisoners in here have a drug problem, screaming, "I need my meds, I'm dying!" Withdrawal and such. Me and about 500 others here feel like they will die without their meds. My father died because he did not take the same medication I need. I'm not sure how long it takes to die. I'm not sure what affect the stress of high blood pressure has, and what damage is being done by high blood sugar off the charts.[2] Yet, I see for myself, half these inmates may also die without their drugs, and likewise had relatives die of the same thing. So what? I do understand this is a world no one cares. Life is not worth much here. Society looks the other way, abandons prisoners. In truth if we die, it is good riddance and saves the tax payers. The goal is to get rid of us. I understand, because it is how I felt about felons. I'm luckier than most.

As one prisoner joked, "The rules for dog kennels is stricter." I am moved in the middle of the night without explanation. This is an improvement.

There are two of us to a small room. Not so bad. My Bunkie is in for beating on his girlfriend. She is posting bail. He is out in a day or two. He was drunk, he is calm and polite when sober, so we get along. Food trays are pushed in through a slot in the bars. Sort of slop, but there are desired items prisoners save, and sell, or trade to others. A single cookie can get you ahead in the phone line, or maybe a book to read. Saved Oreo cookies are treated as money.

The cell is nice enough. Eight by ten. Two cots, a small ledge, two chairs, a sink, an open toilet. Spotless and clean. Room to stand up and turn around if your Bunkie stays in his cot. I've been in smaller places on the trapline in the wilds. There are time periods each day when we are allowed out of the cells. There is a community TV room, a hall with phones. Many prisoners do an exercise routine in the hall, or walk up and down like it's a track. My Bunkie and I get along. I am expected to leave as early as I can, to give him time for his toilet routine. I can wait. When he is done, he leaves and I get my turn. We can step out of the cell into the hall during certain times. Many prisoners get along with no one. We hear about it up and down the hall. All this is a little hard for me. I am in general, not a person of routine. I spent my life eating when hungry, sleeping when tired, whipping it out and peeing wherever I need to, behind a tree. I have never in my life owned or needed an alarm clock. I rarely have needed to know what time it is, even to the nearest week.

My observation is, there must be some effort made to pair people up who might be expected to get along. What is going on is not as random as I first thought. *It is in the prisons best interest to not have riots and major fights, deaths, etc.* "At least visible deaths with witnesses." To gain such knowledge, I think there are hidden cameras, microphones, informants. Believing this, I am carful what I say and how I act, believing there is zero privacy here. In the beginning, before I figured it out, the goings on here were more terrifying. Contraband is common, expected, tolerated. There are drugs, cigarettes, and a variety of forms of abuse and violence. I assumed at first, all random and out of control. I assumed any of us could wake up dead, *or is that, die waking up.* There is however a method to the madness, and a way to survive, for the swift and smart. *Repeat after me,* "We are not all equal here."

One big guy at the back of the phone line did not like being last. He walks to the front, takes the phone, wraps the cord around the talkers neck, and begins strangling him. Everyone else quickly goes back to their cell to stay out of this. Guards come. All they do is say in a kind voice, "Now what did we tell you about this. That is not nice! Let him go." That's it. So it is important to know who the psychopaths in the group are. This is not foreign to me. In the wilds is this same personality type. Those sociopaths who go to the wilds to escape, be alone, and try to stay out of trouble. Basically I take the policy to avoid everyone here, until proven they are sane, and can hold a conversation. I make a list of the good news to keep cheerful. In my diary:

There are no mosquitoes! I have a good cot by a window. I finally reach Iris by phone and all is well on the home front. In the middle of writing, medical call.

My blood pressure is taken. 130 /85, better than usual. No meds. Blood sugar seems sort of ok. Odd. Well there is little stress here of the kind I have in the outside world of having to make a living, pay bills, deal with this and that. The food is not great here, but it is simple, and not much. Stay away from sugar and starch, and I'm ok. Most prisoners want the cookie and the noodles. I can easily trade for any salads, vegetables we happen to get. I'm losing weight. This always helps my kind of health issues. Yet, a prisoner says, "Yeah, I knew a guy here who was diabetic. Not taken care of, lost his leg." Is this true? There is a great deal of misinformation and negative news passed around. I write in pencil on a paper towel:

I'm transferred to B wing. Not looking good. I measure six by six room. Open toilet, no TV access, no books. Possibly this is 'just before getting sent out of state.'

---

No. I am not getting transferred. I write in my diary,

Saturday. First time in forty years I am not setting up at the fair starting today. It's early August. Iris visits. She spends half a day waiting, to see me for half an hour. I fill her in on the 'no meds' issue. Doctor here says the VA will not cover meds, and so I am being billed for my medication. There will be no diabetic coverage because I am diagnosed 'pre diabetic,' meaning in and out, not really a problem. Tracking my blood sugar was not authorized. It may not be life threatening. If it becomes life threatening something will be done. There is no money for prevention. So if my leg needs to be amputated, that will be covered. I'm wondering if I can make it six months. I feel for those stuck in prison for years.

Sunday: Worried somewhat about my diabetes. My feet look bad. I can't feel them.

I observe there are female guards checking on us. In the lavatory, showers, no privacy. I'm guessing the male guards do not have the same freedoms in the woman's dorm. I conclude this has to do with intimidation, punishment, humiliation. Because I understand, I do not let it bother me. A lot of prison time is spent reviewing my case in my head. Going over my arguments. But what good is that now at this point? It's done and over, but not in my head. Trauma can be like that I'm told.

Thursday: call Iris. She tells me everyone we know at the fair says hi, wishes me well. One of the clerks in prison knows me. She has one of my claw jewelry pieces I am in prison for selling. I sold it to her a few years ago at the fair. She reminds me.

A new guy named, 'Mexico' tells us his monitor bracelets came off, loose screw. "I called immediately!" So why is he back in jail he wonders? No one believes a monitor screw mysteriously came loose, and he called anyone about it.

I reply, "Obviously none of us belong here right? It's all some great misunderstanding!" We all laugh.

Saturday: I am groggy, dizzy after progressively feeling worse. Falling asleep on my feet, can't speak. I can overhear two people talking. A guard and a nurse. It's determined I am not about to die in the next hour. Their shift ends in an hour. I'm somewhat scared of being put on insulin and not being able to ever get off it. I'd rather tough it out. I assume, like them, I am not dying. I hear, "Yup, this food is terrible for diabetics!"

The tone is the same as two children observing a fly spinning on its back after being sprayed with poison. It may live, it may not. Let's watch and see, and place bets. No, why bother, and walk away.

No, they do not have $50, or time for pills and prevention. I'm not worth that much. There will be thousands of dollars available if my feet need amputating, or I need a new kidney. I assume because someone gets billed and makes money. *No, my guess is I will make it. But what irreparable damage is being done? I have taken good health for granted most of my life. Lack of control over my life in general depresses me. My very life depends on the monsters in charge here.*

I remind myself many others have it worse than I do. Like I have someone to write to. Many inmates have no one who would read their letters, or write them.

"Anyhow, I never learned to write."

"I could write something for you if you like." I help an inmate write his mother.

Another inmate stops by and overhears the dictation. I help two other guys write letters. They want to trade me cookies.

"Nothing is for free man, take the cookies."

"Naw. Diabetic, can't have sweets. What else are we all going to do here anyhow, but help each other out, huh? Not like I have an appointment anyplace!" We all laugh.

I get in trouble over writing letters on the back of forms. For a while I have nothing to write on.

"Commissary day is coming up, Dude!"

I heard about this, but missed the last one, as I had not been here long enough. I also have to set up an account. I was told I would not be here long enough to bother. Since I do not believe much of what I am told anymore, I begin the process of setting up an account. I think I am going to be here six months. This requires someone outside creating an on line account to deposit money for me to draw from. No money, no outside contacts, no get nothing. Some guys here have to beg for toothpaste. Everything here is generic. It is not allowed for anyone to have much that is different from what everyone else has. There is no such thing as picking which brand of anything you like. We all have the same exact prison issued tooth brush, clothes, and blankets. Pillows are not allowed. I suspect kickbacks are involved with suppliers because some brands of items are expensive and low quality.

> Hey Iris!
>
> Got your card! Thanks! I have robins outside my window to watch. A lot like watching our feeder at home. Glad you solved the mouse problem! Hopefully this is the worse problem you come up against!

Tuesday: So only three sheets of paper to an envelope and nothing but a letter is allowed huh?

I'm having trouble with the rules. My previous life had few rules. I just got my commissary stuff. Pens, paper, tea, foot powder, jolly ranchers, aspirin, and used up my weekly allowed $24. I was able to trade for stamps. I will have to set letters aside until I can get envelopes. I'm just getting the hang of the routine, and how to survive well here. I'm headed into week three, wondering why I am in a state general population cage, when I was sentenced to a federal minimum security farm.

On a Tuesday I am awakened at 6:00 am before breakfast, "Get your gear and come with me!" I assume I am headed out, but could be just going to another cell, or got in trouble, and am headed for solitary confinement. *For conspiring to teach other prisoners how to write.* I have less than a minute to gather everything I have, and follow. All my goods need to be wrapped up in a blanket. I shuffle along in my orange prison uniform. No one looks up, this is a common occurrence. All day long people coming, going, being transferred, and suddenly, you come back from the movie room and your Bunkie is gone, replaced by someone else. I am excited, and assume I am headed for Hotel Fed. Talking to others is not encouraged, so there are no goodbyes, certainly no one to miss. I was supposed to call Iris today. She will not know what is going on.

---

I AM DROPPED off at the state institution in Anchorage after a long bus ride. No explanation. This facility is ten times worse than Fairbanks. Filthy cells, screaming certified lunatics threatening everyone. Blood on the walls, horrible food I refuse to eat. *And I've eaten some amazingly nasty foods in my life on the trapline!* I am in a six by eight cell with two others. One is a young black kid with wide open eyes, scared all the time. He cannot finish a sentence. It is hard to understand him.

"I like peace. But if I had a gun I'd kill everyone. I do not like arguments. No arguments. No sharp. You sharp. No sharp!" He is addressing the third guy, a Native American. When lights go out, the black kid begins beating his fist on the metal cot so hard the ring can be heard throughout the entire prison.

"Everything is fine!" he yells over and over. No one responds, no one tries to quiet him, no guards arrive. It is hard to sleep. I'm sure he is capable of killing the Native and I as we sleep. He's obviously insanely afraid of the dark. Foaming at the mouth, eyes roll to the back of his head terrified. It's not a matter if he is going to kill someone, but when. When he does, the world will be shocked and indignant. If the outside world ever finds out, he is just one of many. As much as a quarter of the population is on the same level.[3]

It is laundry day. Our entire wing of eighty inmates march to the gym, a single open room. We are told to strip down naked. Our various clothes are dropped in different bins as we march around naked, dropping and picking up new items. About an hour later we are told to put our clean clothes on.

Two days later I am put in leg irons, locked to a gang-line of a dozen other inmates. We are shuffled to a plane. I do not know what day it is, or what time. The plane appears to be a small private plane. After hours of flying, we land in what appears to be Seattle, but the windows are blocked. We are hustled around fast, put inside a van with curtains down. I am in a holding cell only a few hours, when many more prisoners are added to the gang-line. One has to go to the bathroom.

We all have to get up and march over to the restroom. We are chained together with two feet between us. The door has to be left open due to our chains. Our hands are handcuffed behind us, so the prisoner has a hard time getting his pants undone and down. The scene is practically a horror story in itself. No one is going to pull his pants down or back up for him. He misses here and there. Now the whole place stinks. We are loaded, maybe back on the same plane. The guy's pants stay half down with poop dripping down his legs. No one is in a position to make fun of him. But for the grace of God, it could be any of us. None of us knows where we are going. The most hardened criminal cannot help but be affected. One is a young Alaska Native who obviously has never been on a plane in his life. It's freak out time. The fear is an odor in the air we all smell and respond to.

All day, more 'fly and stop,' and fly again. I have no idea where we are stopping, or why. On a bus someplace between flights, I get a glimpse of what looks like Reno, Nevada. I'm puzzled. *If I am destined for Washington, why am I in Reno, much further south.* Why wasn't I offloaded in Seattle? I realize I could be taken anyplace. Who would know, and what could I do about it?

The prison system could house us in cheaper quarters than what they are getting paid for. Pocket the difference in costs.

"Yea, we got him in Hotel Fed for $80,000 a year." While I am in the Arizona tent prison for $5,000 a year. This is what I'm thinking. It's Wednesday. In a quiet area, air conditioning, not bad. In a room with about 500 other inmates, but all quiet. Possibly I have arrived with a group of other non-violent prisoners. I do not know what State I am in. We are stacked four prisoners high, with enough room to walk around the bunks if we walk sideways. Zero personal possessions - not paper, pencil, glasses, reading book, medicine, nothing. It's illegal to hide anything under your mattress.

At 1:00 am I am awakened and told to follow. I am no longer in leg irons or handcuffs. I'm put on a bus with other prisoners. At 4:00 pm we are at Hotel Fed in Washington. Most of us have not eaten or been to the bathroom in over twelve hours. I am put in a room with others. One at a time we are processed in. It is 9:00 pm before I am processed in. I am too tired and worn out mentally to take much in. But this is a different place. The first things that hits me are *no bars, no chains, no visible armed guards.* The area is very spacious. There is not a lot of noise. The atmosphere visually, is much like a college campus. A green shirt and pants is the required clothing. This does not look like the loose fitting universal prison orange jump suits. There are no guards. Just various levels of staff to deal with.

It would be possible to simply walk away, or even call a cab. There is a public road through the middle, with no gates. Just put a thumb out and hitchhike. By law there are no secret cameras. It would be foolish to walk off. The prison has my ID, passport, money, credit cards. Without an elaborate plan, there is no way to travel, get a job, have money to do anything once out. I consider it one of the 'tests' to determine if we are material for inclusion into society, is to see if we can do as we are told, stay put, do not walk off. Those who try, are saying they cannot, will not, live by society's rules, and they may get transferred to a more appropriate tighter prison. It's a privilege to be here. Things can be much worse. [4]

"Miles, did you know you could have come here straight off and not done any time in the state prison if you had voluntarily paid your way here and checked yourself in?" I do observe people off and on getting out of a cab, and checking themselves in, from all over the country.

"No, I was never told of this option." Neither the judge or my lawyer asked if I could, or would show up on my own. It was assumed I think, I was too poor. I played the destitute card. "Please do not fine me much, Sir, I am a poor man and have no money." I never answered the question, how much cash I have. I never named an amount. 'Poor' is a relative term. *Compared to who?* I never got pinned down where I had to 'lie.' I showed an official reported income, an amount I pay in taxes. I do not observably show a life with a lot of class. Officials did not dig deep, observing the trappings of the poor all around me. In truth, I spent many years living on $2,000 a year. If I suddenly have $10,000 for the year, that's five times what I was once used to. From my viewpoint 'rich.'

There were no details of the business asked for.

"Everything I make goes back into the business," is correct. I'm all business. My business might require having a 100 grand in cash, conceivably more, much more, in order to purchase fossils. It's not my personal money, it belongs to the business called, 'Miles of Alaska.' No one asked how much my business had, or my partner Iris has. My business records were never found. Receipts were found. That's some unspeakable percent of my business. Bank statements were received with a warrant. I am appropriately, visibly disturbed. Banks do not define my wealth, not even my money.

I offer hefty discounts for cash in my business, that is not illegal. Even I do not know exact numbers, I'm not an accountant. I can honestly reply, "I do not know." I paid my $7,000 fine with cash, and it was chump change. It is not to my advantage to say that to the judge, my lawyer, or anyone. *Well we figured out my public defender is not on my side. We found out soon enough we are not looking for any facts or truths here.*

So 'dang,' I could have come straight here for a few hundred dollars. So thinking I'm pretty slick, is not always to my advantage. However, the state prison experience makes what I see here a vacation. Across the road far off is the prison's farm. There are vast country fields with geese right out my window that has no bars. I see apple orchards. The air is fresh country air. I can handle most any punishment if I can see grass, water, geese, and blue sky.

There are several wings to the prison. Wings are devoted to prisoners of different levels. The rules will vary slightly from wing to wing, as well as security level and certain freedoms. One wing is for prisoners qualifying for, and taking, specific college level classes. The rules here are less strict. I am in unit B, in the middle someplace. I find myself among what would pass as a typical group of citizens. Possibly a little more educated than normal. This is nonviolent crimes, often intellectual crimes. Heads of companies, banks, those who ran numbers scams of different kinds. I meet a lot of prisoners with drug related crimes at the higher up levels, where drugs is just business, run by those who know better than to take drugs, or directly get involved in violence. There are a high percentage of truly rich people here.

"Yeah, I was the fall guy for a big company that sold Monsanto grown corn for organic. I was the bookkeeper. Yes, billions of dollars were involved." Prisoners tell their stories. One of the first questions is, "So what did you do to get here?"

"I was the fall guy," is a typical reply. "The other guys did it, I took the fall." "I didn't do it." "I was framed." I get asked the same. I say, "Fish and Game, cute fuzzy creature crimes. Involving feathers, teeth, claws, ivory, stuff like that." Adding with a grin, "I was framed!" Everyone laughs good naturedly. I find out that out of 700 criminals here, I am the only wildlife offender. I also find out I am the only one who got only six months. As a result, many will never trust me.

"You had to have made a deal, were a snitch, no one gets six months." There had been another guy who got out, who got in trouble over a single eagle feather who got five years. That was only one offense. I had twenty-eight offenses! No way I was let go without turning snitch. I'm a plant here to turn people in! That is the word among some of the more hardened group. These do not hate me, just give me polite distance. Tell me nothing important.

Our wing is one big room, divided up with five feet tall cement dividers, all open facing the center, so no privacy. Each cube is eight x ten feet and holds six inmates. We each get a locker the size of a night stand, about half the size of a high school or gym locker. With a lock, so we can lock up our personal items. The guards have a common key in case they have reason to check your locker for contraband. Mostly, we do not have much thievery going on. I'd say less than out in the real world. Most of us are more high end criminals who know how to shuffle money around, not petty thieves. This living arrangement is not even close to what the web site describes. Where we each have our own private room. A few who earn it, get assigned a different wing where you might get a desk to work at, with only four people per cube. Prisoners tell me, the prison is operated illegally by housing more people in the building than the building is designed to hold. The prison lies about the living situation to the outside world. I shrug my shoulders. I am not surprised, and think prisoners are probably correct. But what are we going to do about it? We are not in a position to complain.

"If I were here for years I'd have a different outlook, I got six months. I'm going to do my time as easily as I can, get along, cooperate, do what I can to improve myself, get out, and forget I was ever here." I'm told from the beginning, "Be careful who you are seen with and who you decide to hang with. Take time to get to know people before you trust them or chose the group you want to be in." An inmate is assigned to me to help me understand the rules and take me under his wing until I understand what is going on. The way the rules work,

"If anyone does anything wrong in our wing we are all responsible. So if you screw up, we all pay. It is to our advantage to make sure you do not screw up." There are other rules that conflict with this. There is an unspoken rule to never snitch, not ever, not for any reason. If you know something, keep your mouth shut. We all cover for each other. The pressure to keep people straight is balanced with leaving those alone who decide to be crooked. Sooner or later they get caught without our help.

The guy I paired up with works in the library. I'll call him Book. Book is really tall, athletic, lifts weights. "I used to be overweight and in bad shape when I got here. I decided to improve my health while I am here."

We are encouraged to improve ourselves. We are stuck here, can do with our time what we wish - up to a point. So why not do positive things we never had time for when we were responsible for ourselves and had to make a living outside.

I am told I will have an orientation class within three days of arriving. Everyone laughs. Lucky if it is within the first month! Maybe never! The prison is overbooked, under staffed, underfunded, under paid. We have to understand.

"Understand what, Book?" He looks puzzled, so I add, "Understand the prison has to break the law because they do not have the money to be legal?"

"Excuse me, but isn't that why we are all here?"

I am smiling and plan to do what I'm told, do my time, and not make problems. I just want Book to know I am not stupid. I get it, I know how it works. Book agrees, and, like me, smiles and nods like this is cool. A blank book gets passed around to new people arriving, and people leaving. Those arriving read what was written. Those leaving write in it. Advice, a few words on what prisoners learned here. Personal stories to inspire and help others make it. One trusted prisoner holds on to it for all of us. The notebook gets passed to a trusted inmate when he gets out. The prison system does not know about it and is not part of this. I think the prison knows, but looks the other way as seeing something positive. The law says we are not supposed to conspire, compare notes, keep private writings that have to do with the prison. Anything that might inspire a riot or cause a group effort to thwart the system. I get handed this notebook.

"Can I keep this for a while, Book? I want to copy some of it down for my book." Word has gotten around I am a writer and keeping notes. I am concerned the prison would not approve! So I make sure to spread the word, my purpose is not to get anyone into trouble. I will change all the names, even the prison location. Whoever is the ears among us for the officials, can pass that along. A lot of prisoners talk about what they do, what they are, and take notes, write things down. Tell other prisoners what they plan to do. There is an amazing amount of feather fluffing, fish stories, concerning their lives. I do not necessarily wish to be taken seriously. I play it down, talk like I do not know what I am doing. I do not want my notes confiscated. Or worse, end up in the hole, solitary confinement for breaking the rules. My thinking is, if the prison is proud of its work, and on the up and up, what is the problem with telling of it? If the prison has a problem with the story of what is going on getting out, then this indicates a serious problem and cover up within the system. I'm not looking for a story, I am just the record keeper. *If it is a good story or bad one is up to you.*

The prison book has an introduction by prisoner Ned 10714-111: You have spent some time here at Hotel Fed. You are about to leave. When you leave, people are going to ask about your experience.

It goes on a little about writing something down to pass on to others arriving. It is followed by names and a few lines written by those now out.

> Wilkinson: "Just because someone is unhappy with their situation and project ill will, it is not healthy to respond to the negativity and act on it."
>
> Callen: "Don't get caught!"
>
> Bruce: Librarian and Attorney; "Every story is real, and worthy of a book, but, alas, how few of us actually write them."
>
> Job: What I have learned here is to live with people with different points of view. The only problem I encountered was myself, accepting myself. This place has been heaven for me.

Someone wrote "rat snitch bitch," next to his name. He wrote 25 points and opinions numbered.

> Charlie: "#1 How critical everyone is of everyone else. #2 How many people take satisfaction in the suffering of others. #3 How immature grown men can be. #4 How many self absorbed narcissistic and sociopathic people there are here. #5 Just how broken I was by watching the behavior of others."

I record dozens of comments, copied by hand with pencil on my commissary issued note pad. I do not know what I might ever do with these notes, how much I might use. I am simply taking notes. It appears some people have good experiences, and some not. Some learned something good and others not. It's an interesting read. Good to see when arriving because I ask myself, *So what kind of experience do I wish to leave with? What is possible? What is it I might write as a contribution when it is my time to leave?*

Book is introducing me to the rules. There are no bars, but there are constraints. The wing door is locked at 10:00 pm. You will be inside! The doors open at 6:00 am, do not leave until then! There are various times of the day when prisoner count is taken.

"Four times a day you must be counted." He adds, "If you are not counted you are missing, an escapee." Not good. So we can be counted in a classroom if we are taking a class, or on one of the many jobs we might get, or counted in the dorm. We are not allowed to be in bed during the day unless we are sick. This is different from State prison, where there are about zero expectations and laying in the bunk reading all day is expected. Here at Hotel Fed, we are expected to be either working or in a class.

There is a dress code for various activities. We have work uniforms, then non-working uniforms, with a code for presenting ourselves to officials if we are called in, or are putting in a request.

"So, Book, I want to work in the garden!"

"Well, to do that you have to earn it. You do that by first taking the horticulture class. Right now it is full, with no openings for a long time, maybe not until after you leave." There is more to this, "Miles, usually we all have a spell working in the kitchen as an introduction. After we do our dish washing time, we apply for a class or better job."

There is 'free time,' when not working or in class. We can go to the library, walk the track around the prison for exercise, go to the recreation room, go to the church. There is a list of the sorts of places we might be expected to be, as long as we are counted during the four counts of the day. I begin a walk about, to check out the routine. At first, not venturing far until I understand the rules better.

I discover the walk path. I want to stay in shape, lose weight, get my heart pumping. I receive my pills here, but think I can work at getting the dosages down as a health goal. The path goes through some remote fields, then near a pond that has fish and ducks. Along the furthest pond is a grass hut! There is no sign, so I have to ask.

"That is a religious hut for Native Americans, for their spiritual growth." Apparently there had been a petition or complaint about religious freedom, and alternatives to the Christian church. I know freedom of religion has a lot of power! That power has reached the prison. I end up knowing some of the key spiritual Native leaders. I just seemed to gravitate towards spiritual discussions. I hasten to add, I am not a religious nut!

One Native is Two Feathers, who is in a wheelchair and one of the spiritual leaders. Tall, skinny, long white hair in a pony tail, and Native hawk nose. I help Feathers get around in his chair, take him on a walk in the chair along the path. We talk about spiritual well being. One of the group, Mushroom, turns out to be the horticulture teacher. Apparently one of the jobs prisoners can apply for is teacher. The subject among us is often wilderness survival. Medical herbs, shelters, knowledge of self sufficiency. I add to this conversation concerning northern climates.

I'm told, "So, Miles, put in an application saying your spiritual beliefs are Native American and you want to join, and be allowed to use the pagan hut." Mostly I just want to sit in there alone, looking out over the pond and wildlife for meditation. Doing a sweat in the lodge does not interest me, nor any group spiritual activity.

"That's ok Miles, we can respect that. Others just want to meditate alone too." I put in for, and get certified as a pagan.

However, there are issues. Many of the pagans smoke. American Indians are allowed some amount of smoking as part of a ceremony spiritual thing. This is being abused by smokers who just want to break the rules and go secretly smoke. Some unauthorized prisoners use the hut to smoke and engage in other illegal activities. One practice is to smuggle cell phones into the prison, and go to places like the pagan hut to make phone calls they are not allowed. All phone calls are supposed to be monitored. No cell phones or computers connecting to the outside world without the prison knowing!

Getting certified to be able to use the hut puts me on a 'person of interest' list. I am not sure hanging out there is worth being on that list. Some of the guys are illegally smoking in front of me. I shift into reverse. *Book is right, make friends slow and carefully.* Two Feathers is one of he big smokers, but also has an illegal cell phone and I hear him running an outside drug business from within the prison. While this is his own business and I am not going to turn him in, I do not wish to be seen as 'involved.'

The one main pagan guy, Mushroom, teaches the class I want to take, required if one wants to work in the garden. We get along well, and have a lot in common. For example I know his brother, "Jimmie the bead Man? Sure I know him, he drops by Nenana in his ancient truck, drops the tailgate, and we trade for antique beads!"

"Yup! Sounds like my brother all right!"

The sign on the class door reads, "No room! Class is full!"

Book has told me we are expected to find our own jobs if we want to get out of working in the kitchen. We have two weeks to find a job or class, or we will be assigned work, at the bottom of the food chain. *We are not all equal.* 'Yeah, if we can figure out how to beat the system within the rules, this is encouraged. *It's teaching us how to get along in the real world outside.*

I walk into the classroom before class starts. A prison employee is in charge of the classes. "I know the class is full, but I'd really like to learn horticulture. I do not care about getting a certificate. Can I just sit in class in an empty chair and learn?"

No one has ever asked this before. There is an empty chair. I can voluntarily sit here until my two weeks are up and I get assigned someplace. I begin showing up for class, even though I have not been assigned. My view is, it does not hurt to be around and available if an opportunity comes up, like someone drops the class. *Much in life is about being in the right place at the right time.* So I ask questions, participate. It is obvious I truly love gardening, farming, the outdoors. I am not here to get out of washing dishes. I am not here to look good, or get in good with the prison. There is no ulterior motive. I get along well with the garden people. I have knowledge to contribute. Much about prison is fitting in with the group, the click. There is 'stuff going on,' that requires keeping your mouth shut, being trusted, and part of this group, that has its own thing going.

For example, food is harvested by the workers, and redistributed illegally among the prisoners. The prison employees in charge of education gets a kick back in the form of favors and produce. Do I have a problem with that? Yes, I do. But the problem is not with these guys. The problem is with a system that calls getting good food into the hands of the needy, illegal. This is one of the reasons I am here in the first place. I believe in 'intent,' and 'morals.' If I question a law, I ask what its purpose is. I hear the rules of the garden.

"The food we grow has to get tossed into the compost pile. We can eat it in the garden, but not remove it. The general population does not eat it." The reason? "It interferes with the food vendors contract." There are other issues I learn later.

I'm smart, learn fast, am well liked. Before my two weeks are up, I am told, "We decided to officially let you in the class and we will make room." So there are in fact ways around

"There is no room, we are full!" I bypass the washing dishes phase of my initiation into the work force here. Book is a little jealous. We begin drifting apart as friends. His time of being assigned to me is up. He thinks life should follow a script, you arrive, you wash dishes, and earn the right to be in a class. I have just six months to do. He feels I should leave that class space for someone who has more time to serve then I do.

"It's not fair, Miles, that you are a short timer, just arrived, and land a primo position!"

"Yes, life can be like that, huh. Standing in line with everyone else, and some smart ass figures out how to get to the front of the line. Really sucks doesn't it?"

Big grin. *We are all here because we are scammers of different sorts. Get over it!* The councilor says about this, "Prison is about learning to get what you want without upsetting others overly much. If you can find a job before we assign you to be dish washer, we are glad. It's what we hope. It helps us decide what to do with you."

This class repeats itself every few months. Lifers who truly want in, get in. Many who got long sentences got such a sentence for serious crimes that involve the inability to fit in, be with others, get along, and do not want a class about bugs and dirt. One of the big issues with horticulture is interest, "Ok Miles, what experience have you had? Are you in here for pot growing?" Because this is the class to get the latest, hottest tips, for growing weed. The teacher himself is one of the top pot growers in the country, ready to teach all! Many who are in the class, are here to learn to be professional pot growers. I think it is best for my rehabilitation, from the prison's standpoint to not be associated with pot growing.

"No, sir, no experience and none wanted. I live subsistence in Alaska and want to improve my ability to grow food in a harsh climate." Mr. Education, the prison employee in charge is annoyed. I think he'd prefer I was here to learn the wonders of pot growing; this he understands. He wants most to understand what everyone wants and what they are up to. *He's a control freak!*

I also have my friend Foil who helped cut wood for Iris, who says he can offer me a job in his business in Arizona. He is a landscaper. So if I take some related classes, and have a certificate, it might help me get a job with him! It can help with early release, or getting permission to travel to Tucson, if I have a job offer. This can show an initiative and attempt at changing professions, getting away from that nasty dead animal stuff. *"I learned my lesson, look, I'm excited about being a farmer now! I'm filled with hope and optimism!"* That should please those in charge of running my life.

My perception of my situation is, the prison, the government, does not like 'off the grid.' They would prefer to see all of us well plugged in as consumers, tax payers, purchasers of permits, with regular jobs working for companies the government can control in various ways. To speak of having such an opportunity says I am getting away from my old line of work, previous associations, turning a new page, starting over, under the governments thumb. The prison wishes to help this happen. This is a major plus to land the primo class in the prison within two weeks as a short timer.

I like the class a lot! I will learn about cloning and maybe grafting. Much has to do with ornamental arrangements. The growing of flowers, bonsai trees, bugs, pesticides. It's all interesting, even if I do not need all that. I have never had college class experience. High school classes were a lot different from this. These are teachers without certificates who know from doing; who are incredibly gifted and intelligent. Every time a name comes up in a video we watch, Mushroom goes, "Oh, yes, him. I dated his daughter," or, "Yeah, we went to school together," and has a story about this scientist or teacher. Mushroom understands the process of plant growth. He tells us how much $CO_2$ plants need, and when. His big passion is compost. I am interested in compost, so I pick his brain to learn all I can from him on the subject.

Most of the guys I arrived with, end up with kitchen duty. Through them, I meet long time cooks and food service people. I meet the accountant who keeps track of food in and out. One food worker tells me, "The prison is having an inspection soon. Prison kitchen workers are ordered to put away all the dented pots and pans and put out the new ones until inspection is over." We both chuckle. "It gets better."

He pauses until I stop laughing. "We are taking out cookers and equipment that will not pass inspection and renting equipment that will pass inspection. Re-installing the outdated illegal equipment again after inspection."

I'm no longer laughing. He takes me in back to show me in case I do not believe him. Yes, this is what is going on. He says, "So I run a restaurant for a living. If I can't pass inspection, I get shut down. If I deliberately pull a switch to pass inspection by fooling inspectors, it is a crime, and I come to prison. So I am here to be rehabilitated, taught to be honest. What do I find?" Yes, this is sobering, puzzling, and depressing. If the prison can't pass inspection, why is there no sympathy for private business that cannot pass, or any of us who can't make a living following the rules.

"Why not change the rules so they are workable? Instead of all of us pretending?" Well, we can't talk about this or dwell on it. I'm sure the prison would object to us following this line of thinking.

"Do what you are told and shut up!"

"Yeah, Miles, well, I heard you are taking notes, so thought I'd clue you in here."

I am more careful about hiding my notebook and playing along. My village idiot act. *But wait! Is it really and totally an act!?* My unconscious mind is trying to tell me something I prefer to ignore. I am willing to concede to a certain level of 'not being like others.' In a conversation with prisoners I say, "Society has a lot of rules to follow right? So we look them up and read them. But many, even most of the rules are in conflict, do not work, or reality does not match what the book says."

"Sounds like a good excuse. Works for me!"

"No, really!"

While I have no problem explaining what Einstein meant in his theory of relativity, how time is relative to motion, and a measurement of decay, I cannot explain two conflicting sign instructions. While I cannot make a pitcher of juice by adding exactly four cans of water, I can cook good complicated meals without a recipe. While I forget what year I was born, how old I am, or the names of my best friends, I can remember every bend of every river I ever ran. I know every trap I ever set, and what it caught. I have built pieces of art with thousands of cut out metal parts without a design, a drawing, or a plan. I simply 'begin.' I know what it will look like when I am done. One answer is, I am an idiot.

My reply is, "Did you know Einstein could not tie his shoes?" Makes perfect sense to me. It's obvious.

"Because our mind is only so big, and can hold only so much. If Einstein fills his mind with all of the ordinary stuff, there is no room in it for cool stuff." If I get a puzzled look I may add, "Like a computer. So much memory, right? It slows up and runs out of ram, right? So, you can choose to load it up with computer games or movies. There is no room now for large files or pictures. We choose what we use the ram for." I may add, "So like, I scan disk and defrag daily." Puzzled look. "I wake up in the morning with a blank disk. I see this yellow thing rise up, load that, and say 'Sun!' I go turn my computer on, see my email list, load that up, and say, 'friends!'" This is how I begin each day. New, fresh, and exciting. We all laugh.

"What a nut case, but he's ok!" I smile and nod, *I'm ok.* That's the main thing right? Not ok is not cool. People come to me to be entertained, not really for any knowledge.

"Listen to this guy, isn't he a riot!" Safe. It's all about being safe.

*Like in the movies. The days of Robin Hood. The sheriff of Nottingham rides into the village swinging his word, demanding taxes from the merchants in a shake down. He frowns. His eyes look over the street. In search of anyone not afraid, looking uppity, or defiant. His eyes meet the eyes of the village idiot, and keep on moving. The village jester outlives many kings.*

I am here in class getting really good grades. I have been curious how I would do on recorded tests. I have not taken any tests in thirty years. No, I am not a genius, or making honor roles, just shy of that. Same as in high school, a B+ average. Sort of what I want. I might do better. I do not want to. Safe, is doing well, without standing out. Out of forty people in class I am number five for grades. Prisoner advice is, "Do not stand out, not for good, not for bad. Go un-noticed, that is best." The focus should never be on you. That might be good advice out there in the world as well. That is what has gotten most of us into prison. We got noticed.

"Hey, Book! You work at the library, right? Is it possible to get access to laws?"

"I can get you on the internet. There is a site called LexisNexis. It allows you into the law library and no place else. I can get you the password." I am not sure how the prison will feel.

"Book, I am told I can't have access to a computer because part of my crime relates to computer crimes. Like I can't take the computer class offered that gives me access to the internet."

"This is different, Miles. We are all allowed access to laws so we can work on an appeal and communicate with our lawyer. It's the law. The prison system may not tell you what the law is, and what they have to allow. Through intimidation and threats, they steer us in another direction. But if you know your rights and put your foot down, they can be made to back off."

"Ok, up to a point. My objective is not to upset anyone and make this a battle." I still have not had my orientation class yet, as promised and required by law. I tend to gravitate towards libraries wherever I am. *Not that I am a book worm or anything like that!* Yuck! I prefer to associate myself with the working class, not the Geek crowd! If forced, I tend to mingle with the tough guys. I do not mingle with the skinny, pansy, glasses wearing, church going, intellectual, stuttering, bunny kissing, losers. *It's possible however that is what I really am. Perish the thought.*

One of my bunkies is a member of a mafia Don family.

"But not me, Miles! I'm in the used car business!" I nod that I understand! He shows me pictures of his cars. Mexican with long greasy curly black hair. A handsome weight lifter with a tan. In every picture, decked out in spotless expensive suits, with a different pretty blonde on his arm in each picture. He dresses like a member of a Mariachi Band. Next to the Rolls Royce Phantom. Here is the Jaguar. "This was my Cobra." A whole album filled with cars. Here he is at a fancy party with movie stars. I look and nod.

"Great money laundering business. I'm impressed!" I know a tad about business. I know that no one makes this kind of money selling used cars. Not him, in the role he is showing me in these pictures.

An indignant, "No! Not me!" Offended look. Pause. "If there is a little going on the side, it's nothing anyone needs to know about."

I nod, sure, I understand. Hot cars, fast women, or hotter women and faster cars, someone has to be there providing a service in a niche market. A necessary segment of society. There is a place for everyone. I have no serious problem here. Happy people with tons of money. No one seems whacked out. No one looks unhappy. Someone has to fleece the sheep, I'd rather not. [5]This is more understandable than rules no one can live by, made by people who do not follow them, enforced by brainwashed goons, leading brain dead sheep.

*Selling used cars. That's like Clint Eastwood being in the lead business.* Muscle is all right. He does not come across as mean, or a user, or selfish. He tries to help others. Lends money, gives advice, tries to make prison a better place for all of us. He often acts tough because he is afraid. He thinks only the tough survive. He does not want to end up as someone's girlfriend. I notice we all cope in different ways with a variety of fears. Partly Muscle is a mover and a shaker here who has connections that can make things happen. I like smart people. I like people who have life figured out and run it on their terms. But while doing so, move some of the pie onto other people's plates out of kindness.

Muscle stays out of trouble. He appears to be able to run a little business from prison. I overhear him sometimes on a prison phone giving instructions to his family. Sort of code. Appears to be giving orders to buy this, drop that, collect this debt, forget that debt. Tracts of land, shopping malls, high end cars. I do not make the rules the world operates under. I am not even pleased. But given the facts of life, people do what they gotta do. I would not work for Muscle, or even be his partner or close friend. He's an interesting guy to talk to and know. I would not go out of my way to throw a monkey wrench in his gears. I like to learn how the world operates. Who runs things. How it's done. Survival. But he's in prison! Oh well. He says when he gets out, the family is already waiting for him to fill in. It was necessary someone in the family do time.

"I was elected. I got no family, wife or kids. I'm young, and can run my part of things from here. I'll be compensated. It was a family decision, or more, me volunteering. Mostly to protect my sister. I got five years. In return for protection when I get out." No other details about the business, his real family name, who deals are made with. He's in the used car business. That's all I know.

"Yeah, Miles, the police are ok. They serve a necessary useful purpose. They have to look good. We all have that need. So the family made a deal." I gather the police help protect the family turf without unnecessary risk and bloodshed. Now and then someone has to put time in so the public feels the police are doing their job. Makes sense to me. Stuff your mother never tells you and you do not learn in school. Fascinating.

There are people here who have privileges others do not have, that money can buy. No proof. Muscle never seems to eat with the rest of us and disappears at meal time. I jokingly said out loud to the guard at the meal line, "Hey! Where's my steak and eggs?" Everyone in line laughs. The guard seriously says. "$75. And puts his hand out." I think he meant it. For $75 a meal, you can come back and eat with the guards and eat well. Likewise, there are those who get good grades in class who attend half the class and are bored, never open a book, do not care, do not study. Talk is, they pay for the grades, pay to get special treatment. Prison for the rich and famous, or their wayward children. It's just interesting to watch, and see how it works. I actually feel sorry for them! No sense of accomplishment, few rewards; all handed to them. No respect from others. Lonely and alone.

I am absolutely not looking for proof, or taking names! Make the sign of the cross. *I'd never get out alive. It's all made up! All just fiction, a story for entertainment! You know me, who can believe anything I say!* We are not allowed to take pictures, record anything. Our mail is read, all phone calls monitored. Every base is covered. There is no way to get undesired information or proof of anything in or out. There is only one true story backed with proof, the prison's. They have been at this many years, know what they are doing, and manage to survive. It's their rigged game, not to be bet into.

"Hey, Miles." Long pause as a tall black guy sizes me up. "So I hear you know a lot about what is going on. A writer. Smart. I could use a guy like you. Might have some work for you. In return, maybe make things here a little easier for you." He waits to see my response. I size him up as well. Well dressed, hires someone to work for him, polish his shoes, do his laundry. He neither works, nor has any classes to attend. He is vague about what he does with his time, where he spends it. Vague about what he is in for, and how he makes his money.

"I deal in land speculation mostly." Connected with stock market inside trades. "There are a lot of ways to make money, as you know." He needs a publicity man, writer. Make him look good, you know.

Well first, I never bet into another man's game. I'm not working for someone else. People like this tend not to pay well as they got rich off other peoples work, not by being generous. Black thinks I am going to be flattered and grateful to receive his notice.

"I'll think about it." I know he does not want people who will think about it. He does not want smart people. He is looking for worker bees who do what they are told.

"Hey Miles, I hear you know a little about import-export in Alaska." An oriental business guy waits for my reply. I give a non committal nod. "I need some stuff imported. As you know, Alaska is a good way to get goods into the country. I hear you might know a way to avoid customs." I do in fact know how it could be done. As an intellectual endeavor. I observe—and see—a series of 'could be done' concepts pass through my thoughts. With a smile and a 'Huh.' I'm talking about smuggling people, guns, bombs, electronics. Whatever you want—by the ton. I'm not especially interested in endeavors that hurt people or are high end serious crimes that carry the death penalty or life in prison. I certainly would not talk to a stranger in prison about any such matter I know about. Cut me in if I told him? I think not. Cut me is correct. In theory, millions could be made. Many in prison are here looking for knowledge, partners, ways to learn how to be better criminals, making their connections here to better run their business when they get out. Or, snitches trying to sell information.

The prison system sort of knows what it is coming down, from practice. My guess is, certain people are watched. It is noted who they talk to, when, for how long, and keep notes. People with certain crimes are watched, to see who they befriend and what that person's crime is. Connect the dots. Some associations are allowed, if it benefits someone watching. Such as, "We do not care what you smuggle, but in return we have a few, let's say, 'sensitive' items we need moved. That we'd like from time to time, to be part of your load." Playing with the big boys can be big money, but comes with a price I'd rather not pay. I play the idiot card again. Big grin.

"Yeah, I got this friend with a small plane who flies into Siberia under the radar going back and forth." I do know such a person, but it does not take much smarts to see the flaws in that plan. I let on I have no idea the plan is flawed.

"Well, not really a friend. I just heard of this guy." Now I'm just another bragging moron! I see that pass through this Mr. Oriental's noggin. I nod like it is the greatest plan devised since the great escape!

"I shee!" nod, nod. "Vawy goot." He's going to talk to me later. *Yeah, right.* This other guy is in prison for book fraud, a writer like me.

"Miles, you should talk to the guy. A lot of best sellers under his belt! He might be able to help you get published!" I heard of this guy. I notice him, observe him in the TV room. He appears not to be kind. His seat is reserved so no one can sit in his chair. He is rude, a user, abuser, and a scammer. I once mentioned to him that I am a writer. He does not look up, "Hmm," is all he says. He is not interested in writing, talking to anyone who writes, has no love of the written word, not interested in helping anyone. I guessed that already.

Others want to know if I can get them elephant ivory, bear galls, and other valuable animal parts. Trophies of different kinds. They have connections, customers for me.

"Nope, out of that business."

"I know but..." wink wink. *We all say that right*, "But between you and I....?" I never was in that business. But why say so, when no one would believe me. I give a 'my hands are tied' look. I have no idea who is a snitch, who is who they say they are. It is wise to keep all talk in the, "I am shocked, sir," format. One prisoner is a well known Alaska pilot who flies drugs in from overseas. He walks away from the plane and writes the plane off, buys a new plane for the next trip. He has some interesting stories to tell. Been at it for decades. Some of the others prisoners have used his service. He did not exactly get caught. He upset certain people, and got in trouble over plane registration issues. He smiles, is not upset.

"It's just business. I'll be out soon." He's another who seems to eat elsewhere, and pays people to look after him. No job, no classes. He reads the paper out in the sun a lot. He might take a stroll to the pond now and then. He's content for now, doing his time. I gather his flights are carrying high grade bud. No hard drugs, or plane loads of money. He'd be a good person to keep in touch with if I were a criminal.

# SECRETLY WILD

Prisoners wanted connections to acquire huge grizzly claws like this that I am at the source of and could acquire, Difficult to deal in legally. I avoided the subject.

MILES MARTIN

Speaking of being legal. Here is the paperwork proving legality of grizzly bear claws I speak of.

# CHAPTER TWO

## FEDERAL PRISON, PRISONER STORIES, HORTICULTURE CLASS

"Flying what Miles?" Book wants to know.

I tell him, "I have some Russian friends looking for a good way to get mammoth tusks into the US without paying the Russian or US mafia. The government takes half the profit. It's a multimillion dollar business. I could play middle man. I trust these Russians with my life."

"So, what would the crime be exactly? I can see the headlines. 'Depriving a country of its museum displays, taking a country's culture away for profit.'"

"Yes, that is how it would read." The truth as I believe it? The money collected in permits does not go back to the people or the country. It goes into an officials private pocket so he can buy a jet. When I do business, I make sure the supplier in the remote village gets his fair share of the find. More than he gets now. It would help out the people and cut out the government. While being a crime. A crime against who? Some guy who needs a new jet is victimized?"

"So, what's to stop you, Miles?"

"Well, any time big money is involved, there is risk and stress. I chose a simple life with less stress. My crimes were low level that had no victims according to the judge. If I was a real criminal with money on my mind, I could have dealt in trophies, and more profitable items I had connections for, access to, and customers wanting. I'm not a criminal."

"We all say that!" Of course, money is not my God. I have enough money. I'm just saying, "If I wanted to, I see a situation here." Possibly one with minimal risk and high profit.

"This is certainly the place to make good connections. A good reliable pilot would come in handy for a lot of ideas. Moving this and that below the radar. If a person was not a criminal when they arrived, it's certainly a good place to become one huh?"

Book ran a scam on a senior nonprofit program and collected a lot of money, the charges say. Someone looked it up on the computer. Stealing little old ladies life savings. Now no one back home talks to him. He lost his wife, kids, and parents. None will write to him. Book is not bitter. He wants to try another life, and make up for what he has done. He seems sincere. Proof is in his actions, how he helps others so much.

We have mail call every day. The rules change by the week. Usually one of the prisoners we elect goes and gets the bag for our wing. We hang around the lobby as our names are called out. Now and then the one elected gets sent to the hole. Or someone commits an offense, and the punishment is no mail delivered. We have to go across the yard and wait there by a different method. A commissary is open for us once every two weeks. We have a limited account to draw money from. There is a lot to buy. Ice-cream, candy, paper, stamps, flip flop footgear, prisons hats, and sweat shirts. Some instant foods. There are four microwaves in our wing for us to cook meals in. We can buy canned tuna, crackers, things to make other things.

Some long time offenders have microwave cooking down to a science! It is possible to create an edible pizza! The crackers are ground down to the basic flour. Paste comes out of some other product. Cheese comes in sticks. Often we prisoners trade for things we do not know how to cook. Book tells me, "Some of these guys have no outside money. They rely on any trades they can do by cooking, doing your laundry, and cleaning your cube." I know even though there is no money here, someone does something and you owe them. They give you a list of what to buy them when your turn comes up at the commissary. *This is not legal.* Yet, some of the trades get overlooked, and is acceptable to the prison. *So why not just make it legal!* I wonder. The rules say clearly it is not allowed, and is punishable. I tell Book what I notice.

"Like we cannot pay anyone to do anything for us. Yet, we all chip in to have the cube waxed and buffed. Technically, we are all responsible for our own area! Yet, only certain designated people have access to the buffer and wax. Since everyone in the cube chips in and pays, it is not realistic to say, no this is illegal and I want no part of it! For this to work we all have to chip in, right? It is quite obvious we pay, because only one designated person in the whole wing has access to the buffer! The prison knows that! So why not just make it legal and spelled out!" There is no answer. "Likewise, we all get our hair cut! The only way to get it done is to pay the barber. We all pay. No pay, no haircut. No haircut, we get written up for not being neat and clean." There is a barber shop. It's obvious, we all go in and pay, it's illegal. Spelled out in the rule book. I quote:

"Haircuts are free. Do not get caught paying!" How do we not get caught? We are all criminals, every one of us. At any time any of us could get sent to the hole over this. The system can now pick and choose who to send to solitary confinement with the reason, 'paying for a haircut.' Book has no answer. He does not think about it, few do. They just understand how it works. Do they read the rules, and then simply ignore them? Why are we all here then? So which rules can we ignore, give me a list please. No, it does not work that way. So we have to guess? Idiot Miles again, what a great act!

I'm sort of nervous and under stress over rules we all break, and me being the one to take the fall.

With Book's help I check out a variety of reading material I have had on my mind for a while.

"I wish to reread many of the old classics I read when young, and might find ideas, or quotes from heroes, by way of explaining myself in my own writing!" I begin with Mark Twain. I like the easy style for ordinary people. Not necessarily best English form, but a great story teller. When Mark Twain wrote his biography he had this to say about it. 'In the autobiography it is my purpose to wander whenever I please and come back when I get ready.' He says later on: 'Start it at no particular time of my life, wander at my free will all over my life, talk only about the thing which interests me for the moment, drop it the moment if it's interest threatens to pale, and turn my talk upon a new and a more interesting thing that has introduced itself into my mind.' An interesting concept of the truth about yourself. Partly interesting, in that Mark Twain was a felon. He was wanted in another state for engaging in an illegal dual.

I read about people who helped form our government in my quest to discover how it was formed, why, and what the intent was. *How and when were our government goals changed, and how did that came about?* I no longer blindly trust what I was taught in school about history. Mostly because it is not matching reality.

I read from Henry Adams 1850. "I like criticism, but it must be my way." Later on, "This is the journey I remember. The actual journey may have been quite different, but the actual journey has no interest for education. The memory was all that mattered." An interesting view on reality, and truth, when speaking of ones descriptions of what you believe the facts are of an event. Of interest is, this is not just some idiot speaking nonsense. "When I was younger, I could remember anything, whether it happened or not, but my faculties are decaying now and soon I shall be so I cannot remember any but the things that never happened."

"I agree, Miles, if any of us here in prison ran our business the way the prison does, we'd be in jail. It's run as a crooked business." Statistical facts say $80,000 a year is spent by the public per prisoner. Most prisoners agree on an estimate that no more than $10,000 actually getting spent per prisoner. The missing $70,000 is skimmed off by corruption and mismanagement. In other words, a prison guards family could and probably does live off the money skimmed off one inmates incarceration. The list is long, of things we observe and are part of.

"Not just the kitchen inspection fiasco I recorded, Muscle!"

Mushroom and others at horticulture tell me more facts about the garden.

"Miles, the prison is telling the county we are only using rainwater to water the garden." I read this myself on the internet information about Hotel Fed. "We are not paying for, nor allowed to use the city water. Yet, city water is hooked up. We use it, and it is all we use. We use a lot. The city is puzzled where all the water is going. The prison plays dumb." Mushroom should know, he teaches and runs the program. He is the one who turns the city water off and on. Water rights is a big issue. Not paying for water is a big issue. We are all ordered to keep the secret, if we know what is good for us. If asked by any inspectors, we are to be part of the cover. The prison is stealing water from the citizens of the area, then lying about it.

I observe, the city water coming on, and watering our gardens. It's a lot of water. The advertisement on the web page states; "Depends on its own water for gardening by the use of rain water stored in barrels." No such barrels exist. In the same way there is not a room for every prisoner as advertised. We are illegally over crowded. The part of the prison that is minimum security was built for 500 inmates, but in reality it houses over 700. There is a small creek running into the pond by the prison where the public goes fishing. I see our septic overflow running into the creek, with toilet paper and turds floating into the pond. Few prisoners see what I see, get told what I get told, have access to what I have access to. I have worked my way into positions of trust among the guards and the inmates.

"If any of us ran our business under such conditions, we'd be shut down!" I'm not trying to take sides or complain, protest, hope for changes. I am the scribe, the recorder of events. If the story was about all of us getting steak and eggs every day I would record that. I would proudly record how the prison is self sufficient, using rainwater and compost with no chemicals. It would be so cool if the food we eat was grown by prison. I'd be happy and proud of my country to write that. I'd prefer to have that sort of story to write. I want to love my country.

"Another reason, Miles, we can't serve this garden food to inmates, is we do not have a certified sprayer putting chemicals down. It is us prisoners, who may not know what we are doing." *Or maybe purposely poison the food? But no, it is all organic, no poisons used.*

It is still early spring. Not much is seriously happening at the garden. The winter food is winding down. It will be time for spring planting. At this time there will be a greater need for garden workers. I am assured I will be one of the first picks for working the summer in the garden. For now, there is a lot of classroom learning three hours a day.

I get up about 5:00 am, as I am used to. Few others are up. I can use the microwave to cook a meal with no lines. I can use the phone, internet, email, when there is no line starting at 6:00 am. We have access to email. The computer reads our fingerprint to access it. The prison knows who used what computer, and when. I can email simple text only, and am charged by the word count. I am able to give a simple hello and the basics to Iris. We cannot email anyone without that person getting on an approved list. The emails are monitored. The computer turns on at exactly 6:00 am. A few inmates like myself, sit and wait. We read or study at one of the computers until computers comes on. I leave the building about 6:30.

There is a feral cat that hangs around we all feed and take care of. It is cold out, so I cover the cat with an old coat when we shut down at 10:00 pm at night, and uncover the cat each morning at 6:30. The cat yawns, stretches, and follows me over to the chow hall. We are not allowed to feed or interact with wildlife, including the cat. It's obvious the cat belongs here, and is getting taken care of. Each wing has a cat who maintains its territory. We bring food out and 'accidentally drop' food from our pocket. We are also not allowed to remove food from the chow hall, or have any in our locker. Prisoners are running entire stores out of their locker selling food. The inmate store gets shut down when it gets out of hand, as determined by the guards. The seller goes to the hole, the goods get confiscated.

I eat at 6:30 am so I can make the pill line by 7:00. I'm not the first in this line because I choose to do emails instead. I get my daily pills issued, and wander over to the class area. I usually drop my books off in front of the door, and head over to the nearby chapel, which has its doors open, and seems like a nice quiet place. There is a desk or two in a lobby area I can hang out at and read or write, while keeping one eye on the classroom door. When the lights come on, I head over to the class, and am the first one in. This a good time to chat with the teacher or other students on what we are learning, and brush up for any test this day. I do that, or read, brush up on the lessons, or write in my diary.

We get counted at 9:00 am. I am usually counted as present in class. At 11:00 am, we get a break until 1:00 pm. There is time to either eat early, or go for a walk on the path. Now and then I take the early morning walk at 6:00 am to see the birds and ducks. I hang out at the library after lunch until 1:00 pm. There is another count at one o'clock so I am either in the library to be counted, or in another class. If not in a class, there is sometimes work at the garden if I am allowed, and I get counted there. I'm not officially a garden worker, but I can volunteer. By 3:00 pm, I am out of class or off work. We have a count at 4:00 pm, so it is hard to plan much. I usually hang around the classroom discussing class material with a regular group and the teacher. Or I'm doing my homework at my bunk.

After count I might go for a long walk if the weather is nice. Sometimes, I go to my cube, or the library to write or read. Dinner at 6:00 pm. It is often a meal I do not want to eat, so I eat something I got from the commissary, or trade for a meal someone else cooks. Or, I have stolen food from the garden to eat. I can often supply one of the prison locker cooks with some stolen garden vegetables, in trade for a meal. I can smuggle out onions, carrots, tomatoes, and hot peppers. The Mexicans really like the habanera hot peppers! The commissary sells a sausage that keeps well. Sticks of sealed cheese can be bought. There are microwave Ramen type foods that can be spruced up with the meat and cheese. Sometimes three to four guys chip food in, and one of us cooks for the group, and we share. I'm not comfortable in the give and take of sharing, so rarely participate in this.

By 7:00 pm, I am at the library working, or reading, on a long walk, or at a group meeting. There are certain approved meetings to attend. The horticulture people sometimes meet for extra information. There is an informal educational meeting where an expert on a subject gives a talk that has been announced, posted, and approved. It might be global warming, car repairs, computer information. It can get interesting, so I attend. Often the meeting is canceled due to the guards punishing us because someone got caught feeding the cat. Records of these group educational meetings are kept and go in a file. This is proof we are being social. That looks good in our records. Many prisoners do not care about the stupid records.

"Miles, these people are not our friends! Their job is not to help us!" Possibly, probably true.

"But they have the big stick, and I want to get away from them as soon as possible."

The prisoners conclude the main reason we are allowed to do anything interesting that we look forward to, is to supply something to cut us off from and punish us with. I agree this is likely. By 8:00 pm, there is often something interesting to watch on TV. There are four TV rooms, racially controlled. One is the black room, one is the Mexican room. One is the Latino and the other minority room, while one is the white room. It is possible to visit a room not of your race. You are a guest and have zero say. If someone else wants your chair, you give it up. You get no vote on what channel we will watch today. If there are problems, it is your fault. In general, it is not a great idea to go visiting where you do not belong.

There are certain programs it is expected we all like and follow, that is the choice, there is no vote. It is not that simple. There are a handful of control freaks. They come in, grab the remote and change the channel in the middle of a program. Dare anyone to stop them. If there is a fight, or even an argument, both parties go to solitary confinement. Some unhappy types do not care! It is all the same to them if they are in the hole or not. They may even wish to be alone for a while. The group gets to them. The rest sigh, and whatever is on, we just watch. The TV room is where 90%

of the fights break out. Some prisoners avoid the TV room altogether. I can go with the flow, and have no problem in the TV room. Now and then someone tells me I am in their chair. I get up, move and apologize. I recall who they are and keep that in mind in any prison dealings. "You wanta tha tomata? You bee-a nice in Tv rooma!"

Mail call can vary, but is usually during TV watching time, so we all leave to get our mail. Lights go out at 10:00 pm. It is good to be around the bunk early, and make sure I am where I am suppose to be when lights go out. There is a count right after lights out to make sure we are all in bed. Another count at 2:00 am, we hopefully do not notice. If there is a miscount we are told, and have to hang around for another count to be made, which might take half an hour. Classes might be late, lunch, movie time, might all be late due to recount. So while there is sort of a routine and ordinary day, it can all get changed. But in general this is my day.

There is a nice shower situation. We have individual stalls with doors. There is usually no line if I choose my time. Bathroom and showers are never off. At 5:00 am, there is plenty of hot water. Cleanliness is encouraged. We can get dressed and undressed in the dark, so there is a level of privacy that is acceptable. There tends not to be homosexual problems. There are a few homosexuals. Some are accepted, some made fun of. 'Couples' often come to the TV room and sit next to each other every evening. Hand holding and such is not accepted by the rest. Some argue like married couples. Inappropriate, unappreciated, advances are seriously stopped. It is a very big infringement. The prisoners will usually get together and beat the offender up, while everyone knows you just fell out of bed. We rarely make sexual jokes, or make fun of, discuss, or mention anything related to our bodies, habits or anything that might indicate 'a sexual problem.'[1]

It takes me a month or more to feel comfortable with the routine. I am not used to routines, and not used to knowing, or having to be someplace at a certain time. I never worked where I needed a uniform, so it is hard for me to remember, or even understand, where each uniform and classy dress is required. Other prisoners are used to being regimented, having a dress code at work, etc. It is common for me to head over for breakfast with a sweatshirt on if it is chilly, or my stocking cap. Especially if I am going for a walk right after. If I have been working on the farm it is hard to remember to change my clothes for dinner. I am used to eating in my work clothes. Others who have family, seem more used to changing before dinner. It's an ingrained habit already. This is a way to socialize us, behave like normal people, get us to adjust if we have issues.

On the weekend, there are no classes. There is often something special on TV, like all day western movies. I am known for carrying my notebook around, being seen writing all the time. During commercials in the TV room, I am scribbling away. This draws comments at first. Maybe I am a pussy. What do I think? I calmly reply,

"The pen is mightier than the sword." If I get a stupid, 'What does that mean!' I say, "I could do more damage to you by writing up a formal complaint and submitting it to the counselor, than you could to do to me with your fist in the short time you had before we both went to the hole." Or even, "If I wrote the truth and sent it to the right place, I could do more damage to this prison than you could do with a riot." Often followed by,

"Wow, I get it! Could you help me write...?" I tend not to get involved in others personal cases. There is a rule against conspiracy, and that can be simply helping another beat the system. There is already a guy we all refer to as 'Doc' headed for trouble, for no other reason than offering everyone free legal advice. He looks up laws and encourages you to fight your case. Possibly the prison does not want us to understand our rights and the law. It is hard to say why. We can only speculate. We can receive help at the library finding the right source for answers.

In this way, I am learning something about how to find and look up laws. The famous 'Doc' has actually been helping me too. Mostly legal stuff, like helping me look up laws the librarian does not understand. It's a bit late to understand my case! Ha! But a little prevention for the future does not hurt.

"Hey, Muscle! I lost four pounds in a week and am reduced on one of my meds!"

"Good for you! I told you losing weight and being healthy was important. Did you join the exercise class?"

"No, I checked it out, but did not like what I saw." I think in this case I am not into organized exercise. One of the prisoners is getting credit for running a class on fitness. A young athletic kid barks orders like you are in boot camp. I see a dozen guys laying on a mat, doing various moves with the legs, sit ups and such. I'd rather jog, and use the pull up poles, sit up benches along the path. There is an exercise room available, but it has been closed the whole time I have been here.

"Yeah, Miles, someone got caught using a cell phone in there after hours. The guards shut it down as punishment. It may open again. It's usually booked and crowded." I look in through the window and see equipment I'd not understand, that does not look like I want to understand. Treadmills with digital read outs, boxing bags, weights. All have a view of a TV screen, so one can watch TV while exercising. The room looks like it would be crowded. Out back near the walk track is an outdoor area with a few pieces of equipment. I see people shooting pool. I see some sort of kickball team, with everyone in a uniform. It is nice to know all these things are available, but team stuff does not interest me, so I watch and do my own thing. I never even found out how you'd join or get picked.

Next to the exercise room is a recreation room, also closed for now, but soon to be reopened. There are art supplies for painting and easels with paintings on them when I look through the window. *I could take art class! Even volunteer to teach!*

"Miles, one thing to watch out for, new people are warned about, is to not get involved in too many things at once, and get overworked, and not do any of the things well. You seem to have a lot going on already!" I do have a full schedule. Another thought crosses my mind. This is prison, and much of what goes on revolves around punishment. I care about my art a lot. So far, no one here even knows I am an artist. It's never been written down, or the subject come up. Is it wise to let on what a good way to punish me is? There is nothing I am doing now, that, if it was denied me, would make or break me. It's all 'interesting,' but none of it is my passion. It might even be nice to take a break from what I do at home for a living!

Many of the activities seem to have cliques and groups that run them. I fit in all right with the garden group, even if most are pot growers. They are into meditation, herbal stuff, American Indian lore, and survival skills. We are 90% middle class whites who live in the country. We are in fact 'at war' with the Mexicans, who are a gang trying to take over control of the garden produce. They steal it and sell it, as if the produce were drugs. Those of us who try to sneak produce out to give away are bypassing the Mexicans, and we get threatened. They want a cut of our action. I see it as the same mentality and plugging in to the same lifestyle as the street drug gangs.

The art group are elderly biker types, with tattoos, into hard drugs, or that mentality. I could fit in if I wanted. The part I disagree with the most about this group is they have a skinhead Arian, white supremacy mentality. I'm White and am accepted and asked to join. I even hang out for a while the few times the door is open. I'm more comfortable with the plant people. The exercise people are like jocks. Counting sit ups as competition, showing off their bodies, muscle guys. Almost in a homosexual way. There are other sub groups that exercise. There are those who simply want to do something about being cooped up! But most of them are like me, they walk, and use equipment on their own, as it is available. The soccer team appears to be Mexican against Latino other minority groups. I'm sure anyone who really wanted to, could join in. But the game calls seem to be called in Spanish.

I'm curious why the prison allows such open discrimination. It seems to me, this leads to fights and problems the prison would not want. Muscle explains it. "Most of these guys are from the inner city, never left their turf. Never been in the country. Never seen a real tree before. Their people and ways is all they know. It's better to allow that. Less trouble in the big picture. Those without a tribe anymore commit suicide. That's not good for the prison."

Among some of the other jobs available is a wood shop. Others work in the warehouse moving prison supplies in and out. There is a bigger farm across the road that is different than the horticulture garden I am associated with. I was not aware at first there is a difference and two different groups. One is more educational with classes, the other is just farm work. Our horticulture part has experimental things going on, with test crops, and ornamental items to get a job in a greenhouse, or in the landscape business. We experiment with winter crops being covered, compared to not covered. We test different pesticides, soils or micro climates.

There are palm trees in huge pots growing outdoors in summer, brought into the greenhouse for winter. We are about 'education.' The farm is about mass production and brute force, putting hours in on a tractor. At my age with diabetes I'd rather be intellectual than physical.

Mushroom tells me, "We used to have a big connection with the university nearby! Professors would come teach, and the experiments recorded for the university, so the knowledge would get shared. I suppose it is a funding problem. No one has time now." He pauses. "We also used to have educational outings, still advertised as taking place, with funding still given to us. The prison used to have a special bus we owned to go to nearby farms, nurseries and arboretums."

"Well, Mushroom, I am happy enough for what we have. This is prison after all." He agrees, and has a good attitude most of the time. He's a skinny Jewish looking guy, in his late 50's, with a lot of nervous energy, and playful prankster outlook. He doesn't believe in grades and sometimes gives out the answers. I find out the degree we get means nothing. It is not approved or accepted by anyone at all. It's a useless piece of paper.

"It doesn't have to be useless, Miles, it did not start out useless when we were connected to the university."

"Well, Mushroom, it looks good in the prison records, to show you participated in its programs and tried to do some good with your time here."

"Yes, it is good for that." It's good for our own personal knowledge.

One word we read and hear a lot is the word 'rehabilitation.' I go around asking, "Have you been rehabilitated yet!" "Are you ready to be reintegrated into society as a new changed person?" I hold my hand out like I am a reporter with a microphone, ready to record the valued cherished words of having been saved. I get a variety of responses.

"Yes, sir! I have been saved, sir!" A military bark reply. One guy looks to the right and left to see if anyone is watching and gives me the finger, scowls, and walks off. One replies, "Yes, Masta, whatever ya say, Masta!" I nod.

"Society will be a much safer place than it was before you were caught. Look what you are learning here!"

"Yeah, I learned how to balance my soil. I understand what my cash crop was lacking. I got some tips on how to save money, and got a new source for Hawaiian genetically altered pot seed."

"Good job! Keep up the good work!" On the side, Mushroom teaches what states are opening up for legal pot growing, and how the laws are interpreted, to stay out of trouble. He's a happy go lucky flower child of the 60's. A little like Wes the Mess back in Fairbanks, but much smarter. I can picture him in tie dye shirt and sandals in the jungle of Hawaii saying, "Hey, Man, come and visit!"

"Rehabilitated? Accepting socialism. Do what you are ordered to do. No one is any different from anyone else. The same clothes, same pay, same ideas. Brainwashed, programmed to sign your name on the dotted line, and be accepting, and happy about life as it is dictated to you, because there is nothing you can do to change it."

"We leave here docile. That's the plan." I get out my Mark Twain book and show the line quoting Twain: 'It is my conviction that each and every human law that exists has the distinct purpose and intention and only one: To oppose itself to a law of God and defeat it!' Later on: 'I do not know anything about laws except how to evade them and not get caught!' A chuckle for reply.

"I guess he succeeded!" I walk away deep in thought, in my private world. The head spiritual guy knows me and accepts I simply want a place with peace around me to think, read, and have a short period of time 'with God,' so to speak. So this priest guy lets me sit at the table by the front door of the chapel. I politely say, "No. I am not interested in being saved, thanks for the offer." *Saved for what? Desert?*

I read more of Twain: "I, like all other human beings, expose to the world only my trimmed and perfumed and carefully barbed public opinions and conceal carefully cautiously, wisely, my private ones."

I am curious, puzzled. That such a well known contributor to society could have such an outlook as I read, and have it work. Not that I out right agree or believe. Just food for thought. I do admire his writing so much. Getting to know the writer behind the scenes is an eye opener. Mark Twain had a private conversation with a young reporter who asks him to tell the truth about his views on subjects like religion and sex. He replies: "I said it would damn me before my time. I didn't want to be useful to the world on such an expensive condition." The truth was obviously not going to set him free.

---

IN HORTICULTURE, Mushroom is teaching us more about 'biochar.' There is a book he quotes, "Biochar Solution Carbon Farming and Climate Change,' by Albert Bates:

"There have been at one time, as many as a billion people living along the Amazon River as long ago as 8,000 years, and up until 1543 when Orellana arrived and described such a population. After 200 years went by, it appears 99.95% of the population had died from the contact. Possibly diseases from escaped pigs, rats off invading boats." This is fascinating background material to me, because I am interested in ancient peoples, and how they lived. It has at least a little to do with being a fossil and artifact hunter. It was writings from this expedition that started myths of

El Dorado, the City of Gold, as well as the fighting Amazon women. The description is of miles and miles of a single city, 100 miles long and six miles deep.

"Archeological finds are adding credibility to the truth of this. So great was the burst of vegetation over open fields and mounded cities, the carbon drawn from the air to feed this greening upset atmospheric chemistry." This was determined by analysis of soils.

The question then comes up, how did so many people get fed? How could agriculture support this many? By our modern day standards, using methods we know, it would not be possible. Therefore, we assumed for a long time, there was an exaggeration, a made up story. How can such an ancient culture know more than modern man?

This fits in with my rabbit cycle theory of civilization. *We have been smarter before, even many times before, in cycles that gets lost when dark ages come.* Because I believe this, I look for answers to civilization's present plight. I'd like to discover social answers that might help all of us. Failing that, possibly understand the future so I may personally prepare for it better. Meaning, prepare for a coming dark age.

Mushroom says, "Until we discovered biochar!" Summed up, charcoal is an important ingredient, very useful in soil, lacking in our modern soils. Because we clear trees and overburden off the land and then plant. In nature, these trees, grasses and vegetation would burn now and then, adding charcoal to the soil. Charcoal chemically bonds nutrients, so the nutrients do not wash away with the rain and sink down to the water table. Biochar is charcoal that has been mixed with compost or nutrients and is 'charged.' It does not take a lot of charcoal to enrich soils. The same principal of carbon charcoal is used in gas masks, and drinking water filters. In both, the carbon chemically combines with what passes over it.

The Amazons had figured that out. They made charcoal, charged it with compost, to spread over their crop lands.

"Today we dig down to this layer in the Amazon. The man made biochar is still full of nutrients after 2,000 years." Mushroom feels this could be an answer for issues the world faces today, with food supply, and issues with soil problems. Man-made chemicals are polluting our environment. Mushroom passionately tells us, "This biochar is something natural, cheap, that works!"

The subject is a bit away from the topic at hand - 'horticulture.' The planting and maintaining of ornamental plants. But is it in Mr. Education's best interest to stop this from being learned? It's prison! Can he make us do anything at all? I mean he can make us attend, but why not allow us something we are interested in that gives praise to Mr. Education's class? People are asking to get in this class, and leaving with certificates that generate more funding. Mushroom tells us, "Biochar is easy to make! Here are instructions for a cooker to make charcoal. It is a way some of you could make a living. Many greenhouses want it, farmers, gardeners. It's a new open field, untapped, and not taken over by big industry yet!" We are unsure if big industry will ever get into this. "In fact, many large companies suppress the knowledge. The manufacture of chemicals is big money." Mushroom finds articles in the news to show us proof of this, as well as court case transcripts we have access to.

One of the farmers here in prison gives us a background on 'fertilizer.' He steps up and takes the microphone.

"After WWII, there were factories still making bombs that might get shut down. The same ingredients used in bombs can be used for fertilizers. The nitrogen based bomb chemicals were put to another use, because the factories were in place to produce it. That does not mean it was best for the soil, farmers, or environment." We learn in class from videos, how chemical fertilizers are a quick fix for immediate profits. In the big picture, toxins are being added, and within a decade it takes twice the chemicals to get half the results. It takes twenty years for the land to recover. We may run out of land. So far, powerful nations have been exploiting the land of less fortunate countries. We are running out of 3rd world countries to exploit.

Many inmates related to farming, are here because they went against the government. Not necessarily against sound land management. Some were intelligent innovators, with new ideas. Or, went against Monsanto, the monopoly in the seed industry. All farmers agree with how the law reads.

"Let's say you have a farm not using Monsanto seed. Your neighbor has Monsanto seed. If pollen from his farm blows over to your farm and pollinates your crop, you owe Monsanto. This is theft of copyrighted patented seeds the company owns."

"If pollen from your crop blows over to this same neighbor, and pollinates his crop, you can be sued. People are losing their farms over this issue." One farmer in class tells us, "I am here for trying to sue Monsanto." *Who knows what the truth is. This sounds pretty farfetched to me. I'm just recording what is said.* However, we see video stories of farmers, court cases, interviews with farmers, company officials, and lawyers. That backs up what inmates share with the rest of us. *Come to think of it, there are a lot of farmers here in prison.*

I AM READING, 'THE JUNGLE,' by Sinclair. Talking about a time in 1906. I consider this a classic for its time, describing the meat industry in Chicago during its peak meat processing time. This book did more to change the way we view the meat industry, workman's compensation and inspections, than any other action taken at the time. The EPA and FDA are direct results of this book. An example of the pen being very mighty! But it had been a long time since I read it! I was a teen! I am grateful for prison time to reread it.

"...sweep off handfuls of the dried rat dung. These rats would be fed poisoned bread. Rats die. Dead rats, bread and meat, all get ground up into sausage. There were things that went into sausage in comparison that made poisoned rats a tid-bit." This was the result of corruption, scamming the public. A fictional story rings true to the common man. The beginning of the EPA. That in itself becomes a source of greed and corrupt power. More than any documents, records, and proof, this story changed the country. I read, and study why. *Did we solve one issue, but create another, considering what I hear in the news of the EPA?* The characters were commoners with simple jobs. The style of writing is not exceptional in my view, only 'ok.' The impact was the story itself. Not especially important people who got arrested for small crimes.

"That they were in jail was no disgrace to them for the game had never been fair; the dice were loaded. They were swindlers and thieves of pennies and dimes, and they had been trapped and put out of the way by swindlers and thieves of millions of dollars."

I pause in my reading to wonder how much has changed since this book was written? I am getting to know some of the prisoners better. I admit it is difficult to get at any 'truths.' I often ask myself, *What would the other side, the victims be saying happened?* I ask, *and who among us raises their hand and says, "Yes, I am a sinner; yes, I am a criminal and deserve to be here as a menace to society?"* Still, time tells all. I can spot the mean ones well enough. The ones who start the fights and problems. Just as easily I can see who is kind and helps others.

Mushroom, the teacher, is one of the kindest people you could ever meet. There is simply no way he would hurt anyone. He does not have mental problems, hidden dark sides to his personality. He has no temper. His IQ is off the charts. He was involved in a great many humanitarian projects, donating his time in life. His story? He got caught smoking pot. He had a large amount. He was giving it away to his friends, along with picking, drying, distributing magic mushrooms. They were a laughing jolly group of young adults. He grew the pot himself. I believe him. I can picture what happened, and how that looked. He's got long hair. He gets high on life, and tells silly stories, laughs, waves his arms in an animated way. He reminds me of Cheech and Chong, the pothead comedians.

Highly intelligent teens who dropped out of college protesting war. Off to save the world in some way. I know how that comes across to a red neck cop. Looks like he does not work for a living. Because he is so very intelligent he makes money just having fun, and not selling pot. But the law says 'distribution,' which does not necessarily mean selling, and can include giving it away free. The law states a certain amount as a felony. What you are doing with it does not matter. He got ten years. I can see it is killing him. Even as he does not complain, and helps others. I can see he misses being in the loop. He is used to discussions with professors and changing the world. He was on the cutting edge of biochar, balancing soils naturally. He had financial concerns going in other countries, helping remote villages in Africa recover soil nutrition. The village can be self sufficient, growing its own food, instead of spending hard to get money on inferior food.

Mushroom showed us videos made of his work in India, Africa, and Mexico. I'm guessing he was well paid as the expert to fly in and solve these kinds of problems. He was fighting Monsanto and genetically altered corn. There are big companies who would like to clean his clock, put a monkey wrench in Mushroom's gears who is stopping villages from investing in Monsanto crops and products. Mushroom is an expert at saving seeds that can be grown again next year. Monsanto seeds cannot be saved to grow again. That's the beauty of their profits. Every year you have to buy the seeds at their price. It would not surprise me if Mushroom was turned in, even set up. How is prison for Mushroom helping society, or him?

He will be a changed person when he gets out. Defeated, out of the loop. Outdated knowledge in his head. A felon can't get the same kind of work. Might not be able to get a passport. Worse, he knows it. Getting old in prison; tired. I can see it in the lines in his face. He enjoys teaching, helping others. But many do not care, do not want to be in class. They are here because it is better than washing dishes. They do not share his passion. Many inmates are not very bright. Mushroom has to step way down to reach them.

"Seed? What's a seed?" It's like asking Mozart in his music class, what a note is. The smartest in all his classes knows how to grow a garden, but Mushroom is possibly the best in the world at what he does. Prison is how we reward him. I can tell that breaks his heart. He's a kind enough person to never lose patience with us. He goes over yet again, what a seed is. I hang my head feeling his pain.

"Sure, Book, I agree, many of us here in prison need to be stopped from what we do. Is prison the answer?" The concept prison was founded on might work! Both punish and rehabilitate.

"Show me a better way, so when I get out I have an understanding of what I did wrong, and a way to make amends." I pause, "Show me by example how being legal looks. Show me by example how it works. Let me see the rewards and the light, that I may see a new path." What is it I am learning when the guards are for the most part meaner than the prisoners. The prison system is more corrupt, dishonest, mean, and illegal then I ever was. I might learn to avoid the stick. This is not respect born of trust, or being right.

Muscle has been listening in and adds, "I might have the kind of respect they better not turn their back on. Drop that stick even for a moment and see what happens." I do not want to have this attitude. I fight it. I understand and do not blame those who feel this way. What does prison and a corrupt system expect us to think about what is going on? We are low life's that can be abused. Nothing can be done about it. Laughed at, kicked, forgotten, tortured, lied to, experimented on, zero rights. Nothing and nobody.

A different glowing story presented to the public. Pictures of the lovely farm, classes offered with certificates, updated top of the line equipment and care.'Look at your tax dollars at work! These people come out with job skills and a positive attitude!' Statistics show otherwise, but it is not the prison's fault!

"That's all you can expect out of degenerates as these." I'm sure the guards and prison officials know how to give speeches and look good in public. I've seen how it is in the past.

Book says, "Yeah, the sad thing is the money is there! If we just had some honest people around, good things might get accomplished."

Muscle adds, "If the educational certificates meant something, we might get jobs! Most of us did the work, gained the knowledge!"

Yes, the university used to work with the educational system so the certificates could be endorsed and accepted as worth something. We learn to grow food, then throw it away. What are we learning? It's not worth growing? Marketing and selling is half the farmers battle. It's like teaching us how to paint a masterpiece, then after class is over, toss paintings in the trash, adding, "Your lesson is over now, bye." Oh well, we can't solve the problems of the world! Certainly not as prisoners! Ha! But we can understand, and help each other, do what we can.

I add, "It is understood we are here primarily to be punished. Teaching us something that does not help get a job might be good punishment. However, this seems like a strange way to dish out punishment because it costs so much!" It is agreed, if this is punishment then it costs a lot of money to run a garden, just to throw it away.

"I'd rather be in a chain gang like the old days. At least getting something positive done. I would not mind working free, and having society benefit. Do work no one else wants to do. Pick crops, make license plates, whatever." Not many others agree with me though. Most would rather just sleep all day and get left alone.

I have to refocus on the good. Stop dwelling on the negative. Here I am in a prison with no bars! I sit in the sun on a bench. Flowers grow around me that prisoners planted. Ornamental trees with pretty red leaves surround me. Blue sky and fresh country air. Relaxing, being fed, without a care in the world. I have a favorite spot and time I like to sit. I watch the people go by for entertainment. There is something to learn from groups I have never been introduced to before. There are some black inner city gang guys that supposedly speak English, who I cannot understand. Every sentence has "moo fook," interjected in it. Mixed with "homey," "The hood," "You know," and "nigga." I wonder how such a person could get a job, when all they can do is talk to each other, and no one else. I can imagine, "That'll be a moo fook nickel change, you know nigga!" I observe an odd introduction gesture of grabbing your crotch and lifting your pants before speaking. As if you were grabbing the handle of a handy man jack and cranking yourself up. I would think such a gesture would be an insult, or embarrassing. Interesting. A, 'My balls are bigger than yours', gesture? How primitive, how odd. *Hey! I'm just the observer here, recording what I see.* I have no idea what it means. I'd love to ask! I wonder if my ways seem just as off the planet to them? Yes, I image my life expectancy would be about one minute in their neighborhood. I smile.

Hmmm, I wonder then if these guys could understand me, from Alaska. I'm interested in if we can open up a line of communication. Hmmm. One black I recognize as someone I have smuggled garden food to. I wave him over. He has to look good coming over, called from his tribe, over here to talk to a White honky. His buddies come over, 'for protection.'

"Wuz up, White boy?"

I say, "Mukluk!" *That's what's hanging.* Black boy looks puzzled. I explain, "Za word from the Eskimo hood bro." He is only a little puzzled. I make the Eskimo hood move. From a dance I once saw. It's like a dog peeing on a tree to see how high he can pee. Everyone understands that. I do the Eskimo hand jive of the Bear Clan brotherhood can ya dig it? Woosh woosh swish, bow the head, move the hands, shuffle the feet and say, "Mukluk." Black boy can dig it. He nods. So I explain further to the jive rap beat, "We all got the moves. We all got the jive. We all from our own hoody bro." Bow the head, move the feet, to the beat of the universal sound of all tribes all over the earth. Spin to the left, spin to the right, "Give me five bro." Hold out the hand, "Give me six bro!" Hold out the other hand with the middle finger up. "Hold on bro! Whoa Bro!" spin, spin "blam, blam." "Say it black boy, Say it White nigga! Mukluk!" Dip like a surfer on the wave. Get the beat? "Whatcha got to trade, whatcha want boy, what I want, what we want? Mukluk!" "Da password to da Hood! Of the Bear Clan bro! Mukluk!"

I show the tattoo of the northern hood, a machete scar from cutting trapline trail. All people in all races know what a scar means. It means you been there and done that. I sing it like a rap song from the northern people.

"We all got the move!" Black boy laughs, but with me, not at me. The others lighten up and laugh good natured at my explanation of the difference between us, but how everything is the same too.

"You want the melon, you want the hot pepper? It's the word! 'Mukluk,' say the password moo fook-r."

They all say "Mukluk!"

I make the move of, "Yeah! You got the move man, yeah!" I look to the right and I look to the left for our captors. No Gestapo around, so I reach into my pocket and pull out some peppers and slip the blacks some hot peppers. It's just us acting goofy doing jive talk. It's our cover. They get it. With valued hot peppers in their pockets, they are bobbing their heads, walking like sand hill cranes down the prison walk.

MEANWHILE... back at the ranch...

I'm in the TV room. I sometimes wander, looking in TV room windows to see what channel is on. This room is empty. It's dinner time. There is an ok movie on, so I walk in and sit down. I'm absorbed in the movie as others come in and sit down. The room is half full before I realize, *Oh, oh!* I'm in the black room. *Dang.* How am I going to get out of here alive? Stutter I'm sorry, and slowly back out?

I holler, "Hey! Has this TV got COLOR?" Everyone freezes and eyes go wide. I grin, "Anyone got any watermelon to pass around?" All the blacks burst out laughing. "God damn, White honky, you be all right nigga!"

"Got a tool a mile long!"

"Yeah, you wanna git chittlings and grits, you hang witch us, White boy!"

I say, "Be nice. I'm the one with garden privileges, that can get you collard greens and chard!"

One guy recognizes me. "Hey, I got sum suppa hot peppa often'n this moo fook White nigga! Just giff'em ta me."

So I got out of there alive, being told I'd be welcome any time.

---

I FINALLY GET my orientation class. The booklet I get handed has 399 rules listed in order. I am responsible for knowing them all.

The very first words in the introduction read:

> "Unit Admission and Orientation is held upon arrival. Orientation lectures will be held monthly."

Neither has happened. This does not inspire me to have confidence in the system that holds my life in its hands. I joke with Muscle, "Reminds me of the time I got my $40 service manual for my outboard engine!" I pause until I have everyone's attention. "Yeah, I looked forward to breaking down and trying it out! This book tells you everything that can go wrong and how to fix it! I got lucky and broke down! How cool is this! I excitedly got out my five inch thick manual. I open to the first page. "Put engine in an engine stand." I look around. I am in the middle of everything, on a sandbar, a hundred miles from the nearest road in the days before cell phones. I could not perform the next step or the next. I look around as everyone wonders what I did! "I got out my duct tape, baling wire, screwdriver, crescent wrench, and fixed it, like I always do!" We all laugh.

"Yeah, a bunch of rules we have to follow, but the institution does not. Just what we need." That teaches us what? Punishes us in what useful way? Rehabilitates us how? [2] I read up on, brush up on, 'the rules,' in case I missed any I was not told about that could be important.

"Rule Eight. No visiting between units." Well, we all go between buildings to watch TV, join our friends.

"Rule 13. All shoes will be neatly arranged underneath the bed with toes pointed inward. No exceptions!" We put our shoes wherever they fit.

"Rule 19. Pictures, etc. will not be attached to the walls in any manner." Every cube has so many pictures on the wall you cannot see the wall.

"Rule 23. Nothing is to be stored on top of lockers." It is common to store folded clothes, books, on the lockers. We have no space otherwise.

I read further about no gambling or card games! Each evening after mail call, a table is set up out in the lobby. Those who wish to participate, play cards nightly, and bet with stamps. Some take it seriously, and owe a lot, others get rich off this. The guards go by and nod. Maybe even join in.

"So, Book, I am back again asking what rules matter, which ones can we break. Why not make the rules workable and reflect how it really is?" I do not understand how others simply know. They get it. They know the important rules from the ones no one cares about. It does not make sense to me, to have rules we all wink about and ignore. Wouldn't it be easier to toss out the rules that are not working?

Book has no answer for me. No one I have ever talked to has an explanation that makes sense to me. This is important because, in my opinion, it is the bottom line of why I am here! There appears to be a zillion rules no one can remember. Most rules do not work and are ignored. So, I also, pick and chose according to what seems logical. But there may be no logic behind it. I assumed I was breaking the same rules others break, or fitting in with the exceptions of those around me. At the edge, but not over the line. I was mistaken.

I assumed wildlife laws are about sound biology. I am guessing the rules are more about politics, power, control, and money. I am also guessing there are reasons the government does not want its citizens to be free; know how to take care of themselves without government help. Living off the land is scary to a government. Not needing the government is not cool. I do not think this is an only reason to get messed with, but it lowers one's value as a prized citizen when there are such issues and questions asked.

"Well, Miles, you can't make such mistakes when someone has a big stick over you. You pay the price. It doesn't have to be fair." The explanation I get most often is, "There are rules that do not work that we all disobey so that any of us can be hauled in any time for any reason. It's just a matter of the authorities wanting to. The secret is not to give the authorities any reason to want you shut up, or out of the way, or part of their statistics."

I reply, "Yes, I understand the sheep do not have problems." *If I'm going to be wild, I can't let on. Move with the sheep, stop and graze when the sheep do. Bleat and look nervous as the sheep do. Let the shepherd walk by, believing he is taking care of me, as he does all the other sheep. Not even the sheep can know.* There is not much room for creative thinking. Here is an interesting note in the handbook. Health care visits will be billed two dollars from our account. Huh. I know prisoners who do not have two dollars.

Some of the work here has pay with it. I think the highest pay in prison is five dollars a month. It is such an insult I said, "Keep it. I'm not interested. Use it for a worthy cause. Help the poor." We actually get prison points for being helpful to others and donating to various funds.

"Works well with others, thinks of others." Goes in a file, and is considered when thinking of early release and such things.

The use of the commissary is explained. It seems a good system. Our prison number lets us know what days we can shop. In this way there is no serious line on any particular day. To get our mail we have to give our prison number in order to make it harder for anyone else to intercept our mail. Someone had hacked into the email system and was emailing prisoner's relatives, saying they needed emergency money to be transferred into their prison account number. There are of course some seriously dishonest people in prison! Da!

Phone use is spelled out. I have no serious issues with the phone rules. If I choose my time to use the phone wisely there is not much of a line. There are times the phones are busy: right after mail call, during lunch hour, commissary days. Early in the morning works well, or on rainy bad weather days as it requires going outdoors and across the courtyard in the open. I feel lucky to have a phone available at all! The phones use voice recognition. Sometimes it is hard to say your name exactly the same way each time. If I am in a hurry, tired or upset, the phone tells me I am not the person I say I am. After three tries I have to give up and wait half an hour. I try to memorize how I say my name, at the same pace, and cadence each time. Background noise effects voice recognition. Still, I recognize the privilege of having any phone use at all. Here is something interesting to me in the handbook:

"English as a second language for non-English speaking inmates. English is mandatory for all inmates." If we do not speak English at an eighth grade level or higher, English class is offered with a $15 incentive for satisfactory completion. I point out this part to Muscle, who is Mexican.

"Miles, remember the old man from Viet Nam?" I nod that yes, this is the reason I show him this part. As far as we know, there is no such class actually offered, as mandated and legally required.

I was on my way to the phones one day. I see an old man out in the grass of the courtyard, happily picking up colored leaves on the ground. I am shocked and go to him to get him off the grass before he is caught! We are not allowed in the courtyard anywhere except on the designated walk paths. Before I can get his attention, a guard spots him and grabs him. The guard is yelling orders at him. The old man obviously does not understand. The old man is carted off to the hole - solitary confinement. A six by six room with no window, nothing but cement and a mattress on the floor. No clock, no music, no reading material. Maybe worse, you lose your bunk and all your 'stuff.' If you are lucky, you have friends who grab it up before the guards come. Friends store it for you until you get out. Otherwise, it simply disappears.

In most cases there is a loss. When you get out, you are assigned a new bunk. Your routine changes. New bunkies to meet, get along with, and fit in with. Gone are your personal shoes, watch, clock, calendar, paper, pens, reading material, letters from home, pictures, and other stuff we tend to accumulate, and get away with keeping in our personal locker. It's not a lot, but means a great deal when it is all you have. You lose the class you might have been in, lose your job if you had one.

This old man gets talked about. He is from a small village in the Viet Nam area. He cannot speak English. No one among the prisoners can communicate with him. I had seen him around as a happy smiling elder with a good outlook on life. He gets out of the hole in two weeks. Has no idea why he was locked up. I have learned, that if no one else is around me, it is time to ask myself why. We are never completely alone, so probably we are someplace we do not belong, at a time we are not supposed to be, like count time.

I run into Old Man in the TV room. He is trying to figure out what the show is, and when it is a good time to come in to watch TV. There is sort of a schedule in chalk on a board. We may or may not follow it, but it is an indicator for at least the favorite shows. The Walking Dead I think is the name of one favorite that I watch, but do not care for much. Sort of an end of the world zombie weekly story to follow. Another favorite, I forget the name, is about a railroad camp during the early days of rail building that features a crew that travels as the tracks are laid. There is a deadline and all kinds of intrigue and characters and plots within plots. This is the show the old man wants to catch. I show him on the board, point to the TV, point to the board. Spell it out for him. Basically saying, "When you see these letters on the board next to a time and day, this is when to be here for this show!"

He understands and is grateful to have it explained. He now knows how to catch his favorite show! I like this guy, so sit next to him, and teach him the basics of how to learn what he needs to know. All of us help. Over time he can talk. He is very smart. He fought for the Americans in Cambodia and got wounded. He helped load big guns. He shows us scars from explosions. He cannot hear well due to war injuries. His story of how he got here? He was hauling vegetables across the border with his wife; a driver for someone else, getting paid. He was stopped at the border and searched. Drugs were found hidden in the truck. His employer had not told him there was a secret illegal load going across. His wife was let go if she gave evidence against him. To save herself, she lied. So here he is. He does not know where his wife is, or his children, or how to find them. He will be here four years. His wife does not know where he is or when or if he will ever return.

It is hard not to believe the story as he is so quiet, considerate, easy going, non violent. He behaves the part of a country man living a simple life that got caught up in something he knew nothing about. Maybe even someone who deserves a medal for his role during the war. We all watch after him so he does not get in trouble again. I sneak him herbs and garden—things I think come from his area that he might be familiar with. I risk going in the hole smuggling food out to the rest of us. Old Man likes bokchoy best. He knows how to stir fry in the microwave. The commissary has soy sauce and minute rice. Sometimes he cooks for me in return for garden produce. This is not something I expect. I let everyone know I am bringing food because we need it, and it is the right thing to do.

Selling food is more of a crime then stealing it and would get me in trouble. I suspect giving it away is overlooked and tolerated. There is so much openness about it, the guards have to know! At evening count there is the smell of home cooking throughout the barracks. We hide it quickly in a locker if there is unscheduled inspection, which is often. There are even designated lockers for contraband. Inmates can give up locker space in return for stamps. Or, we grab a locker from someone in the hole and the guards are not sure whose locker is whose.

We are not allowed to have pointy objects that might be considered weapons. Yet, we need a knife to cut vegetables and create meals. There are secret hiding places no one owns, and fingerprints are wiped off. If the knife is found, no one knows anything. Most knives like this are Ulu shaped, made from some sort of bread kneading knife it is possible to make disappear from the kitchen. Something hard to use as a weapon. If caught, there is more than the hole. This is getting caught with a deadly weapon and adds more jail time. I am unwilling to take a chance, so am never the one to use this item, even though I know where it is, and watch it being used every day. Now and then an Ulu is found by the guards. I have never seen anyone get found with it. Again, I suspect the guards know we have a way to cut up our food and overlook it, but now and then grab one, to let us know what will happen if we use such a tool to make trouble. Or, it simply looks good that the guard is doing his job, if now and then he confiscates something to prove his diligence.

There are sometimes locker inspections, supposedly 'random.' Certain lockers get searched more than others. Leading me to believe there is in fact a method to the madness. Prisoners are hauled off to the hole. All around me there are lockers opened. [3]

I DO NOT GET along with everyone.

"Hey Shorty!" A big guy comes up towering over me, trying to intimidate me with his size. Since I do not respond with fear, he ups the ante. "What if I decided to beat the crap out of you right here, Shorty!" Ha ha.

"That would not be a good idea," said with a straight face, calm tone, looking him straight in the eye.

"And why is that?" Said in a tone of, he hopes this is a good story.

"Do you know who I am?" He blinks and wonders why that matters!

"Besides a punk pussy short reader of books?"

I explain who I am. "The guy from Alaska who killed a moose with a knife." He is not impressed. Is sure I have made it up, as everyone brags and makes things up. Since I do not want a problem with this guy, I have to nip it at the bud. I try another tactic. "I'm an animal trapper. I understand traps, snares, and methods of hurting you without even being around." I give an example. "I know how to string shoe laces together and make a trigger spring so when you climb out of bed in the morning, you could find yourself hanging from the ceiling by your foot or your neck. I will not even be there." I pause and add calmly, "I do not think I am someone you want to mess with." I smile. "Let's be friends instead, ok?" I put my hand out. This lets him off the hook proving his manhood.

"Sure thing. Dang! You make a good connection all right! The hit man from Alaska."

I have met this type all my life. It was a problem I had to do something about… well… a couple of times. The problems were solved. It would not help my time here to get known as the hit man from Alaska, so I make light of it, and let it pass. *I was just bluffing.* The truth will not set us free. *There was that commercial boat operator that did not like me parking my ugly houseboat at the same public dock he parked at.* "Never mind." I can't recall any details of when, where, and how. It might only be my imagination.

In general, there are not many confrontations in the prison. One fight broke out in the cafeteria over a banana. Both got an extra year added to their sentence. I wasn't there, but Mushroom told me about it. Is a banana worth it? Is proving my manhood to a degenerate goon? I think not. There are guys walking the cafeteria when everyone is done eating, picking up packets of sugar. It is possible to trade sugar for stamps. Stamps is the unit of currency here. Everything is valued in stamps. Legally we can't have more than one book of stamps to our name—another ignored rule. Sugar, I am told, is used by the collectors to make alcohol. I'm not sure what the active ingredient is. It might be one reason we are not allowed to take food out of the cafeteria like apples and pears. Some idiot will figure out how to collect them and make an illegal drink.

All of us from the garden are watched for any indication we are fermenting garden goods. There is more activity at the garden as time passes. I am accepted as a full time employee. That had not been promised me in the beginning. I was told garden privileges are limited. Only fourteen out of the 700 are working in the horticulture garden, which has to do with the valued greenhouses.

I had no master plan. I show up to class early and help set up. I stay late and help others with homework, or engage in after class discussion. I volunteer to do the dirty grunt work at the garden no one else wants to do. I'm a hard worker who does what I am supposed to on my own. One day the teacher says, "You, you and you, head over to the garden." Pointing at me among the seven picked. No one questions my right to be part of the coveted garden crew.

"Yo ho, you hoe," we marched off down the magical road like the seven dwarfs with rakes, hoes, and a wheel barrel. I am eventually given a number related to chits for checking out tools. It usually takes a year to earn that right.

I especially like working with the flowers and take it on myself to plant bulbs around the prison grounds. I sometimes do this on my own time. One advantage is, this gives me access to many places, people, and things few others can get near. A guard says, "Halt who goes there!"

I can hold up my bag of bulbs and trowel and sheepishly bow my head and explain without making eye contact, "I am planting flowers, sir." *I'm one of the pussies, don't mind me, masta, Sir.* That is how I got access to the drainage ditch dumping sewage into the lake. I dutifully write that down in my notes.

There is a lot of grunt physical work to do! All the property needs mowing. Leaves need raking by hand. Weeds need pulling. Groups of us get assigned areas to work. Some areas are more desired. I do not mind, as low man on the totem pole, getting the worst area. I have one guy with me. No one especially wants to work with him. He's gay. Few mind that. He has a gay female outlook on life. He hates to get dirty, is afraid of... spiders, thorns and more. Woman is very emotional and passionate about life; cries easily. He's my working partner. I sigh. He's ok. We all have 'stuff' to deal with. Baggage. We are all here; do not want to be, and live in our own hell. We all show it different. My way is to work hard and carry much of the load for the two of us. In return, he gasses up the equipment, sharpens tools, drags bags of leaves off. Covers for me—which might involve my making my way over to the grapes to snaffle a bag full. That's all he knows. I could be checking on the Mexicans instead.

"Miles just went to get the shovel, you didn't pass him?" There are, 'things going on.' I am made privy to the inside knowledge as I am more trusted. My crew swiped a microwave oven. We have it in our garden hang out shack. We are able to do our own cooking there. Those few of us who have access, are eating fresh produce daily. Tons of rules are ignored.

We are supposed to be issued gas for the mower and power tools—one tank at a time—issued by a guard. That could take days! So we have a five gallon can hidden. We do our own filling. Now, technically this is material that could be used to make a weapon, or bomb! The prison of course would never hear the end of it if a Molotov cocktail was tossed into a guard shack, or some such. None of us think like this. We just want gas so we can take care of the garden and do our job! Most of us take pride in, and care about the garden. We want our area to look nice, so work hard and do a good job. Working together, we know each other and trust each other. *Sort of.*

The garden work is wonderful! It is away from the main prison across a road. The prison sounds are far off and can barely be heard. We are alone out in the trees and growing things. Away from many of the rules. The prison gives us seeds and supplies. It is limited due to budget, but we make do. Mushroom wishes we could afford lime for the compost, or get some worms for the compost. But what we do works! Mushroom is in charge. He and I get along great, so this makes my job and classes go well. I'm almost the teacher's pet and there are issues over this sometimes, but we deal with it. Woman does not make any passes at any of us. Hopefully I am not his type.

"So, Woman, what is your story for being here?" We are on a break, sitting on a bench overlooking a vast spread of gardens. There are a variety of areas, set up to showcase what different ornamental designs are available, that one might come across on a job. We are in the swamp garden. This area gets flooded with illegal city water. We grow bamboo, ferns, swamp decorative vines of all kinds draped over arches. We have been pulling invasive weeds and blackberry bushes. We are eating tomatoes from the garden like fruit.

"I don't want to talk about it! I just don't! It's so awful!" I sit quietly and he gets over it. A shrug. "I'm here for selling unpasteurized milk to the public." He owned a dairy farm. "It's a growing thing you know. Studies show unpasteurized milk is healthy! A lot of people want and ask for it."

I reply, "Yes, I heard that. I also heard there are hardly any cases of people getting sick from it if the milk is fresh and handled right. If you take it right out of the cow and hand it to someone, it is perfectly fine."

"That's true. I was mad at the system for taking such a large cut, and requiring such hefty fees and permit costs. I couldn't make any money. So I cut the middle people out. Nothing but organized crime anyhow!" He had a customer list of those who wanted this milk. He was not hiding, lying, or misrepresenting. His neighbor set him up. "They did not like me because… well… you know how it is with me." A pause. "They also wanted my land, and I would not sell." Another pause and sniffle. "So they recorded several transactions and kept records, took pictures, and had evidence against me. Next thing I know, I am in handcuffs being carted off. I never saw my farm again. My neighbors have it now."

I'm not sure this is all it takes to get carted off or not. Seems like there would be more to it than that! Woman does not know what he will do when he gets out, he has nothing. I hear of a partner… boyfriend, maybe… if he waits. I'm not sure if he is in the dairy business, too. I notice the questions Woman asks in class. He is moving in the direction of selling activated biochar to nurseries. It's a new big thing now.

Mushroom has been showing us diagrams of how to build an industrial charcoal maker. Explaining where the markets are. He has people on the outside that might help us get started if we are interested. This would be illegal. Felons are not supposed to know each other, visit each other, work together, associate with, or help each other. At least while on probation, which for most of us is a long time. So, whatever plans get made have to be kept low profile.

"Miles, the purpose is to make sheep out of those of us who are not." So for all the sniffling and squishiness, Woman has balls.

"Well, there are snitches, so keep this low profile, Woman." He nods. Woman trusts me after working together for a while. There is a great deal to be quiet about. The gas, the microwave, where the grapes go, the use of city water to create a swamp garden.

"Tomorrow we are supposed to take out all the raspberries, did you hear? We need to talk to Mushroom."

Woman nods. None of us wants to lose the raspberries. We worked hard to get them to grow well. Suddenly the head of education working for the prison, our boss, decides no, he doesn't like them. No other plans beyond his joy of yanking our chain and seeing us in pain. Taking something away he knows we value, just to watch us squirm. Partly Mr. Education needs to go along somewhat with what we do and our plans for the garden because we know certain things he'd rather the world not know about. It's to all our advantages to work together here. So while we say, "Yes, Sir!" and salute. We can often simply ignore Mr. Education. We are not employees, so what is he going to do, fire us? Mushroom has already got a plan.

"There is another place towards the back, few officials get to. An old ditch, perfect for raspberries. We can put them there and maybe later move them someplace else, or back where they were." In this way we will not lose the plants. I did not know it was possible to keep them alive a long time without planting, by just keeping them wet. They are heirloom plants and somewhat special. The berries are unique, the vines hardy and tall. Resistant to mildew and other culprits that prey on plants. Woman and I are assigned the task of moving the plants, while the rest of the crew covers for us.

There is a specific routine that needs to be strictly followed when taking off on a job. The officials need to know ahead of time what tools we need next day. We all have chits. Each tool is signed out. These tools are weapons. We are responsible for them. If one turns up missing, we go to the hole. The entire prison is in lock down until the tool is found. "Do not misplace your rake, sheers, or shovel!" We have to have a specific project justifying the tools, and have a job done to account for the use of the tool. So getting tools, and time for moving raspberries takes some finesse and cooperation between us. Going to the hole has little to do with being a bad boy.

As Muscle puts it, "It's like being Jews in a concentration camp." Well, whatever. We can justify how we want things to be, what works for us, that helps us do our time. If Muscle wants to be a martyr, I understand. But when he gets out, I think he will have to sing another song if he wants to stay out of prison. Prison may not let him out if he does not sing the song of redemption and rehabilitation. Meanwhile, Woman and I are saving raspberries, and hope we do not get caught.

Horticulture class is in the morning. Hands on work connected to the class in the garden is in the afternoon. Sometimes there are lessons in the field. We go out to identify bug damage. What kind of bug, how bad the damage, what can be done to target one type of bug. We walk around with notepads taking notes for tests later. We may spot leaf damage and bring this to class for a discussion and lessons.

Now and then we escort higher up prison officials on a tour. Sort of show off what gets done with the funding the prison gets. We prisoners help justify the program. Show how much it helps us. Show them we are well along the path of rehabilitation! We rehearse ahead of time the route we will take. Keep them away from specific areas we are ordered to avoid during the tour. Like the outlets for the stolen city water that feeds our swamp garden. There are areas we keep ready, put great effort into, implying the whole rest of the vast estate looks the same. I'm a good talker, so I am often elected to make the speeches. I am much like the Wizard of Oz. "Do not pay attention to that man behind the curtain!"

"Miles, you could sell snow to Eskimos!" The work crew asks if that's what I'm in for.

"You didn't try to sell snow to Eskimos without a permit did you?"

Someone whispers, "No it was eagle feathers."

"Did ya kill the eagle, Miles?"

No use reviewing my charges. If I say "No!" who would believe me. How else do you get here without doing something terrible! Even I think, "Yeah right, and what's the other side of the story? What is it you left out?" Yes, I have the gift of gab. I could convince ordinary people red is really blue. It's a gift. I try hard not to abuse it. I resent having to be unethical and cover for a prison that was not so kind and understanding when it came to covering for me.

Mushroom says, "The system is not working. The public knows it. So they can give as many glowing reports as they want and tell the world how they can't understand why prison doesn't work when any inmate could explain it. It's not rocket science. Try running an honest business following rules we all have to follow, or change the rules so they work."

Woman and I move all the raspberries. "Hide them in a low ditch for a week. Mushroom says if the roots stay wet they do not have to be planted for a while." He's the expert.

Soon Mr. Education will forget what he said, and we can replant them. "The secret to getting along with him is to say, "Yes sir!" and do what he says without argument. It's much like moving a rock pile from one place to another and back again, it doesn't have to make sense. He just has to come up with something for us to do every day."

"We could make suggestions?"

"That would imply a relationship of respect that does not exist." Yes, we are treated like we are stupid, and barely know our names. So we play the part expected of us. It is believed, if we are creative, it is used to commit crimes.

"Define crime!"

"Anything the sheep do, that those with the power and the stick do not like."

"So what happens to the sheep participating in the rule making?" We get into such discussions in horticulture class!

"After all, running any business is about how to do so legally. Of course, we have to know what that means before we even get started!" Woman is given a solution for example. "You could sell shares in the cows. It is legal to drink raw milk from cows you own. So all the regular customers buy shares and jointly own the cows. That's how it's done by those who want to be legal, Woman."

I add, "I own shares and am part owner of cows where I come from. I get yogurt, cheese and milk from my cows. Never been inspected, pasteurized, sterilized or permitted. It does not even taste like what you buy in the store. Real cream on the milk; have to shake it and mix it to drink it." We are all wondering what kind of jobs we might have when we get out. Lucky for me, my web site is not taken down. I still have a business. Most of these guys lost it all. Their car, wife, dog, bank account, home was all lost. What will they do as a felon? By law, we have to tell prospective employers we are convicted criminals. Various ways to go into business for yourself are discussed in class. Along with how we can feed ourselves from a garden if we are out of work and have no job. Many of the guys own land.

Mushroom is in favor of self sufficiency with a few chickens, a cow, a small garden. He envisions trading extra food for services in a rural setting. We see educational films on how problems are solved around the world or in the past that could be applied to modern times.

"In old times the animals were kept on the bottom floor and the people lived upstairs. Heat from composting straw and the animals rose to the upstairs and kept the home warm!" We are supposed to be studying more on how to get jobs in nurseries.

"Realistically, that is not likely to happen as a felon, guys." Likewise, the landscape business. "Rich people who need landscape work done are not likely to want a felon around." Likewise, felons are not likely going to be part of government contracts.

The prison system says differently. Counselors are eager to work within the system with job placement through government programs. We go to meetings and are handed fliers giving toll free numbers about low income housing, subsidized programs for the poor, government loans, how to get them and what not. It looks to some of us like programs that are about keeping government bigger, linked to the prison system being part of the cycle of bigger government. For all we know, the prison gets kick backs, or credit for job placement, and thus more prison funding. The counselor and prison look good when we are kept within the same system. Those of us who go off on our own are no longer in the system. Our statistics and success stories disappear. What good is that? When we can be fodder in the government cannon of programs! We are a commodity once we are in the system. Passed around like coins.

"Or pieces of meat!" *Pieces of ate!* "Yeah, someone gets paid to find us, someone else gets paid to prepare us, another gets paid to wrap us."

## MILES MARTIN

I grow a lot of my own food at home so wish to learn from other prisoners who know farming well.

# CHAPTER THREE

## READING OLD CLASSIC BOOK, DOING OK, HALFWAY THROUGH MY TIME

We all know to smile and say thanks, if we expect to get let go. Mushroom takes helping the fellow prisoners seriously. He wants us to do well when we get out. So much of the horticulture class is geared towards helping us get work, or at least taking care of ourselves. I have knowledge on how to put up food. Now and then I contribute information on drying food, canning and pickling. Only some of the guys are interested. Realistically many are city people! Have no intention of getting out to the country! That is not their idea of escape!

We see a film on city farms growing high end herbs for fancy restaurants. One guy grows basil in the back of an abandoned truck in an inner city someplace. He makes a living at it! *As a street lifestyle he may not need to make more than $20 a day to survive.* In other areas, locals get together to clean up abandoned lots and reclaim them. Often the city supports this as it increases the value of the neighborhood; gets it looking better. Sometimes the land owner does not mind having his unused lot cleaned up.

"Farmers markets are getting popular all over the country. People are often willing to pay more for local, fresh, and organic." Small worn out farms that have been subdivided until it is hard to make a living working for Monsanto growing corn, change. They go organic - revitalize the soil, use less equipment, cut costs, and grow less, but better quality. Selling at farmers markets where they do not lose so much of the profits to middle people.

Mushroom: "Yeah, this is professor Dork. He and I had a biochar business together in the 80's." Or, "I learned what I know about letting bugs help us from this guy."

In another film there are some asides, a personal touch, and story included followed by questions and discussion from the inmates. I envision college being like this. Even if the piece of paper we get at the end means nothing, the knowledge we get is still with us and can be useful! Not everyone agrees, but this view helps me with my prison time. A feeling of accomplishing something while I am here. It's a spiritual belief I came up with on my own over time. *If a God made us, the best way to show respect is the same as with any gift. Take care of it, honor it. Do not waste it!* This is my view of life. Not to waste it.

I assume anything that gets prisoners thinking of careers away from what they did as criminals is good, and part of rehabilitation. Talk of a new set of friends, excited to be off in a new useful direction is a good thing. I make sure anyone who might be a snitch hears about being saved.

"Praise the lord I had the opportunity to come to Hotel Fed before it was too late!"

"Miles, don't you think you are kissing ass too much, selling out, becoming one of the sheep?" Muscle is concerned I'm getting brainwashed here.

"Muscle, we are not going to fight the system from here within. Our first priority is to get out. As early and smoothly as possible." Muscle nods that he understands. I go on, "Many of my heroes were captured by the enemy. They survived, got away, and lived to have other adventures. Even contributed something positive without being sheep." I think of an example. "If Paul Revere had been caught by the British, the rulers and government at the time, how do you think he would have been treated? One side would see him as one of the worse examples of a human being, the other side treats him as a hero. What is the truth?"

"Miles, while we are prisoners, we do what we can to survive, and this is the most important thing. To live to fight another day."

"Well, I would not want to come out and say our government is our enemy. Get caught saying that and you will never see the light of day." I pause. "More like, we care about our country and its people dearly. We can think of no other place that is better. Nor any other form of government we think would work better! We want to help things change for the better. For example; getting back to the constitution we were founded on. By voting, getting involved. Finding out what is going on, and trying to influence people, educate people. If we get those in power who represent us to agree, how could that not work?"

Muscle of course is Mexican, but a US citizen, I assume. "Yeah, it is better here than Mexico, that is for sure!" I have heard rumors of Mexican jails. It gives me the shivers!

"Miles, someone told me in Russian prisons, all inmates get laptop computers and access to the internet."

"One of the issues we face is, how do we know the truth? There is talk, rumors. How do we sort out what we hear? What is propaganda?"

"Much of the world deplores the US for the number of people we have locked up, and how we treat our prisoners." I do not even know this for a fact. I only know the news media tells us this. "I only know about my little world and my life. I just want to get out in one piece and get on with my life. A lesson learned, no hard feelings; live in peace."

I'm not sure Muscle agrees since he has a family business to get back to that is not likely going to change. I also know that everyone looking out for their little world and not caring about the next guy is part of why things could potentially get out of hand. It only takes a majority to do nothing, for a minority to run things how they want. We mostly agree here in prison is not the place to point this out.

I'M LOOKING out the window at hundreds of geese settling in for the night along the big pond. I value the view. I'm counting my blessings. We got a new guy in the cube. He got out of solitary, and knows a lot of people. He is Latino. Doesn't fit in well with the rest of us. Doesn't want to fit in. We guess already he is going to be trouble. We know he sneaked a cell phone into the cube. That could get us all in trouble. He doesn't care.

"You think I care, White boy? You stay out of my business, we'll get along fine!" Fair enough. I'm curious how far his outlook on life will get him. I like to study the various ways of the world, in a quest for survival methods, happiness, making a living. I watch, I observe. Muscle and I look at each other and shrug, both thinking the same things.

Our other bunkies come and go. They are tolerable, no one to remember. One inmate near us a few cubes down is in here for computer hacking. His story is, he had been working for the government, trained by the government, and had simply done some unauthorized spying and hacking on his own. When he did the same thing for the government on assignment it was ok, he got paid for it. He has some interesting stories of how hacking works. I figure he must know something to have such details of how it is done. He is an international hacker. There were news articles about his arrest in the paper to look up.

He is a good one to get information on how to secure your computer. His overall advice is, "There is no such thing as a totally secure computer. Not ever, by any method." It is even difficult to destroy a hard drive.

"I heard magnets wipe the electrical codes recorded."

"Yes, but in a uniform way that can be uncovered." He adds, "I had a device where I could walk past a computer and download everything on that computer as I walked by."

I look dubious. "The public does not have access, and may not have knowledge but the capability exists. I did international hacking for the government." Mr. Terabyte explains a method to secure a computer, but the words were over my head. A program that randomly changes IP addresses between two computers rerouted to other locations by other like minded people. "The best simple way is to have a computer that never connects to the internet, and never shares external drives with computers that connect to the internet." He pauses. "Once you are in the web, it's over." Another pause looking at my dubious expression. "I can hack into cell phones, cars, anything with a computer chip. Yes, I can take over most cars. I even hacked into a digital pace maker once. I just started getting a little too curious and too creative. I made my boss nervous. I'm here to think about it a while." That's all he was willing to say. No names, no specifics. I'm not even sure he meant the US government when he referred to 'government he worked for.'

Terabyte likes to walk, so sometimes I see him on the path and we walk and chat. Nice, quiet, calm fellow, Oriental.

"No, I do not help out Feather anymore." We walk by Two Feathers and I only politely nodded. He can manage his wheel chair better now after building his strength up. I used to push him around the path. He is with the smokers. He talks a lot of anti government I do not want to hear. He swindled a Native Corporation and sold cocaine. He plays on his Indian heritage to get sympathy and followers. I fell for it myself for a while. I got permission to use the Indian lodge, so I am spiritually native. Well at least if I want to stop in and rest a spell on my walk I am not out of bounds. I have permission to be there.

Terabyte does not talk much. I am not even sure what country he is from. Highly educated, no accent. My father was Dean of a college, all my young life I have been around educated people, professors, geniuses, and such. There is a way about them hard to hide. That all educated people in every country have in common. A certain confidence I think. Used to being treated well. Talking like they expect others to listen, without the arrogance. The ability to follow the rules of a debate, and win. Most do not raise their voice or swear. Most dress well. Most are nervous around street people, gangs, a world they know little about. I chuckle telling Terabyte, "Me, I am nervous around insane people." I go on, "If people have the ability to reason, I can usually talk my way out of a problem. The insane are unpredictable." I shrug my shoulders and leave it at that. State prison was scary. Half those people belonged in an insane asylum, not jail. Or, maybe put more politely, needed help, not punishment. "If you are wired wrong it is not your fault." Terabyte only nods, listening. As if deep in his own thoughts, trying to understand a foreign culture. Mushroom stops by and asks if I have seen Fairbanks. I wonder why Shroom would care where Fairbanks is.

Fairbanks is not in the horticulture class, but works in horticulture at the garden. He has already taken all the classes that are offered. He is from Fairbanks, Alaska and says he has seen me around. We know people in common. He knew my fur buyer friend Don and gives me insight into Don's odd personality, even why he got killed by the neighbor. Fairbanks owned a high end restaurant downtown. He is here for distribution of pot. I am not friends with him, because I do not like his attitude. He is working with the Mexicans making a profit from the produce; involved in using some to make prison beer. This is ok with me, but there is a selfishness about his views of the world. Certain parts of the garden are his. The rest of us need to clear anything with him that goes on. Likewise, he harvests an entire crop just when it is ripe, leaving nothing for the rest of us. All the grapes are suddenly gone, or the best apples. These are highly sought after, desired items that store well in the locker, and can be eaten fresh with no preparation. Different then squash, even onions.

Fairbanks and I get along ok. We are not enemies or anything. I sometimes think he has plots to get his way, and get others who are problems for him in trouble. He is gunning for Mushroom because Mushroom believes all the produce is for all of us equally. Mushroom tolerates a certain amount of running off with things to sell. But not when threats, intimidation, and war is involved. Since Mushroom seems to have the ear of Mr. Education, this puts a crimp in Fairbanks's style. He is partly jealous. Fairbanks thinks he got a bad deal for a sentence, compared to the rest of us. He thinks he is smarter than the rest, and deserves Mr. Education's ear as the guy in the know.

"Miles, how come you got just six months for twenty-eight charges filed against you!" In a voice of accusation, resentment.

I do not know how to reply. I do not know why I got the sentence I did. I personally think the prosecution did not have much of a case. I believed however, they had enough they could stick me with ten years if I became a problem. It's about playing your cards. Like the song, "Know when to hold em, know when to fold em." Weigh the odds. Play the game. If you are up against a bully, it is not wise to punch him in the nose. Being a small guy I learned that early in life. There are other ways to teach a bully a lesson. By playing smart.

My opinion is, Fairbanks has now, and had then, a bad attitude the court saw. He wanted to fight to the bitter end and is still fighting. I doubt very much he gets an early out for good behavior. He wants to play hard ball. My take of our situation is, the prison system knows all about people who want to play hard ball, and is ready for them. There is no way to win that game. The system has seen it all before, every trick in the book. Guards take on the job because they love teaching tough guys a lesson. Often, just looking for the least excuse to come in swinging. The tough guy card does not work here. Though possibly most guards would respect standing up for yourself and being tough, to a point. I think this works more in the general population. Most of us in Hotel Fed are negotiators, deal makers like me. *That's option number one anyway.*

I head over to greenhouse number four, not paying attention. A Mexican steps out and blocks my path, giving me a shove backwards. He says nothing. I look up and realize Fairbanks is inside. Probably doing one of his deals, accepting a payoff of some kind. I simply say, "Sorry!" Nod and back away. Now and then I see guards go in greenhouse number four and come out. Usually they stay away from this area. Fairbanks uses this greenhouse like his personal office. Produce gets sorted and handled here. Fairbanks even puts up tomatoes for out of season sales.

"So Woman, we are supposed to clean up the area across from the swamp garden. What do we do about the tobacco?" Woman is a farmer, so has more knowledge then I do about growing things. Mushroom and Two Feathers are growing their own tobacco. I doubt it is legal to do. The guards do not know what tobacco looks like growing. An heirloom Indian variety is disguised in with lettuce, kale, Swiss chard, and tall herbs like dill. Those interested know how to hang and cure it in one of the greenhouses, disguised as an herb drying project for educational purposes. Knowing Mushroom, I doubt any of it gets sold. I think the Mexicans do not know about it, maybe not even Fairbanks.

Woman replies with a shrug, "We just treat it like everything else, we do not know what it is."

"Well, the weeding and trimming will expose the plants more, so I was just wondering." Mushroom is planning to move some mature plants over to a display area near the native hut along the walk by the pond so it is more accessible near where it is needed for smoking in the native religious hut. In this way, the finished product does not have to be smuggled across the grounds. Maybe the plan is to move the plants that are made visible by our trimming.

Mushroom has a work detail the next day with orders to plant ferns, bulbs, and ornamentals in the ceremonial sacred garden across the compound. In full view of everyone, we wheelbarrow tobacco plants five feet tall disguised as experimental ceremonial ferns. The guards watch us do a special blessings ritual over the preparation and planting of sacred ferns cherished by the Oglala Sioux. *And so on and so forth, we bless the sacred weed.*

In my notes from 'The Jungle' by Sinclair, I quote, "The city, which was owned by an oligarch of businessmen, being nominally ruled by the people, a huge army of graft was necessary for the purpose of effecting the transfer of power. Millions of dollars were furnished by the businessmen and expended by the army. The leaders, organizers, were maintained by businessmen directly, alderman and legislators by means of bribes, party officials out of campaign funds, lobbyists and corporations, lawyers in forms of salaries, newspaper proprietors and editors by advertisements. There was the police department, and fire and water departments, and the whole balance banded together, leagued in blood brotherhood with the politician and police. The police captain would own the brothel he pretended to raid."

I rub my eyes from the dim light in the chapel, early in the morning where I have peace, and can read and write. I stare at the compound not yet awake. Deep in thought. I notice things about this main character, Jugar, in the book I'm reading. In my opinion much of his hardships he was in control of, and brought on himself by his poor decisions and selfishness.

The story is, "Poor me, look at how I was abused as an innocent immigrant, used and taken advantage of by a cruel system!" He decides to buy a home when he was not into the reality of his poverty. Anyone in any class who has dreams beyond their economic means, and acts on them, is in trouble. His sixteen year old wife was always in ill health. Money would have been more wisely spent being set aside in case of medical needs. That would have been smarter. While the story is a classic, and changed history, I see flaws in the basic premise it is based on. That premise being, the poor guy had no options, no chance, no way out.

While there was graft and greed all around, Jugar got a good job with very high pay. He was willing to participate in the corruption. He was not as smart as he thought. He pulled a few fast deals and was selfish about it. Jugar was not kind to others, did not look out for, or care about those weaker than him within his family and tribe. What goes around, comes around. He could have made allies among his peers who would have helped him when it was his turn to be down. So, while I understand the points made, I do not sympathize much with the main character.

"Miles, I got some stuff I can show you on the library computer. About looking up laws and legal stuff. Stop by sometime." Book has been talking to Doc. They discovered together, some interesting legal things. In passing, Book says, "Did you know it is common for public defenders to get paid extra to get the accused to plea bargain? In one case we looked up, $3,800." This seems amazing, and cannot be true.

I reply, "Well I suspected at one point in my representation, that the public defender is not my lawyer, not representing me, but representing the public's interest. It did not occur to me this goes so far as to get paid extra for me to take the fall."

"Makes sense though. Getting us to plead saves the court system millions of dollars."

My public defender is probably honest enough. Not mean, not corrupt. I think if he sees a case easy to win, goes for it, digs in more, and spends the money necessary to correct a serious wrong. Based on his opinion. There will not be equal representation. Getting paid more for talking the accused into a deal, is not properly representing the accused. The prosecution is already there with the goal to hang the accused, not bring the truth to light. In a balance of a good justice system, the public defender should be the accused's lawyer, advocate, doing all he can to help the accused, not seeing financial advantages in helping to hang him.

I shake my head to clear it. I can't get worked up over it. The secret might be, to know things, but find a way to make peace. Understand when I can change, accept what I cannot. Look to my own behavior, not be so concerned with what others do. We are not to judge! *Sayeth the Lord*. I have wandered over to the bench I like to sit at to commune with nature. Here are flowers I planted around a type of Japanese maple with small bright red leaves. My legs are stretched out as I lean back to look at the cloud formations. Others sometimes join me. Woman comes and sits next to me, looking upset.

"I am really close to my grandmother. She was taken to the hospital and almost died. I was just on the phone and got cut off after fifteen minutes. I can't call again for thirty minutes to find out what is going on!" His grandpa is falling apart and not able to deal with it. "I was promised an early release so I could go take care of them!" I heard earlier from him, this got denied. I think because the funding for the ankle monitor required for his release got cut. It is hard to be told yes, fill with anticipation, call home with the news, then have the decision turned around. This seems common and part of our punishment.

Another guy stops by I only see around, but do not know. He had chest pains earlier and was medivacced out two weeks ago. It was a week before his wife was notified. It is now her falling apart with medical issues, and him at peace. I had heard his story before. He used to fly helicopters for a medical rescue team in Kodiak, Alaska. He has been on many heroic rescues, and received many honors for his dedicated work.

"My brother, who I am not close to, is in real estate." He pauses. "He buys homes in the $40,000 range, fixes them up and resells them for a profit. Sometimes getting $300,000 for them." The story goes, the brother had a partner. The two of them were running a land scam selling houses for more than they were worth, with false documentation of some sort. I could not follow how it was done. It's words and methods

I do not understand. I assume the bottom line was, getting work signed off that did not get properly done.

At some point, the brother is in trouble financially, has to come up with extra funds, and has over extended his credit. The main thing is, "My brother forges my name on some documents, since he can't use his own name." The pilot can't prove his name was forged. Or more, like most of us, he could, for enough money, go to court and fight and maybe win. But had to take the plea. Not enough money for a lawyer and proof he needs. So he is here. Now a felon over one of his brothers scams. I'm thinking he really may have signed his name to help his brother out, though he comes across as someone who is content with the money he made as a helicopter pilot, and does not need to run scams for more. Nor does he seem close to anyone like a brother who he would do anything for. He did not like his brother. They did not get along, and this seems genuine. I'm just listening, taking notes. Part of the issue I find out later is, their father sides with the brother who he favors, and would testify against this pilot. I understand the situation.

In a divorce, my father sided with my ex. He and she could come up with more money than I could. But more, how can you fight family? How would that look in court? Your own parents saying you are guilty. It's more than I could bear. Fine, let me be guilty and everyone be happy. I am here to please. I hope you all feel good. 'Angry' is how most would say I must feel. That is not the word I would choose. Hurt, sad, devastated, alone, fit my feelings better. Leading to distrust, disassociation.

On the positive side, independent and strong. This positive side is why I am not angry. The bottom line is, I am happy! Why quibble about how I got here? I am not convinced the family and ex are as happy as I am. It's complicated, but I see the same in this pilot. This is why I believe him. He devoted his life to others, being a rescue pilot, compensating for lack of family love. It would be hard to fake this complex situation.

"Miles, do you think you will get all these notes confiscated? The prison officials may think there is evidence they can use in it: confessions, evidence of wrong doing, stuff like that." Helicopter seems savvy to the risks.

I reply, "Well, I have changed the names, made it a little confusing so it would be hard to make a case. I'm not calling it the truth. I can claim it is fiction." I explain further, that, likewise, I have made it clear in case a snitch gets wind of this, my purpose is not to get anyone in trouble. But yes, I am concerned. However, every few weeks I send my notes home to my lady. Apparently all incoming mail is opened and examined, but not outgoing. So as long as the mail gets through untouched, I am free and clear two weeks at a time. The officials have not given an indication we are having problems with each other. Do not forget, it is me they call on to give the tour and speeches to the higher up visitors concerning what a great prison this is. I'm a team player, a con artist, an actor. I do not reveal I asked Iris to hide my writings off property in case there is a search warrant looking for these notes.

We all see how things are going with Doc. He is trying to get evidence, sneak pictures, sue someone, prove illegal deeds like overcrowding. He wants the rest of us to sign a petition. "Yeah, he is going to get in trouble all right!" We all agree. Nice guy, wants to help, but being indignant, combative, is not going to help.

"How did he get here anyhow!"

I say, "It would not surprise me if it involved pretending he was a lawyer when he is not! Practicing law without a license, something like that." We all agree it must be something like that. I add by way of good cheer, "As for me? I am grateful I am in a prison with no bars! Where inmates like us can relax on a bench! I breath clean pure air and hear geese in the distance." I remind them what it is like in other countries if you upset the government! We all nod and agree. Except for poor Woman who has not been paying attention, sitting to be someone who should be on suicide watch. I say to him, "You need a reason to make it through this Woman. Only you can make that happen." He just nods he knows. We all know few here among the guards care if you live or die. A few do, balanced by the same number that would like to watch you die. *I suppose this prison experience teaches us about the real world, here as a lesson in a controlled environment.*

In the real world, if a man is alone on a park bench under street light crying his heart out lone, someone would kick him, rob him beat him up, lucky to get out alive. A nice person might call the police. Who will come for him in a straight jacket, stick a needle in him and put him in a rubber room. He may or may not ever get out. What is for sure not going to happen, is someone stopping and giving him a hug, holding him, treat his as the woman he is.

Here in prison he can set and cry his heart out. No one will bother him. If he is not at the next count in half an hour, he will be put in the hole. All means of killing himself will be removed. Whatever pain he suffers, will be endured. He will be asked if he is ready to come out of solitary. If he is not, a guard will shrug his shoulders and leave him there, No big deal. If Woman lives or not is up to him or her. No one here will give him a hug, that's for sure.

A LOT OF STORIES HERE. I hear a lot of, "I should have taken the deal Man," from those who stuck it out and fought, because they felt they were right, and wanted to prove it. Not one person got less time for fighting, nor are there any, "I got off" stories. I hear guys getting five years who might have gotten only community service if they had pleaded. It is hard to believe someone who knew they were guilty would risk years in prison over some community service. Logic tells me they wanted to risk and fight because they were innocent. The good news is, I probably made the right choice. Do the six months. *"Do I want to clear 99% of my name, not be a felon, and get five years? Or, do I want to do six months, say I'm guilty, put me on the felon list!"* I picked door number two. All of us wonder 'what if.' I'm already halfway through my time. I do not know yet when I get out, what the impact will be of 'being a felon,' and how it affects my life. *How much can it affect my life! I'm a senior! I'm not looking for a job!*

Mr. Education comes to the class to give us a test. No, not a test today. "I need you to answer these questions." I look at the questions we are to write about. The first two, "What is the purpose of this class?" And, "Why are you here?" I am resentful to be asked such loaded questions. I assume Mr. Education needs positive feedback to get funding. Wants, and expects our cooperation. I do not like being taught how to lie, asked to lie, ordered to lie. The correct reply is, "I want my lawyer!"

I write: The purpose of this class, and why?? Well there is the why I think I'm here. Why the prison system thinks I'm here, and why the teacher thinks I'm here. These three answers may or may not match. Depending who is asking. I'd like to turn it in like this. There is an hour given to write an essay so I add to this. I'm in pest management class because it is required in order to work in the garden. I love gardens, dirt. Being allowed to be there is worth taking the class. There are no garden pests in Alaska to speak of. The class is not relevant to me, but is to the prison and teachers. So here I am. There is still more time to write. I am bored. So write more.

Other questions:

"How do I rate the class? What is the best use of time?" As if this were college, and we are all paying to be here, or volunteers. *How do you rate our concentration camp.* How do I rate this class? See answers to one and two. It's ok. I'll survive. I think. Rate this class? What an odd question. I'm rehabilitated now. "What a great class!" Is the only possible choice!

Mr. Education calls me in to discuss my sarcasm. I stick to my answer. "These are rude questions, uncalled for. This is prison. How much am I supposed to like it? Compared to what? Freedom? Do not ask questions you do not want the answer to!"

He tells me later, he did not turn mine in. He destroyed my paper. "To help protect you Miles. I thought of all inmates, you could handle it better. I never figured you to be one to fall apart." I'm usually so easy going, happy, friendly, with nothing but good cheer. No one ever asked me for the truth, or my opinion before. *Like the guard?*

Oh yes, like the guard. "Miles, I often wonder how much help prison has been to the inmates I know. No records are kept, what do you think?"

I tell it like I see it. "Many of us come here to find more crime among the guards than out in the world we came from and were arrested for. It's hard to think it's a positive effect." I thought he might deny the guards are crooked and defend himself and fellow workers.

He says, "You know what the difference is between us and you?" I ask him what. "The ones on your side of the bars got caught." At least he is honest. He thinks it's funny. Like I'm a sucker. So why does he think I would leave here with a better outlook on life if the truth is I'm a sucker? *He thinks he can play someone for a sucker and this person will feel good and benefit from that?* No, he just wanted to bait us and see if we'd make up some bullcrap story about seeing the light and getting a new start in life when we get out. The guard is teaching me something; giving me an important lesson. The system is rigged; not legal or fair. Being on the right side of the bars means to not get caught, being on the side with the power and the stick. I thought for a while there was a third option, leave civilization altogether. I'm still searching for answers.

"Well, Book, I figure I am a senior now, not looking to be hired for work. My choice might have been different if I were young and depended on being hired for work! I can picture the biggest impact of being a felon, not being allowed to have a firearm. Since I live subsistence and depend on getting a moose, and spend a lot of time in the wilds, how do I defend myself against bears?"

"Black powder? A bow?"

I look dubious. I used black powder before, so am familiar with it. It's one shot, and half the time does not go off when it should. "Especially when living around water. There is a salt base to it that attracts moisture. Moisture makes the charge not go off."

Book wouldn't know, he is unfamiliar with firearms. I notice again, no one else here has a related crime, or is from the wilderness. Most are not even from rural areas. Firearms to most, means gang guns, Saturday night specials, assassination guns. No one here is even a hunter.

*Well, what about Red?* Oh yes, I forgot about Red. He may not be healthy enough now to hunt, but used to, and talks about it. He was in charge of a union and misappropriated union funds. Unsure of the details. He says he invested union funds to make union workers a profit in a way that was considered not acceptable.

We met when I asked who the book belonged to I saw laying on a ledge by the chow hall. 'Man Eaters of Kamoin.' An obscure hunting book from the 1940's, not very many printed. A book I love and own. Who else ever even heard of it, much less has a copy! It's a true story of 'Corbett,' a famous big game hunter whose job at one time was to kill man eating big cats in India. Very high adventure stories of man eating leopards and tigers. Some responsible for dozens of deaths. One leopard had killed over 300 people! The population of Nenana where I live! Dang! Imagine having the job of tracking such an animal. Vivid descriptions of the countryside, the people, and a period of time now passed. Red and I meet. He has a whole collection of such books. His wife sends them to him. He lost all the books, now out of print, when he was sent to the hole. The guards confiscated everything. Probably tossed in the trash. I had a copy of one book to give back to him when he got out.

Book reminds me what happened with Red. Something we all want to forget. Red has medical issues, heart problems, and chest pains. The prison has a waiting list and no money. The prison doctor gives him pills that do not work because hard pain pills are not allowed in prison, except maybe for absolute emergencies, but the fear is, you will not take them, then try to sell them to addicts.

I could see this argument being true in general population prison. This is non violent, sane prisoners. No hard drug addicts. White collar criminals. Not the sort to try to peddle nickel and dime amounts of pain killers we need to stop our own pain! Anyway, Red is in constant pain and cannot sleep. Sometimes he wakes up screaming. He is not the type to complain, so this must be serious.

One night he has chest pain, and cannot breathe. He calls for emergency aid. It's the middle of the night. He is hauled out of the prison to the hospital for emergency treatment. We think this is the last we will see of him. He's dead. Too bad, what a nice guy. Turns out the hospital decided it is not a heart attack emergency. I'm told by prisoners with medical background, anxiety can mimic heart attacks. Based on this decision, the prison officials decide he needs to go to the hole for a false emergency call.

It is hard to imagine him being able to sleep on a thin mattress on a cement floor. I am surprised he survived. He's in his 50's, overweight and short like me. Looks like the Pillsbury doughboy. White, shinny, pasty looking skin from eating nothing but prison food. Happy round face, bright red hair, and freckles. His prized book collection is gone. I give him back the one book, but the others cannot be replaced.

Yeah, Red likes to hunt. He speaks of his children hunting deer and turkey for dinner. We talk of Alaska; how he hopes to come visit and go out on a river trip with me one day with his boys. Out of 700 inmates, it's just him and I who hunt. We do not expect him to live long. He'll never get out of here alive.[1] He smiles, "When I get out of here I can go see my doctor and I'll be ok!" Red sees my expression and quotes Clint Eastwood, "There are two kinds of people in this world. Those who have guns, and those who dig." And winks with a smile. I tell Red about the book I got out of the library, 'The Virginian,' by Owen Wister.

"I read it a long time ago. It is the beginning of the western books about cowboys." And the beginning of the one liners used by Clint Eastwood. It all begins here. Cowboys are the beginning of the Mountain Man, sort of a sub heading of the same era.

"When you call me that, smile!" is from the Virginian. It is said of this book: "Contains one of the finest dissertations on capital punishment ever written." Concerning evil and illegal acts it states: "It is not safe to say of any man, he did evil that good might come. Was the thing that he did in the first place evil? That is the question."

I find it interesting that the inspiration for the cowboy, and even my recollection of the first cowboy books and TV series, had a lot to do with 'doing the right thing.' Cowboys were heroes. Roy Rogers and Dale Evens come to mind. The Lone Ranger, Zorro, the Ponderosa, Rifleman. Books like the Zane Gray series, even Louis L'Amour. Well, even Clint Eastwood was about righting the wrongs done that go uncorrected. I get the feeling that somewhere along the way the cowboy and mountain man became the villain, the bad guy. Or always were, except in romantic novels. It's just interesting to read the history, and come to a better understanding of what I believe in, where it came from, how it matches others views, and why.

I'm still trying to find laws of interest on the LexisNexis legal site. It's not easy. No one else I meet has figured it out either. I'm narrowing the laws down. I am still on our Constitution. I have gotten as far as:

Chapter 31, Section 1371, Title 16, Chapter 1, #410hh-2, Civil rights and discrimination. Under 136 is Communications telecommunications Thomas Vs Networks solutions in (1999, App DC) Computer and internet law. Section 8003. Of fiscal year 1998. Supplemental Appropriations provides that the national Foundation is authorized to deposit money remaining in the Internet Infraction Fund into the treasury and credit the account.

Oh yeah, here is the interesting part:

"The internet is an international network of interconnected computers. RenoCAclu 521 US 844. A network the US military created in 1969 developed from the ARPANET, the network the US military used to link its computers with those of defense contractors and universities. See 63 Fed. Reg, 31, 741 (1998). Served as a model for similar non military networks creating the modern internet. *"Government agencies cannot escape responsibility for failing to perform their statutory duties by hiring private parties to perform those duties,"* was the judge's quote in the case.

I understand this to mean, the government messed up, and let the internet into the public domain where it must remain. This does clear up the rumor that yes, the military started the internet. The rumor goes, the government still controls the internet, being the original designer and owner. This is interesting, but not what I am looking for. My time is up on the prison library computer. Very frustrating. It takes my entire allotted time to get back to the same spot. I am many layers into the laws. I have to carefully write down the long code that gets me back here. There is no way to bookmark. Getting this far has taken me three months. I am trying to find the laws that have to do with discrimination, and discovering if favoring Indians by race is legal. Heading into where the government is explaining what it expects concerning subsistence. I ended up with modern time internet discrimination laws.

What I want to find, is a law that comes out and says, "We believe in discrimination by race because..." Spell out why. I can see, even understand why, even possibly agree. I say, "Races have a right to keep their language, culture, and customs." I think it may not be realistic for all races and religions to become as one. Discrimination means recognizing and allowing the differences. I just do not think Indians should be the only race to have this right. That's why I want to see the exact wording for why, "Not an Indian" was written on the top of my arrest warrant, as a reason for me to be guilty.

A week later. I'm in the right area now! 135 Civil rights and discrimination general. Way deep down into the many layers is Civil rights: act 1964 forbids discrimination by race, color, religion, or national origin in public places affecting commerce. I go down more layers: Federal Constitution 201 (a) bce and 203-207 Civil Rights Act (78 stat 241) forbids discrimination. Deeper yet. Here is a case to refer to in court:

Heart of Atlanta Motel Inc. VS US. (1964 379US241), referenced the commerce clause of the Federal Constitution 201. And won.

When will I ever find an Indian subsistence case! Geez! I discover a new area to look. Judicial rules of Courts.

2072 (a)Title 43 Public lands Chapter 33 Alaska Native Claims 1992. 1601 Congressional finding Settlement. "b" "Real economic and social needs of Natives without establishing institutions, rights, privileges, or obligations. Without creating reservations. Enables Natives to participate. No provision of the act will (b) Confer on Native organizations any degree of sovereign governmental authority over lands. Including management, or regulation of fish, wildlife, or persons in Alaska.

43US cs$$1601- Extinguished all claims of aboriginal title in Alaska.

I had read this elsewhere during my case investigation. There must be some other law that supersedes this. Because what I am reading is straight forward enough. A deal was made with the Alaska Natives, part of ANILCA, in which the natives all got a million dollars per person, as well as a huge land settlement. In return, Native's became simply 'Americans,' like everyone else. This million dollars per person that amounted to a large pile of money, was issued to tribes, to be handled by tribal council. The natives themselves decided to invest the money and pay out dividends. They are now partners in oil companies,[2] and other big business, making profits off the investment. Investments in the very industries Natives claim to not tolerate, calling it

"White man's disrespect for God and the land." Due to this 'pay off,' Alaska Natives should no longer be able to claim they got screwed and are owed. Natives should no longer have more rights to resources based on race. More to the point, my subsistence permit should be as valid as a Natives. Based on lifestyle, and not race. I argue there are many other cultures, even 'most' have roots connected in the past to the land with a deep respect for these roots. Modern natives are no more directly connected to the land than anyone else. Book comes over and looks at the screen to see what I have come up with.

"Miles, what is the big deal at this point?" I sigh, hard to explain. Possibly many of us inmates are 'stuck' at a traumatic event in our lives we are having trouble getting past. Reviewing the event over and over until we get past it.

"Book, I want to know in my own mind if the law was on my side. Or even what society has decided as a group, as expressed by the law." The government is saying I knew better, deliberately flaunted the law, conspired with others, to the extent I am not welcome in society, need to be locked up, have many of my rights permanently removed. "Am I a bad enough person to have my basic rights permanently taken way?" I want to find the laws I broke for myself, and see what the wording is. Or more, be convinced the government was out of line as I suspect. Not following the will of the people, or the law. "So that I may hold my head up." I pause to think. "It is different if I am punished because I displeased a corrupt government. That is easier to accept." Book smiles. He has been working out and looks like a magazine muscle guy now.

He says, "I'm right, and they're wrong huh?" We both laugh. Yes, that does sound a bit much, put like that! All of us say this! Logic tells me we all cannot be right. I constantly fight an overall depression. It's not easy to find within, the strength and conviction to get up and greet each day. I realize the alternative is to be in the state of mind Woman is. It helps to understand we all feel it. Showing it in different ways.

Among my notes:

> I see a TV special later in life. The subject is having volunteers who wish to be police officers. The purpose is spend six months in prison to understand better where they are sending people and why. Out of the five volunteers, none could handle prison life more than four days.

"Life threatening, cruel, incredibly depressing, and corrupt," is how they universally described their experiences.

---

ONE THING I MUST ADMIT. I pushed some of the laws to the very limit. I was convinced the government did not want subsistence cases to go to court, and be forced to define the issues that would set a precedence. I still believe, the government has wrongfully stepped over the legal line to accomplish its own agenda, and would not want my case to come out in court. Because of this, I felt I could get right there at the edge, and as long as I was, 'within reason' not going overboard, I'd be left alone. I'm not slaughtering wildlife right and left, not going far afield of the intent of the laws. I was under the assumption, if there was trouble, it would end up in court. I understood it would be extremely costly to win a case against me in court. *Prove it! To what purpose?* What purpose was a million dollars or more spent to clean my clock. Why? *Set an example? To who? For what purpose?*

If I am guilty, I believe it is of being cocky about my position.

"Dang corrupt government anyhow!" At the least provocation. Not very smart considering the power they swing. I'm paying the price. I underestimated those who are in control.

---

WINTER IN WASHINGTON is different than in Alaska! Plants go dormant, but some remain green. The grass never dies. There is rain now and then, but no snow yet. There is no total darkness. Our clothing does not change a whole lot. The winter temperature is about like Alaska on a dismal day in summer. I explain this to Iris on the phone as she tells me it is thirty below zero, the northern lights are out, the wood stove is going, six inches of snow is on the ground. Snow machines are out and about.

"I miss all that Iris, but a break for one season is ok. I look forward to next winter in Alaska for sure!" We miss our routine of course. I'm lucky to have someone who stands by me, and keeps the home front going while I am gone. Most guys here lost their family over the issues concerning their incarceration. Got disowned. Woman is having troubles with his boyfriend back home. He does not openly say he is gay, or out right act like it. In fact, I am just told so by others. There is no lisp or hand waving. Possibly this is just a stereotype. I'm not an expert on what it is to be gay. *Can you tell by looking?*

Back in the library on the computer, trying to find the laws. So it looks like Native lands claim was in 1992. Here is something earlier, from 1980. I am interested because my time goes back to 1973. I lived through all this, unaware what was going on as I am living a blissful life of freedom in the wilds with no communication. Civilization and its issues were none of my business.

**Alaska Conservation Act.** P.L. 96-487. Stat. 2371.

(C) Subsistence way of life for rural residents. Purposes are listed. Ending ... provide the opportunity for rural residents who engage in subsistence way of life to continue to do so.

(D) Act provides sufficient protection for satisfaction of economic and social needs of Alaska and its people. Provide a proper balance. No need for new legislation for new areas.

Updated July 2009

Part 242 subpart A 242.4

**Barter** means the exchange of fish and wildlife or other parts taken for subsistence uses, for other fish and wildlife or parts for other food, or for non-edible items other than money if the exchange is limited and noncommercial in nature.

**Customary trade** means the exchange for cash to support personal and family needs, but not significant commercial trade.

**Traditional** means long established consistent pattern of use incorporating beliefs and customs.

There could be a question if I was commercial or not. The question never came up. The charges stated, "Not an Indian." It was obvious by how the case went, if I was an Indian there would be no problem. Not being Indian was the issue. The question never came up if I was true subsistence or not. The assumption appeared, only Indians qualify. The Indians involved in the bigger case I was part of were never charged. I know better than to get excited and review my case with other inmates. I know I am not thrilled to hear how anyone else's case went, is going, will go, or should have, could have gone, 'only if,' and is about to get overturned just any day now.

Rumors go around that all marijuana cases will get dismissed because the prisons are overcrowded. This is a small crime. The president has a plan and, *I will believe it when I see it. I doubt it.* Inmates are all excited and filled with hope.

Highly placed politicians I know and talk to tell me that states are interested in taxing the legal drug business. The Feds do not want this to happen. *The Feds prefer federal dependency?* Likewise, the Feds are the biggest drug dealers. *They do not want to legalize competition?* (The Oliver North and later Snowden stories in the news). I personally believe the international drug business is second economically only to oil. Part of our counselors job is to say, "Why, yes, just any day now you could get pardoned, we are waiting for the word! We'll keep you posted!" The bottom line is, keep us happy, in line, hopeful, and doing our time in a safe way, without suicides, riots, problems. "You're about to get out! I'm rooting for you!" works.

Why would the prison system truly be rooting for us? When they spend $10,000 per prisoner a year while collecting $80,000 and pocketing the difference? Every released prisoner is a loss of $70,000 a year. Enough to support one guard's entire family for the year. It is true, moving new ones in while moving us out looks good, keeps the funding coming, and also works.

Are these upstanding pillars of the community that depend on all this income from prisoners going to voluntarily give this up and lose their jobs? I think not! I learned when you run a shell game, you want lots of activity and inefficiency. Move the money, move the goods, move the prisoners, move the paperwork.

"Whoops! Something is missing! I wonder where and how! Oh, well, no time, pretty busy here!" I've seen it in action, and talked to politicians about this technique when raiding funds. I had a politician smile and wink at me when he saw me figure it out.

I'm strolling along thinking, when a guard's voice addresses me, "Would you mind coming with me?" *Oh Oh.* One aspect of being here is a certain tension all the time. We inmates are randomly whisked off. Sometimes never to be seen again, sometimes a pee test, or to get questioned, or respond to a complaint of some kind. Possibly there is to be a locker inspection. I'm not sure if this is the system itself, or just individual guards who enjoy creating the tension, and consider it a part of their job is to antagonize us. Somewhat like enjoying pulling the legs off spiders, or poking a stick at a scared wild thing in a cage.

It's 6:00 am. I had been headed down to use the computer for email, as is my daily routine. Now being led to the office where the head of our wing resides.

"Would you like to confess?" I look puzzled. *What would I be confessing to?* There are a zillion things. I paid for my haircut as we all do. I'm paying to have my laundry done. Hauling the tobacco to the sacred grounds was too long ago. I just look puzzled and keep my mouth shut. I'm guessing this is random pee test time. My only thought is, *Dang I just peed ten minutes ago, I am not sure I can squeeze another drop out!* The rule is, if you can't produce a sample within two hours, you go to the hole. Some inmates are nervous about peeing on demand, under threats. In general I am lucky that way. I can pee anywhere, anytime, under any conditions. I'm not concerned if this is a pee test, because I am clean.

"Only kidding, this is the random breath test!" I blow.

"No, harder!" Then, "No! Longer!" Well geez, I have never even seen one of these machines. I have no clue how they work. I pass the test of course.

"Reading?" The guard is pointing at my books. I nod. "Personal or education?"

"I suppose both. I am a writer, this is reading material for background." I have 'Mad Trapper of Rat River' in tow. Not the best book for a prisoner to get caught reading. I add, "I donated three of my books to the prison library." Iris was able to send them to the prison for the library. Inmates are passing the books around and enjoying them. The guard seems friendly enough. We get on the subject of prison reform.

He states, as I had heard before, "We have no statistics on how many inmates get in trouble after they leave prison." He explains how the state, feds, county, do not work together or share information.

I reply, "Maybe the prison does not really want those numbers because they are not good?" I'm sure good numbers would help with funding. He acts like he cares what happens to us. I curiously ask, "So why do you think we are here? What is your view on what is supposed to happen here?" He does not reply so I add, "I see more crime among guards in the system here than I ever saw outside in the world I live in. This does not look like a good example of what a legal life might be like if I change my ways. I am not seeing a better way. Where is the light showing me the path?"

After a pause the guard says, "Doing the crime is not the problem. Getting caught is." *Ah yes, the Roman view.*

"So, I am here to learn how not to get caught?"

"Well that is the difference between your side of the bars and mine. You got caught." I nod that I understand the view. The other guard said the same exact thing. I am impressed he did not deny, or try to defend himself. I do not tell him I do not agree. The guard goes on, "So you can write about it, and help bring change."

I am not trusting enough to positively respond. We are not buddies. *This might be a set up.* "Well, if you read my books, you will see they are about living in the wilds of Alaska, being a trapper and living off the land." The guard looks down at my book about the mad trapper. *I get it.* So I open the book, and find the page with the snowshoes the mad trapper made himself. "Check these out. Kind of a northern Canada style using one piece of wood! It might be possible to make such a pair in an emergency if stranded on the trapline!" The guard hesitates and seems satisfied. I am let go. *I am not admiring the mad trapper's way of dealing with being asked questions, by killing mounted police. I am admiring the cool snowshoes he made himself.*

It's possible the random breath test was not random. This could be about what I am writing, and if it needs to be confiscated. *I need to get my latest words out of here and sent home. It might be good to create a fake paper trail at this point. I have to see myself as a criminal, with a need to hide things. I have to stop being so open and honest, like everything is cool, and right, and not a problem.* Word is out I am a writer, with people reading my books now. Many see me taking notes. What am I writing? Inmates come to me with their story. They think I might write their life story. *I'm not focused on criminal heroes, see!*

"Miles, I am a lawyer, did I tell you? You are right, the subject of intent, morals, ethics are not legal questions in a Federal court. That was given up in the 1980's. The court was losing too many cases over ethics. Who pays for that! It's all about money. The Feds are all about conspiracy, Miles. That's what turns an ordinary state crime into a federal crime. Two people who conspire have now committed a federal crime." I reply,

"I know about the Lacy Act and crossing State lines." I'm not sure this guy is really a lawyer, or more like our buddy Doc, who might only need attention, and is a wanna be lawyer. My public defender said the same exact thing, "If you use the words moral, ethics, or constitution, what you say after that will be rejected as inadmissible in a court of law." I spot Woman coming towards us. "I see you are still among the living, Woman." He wanders off towards the garden and greenhouses where we work.

"Thanks, Miles, you were a big help."

I did not think so, did not see how I was. Telling someone they either need to sink or swim is not being there for someone. "But it's honest at least. No one would care if I was dead or not here."

"Well sure, Woman! I enjoy working with you in the garden. You are easy to get along with; smart, knowledgeable about farming, I'd miss that." It is not much to offer, again, it is the truth. I'm not going to say, 'Come here for a hug, I love you.' None of that stuff! We never get into personal conversations like what role he might play - the female or male and such. Frankly, "Yuck!" He's human; I like him, that's honest. When I have a choice of who I want to work with, I choose Woman. He did not make fun of me when I did not know how to gather leaves with a leaf blower. He just showed me, no big deal; I spent most of my life without electively.

AS WE WALK along I overhear, "No that was not an inmate who stabbed her, it was her husband!" I stop and want to hear about this. There is a new female guard checking our wing. A real fox! Kind of a gothic lady with tattoos. The kind who dresses in black and wears black lipstick and nail polish. She has a cruel scar across her throat. We want to know how she got that. She hates men, so we assume, 'some guy' slit her throat.

"Yeah, Miles, I think you are right, a woman out to get even for wrongs done her. What a waste of a perfect body." Long dark hair, short, trim. Into druids, spells, zodiac, candles, skulls, and tattoos. I'd know how to sell her stuff as a customer. *She'd pay $300 for a wolf skull.*

Another inmate says, "Her husband used to work here with her! Long time ago. I was here." We are all listening. "She started sleeping around, mostly with other guards. Seven to eight guys." All of us are listening as we group around. "So her husband finds out! Waits until she gets home one night and jumps her! Stabs her a bunch of times in the throat. Leaves her for dead. That's why she wears the high collars. She recovered. Husband is doing twenty years hard time."

"Dang," we all say in awe.

Goth comes by looking foxy. Stops at my cube. Finds a locker that belongs to Muscle. Sees a piece of one inch square tape on the inside of his locker.

"What's this huh! Answer me! What was stuck here!" Wants to find a reason to send Muscle to the hole. Daring him to protest. He's been around the block a few times and knows how to handle her. She stomps off looking for someone else she can send to the hole. She was trying to get him to confess to having an illegal picture taped in his locker.

It's getting close to Christmas. I am near the cafeteria door. Here comes Goth. Livid; someone is playing Christmas music someplace. *What right do we have to hear Christmas music!*

"Shut that off now!" I say to the inmate next to me.

"Someone needs to gently suck that anger out of her. Make it all go away."

"You volunteering?"

"Sure! You set it up!" We both laugh. No Christmas music. No, she wouldn't be my type. I suspect she has a cruel streak, even before she got married. Born that way. I feel sorry for her. Possibly, only possibly someone would get through to her, overwhelm her with kindness and forgiveness. Forgiveness? For playing you for a sucker for being nice. Probably it is too late, should have been done when she was in her teens.

The Mad Trapper: "Legendary giants such as Hugh Glass, William Subtle, Jed Smith, John Cotter, and Mike Fink, were characteristic products of a violent existence, where to be alive meant to be quick with a knife and a gun."

I know all those names. Read each biography, followed each story. My childhood heroes. I would not sum up their lives with the bottom line, "they were living in a violent arena, so had to be quick with a gun." Though this could be how such lives are viewed from a civilized viewpoint. I got out of the same lifestyle when reading about it, that they saw the wilds as sane, safe. Civilization as the violent environment to be in.

I get more inmates coming to me who want to tell me their story. Mostly, how they are innocent! I need to tell the world! Help get them free! "So Miles, what stories will you write? Am I in it?"

"Well, I have not decided yet how the book will go. I am just taking notes now. When I am all done and out of here, I can look it all over and decide how it goes together. It will all have to go in a computer first." I get a nod that this makes sense. I add, "I am not trying to get anyone in trouble, not the prison, the guards, or trying to change anything. I'm not angry or trying to get even. So I am changing names, making sure no one faces any problems! You know the prison would not let me get out of here alive if I told all, with evidence and details!" Most inmates nod they understand. I'm categorized as the harmless bookworm pussy type. That's how I like it.

> Inmate #1 story: "My real crime was meeting with the wrong people! We met once a week. A group of us. Talking about the loss of our constitution. Patriots who believe in our country. We did not do anything. I heard there was a government plant among us. We had no proof. Our friends thought we were paranoid."

I nod that I can picture the setting and have sympathy. It's best not to interrupt and affect the story.

> "Most of us ended up in trouble over other issues not related to our group meeting. I'm here over tax fraud charges. I had to lie to get the deal. No money to fight."

I just record the story. I have no idea what really happened.

I tell inmate #1, "A guy in Fairbanks named Schaeffer Cox went to prison on anti government conspiracy issues. As far as I know he only talked." I followed the story in the news—if we can even believe the news. He had regular meetings in Denny's restaurant with anyone who would come and listen. Got up on his soap box and told listeners we are illegally taxed. We no longer have a constitution. We need to fight for our rights. No specific plan, though he had friends who were more serious and had a hit list. They made threats to real people. As far as I know, Schaeffer was not part of that. He was young; looked like late twenties. A military friend told me the pictures in the news used as evidence against him are bogus; pictures of hand grenades and a machine gun seized in a raid of his home. Of course the public is shocked, and glad such a dangerous person is off the streets! My military friend recognized the equipment in the picture. The grenades are dummies—harmless—cannot be made active; used for training and legal to own as displays. The machine gun had a solid barrel; also cannot be made operable and legally sold as a replica for display. So while Schaeffer had these things, and thought they were cool, they are harmless displays, not weapons. There was a trial and a conviction! Schaeffer got twenty-six years under the new 911 Homeland Security laws. Nothing was mentioned about anything he had ever done beyond talk. I found it interesting the 'fake' weapons were lied about. If there was a real honest case against him, why lie?

"Reminds me of the speeches we'd heard in the 60's from excitable teens wanting to make the world a better place, protesting Viet Nam and such. Almost like a rebellious stage in life teens get over as they grow up. I doubt locking them up for life would help them, or society." Inmate #1 does not come across as strong anti-government 'we need a revolution' type. He seems impressionable, looking for a cause to believe in. I could picture him on his own, backing away from the group if it looked like the group was getting radical. I'm told in the 40's and 50's there were socialist groups in the US trying to get people to turn against capitalism that exploited it's people. Socialism is advertised to be about looking out for the working class. Many working class people felt exploited, so listened, even joined.

Charles Lindbergh, the famous pilot was in such a group, I read. His child was kidnapped. Rumor has it, the one arrested and convicted did not do it. The government wanted Lindbergh to get out of this group. It would look bad for the government to publicly denounce such a US hero. So they take his child to shut him up.

Likewise, I follow the Beatles story. John Lennon is my hero. His story is, he was followed, harassed, denied a visitation to the US mostly due to his political views. That 'radical' music that today seems tame. It is hard to know what the truth is. Would the US harass people, arrest and jail innocent people, plant evidence, trump up charges, do dastardly deeds to shut people up? There are those who would say so, and try to convince us. Do those people saying this have a hidden agenda? Certainly it would be hard to get to the bottom of this rumor! I'm just writing down what Inmate #1 has to say.

Inmate #2: "I got arrested for overpaying my taxes."

*Yeah right!* His summed up story is, his accountant made an error, and he paid 3.2 million in taxes. He later caught the error. It was supposed to be 2.3 million. He wanted the error corrected, but the government did not want to pay back a million dollars it had erroneously collected.

"I own a vineyard in Napa Valley. Supplying the world with high end wines."

I am pretty sure this part is true, because inmate #2 is in my horticulture class. He discusses the wine business, growing grapes, and has a great deal of knowledge he could have only acquired by doing this. He has the respect of the class, and Mushroom believes him. He is smart, non violent, kind to others. It is simply hard to make this personality up as a cover. He has a brochure with his picture, connected to his wine business. It looks very high end. One picture shows a huge volume, hundreds of gallons, of expensive wines.

I feel only a certain type of prisoner is approaching me, wanting to tell me their story. Hardened criminals do not talk to me. Book, Muscle, and others tell me why. "You are a short timer and suspected of making a deal to get such a short time. The deal being, to be a rat."

Some criminals here have an attitude. They are not interested in education, bettering themselves, being good contributing members of society. They want to hurt society, bring it down, be at war. They do not talk to pussy book worms like me. There may only be ten percent who would even come to me to talk. Only some percent of those who talk to me who might not belong here, who could have been set up, ground up, chewed up, and spit out by an imperfect system that makes mistakes sometimes. This is my opinion of what is going on. *Well, when I'm in a good mood and being optimistic.* I answer myself, "Or, this is the view that would lead to peace and happiness. The view my sane successful friends steer me in the direction of. Regrettably now and then honest mistakes get made. Now and then a good apple is in the rotten bushel."

Inmate #2 says, "No one would believe the stories here in prison. Not our friends, relatives, no one. So why bother to write them, you'd end up like Doc."

Doc has been in and out of the hole, and is still determined not to give up and cave in to the evil corrupt system he is going to help bring down. He comes to me asking for help. He is short—like me—but stockier, short neck, gray hair, big luminous intelligent looking eyes. Until I look closer, and there is an intensity born of fire and brimstone, hinting of the passion of insanity.

"Miles, I have used up all my allotted time on the computer. Can you log me on and let me use some of your minutes? I know you never use all yours up. I need to look up some legal stuff and contact a legislator." *Contact a legislator using my name? I don't think so!* "I can help your case, too, Miles, I can teach you how to look up the cases you are trying to find!" Doc has made this offer before, and not come through for me. To do so, he'd need computer minutes handed to him.

"No, my minutes are used up this month, Doc. Sorry! Good luck!" He turns to go, then asks if I signed his petition yet. "When I contact the legislator, he needs credibility. If I can get half the inmates to join me, that will be hard to ignore!"

True. But it is illegal for us to conspire. I feel our hands are tied here in the prison. I do not even agree with Doc - that his way is how to bring about change. We are not in a position to make demands. Already, the word is the prison officials are watching, know what is going on, and collecting evidence to shut him up for good. Doc knows, and is desperately trying to make his move before he gets shut up. He wants to punch a bully in the nose and I think that does not often work. I agree with his facts and intentions. The prison is illegally and very overcrowded, something needs to be done.

I see one of the prison officials stop Doc, smile and engage him in conversation. I wander over this direction and overhear some of the exchange. Doc sings, "Why, yes, I'd love to see those records! And am glad you agree, there needs to be some changes! Glad you are willing to help!" I know Doc is being set up, but he does not see it, being so intent on the rightness of his cause. An insider among the officials, who secretly agrees with him, is just what he needs! Doc wants this so desperately he cannot see reality. Later in the day Doc is in the hole. But worse, getting transferred.

"Yes, when you get transferred it takes a week for your records to catch up with you. Also, it takes a week or more for the system to catch up to you for commissary privileges, phone use, the ability to get paper and pen, stuff like that. So the plan is to keep transferring him every week, until forever." Thus, he will never be a problem again. He will not know where he is, never have access to a phone, or paper and pen again. He will not know what day it is, or if it is day or night. It occurs to me, this information was let out on purpose, to be spread as a lesson to anyone who wants to right the wrongs of the world. No one would want to end up like 'Doc' whose story will hang around for years as a lesson.

"Miles, those who signed his petition are under investigation. Did you sign?" I just smile and wink my, 'Do you think I'm that stupid?' look.

There is a flurry of raids, locker searches. The recreation center shut down, TV room shut off, and just all around, "We'll show you!" actions. I make sure all my latest notes are sent home and out of the prison. Everyone who signed Doc's petition is punished.

> Inmate story #3: "Yes, I'm guilty as charged!" grin. Telling me, "Long ago cigarettes were issued and legal in this prison. Then they got cut off." Pause. "So smokers had to figure out how to get smokes. I cut the inside of a book out so money could be inserted. We had a deal going, bribing one of the guards."

This is a short conversation. He was illegally selling banned cigarettes. I assume a Federal offense.

I have one more of Red's books that got passed around. He is out of the hole and trying to recover his books. He says I can read this one before returning it, 'Temple Tiger,' by Corbett written in 1905.

"This leopard about which questions were asked was credited for having killed 300 human beings. I knew the animal under the name Panar Man eater. Two animals between them killed 836 human beings." It is hard to imagine such days and events. I'm guessing such events would have an impact on your view of nature, and the world. I'd about sell my soul to be in his shoes. What days those must have been! Guessing someone who was armed, who could take care of these leopards would be a hero. Now a highly protected animal. Kill one, and you will be lynched by your own people. Times change, as well as customs and our view of history.

My unit counselor has to do an interview and evaluation every few months. She asks, "Have you been rehabilitated?" I have the Alice's Restaurant story by Arlo Guthrie swimming in my head. *In two part harmony. Kid, have you ever been arrested? And I began to tell the story.* Later in the story, *Arrested for what! And I said, 'Littering' and they all moved over on the bench till I said, 'And creating a disturbance!'* There is only one correct answer. It's not a question.

"Yes, ma'am, I've been learning a new occupation, doing well in class. I have a job offer when I get out." That's what they want to hear. She gets scammed all the time, so I know what matters is facts and evidence. I really am getting good grades in class. Attitude is important as well, I am sure. There can be no hint of rebellion, dissatisfaction. Rehabilitation is all about being grateful. I really do have a job offer. She's impressed, which is what this is all about. We are beginning the very long process of getting out of here. Later in my cube, "Muscle, she is the one who asked about rehabilitation. She did not ask how my punishment is going."

"Are you hurting Miles? We can always increase the pain and punishment!" I smile.

"The pain is seeing a corrupt system, being disillusioned. How can I survive if my country doesn't, and how can my country survive being crooked? But no, we do not talk about such things. I was in the military - Navy."

Muscle nods. He can understand the comparison.

"I had an honest conversation with an officer in the Navy." I explain how I told the officer there is no need to create hate in me so I can do my job and kill people. I understand war and what it is. Just teach me my job. Teach me how to shoot. Point to the one you want killed. If my orders from up higher are to shoot you, that's what I do. I do not value your life any more than a peasants in Viet Nam." I have no enemies. But I understand war, and understand taking care of business.

"So, Miles, what did this officer reply?"

"He was scared. I thought this was good. War is a scary thing. Engage in war and be afraid." I pause. "The US wants what it does not have, and is willing to take what it wants by force. I'm sorry about that. But, this is my country. I am asked to defend it. I owe my country. There are objectives that are higher than my personal opinion. "I understand I need to be a team player. Count me in. I'm seventeen years old."

"How does that relate to prison, Miles?"

"Maybe it doesn't. It's just that I wonder why my chain is being yanked. What this crap is about, rehabilitation. Let's call it what it is, punishment, and be honest here."

Muscle says, "A father beats his child with a belt screaming, 'have you learned your lesson yet!'"

We agree, 'classes' are not about helping inmates. It is about getting funding to skim, and appeasing the conscience of the public. It's about how things look. Possibly things learned here can be useful, but not in getting a job.

Or, the issue is something else. I joined the Navy voluntarily. Why not teach me a job and help me do that job as best I can? I loved my work! I volunteered to work extra hours. I enjoyed teaching others. Yet, the system, the higher up officers, treated us lower workers as if we were the enemy! Got many to hate the job, hate our country, hate the military! Why? It is like working for the enemy when they do that. I had to overcome all this negative treatment. Punished for having our hair cut wrong, or shoes not shinned enough. Out to sea with only us workers around trying to do our job!

"That is like prison in what way, Miles?"

I explain. "We did not volunteer to be here! We are told the reason we are here, when obviously there is a hidden agenda and we are here for other reasons we are not told about. We are not here to be rehabilitated. We are not here to pay society back for our crimes. So, then, why are we here?"

"Have you met the new guy in horticulture?"

There has been a shifting of students. I passed horticulture, one in the top five in the class of forty. I am taking another class. Actually two classes at the same time. 'Pesticide Management.' That is not an appealing class! Not enough inmates signed up for it. Money was funded for it so it will be taught. To give us incentive, Mr. Education announces, "If you take the pesticide class, you will also get in the horticulture class and have access to the garden." The incentive for most is access to the precious garden and its goods, and escape from the main compound.

So there is a new guy in class. He talks to us soon after arriving. "I have a lot of knowledge to contribute. I have a PhD in marketing, taught college level farming, herbicides, farm equipment. I own extensive farms making a lot of money." He is here, likes to be busy doing things, and wants to work with us in some way. Mushroom gets a private meeting started to discuss what can be done. A dozen of us who work well together and want to accomplish something get together. Mr. PhD addresses us, "How can we make our prison horticulture program easiest for those in charge of us, so it looks good for them, at the same time benefits us with the most education and ability to get jobs when we get out?"

So this is the task we are tackling. We know Mr. Education and staff are over worked and have little time to work out a plan. We reason, if we come up with a plan and are willing to do the work, it makes it easier for the prison, or in the civilian world, 'the boss.' This concept is like farmers, or factory workers, getting together to help the business run smoother, make more profit, and at the same time make it a better working environment for slaves, without having to pay them more or increase production costs. A win all around situation.

We have several meetings to review inefficiency and issues we can address. Mushroom talks about the compost. I support that adding, "Mushroom has talked about how worms would help the compost a lot. They cost almost nothing. It would be an added part to the education for us. The increased nutrition of the soil would increase garden production and quality."

Mr. PhD adds, "And if the prison garden could produce better food per acre then commercial farmers are now getting, this would be of interest to farmers, government and university! An increased production keeps costs down and encourage natural organic goods. This makes the prison look good, and is a good way for the prison to justify more funding." "If the university is interested they may get involved and offer credibility to our certificates."

It is agreed if we come up with good numbers, the university might show more interest in recognizing our certificate as valid, and endorsing it. This helps us get jobs when we get out. There are some other ideas that cutting edge farmers and scientists among us propose, and could collaborate on, that has not been done in the farming industry, ever. Biochar is the cutting edge of farming right now. No one knows yet how composting and worms effects the biochar process. We have scrap lumber and it is suggested we build cold frames to test. Landscaping ideas discussed. We are like a garden think tank of brilliant people.

The prisons answer is "No!" "Absolutely No!" "Maybe all of you should go to solitary confinement!" Prisoners cannot meet in groups outside of a class - it's subversive. Prisoners do not propose ideas! Prisoners do what they are told and shut up! This is part of your rehabilitation! Our crime was to go off on our own 'thinking,' coming up with ideas. Our crimes out in the real world mean: "All of you were way outside the box, trying to re invent the wheel. Prison is designed to take that out of you, and turn you into worker bees who do what you are told!" If this is true, there is an issue here. Mr. Education has told us there is no work for us available when we get out. He is honest.

"The class being taught is outdated material." Only Mushroom is keeping us updated, and teaching cutting edge garden science, but outside the class curriculum. Mr. Education is taking a chance allowing Mushroom some flexibility. The tests do not reflect any of Mushrooms teachings. Mushroom argues to Mr. Education, "If the students understand what I teach, they will also understand the basics. One of my jobs as a teacher is to get students interested in the subject. If they are interested they will learn."

The book material is dry, boring, and dates back to the 1950's. Mushroom adds, "Good attendance, good grades, happy prisoners, reflects well on you and the prison. It is not costing any money." Mr. Education admits we are not being trained to get jobs. There is no way to take what we learn and go out and be farmers. It's a huge commercially run industry for the most part. Few independent farmers anymore. The pay for farm workers is about the lowest wage of any business in the country. In fact, migrant workers are usually hired. Same with landscape. Illegal Mexicans do the work at slave labor prices, for the most part.

Most inmates here are used to big money in the drug business. They will not be happy with worker bee slave labor incomes. Mr. Education says, "The average drug dealer here makes $100 an hour minimum wage. Is he going to be happy as a farm worker for three dollars an hour?" No one in here was poor when they got caught. Maybe they are poor now. All they had was cut off, taken away. Now what?

"You are the walking dead." Mr. Education is just being honest, and telling us how it is *from his perspective*. It bothers him a little. He has been here since the prison was built. In fact he helped design the prison! He is the one who laid out the farm design and convinced the prison to have a farm and horticulture center.

Mr. Education is on the outs with the rest of those who run things. The rest call horticulture and the farm a disaster. A waste of time and money. By law, we are required to throw away all food we grow. So who cares how efficiently we grow it? Or how much? Or what quality it is? It's going in the garbage. We are doing nothing more than moving a rock pile all around the compound. Who really cares to discuss what kind of rocks, how big, how fast, cost of the hammers, or what the pile looks like? Even Mr. Education understands that indeed, crime does in fact pay. Look at the prison system.

There are too many legal issues the prison cannot overcome by putting the garden to use. First, the garden food interferes with the prison food vendors contract. How can a food vendor make any money when we are undercutting him with free food we provide! We cannot get the garden legally certified on any number of levels. There are no qualified people in charge. Who is spraying the pesticides? A certified person? No. Where do the seeds come from? Are they certified? No! We save them from plants we grow. That has not been proven safe. You can't cut Monsanto out of a commercial enterprise.

Has the compost been certified safe to put on food for human consumption? No! You cannot use any compost you choose, and offer it to the public. You have to use certified fertilizers you buy through certified sources using certified chemicals. Or register organic, with even more restrictions and inspections. The list is long, from planting to watering, soil treatment, harvest, preparation and serving. The prison cannot afford the permits and can't run a legal business. It's flat out stated, "It's not possible to run a legal prison and stay in business."

"What message is that for us inmates when the prison can't teach us anything legal?" Sometimes I think Mr. Education is frustrated, disgusted. How different the prison is now, from the vision he designed and began! His hands are tied. He cannot help us. He cannot allow us to meet and talk. That is a crime. We might be conspiring to have a riot or prison break. Mr. Education has little clout with those in charge. In fact he is on his way out, retiring this year after fifty years being here. No farewell, party, gift, thank you, certificate of appreciation is planned by the prison. That speaks for itself.

Mr. Education confides he has a son going to prison. So what does he think of prisoners and what sort they are now? Mr. Education might even be on our side. It might be why we have it so good, with the microwave we can cook our meals on, the ability to steal the food so easily and distribute it to others. Very little goes in the compost. In fact much of the produce comes back off the land and into the classroom. We can call it, "For educational purposes for the next class lessons." But in fact it is a food distribution point. Mr. Education gets his cut.

"I could use some beets, some shallot onions, and lemon grass." We make it happen. Much of what we grow depends on what Mr. Education likes to eat.

Beets and potatoes from my garden in Nenana.

# CHAPTER FOUR

## GREEN HOTDOGS, CHRISTMAS IN PRISON, CORRUPTION

I drop a watermelon off in the black TV room. "Moo fook, look, it da White foomer!" The blacks all gather around me and joke around, telling new guys about the day I was in their TV room and let me go because I had balls.

I nod, "Yeah, these two watermelons are a reminder!" They appreciate my gift, as I am taking a chance going in the hole doing this. The horticulture program is dominated by, run by, Whites. We control the food flow. You do not have an in with the Whites, no garden food. These guys have no in, and are not going to kiss ass to get an in. I do not ask them to kiss ass, I ask for nothing. Beyond not to set me up, snitch, turn me in, or I go to the hole! In truth, I do not understand the Blacks, may not even like them. Our cultures are too different. I do not care for the rap music and crotch grabbing. I do not care for all the 'moo fook' talk

It does not matter if I like them or not. Some famous person said, "I do not like what you do, but I shall defend to the death your right to do so." I am a very strong believer in personal rights and freedoms. We do not have to like each other and get along. You deserve good food; if it is in the garden and you are an inmate, if I am part of it, we are all equals.

Or no. Not quite. We are not all equals. However there is some minimal level we all deserve. The Mexicans are still messing with the whole farm scene. Claiming turfs, grabbing food in large amounts and selling it. I'm not distributing enough to bother them. My concern is, this could all come to a head and none of us can have any food. It will go to the compost as it is supposed to. Mr. Education does not like it. Mushroom thinks the Mexicans have something on Mr. Education. Or, Mr. Education is in on a money deal and getting paid off. It is hard to figure Mr. Education out. He appears to play many sides of the fence.

"Miles, I need you to come by at nine o'clock tonight." Mr. Education points to another horticulture person, "You, too!" Adding, "Wear your dark clothes!" We look at each other and shrug. We have no idea what this is about. We show up in the dark. No lights on. A truck pulls up. Looks like a delivery truck. It's Mr. Education, "Jump in." We jump in and leave the prison grounds. This is totally illegal and could get us more jail time. At this point we would be officially escapees. *Probably legal to shoot us on sight.* I have a six month sentence, why do I want to risk ten years added as an escapee?

Mr. Education comes back to the prison by a back road that gets us into the farm. He turns the lights off and keeps driving by moonlight into the prison garden area. He wants us to dig trees up he points to, while he goes and gets boxes of grapes already hidden on the grounds. Grapes the Mexicans boxed up. We have ornamental trees dug up. The root wad is wrapped in burlap as we have been taught in class for transporting trees. Mr. Education points to the back of the truck and we lay the valuable trees there.

We drive to an undisclosed location off the prison grounds and drop everything off in a warehouse. We are returned to prison and dropped off where we were picked up. No explanation. That's it. I assume, part of our education. There is no one to say anything to. Not other prisoners, no one higher up. We could get five to ten more years added to what started out as a small sentence, for what we just did. Rehabilitated means doing what you are told, and keeping your mouth shut.

I would not mind the old chain gangs. Doing slave labor. I agree we should repay society back somehow if we have wronged society in some way. *Let us make up for it!* Make license plates if that is all there is to do. What a waste of a resource. We have some very talented people in prison worth $100 an hour. Why not put it to use? We have computer experts, cutting edge farm techniques are known and could be practiced here. Not all of us are rebellious, or hard to control and manage. Prisoners could not only pay their way, but make a profit. I believe this. Imagine prison not being a heavy drain on tax dollars, but be a profit maker! Not a burden on the back of tax payers, but a prison work force of cheap labor! Maybe only minimum security inmates. I am not sure hard core degenerates could be made to work at a profit. I'm not knowledgeable about such things.

I piece together rumors and facts, and come up with what I think Mr. Education is about. He helped design this prison; was one of its founders. He had a vision and put his work and money into it. When it was finished he wanted to see it work. He becomes the farm educator. A big step down in pay from a top engineer! Time goes by. His pay goes down due to funding and budget cuts. The farm dream is not turning out as planned due to changing laws. Maybe even due to the inmates themselves who are not as motivated as he had hoped. Few others have his dream and vision. Politics get involved. For years, he says, "We could teach prisoners! We could have them working, feeding themselves, saving money, even making a profit!" It doesn't happen and now he realizes never will. But he's been here a while. He cannot go back into the old job because he is now out of touch. It is easy to collect the money on this job and take the soft route. Prisoners are not employees. You order them to do something and it gets done, 'or else!' He sees profits to be made all around. No way is he going to toss this good food in the compost. Officials want it to disappear? He can make it disappear! So instead of making money for the prison, he makes money for himself, the heck with inmates or the prison system. They want to mess with him? What goes around comes around.

How evil is what he is doing? He gets Mexicans to harvest his crop, sells it, and he and a few others line their pockets. Better than what happens when the same food goes in the compost! A few trees no one ever looks at or cares about, worth a lot of money disappear, inmates now have a job replanting and learning how to take care of trees. I could imagine being in his shoes.

I was even headed that way once with a government job firefighting. I was barracks manager. Took care of ordering things. I'd get asked to do favors, order things not necessary for the job, but handy to have at one's home. Blankets, fire extinguishers, furniture. One reason I did not pursue this direction harder is, I just did not like getting into this situation and getting put on the spot. Many people owed others favors. Material got moved around. It's almost expected. It's the government! Often the person who takes the fall is the most honest, trying to do the right thing, who gets turned in for miscounting rolls of toilet paper while the boss misappropriates thousands of dollars of goods, and has an entire distribution network with everyone paid off, while keeping out of trouble. Rarely arrested.

This is one reason I prefer to be self-employed and not dependent on what the boss wants done. Now in prison I am forced to be here playing the game. Those who do not cooperate get sent to the hole. There are some inmates below the radar who sail through unnoticed. I am rarely unnoticed. From day one, I found an in to get out of washing dishes. I'm guessing from the start I was earmarked as one to keep an eye on. Smart, makes things happen. I'm helping others, getting things going. What's my game?

I'm not a problem. I can in fact be included in the game. If I play it right, part of the cut. Part of the exchange of favors. Problem is, I do not know how. I am not sure how the details of this work. I can spot the big plan without the ability to fill in the details as a cog on the gear.

"Miles, have you gotten your high school diploma to the prison yet?" Mr. Education address me before class. We are not allowed to take educational classes unless we have graduated from high school. If we have not, we must get a GED first. There are classes offered for that.

I never saw my high school diploma! My father signed me up for the Navy. I was sent off as soon as it was known I graduated. I did not stick around to be in my graduation ceremony or attend the party. I assumed my diploma was sent to my parents. I was never told, and I never saw it. How can I, at this late date in life as a senior, find it? "I have papers from the Navy showing I graduated with honors from machinist mate school, firefighting school, damage control school, nuclear school. How could I have gotten in those schools without graduating from high school? I would not have been allowed!" It appears to give prison officials pleasure to yank my chain and have me jump through hoops. The more I think this is nuts, the more they smile and nod.

I have had Iris working on this for two months! She has called my school and been put on hold; written them; been promised it is in the mail, to no avail. Now I might get kicked out of class and not allowed in the garden. Maybe washing dishes.

Mushroom tells me, "I keep saying, Miles, you have to pay off Mr. Education. Slip him some stamps and he will make it happen!" *How many stamps? What to do, just hand him stamps and say, "Here is your bribe, could you please get my diploma for me?"* I've never bribed anyone, or paid anyone off under the table before. I'm resentful, and want to get the diploma myself. Here we are, down to the final few hours and I will be out of class.

I go in to see Mr. Education. I have a few books of stamps worth maybe $20. I simply set the stamps on the desk. If we are being recorded, I do not want a conversation. Apparently he doesn't either. He pretends he did not see me put them there. Without hardly looking, slides them into a drawer. Waits, says, "What can I do for you?"

"I need my high school diploma so I can stay in class." I hand him the phone number and address of the school. He dismisses me. An hour later Mr. Education has a copy of my diploma that arrived by fax. *See how easy it can be when you cooperate, become a team player? This is what hell is, being beholden to a dirt ball like this. We are both criminals, and he calls the shots.* It's a life rule I live by, not to bet into other people's games. I have a 'thing' about people making me do things, anything, even for my own good. Freedom is everything. According to Christian beliefs, not even God can make me do something. God and I had a talk a long time ago and one 'condition' I put being on speaking terms is, "You do not order me to do anything, it's my choice!" God said, "Agreed!" We shook hands on it.

The quality of my prison time is in the top one percent. My locker has never been inspected. I have never been reprimanded, in the hole, got points against me, turned in, snitched on, been part of anything negative, called in as a witness, had to turn in an inmate. Inmates are falling all around me like mosquitoes. Two Feathers is in the hole for smoking. *Again.*

Even Mushroom ends up in the hole! I can't believe it. Our beloved teacher! It's a holiday, no work today, no classes. Mushroom asks me if I want to go over to the garden to work on our day off!

"Well, sure, Mushroom. But the rules clearly say no work. We are to remain in our designated areas."

"Well there are exceptions. I am the teacher. Someone has to go over and water the plants, check on things at the farm. You can be my helper!"

"Not without authorization!" Where we all are is the single most important thing the prison has the task of. If we are not where we are supposed to be, we are escaped prisoners. No one else is over there, I'm not going. The prison does not care about the garden. If the garden does not get watered and everything dies, the prison does not care. Any more than a prison cares what happens to the rocks inmates spend time moving and breaking up. Mushroom cares, and cannot accept the prison view.

So Mushroom goes alone. The plants may die if he doesn't. The afternoon count takes place and 'someone' is missing. Another prison count is done. Someone is still missing! Another count, taking names, is done and reviewed. Mushroom is missing! He is found at the garden, working. He forgot the time. It is such a nice day, and work needed to be done. But getting work done is not why we are here. Nor is being useful. Nor is the garden important. Keep busy.

"Most important is, we know where you are at all times!" I got that, Mushroom did not. This is part of why I am unwilling to let anyone here know I care about art. Gardening is nice, I can live without it.

Mushroom caused a lock down and recount for the entire prison. He's in solitary confinement. I'd be there with him if I had gone.

"Now what do we do about class? He is the teacher!" Someone else takes over, it's that simple. Class goes horribly. Mushroom is a genius. No one can take the place of a genius. We are stuck with the classroom book. The answers are in the teachers copy, otherwise the new teacher would not know. There is no room for discussion as the teacher has no idea why the answer is what it is.

"Would we use a specific pesticide on this bug or choose something general?" It's a question set up to initiate discussion. The merits of each choice. The answer changes if the garden was in an area with a lot of water runoff headed for other land. You would not want a general killer to escape. The answer might have to do with how bad the infestation is, and what stage the pest is in. General pesticides are cheaper and can be used by the land owner. A specialist does not have to get called in. The new teacher is a 'by the numbers person' who does not like to 'think.' We memorize the answers.

It does not take long for the prison officials to realize we need our teacher. Things in general would go a lot smoother. Word is, he can get out, but has to find another job or class to teach, and is not allowed in the garden again. *He enjoys it too much.* Prison is not about joy. There is a farm across the way, where large amounts of produce is grown, and not the same as the smaller greenhouse experimental stuff. There is more funding. In some ways Mushroom might be happier. He can do more with his compost ideas. Anyhow, he is tired of the Mexican war in his garden. Tired of Fairbanks conspiring against him.

Likewise, he and Mr. Education are not in agreement. Mushroom does not like to see waste of our garden goods going in the compost any more than Mr. Education! However, Mushroom wants to give it all away to the people and resents Mr. Education illegally removing the goods to make a personal profit. He still embodies free love 60's views - anti establishment, anti materialism, and capitalism. I see this in his devotion to helping third world countries eat.

Mushroom gets away from a lot of issues over at the big farm. My guess is, he is more saying that so the prison does not know they have a way to get to him. If he removes the joy of hurting him, they may take the easiest route and put him back teaching. Especially if they think he'd like to do something else. I think again, *For the same reason I tell no one I am an artist.* Writing is ok. It's not my passion. Prison could take that away and I would not be heartbroken. I'd be a broken man without my art. I'm just on vacation from it for six months. A secret to keep.

One inmate says, "I think of prison as a dysfunctional parent. Our dysfunctional father." Alcoholic parents are much like this prison. I never thought of that. Beat you up for no reason; rewards and loves you the next, forget what they did or said next week. Unpredictable rules that do not make sense, enforced swiftly and harshly. Money misspent on who knows what. Many other comparisons.

The subject of food comes up again. Mushroom is in the back as a dishwasher now. "I wonder why the hot dogs have a bread crust on them today? A crust the cooks put on?"

I peel the crust off and the hot dog is rotten green. "Do you know how long it takes a hotdog to get so old it turns green?" I will not eat it, and do without dinner.

I am asked, "Did you see the chicken that was served three days ago?" No, but I saw the same batch two weeks ago. Not fit for a mink farm. Small deformed wings with feathers still on them. I look around and see a lot of pasty white loose skin on fat people not getting enough nutrition. There is not a lot of sickness though. I do not know why. I'd expect more health problems. There may be a way to kill the germs and make horrible food, germ bacteria free. I heard of some kind of light being shined on our food. A reddish light. A form of radiation. Just a rumor.

Some highly contagious diseases come to the prison sometimes. I'm not sure what gets done about it. Inmates are not told.

"Hey, anyone hear from Doc, know where he is? How he is?" I ask, wonder. No one will ever hear from him again.

I'm told, "He will spend several years getting transferred every two weeks. Never see even a pencil." A guard told someone he transported Doc to a Seattle holding facility for temporary detainment. He might as well be dead. *That's what happens to whistle blowers.* I miss Mushroom at class. I take notes that I think will be useful in my own personal life: *Most common plant virus is water mold. Mild Clorox solution kills many molds. High temperature therapy. Keep plant between 95 and 98 degrees for two weeks, kills most viruses.*

I draw pictures in a notebook of how to do things in steps. There are inmates who speak of ending days; a decline. A time we all might have to be more self-sufficient; know how to take care of ourselves. I agree such a time is possible. I am not so sure everything will end within my lifetime. I can picture necessities getting harder to get; lower quality to the point of unreliability, hard to afford. I can picture being ahead of the curve, knowing how to make things, fix things, and supply some basics like food, shelter. We talk also about having a service, an ability that is needed, important, tradable, for supplies or other services.

I tell my story to the class. "Even though I am considered economically poor in my village, I feel rich. I trade my art, custom knives, garden produce for chickens, eggs, geese, pork. I trade for car work, transportation, clothes, tools, and services. I learn who trades, as others learn I trade." Inmates nod that this sounds like a good way. "For example, as felons there is much we will be restricted on! This, too, could be a predictable occurrence for others like us. More and more felons are not allowed to live like others. Our money is controlled; we have to report this and that. Being monitored, so we can never be a problem again."

"Yeah, many of us become street people, alive, but unable to do more than just function. That's the goal. Our hands are out for government programs to depend on. Stand in line, bow our heads."

"I like the idea of being able to take care of ourselves. Through a network of like-minded people who trade. Cut out all the middle people, permits and such."

Communes of the 60s had this idea in mind when civilization looked like it was coming apart. Black panthers, Kent State, power outages, riots, police brutality, was in the news daily. I'm not sure any communes actually worked.[1] I have heard of, and seen, remote communities that seem sane, and have a workable plan. I have seen roadside food stands, with a can simply saying, "Put your money in the can." And people do. Places with no street people, no drug problems. Where anyone who needs a job has one. Where people look out for each other. Nenana is a little like that, not totally, but we do ok.

"Yes, we have drug problems and crime! But children walk home from school. Women walk dogs alone. Many citizens leave doors unlocked, cars unlocked.

Gardens are not generally harvested by anyone else. Anyone who needs work has it. No one is homeless unless they want to be. There are rarely crimes like drive by shootings, arson, rape." There are other places like this I hear of all over the country. Anyhow, a group of us thinks you can't go wrong knowing where food comes from, how to grow it. Even pesticide class is ok.

It is interesting to know how bugs operate. What attracts them, what stages they go through. How to recognize the good ones. No matter what or where you grow, there will be competition for growth of weeds, and insects that want to share. It is possible; there is enough to go around with an added benefit from weeds and bugs since they often perform important functions - attract pollinators, birds, rodents that help the life cycle of the plant in some way.

I learned that weeds win out over introduced crops in weak soils. "The weed was there first. It is the first to recover from pesticides and chemical exposure." This makes getting rid of unwanted plants an ongoing challenge. Modern farmers spend more money putting down more fertilizers and chemicals to get less and less good results.

"The quality of produce, over all, is half what it was fifty years ago." Meaning, you have to eat twice as much to get the same nutrition out of it as your grandmothers did. We force foods to grow bigger and faster, look better, have better color, but weaker nutritional value. Our crops are not as genetically diverse as they once were. It would be easier for a disaster to wipe out an entire food line. Stored seeds are not as secure as they once were, and getting lost. Mostly, as a whole, we care less, and as funding is lost, this is an area getting cut. Domestic meat industry is the same. Meat value is balanced by increased hormones, steroids, and antibiotics. An animal is a product of what it eats. Eating dry straw is not the same as the moose in the woods eating tender birch buds.

Some of this was really brought to me when my friend, Josh, could not get his race dogs to pass the drug test because he fed them a lot of ground turkey. What is that turkey doing to us? Usually we do not eat as much as the dogs had gotten. But if everything else is having issues, where are we to have a source of healthy food? One solution is, grow it yourself!

Much of this relates to pesticides, weeds, bug management methods. It's good to know, so we do not lose our gardens! There is no way any of us would want to be pesticide specialists. We learn what such a person is liable for and the pay scale. There are health risks. If you accidentally spray an endangered frog, the fine is hundreds of thousands of dollars. Likewise, if a cloud of pesticide drifts over onto someone else's land, there are liabilities. There are strict rules for buying, using, storing and disposing. Rules of who is qualified, who can help. Time limits, permit deadlines. Weather to know, exposure limits. All this, we have to learn to pass the class. Much of the hard part is higher math. How to figure out how much pesticide to buy if you have twenty nozzles 2mm at ten pounds pressure driving five miles an hour with a twenty-five ft. width. I whisper to the inmate next to me, "I'd fill the truck. Spray. Whatever is left over, sell to my neighbor, offer a deal for anyone else in the area, until it is used up." It doesn't have to be rocket science. I believe ultimately there are too many factors, and you have no guarantee of getting it right. Nozzles might be worn, slightly plugged. Using hard water would have an effect compared to rain water. How much air is in the tractor tires would have an effect. The accuracy of the speedometer. The temperature of the liquid as it expands and contracts. Rough ground compared to flat hills slows the tractor and bumps increase the distance. Pressure can vary by a pound and throw all the numbers off.

One inmate says, "If it is your farm, you have done this before. Use the same amount as last time. Guesstimate based on previous experience."

"Ask your neighbor how much he uses."

"That would not be the correct answer on the test!"

"The one with the best math skills is not often the best farmer."

"Google it."

"Ask someone."

"I have a hundred acre farm, how much of this stuff should I buy? Ask the supplier." We memorize for the test, but the real learning is the discussion. We have some real farmers among us to ask how it is done in the real world. Absolutely no one follows the rules. It's impossible. *Maybe the ones who do not follow rules end up in prison. Those who follow the rules have a good life. I have no way of knowing. I do not recall knowing anyone who follows the rules who is successful. If I thought of someone, how would I know they are really following the rules? Are they just the best liars?* I'm not, in general, one of the rule followers. Am I among the few honest ones, admitting it, and asking why we can't set something up that's workable?

Some inmates arrive in class, and just go to sleep as a regular routine. No one interrupts the class, as that gets points against you. Written up. It can affect early outs, when the question is how well you adjusted, and did your time. We can't make people learn or use time wisely. *Some people pay money for this class experience in the outside world!* I'd never be able to afford the time to take these classes if I was out of prison. I joke, "Gosh! I wonder if I will have time to finish this pesticide class! I only have a couple months to go! Can I request more time so I can finish?" The deal for me was do the full time with no really out. The judge could have given me a year. I got the minimum. However, much is out of the judge's or prosecution's hands now, and up to the prison board. There is talk of being out early, but wearing a radio collar. Where I am restricted to the house except during specific short times. This is only offered to inmates who seem to be self disciplined and able to behave on their own, without threat of punishment. My record is squeaky clean. I am a model inmate. Before spring, I will be out, if all goes as planned.

"Muscle, I'm reading a book called Blink, ever heard of it? By Malcolm Gladwell?"

"I heard of it. Someone I know read it and thought it might be a good read for me." We are laying in our bunks, waiting for lights to go out.

"It explores the world of instincts and gut feeling." He and I have talked about the subject off and on. How we form opinions about people at first glance, that so often turn out to be right. "Well, here is a study on the subject!"

The Latino who shared the cube with us is a case in point. Muscle and I both took one look and thought, "Here comes trouble." We agreed this is not fair to the new guy. Give him a chance. Maybe we are stereotyping. Rationalized why we passed such quick judgment. He was not around a month and got hauled off in the middle of the night. He had been smuggling cell phones into the prison, helping people escape, and had hacked into the TV line so at night after hours he and his friends could watch the Playboy channel. He is gone now, but gave our cube a bad reputation. We honestly did not know what he was up to. I do not understand his language. When he talked to his friends who came to visit, I did not know what was being said. Muscle should have, but if so, he would keep his mouth shut as is the inmate code.

Sometimes inmates try to help a problem person stay on the right path. Often though, hardened criminals we just avoid. Many were wrongly sent here, and belong in a higher security prison as dangerous. Sometimes money, politics or plea bargains get them here where they do not belong. Muscle and I were right about our first ten seconds meeting Mr. Trouble, who is no longer with us. My concern is, sometimes people live up to what you expect of them. And that is a big factor in how they turn out.

A group of Iowa scientists proved in an experiment that our unconscious mind has a system by which our brain reaches conclusions without immediately telling us. Psychologist Gerd Gigerenzer calls this 'fast and frugal.' This is now the cutting edge of psychology.

We live in a world that assumes that the quality of a decision is directly related to the time and effort that went into making it. Doctors that are faced with decisions tend to order more tests. We say, 'Haste makes waste,' 'look before you leap,' 'stop and think.'

"Muscle, it turns out we quite often are correct the first time, based on gut feeling." Important, or simply interesting from my viewpoint. I had learned in my wilderness life alone. [2] I learned early on, to get along with, and be friends with, my unconscious. I had the belief at the time, if we do not learn to get along with our unconscious, and the hidden part of our brain, we can become sick from it, and become schizophrenic. It is best then, to come to terms with our basic instincts, even if they are unpleasant. If we are nice to our unconscious, and treat this part of us with the respect it deserves, instead of suppressing it, our unconscious will work with us, be our friend, and help us. I believe this part of our brain was created for a reason or it would not exist.

We do not always have time to think and reason. Part of this gets termed 'street smart.' In a world of fast pace life, drive by shootings, cars zooming by, lights changing, those who survive need to quickly spot developing threats. Something out of character in a pattern, the unconscious spots.

The book, 'The Right Stuff', about fighter plane test pilots like John Glen, affected me a lot. I incorporated the term, 'high Jesus factor' into my common vocabulary from this book. Very much about instinct, gut feelings, fast decisions based on nothing conscious, and getting it right. Scientists at the time were questioning these pilots abilities. If we can't see it, or prove it, then it doesn't exist. Yet, we all know people who are walking disasters, accidents waiting to happen! People I would not get in a car with to go two blocks! Others seem to have good all around them where not much goes wrong. Those, I would follow into battle with bullets flying all around, believing we will be untouched.

Now, here is a book about why! Interesting. Prison survival has something to do with these Blink concepts. As we walk around we have feelings about what to steer away from. Groups of people we spot, deciding which group to go over and talk to. Decisions are made when to haul garden produce from the farm and not get caught. I make no plans. Suddenly I think, "Now!" and it's done. No questions, no debate. I trust my gut. This is a world of mental land mines.

Scientists conclude gut feelings can be wrong! We still need to learn, have experiences, put data in the data bank where our unconscious quickly processes data. Or, maybe has a series of potential answers stored, in case we need action in a hurry. Practice matters. Information matters. Our gut feeling does not work well in new situations we have not seen before.

Muscle says, "When we are treated like dogs, we will usually respond like dogs." I'm not sure how this fits into our conversation. The loud speaker comes on and we have to listen close as the words are garbled. Prisoner numbers are called out. If our number is called we must respond and report someplace! It might be our doctor. A prescription may have been filled, we have a book in at the library, our counselor needs to see us with an update, or we are going to the hole because we got caught. This puts a lot of strain on us as it is a big offense not to report when called. Yet, we can't hear the numbers. Wherever we are, we all stop and listen. "Did you hear my number called?" If we are not sure, we report to the office. This can interrupt whatever we were doing, taking a test in class, or lunch hour.

We can't hear the loudspeaker in the garden where there is no speaker. If our friends know our number they come look for us even though you have to be authorized to come to the garden! As Muscle made the comment about dogs, we are interrupted by the blare of the speaker. We concentrate on numbers being called. Seven hundred people listen as two inmates are called. There is usually a sigh of relief it is not our number. Sometimes we know ahead of time it could be us! We are waiting for the counselor to call us in to sign some expected papers. Sometimes when the loud speaker goes off and we all stop to listen, I am reminded more of a concentration camp than a university campus.

Next day is Sunday, no work. Breakfast is sometimes better. We get pears, rock hard, impossible to eat. We try to sneak them out so we can ripen them in our locker. Likewise, we sneak out old bread for the birds and something for the cat if we can. Which table we sit at and with whom, is important. There are reserved tables - some fore gangs, some are racially determined, others politically, or occupationally determined. The filthy rich have a table. Sometimes others are welcome as a guest—if you know someone. Specific people are welcome in more groups, and at more tables than others. I'm welcome and tolerated at a lot of tables because I am the writer and recorder of stories.

I overhear, "I screamed at the doctor! Guards came, grabbed me, hauled me off to the hole. I'm told it might be a month before I get out. After a week, this one guard who knows me, stops by and asks why I screamed and made trouble. I'm not known as a trouble maker." Everyone at the table is listening. His friends are here. I assume he just got out of the hole, and they want to know why he was there. "I told the guard I think I have a broken bone, and would like an x-ray." I assume that he screamed at the doctor because he hurts with pain of a broken bone. "The doctor told me he had no time. There is no funding, and dismissed me." This guard takes me back to the doctor for x-rays. I had a broken rib and cracked leg bone." He had been beaten up in the TV room in a battle over the remote control. During that week in the hole, the leg had become infected. He shows us where flesh had to be removed. If the friendly guard had not intervened, he thinks he'd have been dead before his month was up, or lost a leg.

Someone else at the table brings up another injury case. "Did you see Bill's finger?"

"Yeah, he's in my cube. He might lose the finger."

Another, a friend of Bill says, "Yeah, he started out with a splinter. Dug it out himself as preferable to seeing a prison doctor. The finger got infected. They call it mercer virus. Doctors removed a lot of the flesh along the bone the length of his finger."

"Miles, speaking of injuries, how come you have had all these hair raising adventures and not had a major injury? Maybe you never had the adventures?"

Eyes turn to me for a reply. I simply say, "High Jesus factor."

"Oh, so you are a God fearing man, huh?"

"No, God does not scare me. We're friends."

"Yeah right! I could use a friend like that!"

"God is your friend already. All you have to do is believe that." I add with a wink, "So I am going to pick up that stale bread roll for the birds, that piece of bacon for the cat, and this pear for myself. Put it all in my jacket pocket, and God is going to spread his cape between me and that guard over there as I walk out the door!" We all burst out laughing as I lighten up the conversation.

"Watch and behold. A miracle!" I get up, as if I am Jesus about to walk on water. With a wink, a smile, and magical flourish of my hand. *Now you see it, now you do not,* and leave. The guard sees and knows nothing. I feed the birds and cat as I go by.

---

THE GUARD at the food line is scowling and having a bad morning. It's Bully. "Excuse me Sir, I'd like to file a complaint. There seems to be a hair on my egg!" I move the tray as if to show him, with a concerned look on my face. He bursts out laughing. I smile and wink as I go by. I look up later as I eat, and he still has a smile on his face. He knows me. I often pull stuff like that on him.

"I seem to have misplaced my wallet."

He usually says, "Don't worry, I'll get it this time." I have a happy relieved look that says, *Wow what a great place! What a great guy! You hear that? He's got my meal covered today.* I assume the guards are human. I do not know it as a fact, but why not assume, and treat them accordingly? It's not going to hurt anything. It might even help. In return, maybe a few guards will think inmates are human! What a concept! So I work on that. I'm aware both the guard and I are white, so closer to being of the same tribe than the blacks he has a hatred for.

*The guy with the broken bone story. So why was he getting in a fight over the TV remote in the first place? What an idiot!*

"Miles, are you in the 'Breaking Barriers' class?" I do not know who this is.

"No, I do not qualify, because my crime was not drug related, and also I got a short six month sentence." I saw the fliers and understand the program. The headlines, 'The Making of a Man!' Your sentence can be reduced if you take this class. *Most of us were men before we got to prison. If we remain a man after, it is despite prison, not because of prison!* This reminds me of civilization's treatment of the Indian.

I have a **past flash,**

I was in the village of Galena in the 1970s. The natives are fine! Happy, rich, sober, admirable people by any standards. I watch the white man move in, or more, the government programs.

"We are here to help!" The Natives I know tell me how they feel. A polite smile thinking it is the white man who needs the help. Time goes by. Government programs are not a request, but required, demanded.

"You want your post office, runway, electricity, oil?" The village had received grants and are now beholden to the giver. Eventually, I see posters offering classes. Offered to 'get your Native pride back!' Fliers for mental health programs for troubled people. Suicide prevention. 'We care' fliers. Clinics are built, white man office buildings, staffed by white people getting paid to help the poor depraved indigenous species. These savages are expected to be grateful to their father the white provider who cares for them.

My **past flash ends.**

---

CHRISTMAS WREATHS and decorations are to go up. It's mandatory. There is going to be a visit from the head people. We have to look good. There is a competition as to who can make the nicest wreaths!

"Like the pumpkin carving contest, remember that Book?" I carved one, filled it with dirt and had growing flowers sticking out of the ears, eyes, nose, and mouth. I was told it was dirty, not fit to go on a desk and it was tossed out. I had not followed instructions. We were given specific paper patterns to pick from. Patterns designed for ten year olds. I was almost written up, except this was labeled 'voluntary.' Imagination is not rewarded. Rehabilitated people do not have imagination. So it is with the wreath contest. As a person certified to go to the garden, it is my job to come back with ferns, cedar branches, holly vines, and such material as might be appropriate for a wreath. We are given cases of empty plastic yellow lemon juice dispensers in the shape of lemons. We hang them on the trees in the compound.

Different wings pick out their material to use, all laid out on the ground in piles. Overnight another wing steals our pile. Ha! So we cannot possibly win, as we have leftover's now. The prison employees have a route picked out they will walk the higher up inspectors. Only this route is decorated, no place else. The route goes up the steps of one wing through a few isles, and out the back door. There is no other place inmates get to see Christmas decorations. The officials arrive, and are filled with praise at the festive air, and, "Look at all the wreaths all over the compound. Isn't that sweet?" I hear one say.

Everything is immediately taken down, swept up, within an hour after the inspection. I'm put with the group responsible for making flower arrangements from the last of our flowers in the greenhouse. Mr. Education explains, "Ok, these are the people who approve our budget. It's good to keep them happy. Try to do a good job. They do not know why we have a horticulture program. This is the only reason the program exists, so they can get flowers on their desk. If you like the class, try not to mess this up." There is one inmate assigned all summer to pick flowers and deliver them to desks around the offices of the compound. He's in the hole right now so we have to fill in especially for the holiday season. This is the guy who promised to teach me bonsai tree cutting. He is the expert on this. *Oh well, I can only cram so much in a six month time period.* Some guys get teary eyes over the holiday. Woman is upset after recovering from another spell of sadness. I've had to cover for him a lot on the jobs we were supposed to be doing together. We have been assigned to the outer limits. Partly because we are not happy with the Mexican deal selling the garden goods. We are not among the trusted, so we are off somewhere where we do not see what is going on and do not want to. There is concern we may turn them in. *But turn them in to who? The entire system is corrupt from the President of the United States on down. So tell who?*

With Mushroom gone, Fairbanks is taking over with a different agenda. I promised Mushroom I'd maintain the compost pile for him. He gives me instructions how to layer it for winter. This is not part of my work assignment, so I have to do it on my own time, almost sneaking over and hope I do not get caught. No one especially minds, it's just not directly helping towards the look of the garden today. Next year is too far off for most in charge to think about. Fairbanks says they will just order fertilizer through an outlet when the time comes, like they do every year.

"If we make our own compost someone is out a job and not making money off us."

The new guy taking Mr. Education's place after he leaves, has no garden skills, and may not even be interested in the farm and garden. 'Education' can mean something else after he takes over. We certainly have no control over what will happen, or how things get done. Mushroom used the compost we make on at least one section of garden, and not the commercial fertilizer we were told to use. At least not on one garden. Mushroom confides in me, "We can compare and see which does better! Keep records." The prison does not care, but we do. Now that he is gone, how will we use the compost?

Putting the gardens to bed is an interesting process. I am glad to learn how to do this. There are a few winter crops to put out that were started in the greenhouse. Some cabbage interests me because we grow this in Alaska. Hoops and plastic go over each row after winter planting. A few pumpkins got left behind. Fairbanks shows us how to cook them in the microwave to make a pumpkin meal. We miss watermelon season! Many herbs are gathered and dried. I enjoy gathering seeds from flower pods; bagging and labeling them for next season. I have to learn all the names. I will not be here to plant them, but I enjoy the process anyway. I want to

## SECRETLY WILD

learn better ways to save my own seeds at home. Red will be here longer, so says he will take over and make sure these seeds get used after I am gone. His heart is bad, and he is so overweight it is hard to imagine him having any energy to get seeds planted. I appreciate the thought.

One prison test we have is to identify fifty plants laid out on the lawn. They are numbered and we have to write the number and its name on a piece of paper. Since I grow flowers at home in my own greenhouse, this is easy for me. I learn about Statice flowers though. *They might grow in Alaska.* What is nice is, they dry easily and keep their color! Like straw flowers. I sneak some seeds into a letter and send them home for Iris to set aside. I send a few heirloom pepper plant seeds home the same way. Mushroom has told me these are special seeds, not available on the market. Few connected with the prison care. Possibly there will be no more garden under new administration. All plowed under. The strain of seeds developed under inmates grafting and experimentation will be lost. Mushroom pointed out the seeds most unique, valuable to save, and why.

The strains were secretly sent out of the prison so they are not completely lost. I get back to reading my book, 'Blink.' When young, I read Freud and Jung's work. In general the unconscious was deemed evil and should be fought, overcome, even eliminated. There was shock treatment as in the movie, 'One Few Over the Cuckoo Nest.' It is nice to see studies that indicate our unconscious can be our friend, serve a useful purpose, as I have always believed.

"Advertisers spend money studying our unconscious to sell us stuff we do not need for prices we can't afford by appealing to that which we have no knowledge of or control over."

It was pointed out ice cream makers discovered they could get ten cents more a cup for ice cream if the containers were round.

"Truly successful decision making relies on a balance between deliberate and instinct thinking. In good decision making, frugality matters."

On the next page: "Only ten percent of those who come into a hospital thinking they are having a heart attack, really are. Yet a single bed to 'check this out further' is $2,000 a night."

With book in hand, I head out the door into the cold morning dew. I stop to uncover the feral cat sleeping by the door. I often put an old coat or blanket over the cat in the late evening. She remains under the blanket undisturbed and warm all night. Before the guards notice in the morning, I remove the blanket. Sometimes she bounds after me to the cafeteria. No, she has not become domestic, or even my friend. She takes advantage of situations. Others take care of her as well. She knows she can go out back where the prison cook leaves more and better food than I can come up with. Other prisoners during the day have more time for the wild cats. There is more than one cat.

Some prisoners, who have no job or chores, spend most of the day sitting at a table playing dominoes or checkers even though we are told jobs are a requirement! 'Work or take a class.' I only assume the way around this rule is with money. A very few have medical reasons. I know some of these inmates spend a lot of time fooling with the cats. It's enough one cat comes around and knows I will cover her with a blanket. This morning she looks at me, yawns, shakes herself, and greets the day as I do. I comment on the cats at the cafeteria.

Someone who has been here longer then me says, "Yeah, the prison does not like wild cats around. About once a year, someone goes around and kills them all. We have to start over when new ones move in." Fairbanks tells me the cats keep the mice down in the garden and make a big difference! Farmers tell me most farms have a few cats around, often wild, that help control rats and mice in the barn. I'm not a farmer so do not know about such things. But we can't get close to the cats. We just help them out and entertain ourselves and them without getting overly involved since they will be removed.

"The prison secretly removes them because by law they have to call the humane society and pay. It's not legal to put poison out for them, or kill them."

I'm puzzled. "How do you know the cats are poisoned?"

Fairbanks says, "I have come across more than one dead cat at the garden with blood and foam coming out of its mouth, and all the cats are gone at once. On a regular basis. It's not a pretty sight. They appear to have suffered a lot."

Blink talks about a variety of distinctive instincts gone wrong.

The author did an experiment; let his hair grow long. He is pulled over and given speeding tickets he never got before when doing the same speed. Once, he was pulled over and thrown against the car because he looked like a rapist they were looking for. All they had in common was long hair.

Why some people get arrested and others do not, is a topic of interest. Statistics listed how many blacks get arrested and convicted compared to whites. Partly based on 'gut feeling and instincts' the officers have. Some police behavior is explained. In a crisis, our conscious mind can shut down while unconscious takes over. During this unconscious heightened state of fear or stress, we can react in unreasonable ways tossing out all training and conscious knowledge. We may even see things that are not there.

A recent case comes to mind - seventeen year old Michael Jordon was shot fort-two times by four police officers who swore Jordan had a gun. He had his wallet in his hands to show ID.

"It looked like a gun!" Say four officers.

I do not believe they made that up. I got the impression at the time, the police believed what they said. *But how could they be so wrong?* I had a similar experience. I faced my first bear. The incident was so terrifying, my unconscious mind took over!

I realized later, it is an old part of the mind that does not understand anything modern. It understands run, fight, kick, scratch. I had a pistol in my hand and was going to use it as a club. I saw all kinds of things in the movie screen of my eye. I wonder if modern day police get 'programmed' to be scared!

"Yes, these new criminals are on meth and hard to stop, hard to kill; why just the other day an officer had his ear bitten off, arm pulled out, and beaten to death with it!" Stories of people simply wigging out in the middle of getting a traffic ticket. Young kids pulling guns. It's not a safe world. Cops read this in the paper, hear it from the news media, from the chief of police, and are primed, ready to draw and shoot. They wake up each day scared. Maybe. I mean it would explain what is going on through this 'Blink' view of instincts gone wrong.

Good to think about, and consider as an inmate going out in the world as a felon. Encounters with the police need to be understood. How to act to ensure survival needs to be understood. At the same time we inmates are fed the same stories about the police! How criminals get shot, guns put in their hand; crooked cops, violent crazy cops all around us. See a cop and be afraid! Run if you can! Never ever call them. You could end up dead. Just look at the news! Why should I trust a cop anymore then he trusts me! [3] Why should I assume he is doing good deeds? 'We' - all of us, - should try to understand what is going on! How is this going to get solved? Is it simply all out war against each other as many street people and minorities feel? 'Blink' has an interesting slant on the issue. Many peers I talk to at home trust the police, legal system, government. They are all white middle class, perhaps belonging to the correct, and protected tribe.

In another book I see this quote: "It doesn't matter how many people vote. Only who counts them."[4] — Stalin.

There is a form of torture going on in the system, hard to define, hard to prove is deliberate. My mind goes back to the state institutions I was moved around through. About twenty inmates are chained together. We have not eaten, or had a bathroom break. We do not know where we are, even what state we are in. Disoriented, off balance, everything new, strange, scary. We arrive 'someplace' late at night.

Prisoners line up as we are marched by in chains, taunting us, leering. "I want that pretty boy!"

Guards teasing us. "Careful! You will be one of these guys toys!"

I'm old, this is not a serious threat to me, or not the direction my worst fears go. For some guys, this is their worst nightmare. They are beyond fear. This snaps some people's minds. Their eyes role back, they foam at the mouth, and fall over in a faint. I've seen this happen with animals I am about to kill. I notice some guys are afraid of germs. A high percent carry a cloth and wipe everything—door knobs, faucets, their hands. Guards pick up on this and make these guys touch stuff for fun. To watch them suffer.

Other guys are afraid of bugs. Spiders, even mosquitoes and flies. They lose it, and scream their heads off. The guards notice this as well. It seems like all humans have some weak spot. Some button you can push that unwraps their wiring. A way to break us. Turn us into putty.

This had been the stated goal in Navy boot camp! The officer in charge said, "Our job is to turn you into putty, then mold you into soldiers!" *Into whatever we want; brainwashing.* It had been me who hollered back, out of a thousand recruits, and no one else, "Good luck!" *Go for it, if you think you can! But why? I volunteered to be here. Why do you want to brainwash me?* Go for it, because I am sixteen and bullet proof. I know I am among the strongest here. I already know I am not the first to fall when we do sit ups, pushups, marches; physical, grueling work. We normally work until the first one drops and an ambulance comes. I am mentally the strongest one here. You will not break me. It is you who might be sorry you tried. In four years of service, I was never broken. Nor molded into what the military wanted. I got out with one of the lowest ratings for respect, yet one of the highest for getting my job done. I considered it the military's loss. I could be one of the best there is, if I was treated as a friend, and not the enemy. *I didn't get the nick name 'Wild Miles' for nothing.* So it is in prison. I am not going to be among those who fall; whose brain fries.

Prison helping people? Absolutely no one is helped. No way. If an inmate gets out of here a decent human being, it is despite prison experience, not because of it. The smart good, become quieter, wiser. The smart bad, get craftier and more devious. The not so bright good, get eaten up. The not so bright bad die, or never get out.

Another prison inspection coming up. I role my eyes up. Guards and prison officials are on edge because they have to cheat to pass. Inmates are asked to help; to 'care.'

"Be sure the cleaning spray bottles you use have the right label!"

"If asked, be sure you say you have had fire drills and know where the exits are!"

"Fire drills? Yeah, right." I say to Muscle, "I had to sign a piece of paper saying I have had a class about safety. I was issued a hazmat suit when using pesticides. There is an eye wash station in my work area. All not true. I had to say it was, and sign a paper saying so." Muscle understands. We all sign things without knowing what we are signing. Part of rehabilitation is doing what we are told without question. Signing statements you are not allowed to read. Muscle says he has seen a lot of inspections in his long time here.

"The inspection is important for the prison to pass. If they do not pass, there are more inspections, investigations and fund cutting. The prison can't pass inspection."

We are asked to sympathize, understand; lie and cheat in order for them to pass the inspection.

"Fine, we understand, but where were they when it was our crime we'd like understanding about?" I say my usual, "If the rules are not workable and impossible to keep up with, let's get realistic and come up with a workable set of laws!"

Muscle nods and adds,"The system is set up on purpose, so anyone can be arrested any time; just pick a crime."

Another inmate, "Fire drill? Most of the guards and officials would as soon lock all the doors with us inside and light the place on fire!"

"Now, don't be so cynical! Only a third would want to see that!"

At the horticulture garden, Fairbanks says in a horrified voice, "All the records are gone!" We are supposed to keep logs on our garden activity. How much gas we checked out, how much pesticide we use, stuff like that. The books are doctored to cover up reality. The inspectors will want to see the log books. Mr. Education blamed an inmate who must have sneaked over to the garden and stolen the books! I happen to know Fairbanks burned the books, on Mr. Educations instructions. Gone are all Mushroom's garden and compost experiment records.

"Oh, wait a minute! There is a back up copy in a computer!" The backup copy is a fake set of cooked books. The head warden seems to think all inmates have their own desk. Inspection is over. Life gets back to normal. I have a new book, 'Genghis Khan-Making of the Modern World' by Jack Weatherford.

"In twenty-five years, the Mongols under Genghis subjugated more land and people than the Romans did in 400 years. More than twice as many as any man in history - twelve million square miles, thirty countries, and three billion people. Done with an army of 100,000 people."

In trying to understand what freedom is, it is good to study great conquerors and how they accomplish servitude.

I read during the TV commercials in the TV room. I look up when there is a loud discussion over something in the news. The subject on the TV screen is a black rhino hunt at auction to raise money, 'to save the rhino.' The news media is putting the slant on this as an oxymoron. 'Killing to save something.' The inmates are agitated and of the unanimous position that the Sierra Club is no good, and destroying the planet, etc. I am the only hunter in the prison. I watch to see what the facts might be, before having an opinion.

The situation concerns an old rhinoceros the government feels should be put down. The original plan was to have the government dispatch it and drag it off someplace and leave it to rot. The Sierra Club got wind of this, "Wow! Just kill this animal and leave it? Let us dispatch this animal if you want it dead. We can offer a hunt and raise money to help other animals. We can raise a million dollars."

The public in general is not seeing any gain in that and is outraged. The animal will get killed. The only question is by whom. One plan is to have a government official shoot it, tie a rope around it, and drag it off, dump it in the nearest ditch and drive off. The other option is to have it shot by a hunter who has paid to be in a drawing that raises a million dollars. I'd rather see the million dollars raised and put back into the system for habitat improvements.

I see how discussing hunting, killing a rhino, and making it big news helps promote and support trophy hunting. In many eyes this glorifies the death. Maybe we do not want to do that. I can understand. I do not trophy hunt nor do I support it. But I am not going against it either. Because, by law, people have the right to trophy hunt in a responsible manner. I assume if it is legal, then the majority support it or they'd vote it out. Or, put pressure on the decision making process to get that changed and outlaw trophy hunting. Getting mad at a group or individual who is following the law does not seem to me to be the right way to address the issue. I am surprised how few agree with me. The million dollars also honors, and glorifies, the value of the life lost and goes a long way to enhancing and buying preserves.

"Hang the bastards that want to hunt a black rhino!" In this way, support the government killing, and hauling it off with no fan fair, and no money. Saying, "There is no funding to take care of the rhino habitat so we need to kill off even more."

"Raise the money through tourism!" One inmate tells me. Nice thought. I know the tourism trade. I doubt very much tourism is going to raise a million dollars over the fate of one rhino. For the most part, tourists want their senior discount on a penny postcard. Donations consist of a quarter. Now and then I hear an outcry, see picketers with signs, 'save the whale,' or spotted owl, but have never heard any statistics on just how much money the public actually puts out to help. I have heard the public is fickle and sometimes does come up with money when something needs doing!

There was a news story about two whales stuck in the ice. The public saw the pictures, heard the story and think enough money was raised to get a bulldozer or ship to break the ice, make a path so the whales could swim to freedom. But this is different. This rhino is old and it has already been decided it is best he be put down. Would the public raise the money to prolong his suffering? I shake my head and get back to my book; the program I am waiting for is not on yet. I arrive early so I can reserve my seat. I now have a sort of favorite spot I hope others respect. If someone else gets there ahead of me, no big deal, but I like to be at least near the window to use the ledge to write on.

Mr. Viet-nam comes in now to watch his favorite program and nods at me. I just look up and smile.

One inmate I do not know well is in the TV room in pain. I look up. He is sitting near me so I asked what is going on. I had only heard rumors.

"I had chest surgery. The doctors will not give me pain medicine." I'm puzzled, and give an incredible look.

"They say they cannot give drugs to people in prison." I wonder if they think he will not take the pain meds, and sell them. "So I go to my team counselor. She says she is not responsible for medical issues. I show her in the handbook where it clearly states the team counselor is responsible for our care, including medical issues." She insisted, 'No.' I'm not sure if he argued, or was in some way disrespectful. *Just curious what the other side of this story is.* "She did not refer me to anyone else. Nor offer any solutions, just, 'No.' He is obviously in pain. It seems reasonable after opening a person's chest there will be pain requiring pain medication.

The inmate goes on. "The next day I have been assigned another bunk, a top bunk in another cube. A bunk painful to climb up into."

Red overhears the conversation. He still has heart issues and pain. Sometimes can't breathe. He is the one who screamed out in pain and was sent to the hole for falsely saying he is having a heart attack. He is in my wing just a few cubes down. I heard him, and saw him taken away. I know him, and find him to be an honest reasonable person, not trying to get attention, or get even by making false reports. Red adds, "They had me in handcuffs standing against a wall when I could not stand. The guard told me to my face he did not care if I lived or died." This is the same guard who got reprimanded.

A Black guy was trying to kill himself. He had a noose around his neck and was about to jump. This guard had laughed in front of a lot of other inmates who came running. He said, "Good, I hope you jump!" Possibly adding some racial slurs. The word is, the prison warden was worried most about the racial slurs, how this might impact the prison. The public frowns on racial stuff. That and religious freedom. "Suicides are normal." "Oh well! Go ahead and jump" is ok. Just do not suggest it has anything to do with your color or religion. I do not say much, but tend to agree that these words match what I'm seeing. The guard was not transferred, and was only verbally reprimanded. Many inmates are laying for him, in hopes of catching him alone. I would not want to be in this guards shoes.

It turns out the 'Black Dude,' was Mr. Watermelon, one of the guys who stood up for me in the TV room. Someone I supplied fresh southern greens to.

The guard's attitude to all of us is, there is nothing we can do; he is in charge of us, we are low life with no rights, and should all be dead. It is a waste of tax payer money to feed us, or keep us alive. Nothing will change those views he holds as truths. We are being trained to be sheep; his job is to sheer us. He comes right out and tells us this openly, laughing at us.

I have a private conversation with Muscle. "Let's play 'What if' for a moment."

"What if what, Miles?"

"Oh, let's say, what if we weren't sheep. Just pretend of course." Muscle follows in the slipstream of the heavy talk, moving as a Mac truck down the freeway of conversation. "You notice how Bully the guard stands in exactly the same spot every single day like clockwork?" I pause at a stoplight in the conversation. The light changes. The conversation continues through its gears to cruising speed. "What if something spooky, strange, and freaky, was to happen in that exact location at the time Bully was standing there."

Think about the possibilities. There is a light right above him.

"Ingredients of this recipe for retribution might go as follows." An empty Clorox jug, a gallon of gasoline, box of tide, a roll of string, a foot of electrical wire, a heavy weight, two picture frame screw eyes, a nail or two, a ladder. All innocent enough items. All items we can get. Get them a week before the event. Set much of it up a few days or week before raising the curtain on this play. Come in after hours as the cleaning guy.

Gas and tide make napalm. Fill the gallon jug. Balance it so it will pour when the weight is removed. String holds the weight. Bare a plus and minus light wire. Hold live wire in a way that a string tied to one, pulls it in contact with the other, creating a short and spark. Have some greasy rags ready to ignite. Run a string across the ceiling down a wall near the door. Screw eyes allow the string to move around the corners. A loop in the string holds it onto a nail.

Bully stands there, someone by the door takes the string off the nail and tugs it. Two wires create a spark, rag ignites. The one pulling the string walks out the door and disappears. Ten seconds later, the small fire burns the string holding the weight balancing the napalm. Pouring napalm ignited by fire all over Bully in the middle of a cafeteria filled with a hundred prisoners, all of who are suspects. As Bully screams for help, everyone just watches. It would be difficult to know who of the 100 witnesses was involved, who to charge. The main culprit was not even there. Has a better alibi than anyone else. He was talking to the Chaplin at the time.

Or, substitute collected toilet goo for napalm, just to send a message. There are other ways to use a cigarette lighter taken from a truck, or a series of relays, solenoid, and delay switches, maybe a mercury tilt switch from the thermostat on the wall. Hook that up to the thermostat, or the handle of one of the coffee machines. The same idea could be applied to 220 watts of electricity, and two points Bully might be encouraged to touch. Many things in the kitchen run off of 220 watts. A car battery and coil could be used. Even a charged capacitor. Give him a jolt. Punish who?

"Who did that!" Would get what answer? Muscle says, "Any of us." There would be an investigation.

Muscle gets it, saying, "Who would want to harm a hard working dedicated prison guard? Who would have a motive? Let us explore the possible suspects. Investigate this most strange event." There could be a note on the string, "In memory of Watermelon."

"Yeah, or 'What you dish out thus you shall receive' or, 'paybacks are a son of a bitch.' Just in case the act itself is not clear."

The Mac truck, which is our conversation, zooms by. We watch and feel the wind of it as it heads on without us. We would not climb on such a ride. For no other reason than we are better people than the guards are. Not all the monsters are on our side of the bars. I do believe however, that Bully trips and falls. He shows up for work bandaged up. A lot quieter.

Woman says, "Bully is wrong. We have options. We are not decent because we must be, but because we choose to be."

I ask in fun, "Was it you who helped Bully trip?"

He looks down and mumbles, "It was an accident."

I suspect Woman has inside knowledge of what it is like to be a member of a minority group. "Good job Woman!" I pat him on the back and he just smiles.

Not all guards are like this of course, maybe even only him. Some are 'ok,' like the one I joke with at the food line. The conversation here drifts off to rumors and second hand information about the horrors of the prison. Some stories may be true, some may be partly true. That is the issues I have. We repeat rumors and who listens? Ha! It's just a bunch of criminals crying they got arrested, saying they are innocent, and whining like babies when life is not handed to them on a silver platter! Anyone who seriously goes after the truth with proof like Doc, we see what happens. Evidence? What kind? Pictures are not allowed, nor tape recorders.

So I learned a lesson, and take note of who is stepping forward to be counted, and who wants to push me up into the lime light alone. We have to choose our battles. Often bide our time. It's not me who has been handcuffed here, received horrible medical treatment, or gone to the hole. I tell Book, "I decided when writing my books, that the purpose is not to get even, expose wrongdoings, right any wrongs. This is a story of my life, and what effects me. Following an interesting time in Alaska history and maybe an interesting lifestyle; choices we make; how to solve basic problems. How to eat, pay bills."

"I read the first book, Miles, and the interest is the hair raising adventures in the wild! The books seem to have changed. By the time you get to prison, your writing may have a different appeal to a different type reader. In other words, those who liked the first may not be interested in the last. The folks interested in the last, might not care for trapping and killing things as a lifestyle."

I tend to agree, but am not sure what I ought to do about it. It is hard to write about a lifestyle I am not living now, like killing bears and getting lost. Unless I write fiction.

"Did you see the movie or read the book, 'Into the Wild?'" It was a best seller that got me thinking. One big appeal is wondering what motivated this kid, what makes people like this tic. What was he thinking? Well, I am that kid, only I lived. I can tell that story of why. We can follow that personality type over a lifetime. See the legal implications; show the strengths and weakness. There are rewards and a price." I pause. "Maybe people can look at their own lives, compare, and learn something about choices, and what happens. I talk of a reality few get very deep into."

"Well for sure you are smart, getting the word out while no real names are used—it's just a story." Book has another line of thought. "Some of these guards know how to get away with what they do. I think they do not treat everyone the same way. They believe in hierarchy; know who to be nice to. They know who they can prey on as well."

I think this is so. I have met the personality type in my life in a variety of places. Maybe everyone has. Bullies, those who enjoy other's pain. I meet women abused by husbands. Husbands who seem like nice enough guys outside the home. There are those as well, who, when they have their way, are very kind; friendly. If things do not go their way, or they perceive a slight of some kind, suddenly go ballistic. Often difficult to prove. Difficult to convince those who know these people they can be the opposite of how they appear in public.

I also know most people who are up to no good and know it; will go to great lengths to protect the operation they have going. They will not operate legally to protect their livelihood. "No, I am not referring to just the inmates!" Mostly I keep to myself. Find a quiet spot to read and write.

I took a lot of notes from the Genghis book. "But eventually the conquerors take on the same characteristics of the conquered." The Mongols were a tribe of warriors used to being on the move. Their skills had to do with weapons; survival off the land. The needs and requirements of staying in one place in large numbers, is different than the needs of a forage gatherer. "Four decades transformed the Mongols from a nation of mounted warriors to a sedentary court with all the trappings of civilized decadence that was contrary to the Genghis legacy."

As they expanded, they also left the plains and came to forests, fields, and rivers. Horses were slower. The element of surprise is missing, compared to charging across open plains. Some of this fits in with my own rabbit cycle theory of civilization. (Reviewed well in past books). Basically, mankind lives in predictable cycles on a time line, the same as rabbits do. The cycle is built into the system. Our cycle might be 1,000 years, instead of seven years of the rabbit. As the Romans fell, so do we all.

The good news in my mind is, "This too shall pass." There is a renewing; a rebuilding; earth repairs herself. We start over with fresh energy. Healthier; happier.

*So goes my theory! It helps me understand what is going on. Do not cry and despair my friends! It is just us, crashing, as we have done for millions of years. It's all predicted; all is in order and on schedule.* I neither hasten the events, nor try to change anything. I'm careful with my own personal life. *I want that to be enough. But is it?*

**Future Flash**

Reading a book that is a study on the collapse of the world as we know it. 'The Five Stages of Collapse' by Dmitry Orlov.

A certain degree of indifference or detachment is helpful, including indifference to suffering. Possibly the most important characteristic, more important than skills, preparation or luck, is the will to survive. Next is self-reliance: the ability to persevere in spite of loneliness and lack of support from anyone else. In a survivable future we would do well to put our emphasis on individuals, and small cooperative groups, rather than large entities.

The author who has studied the subject believes society is not adaptable enough as a whole, and changes too slowly for survival when big changes take place. Governments are slow to keep up and tend to want control; uniformity. Unorthodox ideas and ways offering choices works in studies of our past. This supports my own unprofessional observations. It is also stated the majority do not wish to realistically look at the potential of a collapse of life as we know it. Yet, it is pointed out, collapse has already begun in many areas.

A special on TV showed what is happening in Detroit, Michigan in which entire city blocks including skyscrapers are deserted. Uninhabited. In Alaska many smaller villages are not making it. Inhabitants are forced to move to the bigger cities to survive. Village power gets shut off, with no more services. People all over are losing jobs, then homes, then living on the street. People were used to a middle class lifestyle. I consider this worth facing and being real about. Questions I ask become important - what is it we really need to survive and how do we get that? A vivid film of a woman and her children dying on the street comes to mind. She cannot figure out how to live on $2,100 a month. I'm shocked and appalled. Dumbfounded.

"Lady, I saw a yard in the beginning before you lost it all. Where is your garden!" I saw pizza containers, buying food one can at a time, one day at a time. I saw a computer, a car. "Lady, sell that car, forget the computer age. Grow a garden, walk, buy a freezer and store food in bulk when it is on sale; dry it, can it. Where is your pressure cooker? Lady, I see pigeons on the wires over your head. I have a recipe for four and twenty blackbirds baked in a pie; substitute pigeons and live well!" What are these people being taught about their condition besides, there is no hope, you are doomed? Hope for welfare and the kindness of the rich!

I have had girlfriends like this lady I loved and tried to help. Buying soda for the kids one can at a time out of a machine. I tell her if she buys case lots at Sam's instead, the savings in one year could buy a car. There was no changing her. It was like putting money in a hole. I am convinced if we gave a million dollars to everyone, the poor would be poor again, and the rich would be rich again in a very short time. I am also convinced the poor get taught to be poor and stay poor, to fulfill a social necessary purpose for those 'high up.' Brainwashed is a good term. It is not necessary to fall into that!

Ha ha and ha! I began with twenty-five cents in Alaska. I have never in my life paid a dime of rent. Within a year, I owned my own home. I did not do it with money. I built it. I lived on a boat. Before that I lived under a bridge, in a tent, in a car. I lived like a king on $2,000 a year (not a month) for a decade. I had all I wanted. I became a land owner. Had enough food to share. I owned the world! It is all about outlook, the willingness to be open, change and adapt.

"I'm not special! If I can do it, so can you lady!" I didn't say it was easy, but yes, very rewarding and at the end of my life, no regrets. I have lived, and am living all my dreams. I do not have sympathy for, "poor me!"

**Future flash ends**

I do try to change things actually. I believe in accountability. But people trying to change things is also part of the plan! Slick, huh! I try to change things, but if that is not going so well, I try not to despair. The world will keep spinning with or without my opinions. There is not much room for philosophy in Hotel Fed.

"I appreciate you buying breakfast again for me this morning!" The stern guard just nods as he has his eye on someone with an unauthorized bandana on. A request can be put in if you are Native American, to wear an Indian bandana. But this guy does not look Indian. *Oh oh.* Usually the guard smiles and makes a comment back at me. Sometimes stuff like, "So, when are you getting out?" He knows me by name now. We are getting closer to thinking of each other as humans.

I sit at the Mexican table today, but only briefly. The main man that runs the garden harvest ring is at the table.

"I'll plant more hot peppers for you, if you leave one row of watermelons alone. I got a deal going with the blacks." I do not tell him the deal is I give watermelons away for free.

"I'll think about it," is all the Mexican says. That's as close to, "We have a deal" as I'll get. He can't make anyone plant what he wants. But someone could volunteer to. Naturally I'd want something in return. Seeing as we are not friends. It would look bad to do what the Mexicans want without expecting grease to make the gears go around in return. It would look like I was scared, or he had something on me. Demands might get made of me by others. Respect and survival is, 'It's business.'

Fairbanks scowls when I suggest that I—we—should plant more hot peppers. I add, "This is about learning to grow stuff. Why not grow what people like? Part of being a farmer is marketing right? How to sell it, move it, trade it, unload it, is part of our education." Fairbanks wants a cut, a favor, this is his turf. I'm the new guy.

"Fairbanks, I have an in with Mr. Mushroom. I get along with Mr. Education better then you do. I can do you some favors." I'm unwilling to do something I think is unethical. I realize however my sense of ethics is more my problem than anything positive. All of us inmates have a story, a reason, a justification for who we are, what we do.

"Remember this is the world many of us come from. The land of the tough and the dead." I nod, I understand. "Nothing is free, and there is no such thing as an act of kindness without a snare on the other end of a line of bull."

I simply do not agree. "It is possible to be nice for no other reason than to be nice. When we are nice, we feel good inside."

"Nice idealistic view, Miles. Some of these guys cannot even trust their parents. How are they going to ever trust anyone else?"

"I'm sure that is what the prison system will think if I get caught. I am obviously getting paid to help others; after all, I am a criminal! That's what criminals do, lie, cheat, steal, and con people. Some felons are good at it, and very convincing! But do not be fooled by our ability to imitate humans! The bottom line is, we are all snakes and vermin!"

Muscle chuckles, "You got that right! More than that, we all try to live up to what is expected of us so we are not a disappointment!" *Politics in the garden, geez!* Muscle is more of an intellectual philosopher than he admits. That's not expected of a member of a top Mexican drug cartel. It would be bad for business. Muscle knows I will never tell. Besides, I do not know anyone in his circle of life to tell.

Out camping on the Tanana river.

# CHAPTER FIVE

## WRITE SON, SPACESHIP PLANNED TO MARS, OUT OF PRISON

"Yeah, Miles, the family used the Alaskan pilot once. He does a good job; reliable guy."

I smile. I have had conversations with The Pilot. Flies planes into the wilds, filled with contraband of all sorts. And walks away from the plane. The plane is written off as a loss, its value insignificant compared to the value of the cargo. He's been in business for over forty years. He flies for a lot of the big names. Specializing in flying across borders under the radar. "Miles, what's your view on the drug business? You do not do drugs, so I am curious you would talk to drug dealers."

"My number one priority is freedom. Freedom of the individual to make life choices. My opinion—yours—is not as important as each of us doing as we feel we believe. As long as we are not messing with anyone else overly much." I say it like that because, technically everything we do effects the world and others! Your standing in line at the store effects the quality of my life. I hate lines!

We both chuckle. "Muscle, I do not do drugs. I think drugs cause early death; major body problems. This may even be more than an opinion, but a fact!"

Muscle adds to this thought. "Yes, few of the top dealers do drugs themselves, they could not run a business whacked out on drugs and know it."

I nod that I guessed this. "It is not for you or I to decide what the rewards of drugs are. That is up to each individual. If someone does drugs, I am ok with that." I explain, "I think these people are the walking dead! Just an opinion. But there are a lot of people; a lot of competition for our resources, jobs, space. If there are those among us who wish to willingly raise their hands saying 'Count me out!' I give a sigh of relief we are not having to draw straws!" I say, "So spend your life on a bench with a bag in your hand that has a bottle in it as the train of life zooms past! I will wave 'hello'! Followed by 'good bye' from the window of the train." Some say it is all a disease. A disease that can be cured. I have no opinion on this. Every 'wrong' behavior is a disease. If you look at it in the right way. It may not matter.

"Bummer you caught the disease or inherited it; I feel for you!" Do you belong in jail? I think not. In a hospital? Only sometimes. Who will pay the bill?

I meet plenty of people who party hearty and love the life of the irresponsible drunk. Someone will always feed them, give them shelter, attention. My opinion is, at least some of these people I know, chose this and are not sorry; do not wish to change. I think it is wrong to use tax dollars to cure them. Or even to convince them of the error of their ways. Who says it is an error? Some may want and ask for help! But even among those, the cry for help comes in spells. Tomorrow they are at it again. I am therefore unsure how much should be spent, and under what conditions.

I also feel if we look at the definition of a drug, we find caffeine, sugar and chocolate are also drugs. Is taking these things a disease? Do users of these need help? Should tax dollars be used to buy your chocolate or pay to help you quit? Define abuse of a substance. If you are 100 pounds overweight, and your life is messed up over your sugar addiction, should the law step in and arrest you for that reason? Make you get help at tax payer expense? I think not. Should those who sold you sugar go to prison for it? Some outlawed drugs I put in the same category as sugar, caffeine, nicotine, or alcohol.

Some drugs like Meth, I have no clue why anyone would even try. Beyond my rabbit cycle theory of civilization. When the population needs to be reduced, and some volunteer to remove themselves so that there is room for the rest. *Thank you! I appreciate your sacrifice!* Or are somehow part of a spiral downward trend by causing chaos. I do not like it, but it makes sense. Has a purpose.

I am not in favor of criminalizing the use of drugs or the selling of drugs unless it involves another issue like distribution to minors, stealing to support a habit or putting drugs in food people are unaware of in order to create addicts. Like what was done with cigarettes. I support prostitution. Never saw one... well... once when I was seventeen in the navy in Denmark, but saw how the concept was set up legally there and have no issues with the basic concept.

"Miles, certainly my family agrees." Muscle cannot give me any actual details of his family's operation. "They help out the village. Donate money for the hospital, pay for operations local people need. Lend money at no interest to those who are contributing to all. Drugs are sold outside our area."

"Does that destroy someone else's village?"

"Maybe. But there is a segment of any population that is weak, wishes to cop out; not face reality. The family does not push drugs, merely makes them available to the wanting and needy."

*The oil industry destroys villages, as well as the timber industry.*

I'm not sure I believe this, but sounds like a good line to repeat. Government uses the same promotional line, "Just here to help." There was a documentary on a Mexican drug lord, the biggest in the country. He had never been in jail. It was proposed higher ups did not want him in jail. He got caught once, and was in jail about a week, then mysteriously escaped. Where he lives is known, so he is not hard to find. Locals were interviewed in his village. They support him, saying he donates a lot and supports the entire community. He pays well and is generous; is a good parent; has a good personality and is well liked. He takes care of his own better than the government does. No one goes hungry in his village. He lends money when banks will not, with no paperwork. *(You do not pay, he kills you; easy to understand and not complicated and no fine print. I have no serious problem with the concept.)* I am not sure what to make of all that.

The story matches what Muscle says. I like Muscle. We'd get along on the outside. Of any wrong doings I do not approve of I'd say, "No one is perfect." A great many activities sound great when presented. There is a harsher reality to most occupations.

Some things there is simply a social need for. That need will get met. I decided this when debating whether to become friends with my unconscious or not. Our unconscious wants things that are often not socially acceptable that we repress. I decided to accept myself. Come to terms with 'reality.'

Muscle says, "Miles, I have extra room in my locker with a locking box. I can let you use it if you are worried your manuscript will get found and confiscated. If they come and look for it, it will not be in your locker."

"Thanks for the offer Muscle! I send what I write home in batches so not too much is on hand here at one time. I think I'm ok." I do not think I am writing anything the prison would be interested in, or does not know already anyhow. I rarely involve others in my business. I can take a risk, but do not want others to be at risk on my behalf. My own personal sense of how to live I call ethics and morals. Not necessarily in agreement with how others feel or agree with.

Mr. Education is upset about the garden. Addressing the class one day. "This is not supposed to be about feeding yourself and friends! Horticulture involves landscaping; plants that look nice. Flowers, ornamentals!"

He is troubled not enough students are interested in flowers! This is prison, we did not ask to be here. It is hard to make anyone interested. The bright side is, a few are honestly interested. I am one. At home I grow a lot of flowers. I plant ornamental trees; even buy them. I want to learn how to take better care of them, even experiment with new varieties.

Mr. Education in a rare moment speaks to me in private. "Miles, my son is giving me problems. Getting involved with the wrong people. He needs to get away; do something different. Can you help him out if I send him to Alaska. Maybe help him get a job; keep an eye on him?"

My mind freezes with shock. I do not know if Mr. Education is setting me up for more jail time, or is serious. It would be against the law for me to help his son who he admits is a felon. I'd think it would be against the law to make private deals between a prisoner and prison employee. *Does Mr. Education really think we are buddies? Is he that naive? Why doesn't he have any friends or family to talk to about this?* I am truly sorry his son is such a problem for him. But I have my own issues to deal with. I'm not in a position to worry about Mr. Education!

"If he shows up, maybe I can line him up with a friend who can help." Is the best neutral and most legal answer I can come up with that sounds hopeful, but says nothing.

He's almost in tears and getting emotional on me. However, we do not have the kind of relationship I can actually 'care.' We are not equals. He owns me. I have zero rights. If we have a disagreement he can have me in solitary, or have years added to my sentence. I get laughed at for suggesting I can have a complaint. My rights are less than Mr. Education's dog.

In the garden, I gravitate to tending ornamental plants and flowers. Even though I saw that many hot peppers were grown, they do not take much care once planted. This part of the garden has too much politics and controversy. In the flower area there is less interest, fewer guards and less people around. *Who is going to fight over flowers?*

One of my axioms in life is to find my own pie no one is fighting over, that there is no line behind. It may not be the most desirable pie, but I am left alone not waiting in line for a bite of it. Whatever it is, I can eat at least half of it, then generously share the other half.

As an artist, beauty attracts me to the flowers. Woman joins me, as rarely do prisoners get to be off totally alone on any job. Once in the flower area, we can separate and do different jobs. I ask Woman about dairy farming. "How much money is in it, how much time does it take, Woman?" I ask about raw milk, admitting I know little about the subject. I ask how cheese is made. I want to know if cows or goats work better. Farming interests me. I think I would never be a farmer. Sometimes I wonder about having one cow, a goat, or one pig though.

"Not a pig, Miles. Pigs need groups. One pig does not work out well."

Oh, I did not know that. I decided I like ducks more than chickens.

"Chickens just seem so stupid!"

We laugh. "Anyhow, Woman, I am a forager by nature. I like to live nomadically over vast areas." I know how to gather wild things when in season. I gave a class talk on edible mushrooms one day. Many inmates who are from the big city think about a change. That change is to be alone more to regroup, live a quieter life in the country. It seems like a good idea if you do not want to get back into the old ways with the same kinds of people. Some inmates are just talking, saying what the prison wants to hear. I'm told the number of inmates who return to prison within a year is high. Yet few of the inmates I know are repeat offenders.

"Miles, I think the statistics have to do with the general prison population, not Hotel Fed."

There appears to be no separate statistics for minimum security prisons. I tell Muscle, "If we care about freedom and want it, we need to study control, what it is, how it happens, how it works, how it does not work."

"So we can recognize it and avoid it."

"Or, at least have an understanding of what our problem is." *Conquering any problem usually involves first identifying and understanding the problem.*

I read from the Genghis book. 'The Mongols accomplished in three years what European Crusades from the West and Turks from the East had failed to do in two centuries of sustained effort. They had conquered the heart of the Arab world. From 1250-1270, a temperature change of a few degrees annually severely reduced precipitation that restricted growth of grass and thereby weakened the animal herds. Without strong horses and ample food the Mongols could not sustain a war. They turned to China and took over by becoming part of China. The great capital the Mongols founded became modern day Beijing.' Some of the changes Mongols made are reputed to be why their government worked for so long, and over such a vast area.

Some ideas are hard to sum up, or depend on a complex network. Here is one concept I wrote in my notes. 'Peasants traditionally groveled at the bottom of the food chain in a long line of government officials who commanded every aspect of their life. The Mongols organized peasants into units of about fifty households called a 'She.' These units organized and ran themselves. They oversaw local farming, water, resources and education as a local government. There were over 20,000 schools. It would take over 500 years for the rest of the world to offer schooling to the common people.

Mongols had passports and credit cards to use as they traveled long supply lines with shelters spaced every twenty-five to thirty miles. Europeans at the same time disdained commercial enterprises. Merchants were considered dirty, immoral, undignified for the ruling class as manual labor. Goods leaving the estate should not be going to trade for other goods for the peasants on the land, but to buy jewelry, religious relics and luxury goods for the aristocracy. In a Feudal System, reliance on imported goods represented a failure at home. Mongols elevated merchants and traders to respectable positions. They realized items common in one place and taken for granted, have value and are exotic somewhere else, and marketable.

I stop here to think. I spin this thinking forward to modern times, and wonder if the ideas still apply. Would there be a reason today, for those in power to look down on merchants, commercial enterprise, and free trade? Maybe our rich are against the goods of the world ending up in the hands of the common people? *Because the goods belong in the hands of the lords?* If this is an issue, is it because we are getting more feudal? In other words, reverting back to the ways of the original European ways where we started? Where the common person is a serf, serving a higher class. A class system exists, even though we speak of equality?

Mongols traded for silk and game playing cards. Cards were popular as a pastime because they can easily be carried in a pocket and became a source of great income. The use of cards led to reading, writing and understanding symbols and the written word. This led to written records, stories, and plays. Politically a great way to disseminate propaganda concerning history, accomplishments, and conquests.

I REALIZE IN PRISON, I have the time to ponder, to think, to read, to learn. I am in a structured environment where some stresses are gone. There is time off, where I can be in the chapel reading alone, safe from any brewing prison problems. I'm adaptable. I look at what I can control, and what I cannot control, and make the best of it. I am reading a history not seen in school. I think, because it is not European white man history. I am engrossed in my reading…

> Mongols never got deep into Europe to conquer it, but later trade routes opened up and were shared, helping Europe a great deal. Mongols killed the knights of Hungary and Germany, but not the big cities. Europe had been cut off from mainstream civilization since the fall of Rome and Europeans eagerly accepted the new changes. Standards were quickly escalated with music, food, and cloth. They forgot the early records of 1240 and the invasions of the evil Mongols and Tartars. Europe experienced a rebirth, the renaissance.
>
> We do not have accurate records of how the Romans fell, or what became of them, or the Greeks, or the Egyptians. But we have accurate records of what happened to the greatest empire in human history, the Mongols.
>
> Climate change had a huge effect. From 1328–1332 a flurry of assignations, disappearances, and inexplicable deaths happened among top leaders. Fear gripped everyone. This turned out to be the plague, an unknown death at the time. In China, 90% of the Hebie Province population died. The country lost half to two thirds of its entire

population as it was the manufacture center of the Mongol world. As goods traveled, so did the plague.

In 1345, the plague reached modern day Ukraine. The merchants of Genoa exported goods to Russia and slaves to Egypt. The population of Europe declined from seventy-five million to fifty-two million and then twenty two million. Compare this to WWII, where Great Britain lost 1% and Germany, 9%. Poland and Ukraine lost 19%. Far below the plague of the 14th century.

Plague hit urban dwellers hardest and fastest. Educated classes, craftsman, the church was hit hardest. Diplomatic letters stopped flowing. Transportation failed. In 1348, Pope Clement VI could not enforce orders to leave Jews alone. On Valentine's Day, authorities of Stansborough herded 2,000 Jews to the cemetery and began mass burning. All Jews between Cologne and Austria were burned between 1348 and 1349. In Spain people initiated persecutions against minority residents like Muslims.

I pause in my reading to take in the events of long ago. The class across the path should be open soon. No lights yet, but I keep my eye out the chapel door. As a prisoner in hotel Fed, I read about a fall of that civilization and see some similarities with how it is today in present time! *My rabbit cycle theory of civilization at work again.* I read on…

Europe became isolated. Mongols in Persia and Russia were cut off from China and Mongolia. The system collapsed. Without massive connections there was no empire. As foreign conquerors, the Mongols were tolerated by their subjects, who outnumbered them by as much as 1,000 to one. The Mongols intermarried and became as the subjects, to blend in and survive. Mongols became Muslims in the East. By 1356 all paper currency was useless.

In 1492 the belief in the long-lasting Mongol empire was born again by Europeans who wanted to reestablish the old trade routes. A century after the last Khan ruled over China, Columbus sets out to reestablish the connection.

And thus, modern European history begins, that which we all learn in school. This is the first time I comprehend what lead up to 'my people's history.' So Columbus was looking for the trade route to Cathay that Marco Polo spoke of. He found the USA instead. *I'm trying to go back to the very beginning of my country's history, and briefly follow to present time. What I have been taught is not the truth. What is the truth? Even it if was the Vikings, not Columbus who got here first, why did people come here and what did they want? How did they get what they want? What beliefs did they have and hang on to that are the basis of my country?*

"The 18th century of Enlightenment in Europe produced a growing anti Asian spirit that often focused on Mongols, as a symbol of everything evil and defective.

Voltaire adapted a Mongol play, 'The Orphan of Chao', to fit his personal political and social agenda, portraying Mongol leaders as evil, ignorant, cruel villains. He renamed the play 'Orphan of China' which was shown in Paris in 1755.

Eventually, scientists backed up notions that Mongols are inferior. The term 'Mongoloid' persists today. I read the rise and fall of the greatest conquers in the history of mankind, that has been well documented with records. It's not what I was taught in school. I think about this Genghis as I sit in prison. Some aspects of how he conquered stand out in my mind.

He'd kill all the enemy leaders straight out. No torture, trial or prison. No making an example of them. He'd turn to the rest of the population saying, "You may join us or die. If you join us, you will be one of us. You share in the spoils, will be allowed to work, get paid, practice your religion of choice." Most people will join! I can imagine many did not like their leaders. Most leaders at the time treated peasants as slaves. There was little love shared. Good riddance to those leaders. They ruled, for the most part, with a stick, not with understanding or equality. Genghis was good to his word. He did not believe in slavery. Each citizen had to give one day a week of their time for the good of all. No exceptions.

Next, he did not allow wholesale pillaging. All acquired goods were put in a pile and later distributed throughout his people. This is quite different from war as I hear about it. One concern expressed is that warriors tend to focus on the 'loot, rape, pillage' part of conquering, and do not pay attention to the enemy warriors as much as they should. It's all about how much loot you can raid! It's chaos! In other methods of fighting the enemy ran, the conquerors concentrate on loot, the enemy regroups, comes back and sometimes wins. Genghis had a system with a distribution method all his people took part in.

Those conquered had immediate rights. Word of this traveled ahead of him. His people soon married in. All had work and were described as somewhat happy. Certainly they were treated better than any conquered race I ever heard of. A variety of religions were tolerated, again, very different from anything I ever heard of. I find it worth remembering because it worked. In the end, he did not lose by being overthrown. Weather and disease was the undoing. I think Genghis is the only major world leader who died of old age after a lifetime of ruling.

European scientists set out to classify everything from breeds of dogs to horses and roses. Johann Friedrich (1776-1835) created zoology. Classifications for humans is based on comparative anatomy. The categories implied evolutionary ranking.

In 1844, Robert Chambers of Scotland wrote 'Vestiges of Natural History of Creation' in which the various races of mankind are simply representatives of particular stages in development of the highest Caucasian type. From there, scientists went to the next conclusion. The Mongoloid race exhibited a close relationship to the orangutan, the Asian ape. For example, it sits in a folded leg position much like Buda. The term 'Mongoloid,' expanded to include American Indians and Eskimo, as well as Tibetans, Turks, Koreans, Japanese, and Palo Asians.

In 1876, Chambers associated features of those in insane asylums with having Mongolian facial features. Scientists decided these features derive from the time Mongols raped white women during Genghis's time. Now and then, there is a throwback in modern times brought out by alcohol, and bad nutrition. These imbeciles derived from an earlier form of Mongol stock that should be considered more prehuman than human. Brought out in a popular book 'The Mongol In Our Midst' in 1924.

The book brings us up to modern times, and relations with Japan, China, and the middle east. I smile, and can see how relations could be strained when the conversation begins.

"You, of the inferior race." It's interesting to read one version I have never heard, of how this came about. I mean, it even effects life here in prison. The guards and prison officials are all of the superior race. How did prisoners get categorized as subhuman? I have a belief that it is hard to mistreat those you believe to be human like yourself. Creating an enemy requires dehumanizing.

"We are not harming people." Stopping or winning a war could have to do with somehow humanizing this enemy.

There were some specific techniques Genghis used for winning battles that were clever and unheard of at the time. Now, 'Mongol' means to be an idiot. How interesting.

"Miles, you look deep in thought, what you reading there?" I tend to live in my own world. I'm not playing cards or joining groups.

"Hey, Miles! How come you are not over with the Indians? You joined the Indian spiritual group!"

It's true, I have not had much to do with the small Indian group. I used to dream about being an Indian when I was a kid. I wanted to be one, live like one! So what is going on? The Indian group is running a cigarette smuggling business. I oppose that, as does the prison. Nicotine is a drug; that's being a drug dealer, or close enough. I smuggle food! But that is something healthy being denied us. The prison does not frown on this as much. Live and let live. I do not agree with smuggling cigarettes, but do not wish to stop anyone. I simply chose to go elsewhere.

"Miles, when I was here years ago, cigarettes were issued! We all got a ration. That was the trade value here, not stamps like now! We also got Playboy and Penthouse in the mail."

Different times all right. The Indians get to wear a special bandana under religious freedom rights, that no one else can wear. No other religion can stand out due to its religion. The Indians do not support religious freedom for all. They flaunt their freedom and throw it in our face. I know not all Indians everywhere are like this, but the dozen or so here are. I do not support what they stand for. Even as individuals, I do not get along well with any of these Indians. I feel none show any true respect or connection to the land. All of them appear to be con artists, playing on white man sympathy and guilt. They have no clue what got taken from their people. If what was taken away was to be given back, these are not among the Indians who would be happy, or even survive.

I notice in Alaska something going on. The Natives got compensated for the evil done to them by whites.

"You whites ruined what we had! We had a good thing!" So ok. We give the Indians a lot of money and land for compensation. I would expect from the talk, to see the Natives go back to their old ways and use the money to support that! *If we took such a great life away from the Indian how come they do not want it back?* However, the tribes take the money and invest it in oil companies so they can have dividend shares. The oil industry is the epitome of what the Indians say they hate! So what's this all about? Investing in what they hate in order to make profits. How is this different than the white man they hate? I had assumed I would be close to the Native Americans when I arrived here in prison and met Two Feathers.

These people were the superior race of my youth, who stood for a connection to the land. I met none here in prison interested in eating well, growing food, or appreciating or receiving garden produce. None were hunters of wild game. None spoke of subsistence, living in connection with the land. Oddly, it seemed the blacks had the greatest interest! I never thought about it. I have zero education concerning black people.

"Yes, my parents, and grandparents picked collards! My ancestors lived off the land! I believe in this too!" I did not hear this sentiment from the Native Americans. I am surprised. I do not want to face this collapse of my dream of what the Native American stands for.

"There are only a dozen Indians. It's not a big group. I'm not part of any group, anyhow. You know me; off reading someplace!" I did not elaborate more. I wish I could use the Indian hut by the lake! But a lot of illegal activity goes on there! Anyone known to hang out there is kept under close watch.

"Upsetting a guard who thinks you are hiding something is not a good thing." Everyone agrees with that! I settle for seeing the lake off in the distance when I walk the track. I usually walk alone, notepad in hand.

I meet one of the prison inmate drivers who also teaches at the trade school. I'm sitting on my favorite bench on the walk path that is closest to the garden area where I work. Trade school is next to the garden and bench I sit at. I see some of the guys going to and from classes there. I have seen this guy before. He gets to drive people off the prison grounds and to freedom when their time is up! Now I remember, Driver is one of the guys who stopped to tell me how nice the path he walks every day looks, with hedges I trim and flowers I plant. I planted a thousand daffodils along the path. I'm especially pleased with any compliment because this was a big bag of bulbs about to get tossed in the trash as too old. No one wanted to do the work. I dislike waste! These could not get tossed out! I was on hands and knees, one bulb at a time in the mud and rain getting these planted. *I hate waste. Especially of food, or living things.* I have trouble throwing seeds out, or thinning. This is one of the areas Woman and I are responsible for.

I answer Driver, "That must be a rewarding job! Sending inmates off to their freedom!"

"Sometimes. More often the inmates do not know where to go or what to do. They are scared. I take many to the nearest bus stop and simply drop them off. They have no money, no hope for a job, no family, nowhere to go. No one picks them up, or is glad they got released. It's not my problem."

He tells me his story. "I'm in the building trades. I invested in houses and resold them. Sometimes fixed them up, or had a crew work for me. I got a little overextended and the market crashed." *A lot like the helicopter, Coast Guard story about his brother!* "I had two houses I just bought. I couldn't make payments. I owe a bank 400 grand." The Feds took his houses, his bank account, his dog. Nothing to go back to. "I have a sixteen year old I probably lost, never hear from him." He shrugs his shoulders. Has two more years to do in prison.

"I teach the prison trades. Inmates taking the class get a certificate that means nothing. One of the 'no one gets left behind' deals." He explains how the equipment is thirty years outdated. The codes he teaches are now illegal. He feels it is all about prison job security. How many took the class, how many get processed to get the continued funding.

"I hear and see for myself; it is the same with the horticulture class. Outdated methods, no one could use the certificate to get a job."

He nods, "I try to upgrade the teaching and materials with updated video. The prison gets upset. The officials are more interested in getting inmates into government help programs. Welfare, food stamps, assistance, job search, subsidized pay, alternative programs, outreach, shelters, and food lines. They must get a kickback or something."

None of us know. I suspect it is easier to keep track of us if we are in a government program. Records of how we are doing, connect back to prison funds. [1] What I am hearing, and as I understand the way it works, this sounds a great deal like the Feudal System I read about. Traders and merchants were not welcome, because trade goods belong to and should be controlled by, the rich. Middle and lower class is run by a series of government permits, restrictions, endless paperwork to the point the citizens, serfs, were slaves in the past, and possibly getting that way again.

Mr. Education, who is also in charge of the trade school, says the role of prison is to punish and baby sit, not to educate. This seems an odd statement from the head of education.

This inmate teacher says, "The reported money cuts are in the form of paper, pencils, books, saving hundreds of dollars. While inefficiency in the system and waste costs hundreds of thousands, if not millions."

I get some insight into the food situation here.

"Miles, I have been here three years. The food quality goes up and down with seasons. It's the end of the year now. The budget got spent by the providing vendor, so it's a lean time. This year's food vendor lost the contract for 2014. The vendor is not excited about filling out the last orders of his contract since he got cut off for next year. So we get the dregs. That should improve with the new vendor stepping in." Well this is good to hear anyhow!

"I'll be gone by then!"

"Yeah, and it will probably be me who drives you to the airport. Good luck. See you later!"

I realize that other aspects of prison change with the season. Guards come and go. Politics come and go with new leaders coming and going. Inmates have trouble knowing what the new rules and routines are. The prison does not trouble itself informing us. New leaders usually introduce themselves by showing us who is boss, throwing their weight around. Some of the new prison employees arrive from the prison system at large and have no experience, or do not comprehend this is minimum security! Some do not see the difference, or do not want to. Believing, 'A criminal is a criminal, they are all the same!'

Much like in the book I just read, how the greatest civilization in the world, the Mongols, is now associated with being an idiot. How in the days of the plague and European despair, the problem was blamed on the Jews in 1348. It was not just Hitler in modern times. Soon 'Jews' got expanded to any minority or disliked weak group. Those in power wished to blame 'them' some minority group easy to identify. Hatred and fear got misdirected. An enemy was deliberately created to take it out on. Again, my rabbit cycle theory of civilization. *Here we are again.*

An example is the guard who brings us bags of mail and hands it out sometimes. A new guard hollers, "No one behind me!" and reaches for his gun ready to defend himself. Nervous, scared, concerned he is about to be jumped. The sweat of fear rolls down his red neck. His worst nightmare, the only non-criminal in the middle of prison with 700 convicted felons! The regular guard is relaxed and does not even wear a gun. He only oversees handing out the mail, often asking one of us to hand it out. The regular guard sees us as human. The new guy has been told different from above. I can see it would only take one of us to move a hand fast, hide a hand behind our back and step forward, or trip and fall, for this guard to spin around blasting in self defense, in danger of his life. Such stories are in the news almost weekly.

"All the barbers got sent to the hole!" I hear the word as it spreads like fire. "A pair of scissors is missing!"

Another guard, "Scissors are a weapon. Until someone confesses and turns over the scissors all will be punished!"

This is minimum security; non violent criminals. I have reviewed what could be a weapon many times, in the hands of the smart. Gasoline, Drano, Clorox, battery acid. Pointy weapons could be easily acquired from car parts, a lawn mower blade... well... on and on. Scissors would be a fools weapon of choice.

After five days, it turns out a prison guard borrowed the scissors to take home to do a hair cut project and forgot to return them after the weekend. There was no punishment for the guard; no apology to all the barbers in solitary confinement the past week. We are now lacking barbers. Half of them quit. Refuse to be liable for guards taking equipment. I think hair cutting is voluntary, but they get the stamps and convert them into commissary goods. Most inmates are hurting for money, or so they let on.

The horticulture group is in the same position as the barbers in that we are issued tools that have to be accounted for. Fairbanks tells me that a few months before I arrived there was a war with the Mexicans. Someone took his pruning shears and tossed them on the roof when he was not looking. He had to go to the hole for not being able to produce sheers that he is responsible for. Eventually they were found on the roof. The Mexicans had wanted Fairbanks out of the way and wanted to get a message to those of us tending the garden.

It is easy to make an honest mistake and leave a rake or tool on the job. Now and then we lend a tool we checked out to someone else who needs it on their job. Like one night a wind came up and I did not know there would be a lot of leaves in my area. I borrowed a rake someone else checked out to get my area in order. The inmate I got the rake from did not have leaves in his area, so he got my pruning shears to use. At the end of each day we have to turn in the tools.

We get chits that go on nails in place of tools we take. Each of us is issued so many chits to use. I am allowed two chits, two tools checked out at once. Others who have more seniority get up to five chits. At least no one in my group has gone to the hole except Mushroom, during my time here.

"Miles, are you getting a visitor?"

"I only think so. I'm not sure!"

We are allowed visitors once a week. Few of us get visits because we are not from this state and it is a long ways to come to sit at a table and talk for two hours. A single room, set up like a cafeteria, is used for visiting. *At least no bars between us, like in the state institution when Iris came to see me.* Apparently I have a relative here in

Washington who lives just half an hour away! Well, not a direct blood relative, nor someone I am close to.

After my father and mother divorced, mom answered an ad in the paper. A guy looking for a woman to help him raise his children. Mom answered. There were three kids not being well taken care of. The single father who placed the ad had little money, working, with a minor drinking problem. Betsy, the oldest girl, was ten years old, taking care of her younger brother and sister. They welcomed mom! She raised them as her own until they were grown. The relationship with the father was not great, but mom did a good job with the children, who owe her their very life! Mom is close to them. *All this is mom's version.* I only met them one time - long ago. We did not keep in touch much. In general, mom does not like children! She had to raise her own sisters when she was too young to do so and hated it! Her mother was single during the depression and had to work. My mother had a lot of responsibility she was not up for. I think mom took the 'project' of saving these kids partly to make up for her past. The guilt she felt maybe, for not being a great mother to me and my sister.

It just seems strange to answer an ad, 'Guy looking for mother for kids,' and mom, who hates kids, answers. Betsy, the oldest, seems to have been the strongest. She did well in life. Got married to a nice guy, has children of her own. She is very involved in the children's lives - PTA, sports, events, after school activities of all kinds. Always on the go, and seems to do so happily, with a good disposition. And she lives just half an hour away! Dang! She wants to bring the whole family! The children are fans of my first two books.

There is a process to go through to get approved as a visitor. Papers, a waiting period, an approval, and what not. I guess a background check. There are no casual visits. Betsy shows up with her children and is denied at the door. The children are not allowed. So she has to come back another time—alone. The children are anxious to meet me. I at least see them. I watch them come into the building and stand in line through a window. I see them get turned away. They do not see me. I recognize Betsy even after all the years gone by. Short with long, blond hair and a way of walking easy to remember. Side to side with pauses, as she looks around unconsciously. As if she is contemplating doing something she shouldn't, and trying to check out the surroundings first. Bright blue eyes, not quite lined up. Just enough to make you focus on those big blue eyes. Head goes back a lot, as she shakes her hair in place, always a big smile. I watch her leave. So much for the visit I got all built up for.

But she is back a week later. We get a two hour time period sitting at a cafeteria table across from each other. At least allowed a private conversation. A guard in the room oversees everything, but is not listening in. Others are having visits at tables nearby, but no one is focused on anyone else. All attention is on your visitor.

"So, how is Hotel Fed treating you, Miles?"

"So you know the place as Hotel Fed, huh?"

She laughs and says the reputation for the place is as a laid back easy place to do time.

"Compared to state prison and general population, this is all right. It's still confinement, control."

She understands there are a lot of things I'd rather be doing. As she talks about what her children are doing, I can see she is a good mother, and her children are her world. We talk about the mother we share. I fill her in on mom stories from long ago; what she was like before Betsy met her. She laughs easily and enjoys hearing of life long ago.

"Miles, I and all the kids still have the wolf claws you gave us! We treasure them!" I have no recollection of having given them any. I assume I must have.

"Yeah, that's what I'm here for. Wolf claws, and other wildlife products."

Her head goes back and she shakes her hair in place. She works in a hospital cafeteria. I think orders the food, and is in charge of distribution.

"My husband and I both have to work to make ends meet," she tells me.

"Just part time though, Miles, three days a week." They have a big dog, a garden, no time to do much camping, boating; anything like that; but would love to one day—after retirement. That is a long ways away yet. She's still in her 40s! I try to picture her life and what it is like. She likes to cook, but not much money to get fancy. Her meals have to come out of a can, mixed in with what little they can grow. She has always envied and looked up to my lifestyle and how I live. She wishes her family could live like that! Closer to the land. "Hard to make a living که way though, Miles!"

Yes, I know. I make a joke, "There are ways to make big money! It's either very dangerous, takes being a genius, or is illegal. Take your pick!" She laughs because implied in that, is me being in jail, so guess what choice I made! I add, "I have never felt like I was struggling, or had trouble making ends meet, nor did without anything."

She nods that this seems enviable. "When you have kids you can't take as many risks."

I nod I understand. "Betsy, can you call Iris and tell her you saw me and fill her in?" Iris has been getting letters and calls from me, but it might be nice to hear from someone who has seen me. There are things Iris and I can't talk about because the phones and letters are monitored.

Time is up all too soon! I watch Betsy leave with all the other visitors who are crying, waving, carrying on. It is nice to have Iris writing almost every day. She has taken to doing little drawings in the letter. Usually of the cat. The cat looking at birds out the window. The cat falling in the cactus plant, the cat leaving paw prints on the window. I have a whole collection now. We are not allowed to discuss business, so it is hard to know how the business is going. She implies a few things have sold on the web site. No emergencies. She is heating with wood. She walks to the post office every day, and has her routine.

Nothing about prison life stands out as interesting, exciting, funny. It's not supposed to. Life is designed to be regimented and all experiences much the same. If you are having a unique experience, it is not good. I think of the Johnny Cash song, "Learning a lot of things here in prison momma!...and, there ain't no good chain gangs."

**Hello Iris**, Tuesday, January 1 , 2014

I am reading *Brave New World*, a classic about the future, written in the 30s. It describes prison to a T—what it's for, why we are here, how it is accomplished, etc., etc. Being reminded what it's about is a big help, for 'confusion' combined with 'stress' is a main objective. Yes, it's all necessary, I understand why. The author describes something called 'the feelies' set up for the masses. Written before the age of computers, even before mass TV or movies. Beer and a TV. I smile. But no, not everyone fits that mould, nor was meant to.

There were tasks to be done, other than working in factories or being among the sheep. The savage in *Brave New World* was in high demand. He lived in the natural world! How cool is that! The feelies had to be created based on his story and input. It was a sensation! It went viral as we'd say today. His civilized new friends had to go to concentration camps on remote islands. Sigh. But yes I can understand why! It simply wouldn't do to have a bunch of people with wild ideas thinking they might live outside the feelies! Who would pay for all that? Good grief! What a decision to have to make though, for the good of the people.

Mustafa Mund, the controller, quoted, "Factories do not run when people are out in nature." Unless of course you stay in a lodge, eat the prescribed foods, buy gifts; you know… contribute… consume. Imagine not contributing. How selfish is that! Geez! What an inspiring book. It helps one do their duty. Anyhow poor controllers. No one taught them what to do when it snows; can you feel their distress? Future generations will want to know how we lived back in the days before feelies. Take care! **Sunshine Miles**

I'm zeroing in on my last day. I have to bring a check off sheet around to get signed off. I see the doctor, go to the library, see Mr. Education. After six months of repeating my prison number at least once a day, I have to get my prison ID out and look at it. *I am not a number!* My unconscious is already disconnecting me from here and wiping out the memories. January 10th at 10:30. As I check out, I get finger printed.

The guard printing me casually says, "Lick the ink off your finger, it's edible ink." Without thinking, I do as I am told. It is not edible ink. The guard laughs, gets a big kick out of this. He does it to everyone. Proof we have been rehabilitated, and will do whatever we are told, like robots. I smile with him, *Yes, very funny.* The transportation guy I met earlier, is here to drive me to the airport! No guards! I have been given $100 cash to get back to the point I was picked up in Nenana. Saying cab fare is $100. Even though Iris is picking me up in Fairbanks. I have only my prison clothes. I was given a donated civilian jacket. Our prison pants and shoes are sort of normal looking. But only sort of. *I mean who wears green pants*? I'm a little scared, unsure what to do; how to behave. I've been brainwashed and know it. I can only imagine how it is when your time has been a year or more! I am not used to unstructured time. I tip the driver as expected. And I'm on my own!

I am unsure how to pick up my ticket. I have not done much on my own in six months, and been threatened with punishment for doing so. I realize now, I have been told what to wear, when to get dressed, when to eat, what to eat, and how to eat. I have been told how to walk, where to walk, when to walk. I am not used to people around me who are not fellow inmates. Chattering children and women are unfamiliar. As is music, traffic, and bright lights. The feeling is much like coming out of the wilds in my younger years. I am sure I will get used to it. It's just hard adjusting. Perhaps being a senior makes it harder as I am less adaptable, less willing to adjust to change. My brain does not take new things in fast anymore. I keep to myself and do not talk.

I arrive on the red eye in Fairbanks at 1:00 am. One of our friends who drives, brings Iris in from Nenana. We do not drive in winter. The Northern lights are out. I have orders to report to my probation officer when I arrive. I am not sure how to arrange that at 3:00 am. It is 100 mile round trip to go home and come back. I am to get a monitor for three weeks, and cannot leave the house.

My German friends, Helm and his wife come to meet me and say hi. Helm begins to cry when he sees what has been done to me. This reminds me of the woman at the pipeline camp who burst out in tears when I turned to face her after my rescue on the Yukon. I am not the same person I was when I left. A lot of the wind has been taken from my sails. That's the objective. I'm thin, white, do not talk much, keep my eyes down. I'm worried about reporting in. I am able to report at 5:00 am for my ankle bracelet. But it is not turned on for a few days. Iris tells me, "I had to buy long distance for the phone so the ankle bracelet will work." I will be allowed to leave the house for an hour a day to go check mail and a few hours a week to go get firewood. We realize the monitor is limited to seventy-five feet, and I cannot go to my shop! Even so, it is good to be home! Iris took care of the home front, lived frugally so our cash is intact.

Being on probation, I have to report in monthly. Luckily, not in person. "Iris, when I was told I was being released, I was told I would be a released to Anchorage, and I'd have to report to a probation officer there!"

"That's 300 miles from home, Miles! A 600 mile round trip and you do not drive! How could you report in?"

"That was the closest place they could find in their computer. Lucky Alaska is even considered a state. Often computers find Seattle as the closest place to where I live." We know that when we go on line to look for shipping costs. We talk to companies when ordering items. The United States ends at Seattle. Luckily the prison counselor listened to me when I showed her where I live on a map. I will be able to report in by mail, filling out a four page form each month.

I believe my good record in prison allowed some leeway when being discharged. Many inmates would get ordered to report to Anchorage and nothing you can do about it. Find a place to stay until you are off probation, or remain in jail instead! I took classes, contributed, donated, volunteered, and this is the result. The ability to get discharged to my home instead of a halfway house far away.

I review conditions I have to live by, or risk going back to jail. Going back to jail for a probation violation can mean three years in prison. No trial, no recourse. Simply upsetting the probation officer. That's a lot of power in someone's hands over my life. The issue I begin to see is, many of the conditions are 'impossible' to live up to.

I can't meet with other felons. Ok, how do I know if someone is a felon? Do I ask everyone I talk to, including store clerks, customers? I skip over that one. I cannot be around guns. Meaning I cannot get in a car that has a gun in it, or into a home that has a gun in it. In my community of 300 people I'd guess there are at least 1,000 guns. Even if I ask when entering a home if they have a gun, or if someone I talk to has a concealed weapon on them, I think there is no legal obligation to answer that question. The question is culturally inappropriate and rude. So I move along and hope this works out ok.

I cannot have on my property anything that could be a weapon or dangerous chemicals. This concerns me the most. The probation officer is visiting my home to inspect my living conditions to determine if I may live here. I ask about 'anything that might be a weapon'. *What about my ax, machete, chain saw?* The probation officer is a woman who appears to be nice, friendly, full of smiles, easy to get along with. Thin and good looking, well dressed, hair pulled back tight like a librarian. *However, a city woman who may not understand remote village life.* She answers huffily, "Everything in its appropriate place!"

"I keep my ax by the door so I can split wood near the entry way and get kindling into the house, is that appropriate?" My concern is, she feels intimidated, scared, threatened if she arrives and sees an ax by my door. Big headlines, 'Felon has ax by door as probation officer approaches! Felon shot dead in self defense.' There is no answer. I want to ask about chemicals, but see she does not want to answer these questions.

I have enough here to make napalm. I have acetylene and oxygen. I could make one heck of a bomb if I was inspired to. I could toss gas on anyone, followed by a match, and do a great deal of damage. In fact, I can take a great many things and get innovative if I had evil intentions. You could not keep dangerous things away from an active mind. I am labeled a non violent criminal, so what is the big deal here to tell me all this I am expected to live up to. Could the probation officer see battery acid and decide this breaks my agreement, and send me back to prison for three years? Trying to follow impossible agreements? So, now I need to live scared, because I am breaking my agreement? What is wrong with a fair agreement that is possible to live up to? I've asked that all along, all through the legal system.

Iris knows I bring up the fact all the time, that 'everyone' rides snow machines and four wheelers on our city streets and alongside the highway. That is illegal. Almost all of us do it, even the mayor. It's how many of us access our firewood. To get there we have to go down our streets. Even five to ten year olds zoom around on our streets. I remind Iris again, *The good news is!* Yes! Let's hear some good news! I still have a web store.

"I can focus more on the local rocks, my knives, and do some work with local wood. I finally came across a concoction that works well with wood for stabilizing, dying, and making suitable knife scales and carving wood."

"I know you have tried a dozen products, Miles." Yes, it was common for me to spend $100 on something new to try, and have it not work out. Walk away from the investment. Walk away from the material I tried to work with.

I can work on the pictures on the web site, make the site look different now that I have time at home, and can't leave for three weeks. *No, I am not ready to work on my prison notes. It is too fresh, too much an open wound. Let's wait until I can reflect more with an open mind.* I can focus on my books more in general as a long term business. The books could make a nice retirement, as once the books are done, all I do is reprint them. Well… do some advertising, but this is something I can do when I get old and unable to do much more than sit!

I have a lot of emails backed up, but am not feeling up to answering. One is from a long ago friend who found me again in a google search. Andrew was a high school friend. He emails me a memory I do not recall, from the 1960s.

Do you remember when we got a ride into Lansing, to see 'The Jungle Book'? It was January or February. Our plan was to take the bus back. The movie got out around 11:00 pm. It was cold, so we jogged to the bus stop to keep warm. We were the only ones out. After waiting and freezing for a while, we discovered that the last bus had already come and gone. You had an admirable phrase, "Let's motivate our carcasses to a more promising premises." So that's what we did. We headed towards East Lansing, finally coming to a 24-hour Laundromat. We used the pay phone to call a parent to come rescue us. I still enjoy the movie, partly because of our adventure.

I smile, that he has good memories from our friendship. We used to play tennis together. His family owned a tennis court. I look over emailed pictures he sent that I keep in a file. Wife, kids, grandkids now. Nice home, nice job. Very civilized. I'm sure he has never been arrested, and never will be! Among the protected. The police, the government is there to help and take care of him. He donates to Friends of the Animals, doing his part to save the planet. He pays a lot of taxes so everyone is happy. I smile. What would I have to say to him? *I can talk about my art and new web site!*

Here is a long ago letter from my son Mitch.

**Hey Dad**, Those are some really cool looking ice sculptures. I guess they do similar things with beach sand here in Hawaii, but I have yet to see any in person. It has cooled down here a little this month. It has also been super windy. A lot of the people in my classes are crying about how cold they are and it makes me laugh. I am still walking around in shorts and tee-shirts all year round as always.

My classes have been going well this semester. I have a much easier work load than any of the other semesters. I am only taking three classes and all of them are pretty easy. Which allows me to work on revising the three papers I need to submit for my culmination. I have been stressed out about that. I really just want it to be done and over with. I am not exactly sure what to expect and what kinds of questions the professors will ask me.

The only other thing that is going on is that I have finally gotten around to getting a passport. I might be using it to go to Japan at the end of the summer. My department is doing that summer institute thing again only this time it is the Japanese university that is hosting. A free trip to Japan would be really great. My fellowship is ending this semester so I am going to have to move, and rent is going to basically double.

Anyway, not much else going on really. Spring break is in two weeks. I do not really have any special plans. My goal is to have my revised papers all finished up by the end of spring break and sent to the professors. Other than that, I will likely be playing a lot of board games with other people in my department. There is this one game that we play that is notorious for being REALLY long. Most of our sessions at it take 12 hours. Each person plays as an alien race and you try to take over the galaxy earning points through conquest, war, expansion, trade, politics, diplomacy, technology, and things like that.

It is a game of making alliances, breaking alliances, trust, and betrayal. It is a lot of fun. Most of the time I am not really trying to win too badly. I just like to mess around in the game. I might take a side with someone to help them win. But last time we played I ended up winning completely on a fluke. I ended up in a situation where there was no way I could lose so I took advantage of it. So now I have to try to protect my title. One of the best parts of the game is the plotting and alliances that form outside of the game in between game sessions. We have this running joke about openly making "secret alliances" right in front of everyone else. So now I expect that everyone is going to be gunning for me next time we play. I have put a target on my back when people used to write me off as not a threat. Clearly there was method to my madness and I must have been playing the long con. I am really looking forward to playing. Well I hope everything is going alright with you. Talk to you later. **Love, Mitch**

Once again, a very different life. He takes after my father. His mother encouraged that. Having a son was the most important thing in her life. I let her raise our (her) son as she wanted. She and he are happy. It's all for the best. I rebelled at first, wanting to be a father. Oh well. Long ago. I have specific events along a time line as memories and turning points in our relationship. Some recorded in earlier books. Mitch was interested in magic for a while. We were both happily talking on the phone about the wonderful world of magic. Which leads to art and music. A magic show is on TV! We are living apart. I call him to ask him to watch the show so we can discuss it after! His mother tells us no. He has no time for this show. Mitch has homework to do. How thoughtless of me to interfere with homework. No, there is no good or better time.

We email each other and stay in touch. I remember emailing him pictures of the ice sculptures at the ice park in Fairbanks. He is in Hawaii now, where I was born. No, I do not suppose he understands my being arrested either. He is well entrenched among the protected. Police and government are nice to him, his friend, there to serve. I can see his mother now,

"Mitch, aren't you glad you listened to me and did not spend time with your father!" Sigh of relief all around. No, there is not much to say beyond blue sky and good weather.

Though it occurs to me later, when rereading his letter, this game Mitch refers to is a little like living as I do, only pretend. At least the pull, the interest, is there. The life of Indiana Jones.

I'm a felon now. It is hard to look at the world through the same glasses I once did. Being a felon wipes out any good I may have done with my life. An outlook I get all around is, "But what does any of that matter? You are a felon! Get real!" That's a conversation stopper. Nod, walk away. It will be hard to overcome this, if ever.

**From my diary**. In the news:

'Mars One' is a group serious about going to Mars 'soon.' Recruiting people for the trip, and in the process of building the ship to do so. NASA has a stated goal of having people on Mars by 2030.

There is a list of volunteers. More news off and on, as I read updates. A date within the next decade to be mining asteroids. Already discussing permits and mineral rights, and who gets what percent, what the taxes might be, who owns an asteroid. There is a space station already, in the news, a late trip reoutfitting with supplies that are getting low. Some people have been at the station over a year.

With this in mind, such first visitors to Mars will have to have the skills I know, possibly the same personality and qualities to survive. They will not be sheep. People headed to a new frontier with a great deal unknown, possibly alone, not returning ever, or for many years. I never did see myself as 'stuck in the past.'

"What does it take to increase the odds of staying alive? What are our basic needs, if we remove what we only want? What is possible?"

If some modern cutting edge technology is practical and useful to my chances of survival, then I am interested. Though it is common for old, outdated, tried and true, methods to be a good, even the best choice, in most situations. There were times I saw myself in the great alone, as someone stepping off the Starship Enterprise into the vast unknown of another planet, having traveled through a wormhole or the Star Gate. I asked question like, "What is time?"

My life reads like science fiction, but along the same lines as Jules Vern. A story that one day in the future may take on a different meaning. A text book, a profile, a psychological study, required reading for those stepping onto a ship headed for Mars. What happens when we have no light? How do we handle sitting in a quiet room without electric, or light, slowly starving and freezing. How do we find people who can do that?

**Diary ends**

I'm struggling with my sense of purpose. 'Why am I here?' In the wilds there was no question. Maybe no time to ask or wonder! I had to get the fire going, the snow melted, the moose skinned, the wood cut. I, and the world all around me changed. I am the trails I cut, the cabin I built. I am what I eat. What I ate was a direct link to the land. Civilization is a blend of all of us. It is more difficult to remain an individual, with a list of things done I am responsible for, that I can point to and say 'me.' I still eat from the garden, from the moose I get, fish traded for.

This has me wondering already, what I will do in the future about getting a moose to eat if I cannot have a firearm? I am told I can have either percussion black powder, or bow and arrow. Iris and I find a compound bow at a pawn shop in town. I try it out and find it is amazingly strong and accurate. Not like the re-curve bow I had as a child. I explain to Mrs. Probation Officer, "I have a friend who raises pigs. I am thinking we might get a couple of pigs to raise, so I do not have to hunt." Just an idea I toy with.

Mrs. Probation says, "Well, that is an animal product. I'm not sure you can do that!" *Imagine then getting arrested and hauled off to prison again because I have a pig I am raising to eat.*

I ask about the bow, as I am told it is legal, but want confirmation.

"Well, it is a weapon! You can't have a weapon!" She pauses, "Just let me know where you keep it, and every time you move it and put it back, let me know!"

*Yeah, right, in your dreams.* I'm discovering half the time I can't get hold of her when I have a question. Days can go by, she's busy. If I upset her, bother her, she can send me back to jail because I have an ax and Clorox. I have to think, *Yes, good point, if I had a pig I might try to illegally sell its parts, or sharpen a leg bone and stab someone. You just never know what to expect from us felons!* I understand I need to put this Mrs. Probation at ease. She thinks I'm a monster; that all felons are. There is little use getting angry or upset as it just proves she is right. Normally, I would simply avoid such a person in the way any of us avoid people who have power over us and hate who we are, and what we stand for.

I have gone through a lot of trouble in my life to make sure I am not between a rock and a hard place. Making sure decisions were mine to make. Making sure I had no boss, no employees, fellow workers I was forced to deal with. I pick and choose who I wish to be around. In my business life, I have, and do, tell customers to go shop someplace else. While at the same time struggling to understand and be open minded about customs and differences between people. Still, a sick person is the same in every culture like those who enjoy pulling legs off spiders. Now, here I am in hell. 'Hotel California.' Where you can check out, but never leave. Kissing a monster's behind, because I illegally have the dangerous chemical gasoline at my disposal, and signed a statement saying I didn't. It might be best to simply have as little to do with my probation officer as possible.

"Isn't that a little bit overboard, Miles! Geez!"

I reply, "Well, if raising a pig for food is considered a problem..." I leave the sentence open and give a shrug for a question mark.

"Hmmm. Yes, well I see your point."

I add, "The statement I signed reads if I make a false statement, such as knowingly have access to a dangerous chemical without saying so, the punishment can be five years in prison and $250,000 fine. Would that get your attention if you signed such a statement?"

I was making blank blades faster than finished knives, and getting way ahead on blades. I decide 'kitchen knives' is a safe venue, compared to being a felon selling 'hunting' knives. I tell Iris, "It seems to me there are fewer hunters in the country.

Fewer places where anyone would wear a sheath knife! Everyone cooks and could use a good knife in the kitchen! Plus, a big chef knife gives me lots of room to do my steel etching designs."

"Yes, that mammoth hunter handle theme sold, Miles! I got another buyer if you make one!" So that is on my list once I can work in the shop. I had thought at one time there will be a lot of people wanting to get back to the basics, considering the uncertainty of our economy.

"You know, people who want to know how to live off the land, grow, and hunt their own food. A knife is the single most important necessary tool to do so. Yet instead, the knife rage is zombie killer knives." *In the ending days, people are worried about, of all things, zombies!*

I want to be testing wood. I have this 'stuff' I want to try, called cactus juice. It is used to dye and stabilize wood for knife handles. This is something I want to get into as a new business. I have to try it out and perfect it better, but is much like stabilizing fossils I have had experience with.

It turns out Iris is going blind! Cataracts so bad she cannot see well enough to walk, drive, or read. We are working on an appointment for her in Mexico with an eye doctor she met on line. A woman who specializes in cataracts, for a price we can afford!

"Miles, they want $10,000 here in Alaska! For just one eye!" We can get it done for $1,100 in Mexico. Locals are willing to take up a collection, pass the hat, raise the funds for Iris to have her eyes done for a total of $20,000. It would be good to take care of this ourselves instead of burdening our community.

---

I STARTED a worm farm a while back, but it has been neglected for months now. I keep worms in a plastic tote in a back corner. They have been dormant all winter and need to be awakened, fed, and multiply so we have worms for spring garden! Alaska has no worms. I am especially interested after my knowledge gained in prison from Mushroom. The greenhouse roof broke from heavy snow. By March I will need to get the greenhouse going. If I need materials, I have to measure and write all that down!

I had not known Iris was going blind!

"I did not want to worry you in prison, Miles!"

The seniors say again, "We want to take up a collection, help you out, get you in for low income government help."

We'd rather pay for it ourselves. It's critical at least she gets to Mexico, even if I cannot. "Our friend Foil can help her get across the border and back if she can't drive or see!"

I FINALLY GET out of the ankle bracelet, but not much changes. I am not allowed to leave my area without permission. If I make over $300, or spend over that amount, I have to report it and verify why with proof and a legitimate reason. Thus, I am not encouraged to make money or do well. $300 is nothing. *I used to average that per day. I mean... I think. I'm not sure. I have no proof of that. Gross of course—not profit.* $300 is the average price of a custom knife. Some sell for $1,000.

There is no, "Good for you!" Oh no. There would be a frown, and I know it. What is desired is I get on various government help programs. Mrs. Probation would help me fill out the forms and help me get on welfare, food stamps, weatherization, fuel assistance, assistance of all kinds. There are senior programs to learn about, she has the information for me.

I tend to dwell on the positive. Mrs. Probation stops by and I excitedly want to show her the latest art I have done, a kitchen knife I made for Iris. She arrives with a back up body guard who is armed.

"Step back!" She sternly says as the body guard gets between me and her, hand on her weapon. The knife is across the room not near me. I forgot. 'Knife' would be a key in word to someone living in fear of psychopathic felons. I apologize. *What was I thinking?* Luckily everything is ok. Mrs. Probation wants me to store my knives in the shop, no knives in the house. There is no arguing. Asking questions is discouraged. There is only one correct response.

"Yes Ma'am." Eyes on the ground. Shuffle the feet in slave fashion.

Iris asks later, "How am I supposed to prepare dinner without a knife?" I gather some knives are viewed as weapons, while others of the same size are not. I notice this on E Bay, when looking around on line. A knife will be called a letter opener, but from the pictures we all understand it is a zombie killer. Since that might not be legal, we call it a letter opener. I understand by this, it would not be good to make machetes, swords, daggers, concealed weapons. They are 'kitchen knives,' like paring knives, chef knives, or generic 'utility' knives.

It seems a paradox that I am not allowed to be near anything that might be considered a weapon, yet am told I can continue my custom knife making business. I am working on a series called, 'Ladies of the Night.' A variation on what men wear as neck knives—a knife worn as jewelry. The sheath is a work of art. One design is a humming bird, where the beak is the blade. The sheath is a flower. The handle is mixed colorful materials that make it look like the body of a hummingbird, with a gem stone eye. The flower, as well, is colorful and artistic. It is basically a piece of jewelry. I advertise, "If you have little else on, you can be armed."

I believe in women's rights, all people's rights. Women should not live in fear of men or anything else. "It's a niche market. There are a lot of choices out there for guys. Macho knives, hunters, skinners, etc. Who specifically address women?" It's not my only idea, but the 'Ladies of the Night' series is popular. All kept in the shop. The 'no animal parts' issue is like the knives. Mrs. Probation interprets that as not allowed to raise a pig to eat. So am I expected to be a vegetarian? Could I be ordered to be one? I assume I can't be a trapper, but can I fish? Hunt for food? What about a wide range of animal products: shoes, belt, leather of all kinds? Leather sheaths for knives I'm selling will be an animal product.

My accountant friend Bean, tells me, "The objective is to make sure you do not sell illegal animal products ever again. There is little trust. The restrictions are tight enough they can rein you in over any tiny infraction if they so choose. Just do not give them reason to choose to!" I am dubious, but think he is right. I answer, "This is fine, in theory. In practice the authorities can reel me in for any reason whatever, because they do not like me. Because someone has that kind of personality that likes to hurt people. Because I am among the unprotected."

Bean nods. "You mean like the Fairbanks four?"

"Yes, exactly!" This is a case in the news. Four men were convicted of murder. There were four separate trials, and four convictions.

Now, eighteen years later, a big investigation. For many years the state had the confession of someone who says he and another group committed the murder, with details only the killer would know. This comes up after the trial of the four who are considered guilty.

One of the convicted says in court, "The interrogating cop turned off the microphone and told me, "If you do not tell me what I want to hear I will make sure you fry!'"

People among the unprotected, hear the news, spread the word, that the police can treat you however they want. Make you disappear, plant evidence, beat you up, kill you, rape you. Nothing you can do about it.

"Do whatever the police say, and hope you get out alive." This is the belief among street people. Being someone who believes this, I am not excited that the laws are not workable and can be applied whenever, to any of us, but mostly to the 'person of interest' list. How can one get on that list? The ways are numerous. Being a democrat, registered gun owner, member of the Trappers Association, meat eater, per owner, supporter of zoos. Any way of thinking; out of favor with the present administration.

I figure out probation is not about finding out what I can get away with or do. It is about accepting my responsibility and punishment. It's not about asking what I can do; what my rights are. It's understanding what I can't do. This is hard because this is not what I have been taught when studying our criminal system. For the protected, 'probation' is a time after punishment. Paying a fine and jail time is the punishment in which I contemplate the evil deeds I was arrested for. When this ends, 'probation' is about getting readjusted, integrated back into society, sort of a recovery time. A transitional period while you look for work and try to stay out of trouble. Part of the reason for this time is to ensure criminals stay on the straight and narrow and do not fall into previous bad habits. Probation is about help with the assistance of someone who will teach you how to be honest. Help get your life back together. I can appreciate the wisdom of this. Probation should not be continued punishment.

Bean wonders why I chose my lifestyle and occupation, deliberately among the unprotected. He knows I am white and born in the privileged class. "Why didn't you stay in that privileged and protected class?"

"Several reasons, Bean!" I chuckle. "Partly I didn't know what I was getting into. There was no advice on career or future, going over pros and cons of choices." I explain how, when I was a child, mountain men were heroes. I have explained this a zillion times, like a broken record I say it again. I assumed I was among the protected, as they made our country! Are part of history! They killed off the savages and made room for progress!

"Remember the Alamo!" I smile at my deliberate sarcasm. Some well known mountain men died at the Alamo. Some survivors became Texas Rangers— the only law around. Their job was, among other things, to practice genocide on the Indians, to open the land for white homesteaders and trappers. The land was owned by Mexico and Indians at the time. These Rangers were 'outlaws' according to the Mexican government in charge. Sam Houston, who Huston, Texas is named after, was one of them. He had spent time in a Mexican prison. It was the equivalent in modern times of hiring the mafia in a lawless land. Law was whatever the rangers said it was. Ordinary street thugs were afraid of 'organized crime'. It depends on who is in charge at the time and how history records events. Once tame, the past never happened, is forgotten, becomes unmentionable. "No one told me that, Bean."

Bean gets it and nods.

I give another answer to a complicated question. "Another reason, I needed attention. Choosing something different worked. It was the 60s when it was common for teens to be rebellious. Going against the establishment was normal thinking. "Tune in and drop out" are bywords. Going to live in a commune was hip. Robert Redford in, 'Jeremiah Johnson,' reached a lot of people. Being in the wilds on Dad's summer vacations was among the few times I saw my father relax and smile. Our quality time together made an impression. I was good at wildlife skills, so considered this doable. There was stress living up to my father's level of education, with us having the same name. I did not want to be a chip off the old block; life handed to me on a silver platter. I wanted to earn respect, not demand it. Being in the wild is something a young unskilled person could do without an education! I could do this as a loner, in control, with no boss, no one holding me back. I needed no one's consent, permission, or help. The thrill of owning your own land by homesteading is a big attraction! I believed civilization was flawed. I believed living out in nature was more healthy.

"I was part of a budding green movement without knowing it, before the various protection organizations got big." I shrug my shoulder and assume I have said enough. That was then. This is now.

"So, Miles, why the animal parts business? Not all mountain men or wilderness people get into that."

"Again, several reasons." Where to begin. "Most of my mountain men heroes were trappers." There are not a lot of ways to work and buy supplies in the wilds. Trapping was a usual choice. Also, when it came to attention, people wanted, expected bear stories. If I am selling my art or anything else, I must first grab your attention. Bear stories do that. The public determined that, not me. I tried to tell other stories. People wanted bears, danger, thrills. I gave it to them.

Also, not wanting to be wasteful, I looked for things to do with discarded animal parts that trappers and hunters normally throw away. As an artist, it seemed natural to use animal parts in my art. I did not have access to normal art supplies like gem stones. This is what was asked for, and is popular at shows I did. I admired Indians, and their art includes a lot of animal parts. As a trader, wheeler and dealer, I often got paid by remote people I met, and did business with them in animal scraps I thought I might use for art, that my peers put little value on. It did not bother me being the garbage man, making a living from my peers garbage.

"The ultimate in recycling." I explain how I'd get asked for specific things, and tried to acquire what was wanted. Stayed away from trophies, but teeth, claws, skulls, were asked for. I got enterprising, and discovered the untapped internet as an outlet.

"The rest is history," I say with a grin.

An analogy comes to mind. I sometimes have to put things in perspective when I see puzzled looks on the faces of those I am trying to explain something to.

"Bean, it would be like you having connections to wilderness people." They ask you for broken glass, copper wire, plastic jugs. They have no source and will pay dearly. "Five dollars for a piece of broken glass to make an arrowhead." Wouldn't you begin collecting broken glass from your civilized friends almost for free and selling it to your wilderness connections?" I add, "These wilderness people have no way to make glass or plastic, so value these hard to get items that you and your culture call garbage." It is difficult to understand, that to the wilderness people, duck feathers is what you spit out when eating dinner. Bear claws, moose antler has a very minor value, because after you have one to wear, what are you going to do with the other nine? Dogs drag bones through the street, that I find a market for.[2]

There was more to it than that. I decide to add, "Well, being forced out of a lifestyle had a big effect on how to make a living. Beginning with not being allowed to fish for sled dogs, and having to use a snow machine. That put me out of the trapping business." I explain how art got harder to sell as pipeline money disappeared. I had to be around town more to sell my art. I still had all my wilderness connections in the villages and among trappers, due to my nomadic subsistence life on the houseboat. Those needing to sell and make extra money from trapping surplus, like carcasses, learned to come to me. That never stopped, especially as times got tougher for these people. I had trouble saying no. It is a business I understand, have a lot of knowledge about. It took years to get a reputation for knowing this business. It was a niche market at the Tucson show and even at the Tanana Fair; certainly the internet. Few vendors specialized in animal parts. Few who had access to animal parts in the wilds, had computers, or understood the internet for a decade or more. I understood this is something that can't be copied in China. There are not many people with skills and connections in 'both worlds'. Tarzan with internet skills. My civilized upbringing with a father who had a degree in marketing and psychology. I grew up with some of the top professors and scientists in the world at my dinner table. People whose names I recognize in science magazines.

How am I going to compete in Tucson, the biggest show in the world? I understood what Genghis did when he conquered the world. Goods at the source can be cheap and common. Move them too far away and they have a high value. I am at the source for a lot of animal byproducts. I know how to offer them around the world.

On the internet, I am the one people came up with when searching for teeth, claws, bones, skulls. I say, "I did recognize some changes over time. More irritability from the public over animal parts!" But I always dwell on the positive, tend to forget the negative. People to me seem mad in general about everything. They fight over a place to park, so seem impossible to please! Feel sorry for such unhappy angry people! I try to put this in a perspective civilized Bean might understand better. "Suppose you had this business built up over many years, selling broken glass and scrap plastic to people of another culture you have built connections with." Over time, those who said they wanted broken glass, rusty parts and empty soda cans now tell you it is unethical, wrong, even illegal in many cases to offer this garbage to your customers. For reasons you do not understand, because you are from another culture. You are told, "You must allow these items to go to the dump; you may not repurpose them to make a living. If you do, you will become a felon." This seems very odd and contrary to the bigger directive of, "We are running out of resources and have to learn to be frugal!"

"I was not paying enough attention, or recognizing the signs. What were my choices? Like most of us, I balked at having to change." Bean only nods. "What happened, Bean, is not the end of the world. I have few regrets. I lived a lot of years doing what I want, how I want, staying out of trouble. It could be worse. It would have been devastating to have this happen at twenty years old!

"Except you would have been young enough to go for a new occupation!"

"True!"

I have some other concerns about my probation, and even the original arrest. That there could be more to come! Tusk expresses this when I contact him. I am reluctant to keep in touch with my old suppliers and animal parts friends. Tusk was just a fossil guy, but is a suspect in setting me up and providing evidence. He says, "How come there was no problem over the mammoth ivory, Miles?" He suspects I get the ivory at the boneyard, a federal preserve where it is illegal to remove fossils or anything else because it is public lands.

"I'm not sure myself, Tusk." We both know the Feds have told us there is no such thing as legal ivory of any kind, including fossil mammoth. We have been told, "Because the sale of mammoth ivory promotes the sale of elephant ivory." And, "It is hard to tell the difference, so elephant ivory can be disguised as mammoth ivory!" Neither Tusk or I believe either of these statements is true. If anything, the sale of mammoth is an acceptable alternative to illegal elephant ivory and takes the pressure off elephant ivory sales. That is the opinion of those in business among both buyers and sellers. We have never heard of a single instance where elephant ivory was disguised as mammoth. People spending that kind of money know the difference. It is not hard to tell, the hash pattern is different enough to easily see with the naked eye by even an amateur. Elephant ivory is worth twice what mammoth is. It is hard to imagine anyone disguising a valuable material for one less valuable, with a lot of work to make it happen, and an easy way to tell the difference. Mammoth ivory is rarely white, so will not be a substitute for elephant. Environmental impact of harvesting mammoth tusks is minimal because it is 90% byproduct of the gold mining industry. Some, like what I find, are falling out of cliffs and disappearing in the river.

However, Tusk and I know that on line auctions and outlets like E Bay, have banned the sale of mammoth ivory, due to the word put out by the Feds. Or, even their own sense of doing the right responsible thing voluntarily to help save the planet. However, the laws are clear. Selling mammoth ivory is legal.

"So, Tusk, will the Feds follow the law, or will there be an effort to make an example, and illegally charge me?" Or, the only way to legally charge me would be to show I acquired mammoth ivory off of federal land. A big question.

"Tusk, maybe in the initial investigation they could not find enough to have a solid case. Maybe they want to make this a separate case and are still gathering information and waiting." After all, my computer is now compromised. "I'm pretty sure my web site was left to me, and my computer returned because the Feds are using both to get information on my friends, and looking for customers coming to me asking for illegal items. There is evidence the Feds have sent emails from my site that I never wrote." Using my web site, and all it has stood for, as a front for their own operations. I can't prove it. I just believe it, and see evidence. I have had people ask me directly if I sent this email. Emails I did not send. Originating from my email address and web site.

"I had a computer problem and went to my server. The gal I spoke to was puzzled. Told me I am not the administrator of my computer. The administrator has a GCI address. I think she divulged information she was not supposed to tell me. But I get the conversation back on track. "So there is a possibility other charges can follow. This could explain why no fossils were confiscated or part of any charge. They maybe could not go back and charge me again for something that has already been covered."

# CHAPTER SIX

## TUCSON TRIP MOM, SOCIAL SECURITY, COMPUTER TAPPED, MY BOOKS ON AMAZON

"Do you still have all your fossil material, Miles, if it was not confiscated?" Tusk is interested in buying. *Because he is working undercover?*

"My probation officer says I can have it, but not sell it. She considers mammoth ivory an animal product. Fish and Wildlife, who charged me, told me fossils are no problem, and they are not concerned." They may have figured out I get my fossils legally, even though many think I hunt the boneyard. I allow people to think that for reasons I explained before. It is possible, maybe, to analyze pictures digging them up, examine dirt in fossil cracks to determine exactly where it is from. There is no match to the boneyard. I am not sharing this with Tusk. If Tusk knows where I go, he may go, or send his workers there to tap into my source. There is enough money involved to be a motivator. I'm not sure Tusk has done this to me, or anyone I talk to, but our mutual friend Knife has done this to me before.

Knife found out I had a supply of something, did an investigation, found out where, and cut me out. If Tusk and competitors think I am up to no good at an illegal place, they will not want any part of it. It's a tight wire for me to walk. However, if he tells the Feds he is sure I go to the boneyard? I hope the Feds will ask how he knows! What proof could he offer.

"Everyone knows!" Hopefully, such a reply is not going to work in court. However, my original case never went to court. It was all about what the Feds wanted, and made happen. The same could happen over fossils.

"We know this, we want to plea bargain. If you do not bargain with us, do you have hundreds of thousands of dollars to go to court? Because we have unlimited funds." So, Hmm. Waiting for the other shoe to fall.

Tusk put it well. "That case is in the news, Miles, the female guide who got in trouble over a single small tusk from a remote wilderness river way up in the Brooks Range." We both know that is nothing. A tip of an iceberg. This is weekly business for Tusk, who has reason to be concerned, too. Unless he has immunity because he is working for them. So here we are. What do the Feds want? Lifetime 'friends', Tusk and I, not trusting each other, not working together anymore. In the big picture, the business will be brought down if those of us running the network can't trust each other, or our customers. We speculate on how much time we have.

"A decade?"

"Miles, I am phasing out. I will move to moose antler."

"Just as many issues, Tusk. Feds raided what's his name, down by Trapper Creek. Bill Merry. He told me he was asked if any antler sheds came off federal land. Nothing can come off federal land. Not a rock, twig, flower, or antler shed."

"If you sell, it you mean."

"My understanding is it can't be removed, period. It belongs to all of us, so no one can have it." We agree the laws so far have not been enforced. But could be, are beginning to be.

"In the lower states, more, I think. Yeah, I recall there are issues picking up arrowheads, any artifact, antique, treasure, stuff like that. I have heard it from dealers at the Tucson show. I had a customer who told me he could not cut a twig off a tree and asked me to sell him one."

"I notice, Miles, more and more land is coming under federal control."

The main thing is, things are changing. I never answer if I have any fossil material, how much, or where it might be. *We are living in the end times of distrust.* I'm not upset. Mankind has not been very nice to the planet.

"One third of the land is occupied by man. One third by forest, which is shrinking, and one third by desert, which is expanding." Quoting Horace Mann, pioneer in land management. As we feel the squeeze, we react as any living thing does when pressured.

Tusk agrees, only views this from God's point of view. He begins quoting the Bible. Speaks of those who will be saved. "Have you accepted Jesus Christ into your life, Miles?"

"God and I get along." Which does not answer the question directly. For sure I am not interested in a spiritual debate with a man who probably helped set me up. In his place, I would not have done that. I understand the viewpoint of the intent of the law. Protecting nature and resources. I understand the laws will be different in big cities where there may only be one tree per million people. So, sure, if everyone got it in their head to take even one leaf, the trees would die. However, in Alaska there are a million trees for each person. Taking care of nature will look different.

"Tusk, if I ever come to visit, and begin the conversation with a cough, and tell you the dust is bothering me, know that I arrive wired, and forced by the Feds to help bring you down." Tusk only nods, out of concern we are being recorded. I notice he does not offer me the same courtesy, a way to warn me if he is forced to work with Fish and Wildlife. *Maybe because it has already been done?*

An officer did say to me before my plea bargain, "You do not want to hear it now. But down the road we will ask you to help us. I'm just letting you know so you can think about it."

I had looked puzzled and replied. "I'd love to help bring down criminals like Jessie, but I do not know any criminals. I do not see myself as one, and do not knowingly associate with criminals. All my friends and associates are honest people."

Jessie was the true criminal that got me on the radar. The one under investigation when he contacted me. The one trading guns and drugs for fresh ivory. At first, I thought the government assumed we were partners working together. That this is the problem! But no. I heard some of the evidence on tape. There is a phone conversation between Jessie and an undercover agent where Jessie clearly says, "Miles? I can't work with him, he doesn't understand the money that can be made. He doesn't want to do what I want, so I found someone else!" Called me names. Clearly not on working terms. This would be obvious to anyone listening. This recorded conversation is early in the game, even before Jessie had done anything illegal. He did, in fact, found someone else to take my place, who would do his bidding.

I thought it would be hard to prove, that he and I were not working together. Because at first he conned me into believing his dealings were legal and above board, so I was interested for a while. Long enough to be recorded discussing business.[1] The Feds and public defender convinced me I could not prove my innocence. When they had the proof of my innocence themselves. *Much like we hear how the Fairbanks four were handled. Take the deal or know our wrath!* Oh well, I can't complain overly much. I mean, my punishment was minimal compared to Jessie! He got twenty years. But again, I am not sure the Feds are done with me. Others are obviously not sure either. I'm a marked man. Many former customers, suppliers, friends do not know me anymore. Out of politeness, I do not ask anything of them, or put them on the spot. I understand. My emails are being read, my phone is probably tapped. I doubt I am being followed, but if I carry a cell phone everywhere I go, and for how long, am I being recorded. Even when the phone is off. I leave the phone with Iris while visiting Tusk.

"Do you trust Knife, Miles?" I never did know Knife well. He is a local knife maker. Many who deal with him say he is odd, hard to figure. I used to sell knife materials to him. Once, a sliced meteorite. He was a buyer of musk ox horn and fossil ivory. There is not much I got from him. He does not like to trade. Knife makes his own Damascus steel, so I had hoped to be able to trade for some local steel. "Yeah, Miles, he wants $500 for a blank piece of steel you have to work into a knife."

"Yes, I know."

"Well, I hear he gets over $1,000 for his knives!"

"I heard that, too." I did not answer if I trust him or not. I had an odd dealing with him just before I went to jail.

I knew there was going to be a confiscation of any animal product I had. I knew ahead of time this was likely going to be part of any plea deal. My friend, Foil, was around at the time, helping Iris cut firewood to burn while I was to be gone. Foil says, "What are you going to do with all that moose antler, Miles, it's quite a pile!" Perfectly legal for anyone else to have, but not me due to the upcoming plea bargain. The deal does not go into effect for a while. Foil tells me he thinks Knife would buy it.

"I can't sell it, Foil. But it can disappear, get stolen, not much I could do about that." Foil nods. He borrows our car. The main part of the antler pile disappears. I can have no knowledge. I can 'guess' without any proof.

Foil comes back. "Boy! That Knife guy for sure is not your friend, Miles!" Foil showed him the pile of antler and asked $5 a pound, indicating that it was his. That's a low price. Eight dollars is the going wholesale rate. Knife had counter offered $3 a pound. It should not have been any of my concern! But Foil is asking me an opinion on value, and should he do the deal?

I said, "No way in hell! Scr&%w him. For $3 a pound, leave it at the dump transfer station and let people help themselves for free!" That is the more legal thing for me to do anyhow. Take it to the dump. No problem there. Apparently Knife knew it was originally my material. He recognized the car. So what. Nothing going here between Foil and Knife would be illegal. He does not have to recognize the car unless he feels compelled to. My name never came up. If the situation were reversed and it was Knife in a bind? I would say if asked, "Car? Why would I leave my shop to go out in the street to look at the car a customer drives up in? All I know is someone I do not know comes in with boxes of anther and I buy it as a legal material I can resell." I'd have been happy to pay $5 a pound, knowing I can get $15 a pound. I'd buy it all. I made deals like that all the time. Spend $1,000 or more. Re-sell it to people like Tusk, Crafty, or Knife for the going rate of $8 a pound. Make a quick $500 for an hour's work. Knife knows the business, knows the drill. We all know each other. If I suspected it was Knifes' antler he needed to unload for quick cash? No problem. Good luck, glad to help him out. I consider us all 'family', 'in the business', looking out for each other, covering each other's back as a tribe, a subculture.

Anyhow, if the Feds confiscated it, they would auction it off locally. My competitors would pick it up for ten cents on the dollar. Why let that be in my craw? Maybe laughing at me, "Hey, Miles, got your materials for next to nothing! Thanks!" No, it went to the dump. We actually saw some natives eyeball it, wonder why any idiot would throw this away! Loaded it up and I was glad. A financial loss, but I had acquired most of it from natives who roam the woods and rivers gathering moose antler sheds. Even children earn extra money on the homestead looking for antlers and making a pile for when they come to town and see me.

"What you thinking about, Miles, you look deep in thought!"

"Yeah, Tusk, just thinking about our buddy, Knife." Foil later made other items disappear, stored in an undisclosed location. Technically 'his.' All my guns, fossils, what not. Iris could have much of it legally, but not on the property. Easiest to keep it out of the family. One dealer friend made some fossils disappear at a time they were still mine. I got ten grand at the going price. Enough to cover most money emergencies I might have. Not nearly the hundred grand I might have used for a real lawyer. But if I had it, I would not have spent it. That's a rip off price. Not sure an aggressive lawyer getting the Feds angry and digging in their heels would have got me a better deal.

**Tucson Feb 10<sup>th</sup> 2014**

Just two weeks after my probation started, my probation officer will allow me to go visit my mother. Mom is getting old, and it is believed seeing relatives who have clean records is a good thing. I will not be allowed to go to Mexico to get my teeth worked on, even though I have my passport. The eye doctor in Mexico wants to see me as well. I am not getting good service from the VA, and prefer to pay my own way in Mexico, rather than get on a low income help program.

Iris has to see the dentist about new dentures and the eye doctor. I may as well join her? I lost at least one tooth I did not have to lose in prison. There is money to remove teeth, not to clean or do fillings. Or, at least as a short termer. Mrs. Probation had assured me I would be well taken care of in prison. "All fixed up!" *I got fixed all right.*

**Diary ends** – but thoughts are stimulated by the entry.

I am glad to be allowed to go see my mother. That privilege is treated like the greatest thing since sliced bread, 'mother and son' how sweet. *My probation officer is a mother.* It is good to love my mother. However, she was not a good mother. We were never close. She never wanted to be a mother. I understand, and forgive. But that is not the same as love. Happiness and good health is not in the direction of loving or depending on someone who neglected you. We got closer later in life, after I got stronger. We get along. I like her. That's not the same as the highest priority in my life. *"Yes! Go! Be with the mother that neglected you as a child!"* Great. Big help. " *Oh no! You can't travel because you need medical help! Oh no, you can't go to earn any money to pay your bills!"* What message does that give?

---

It is good to see the sunshine. I smile. It is nice to be with Iris, my partner. I help mom by painting the trim on the house. I decide to paint the bench she likes to sit on. I paint flowers all over it. She loves it! Mom does not go for walks anymore. It is harder to get her to go out anyplace at all. Going shopping with her is an exact routine. We have to take the correct turns, go to the right stores in the correct order. We stand in line to buy one tomato. Go to another store to get a can of juice.

"I like this brand! It's the only store that has it!" Smile, nod. Stand in line. It's ok. Just ok. It is being with my mother. No. We need to go back to the store. We forgot something. She is too tired. Iris and I need to go back. All day, and all we got done was acquire a bag of groceries. Hardly any room to put dry goods in mom's shed. The shed is full of empty boxes she collects. She might need them one day to pack something.

Our visit interrupts her routine. She and her younger boyfriend, Ted, do certain things at certain times. It's harder as she gets older to work out another routine. She laughs, "Just getting up makes me tired!" And, "I'm old, I can get one thing done in a day. That's it!" She still cooks with Crisco. It's hard to eat her cooking as a diabetic. She is diabetic now, but refuses to change what she eats, or how she cooks. "I'm not giving up the little pleasures in life! What's the use of life if you can't enjoy it!"

I tell Iris later, "That outlook might work when you are in your 80s, but not in my 60s. I'd rather adapt and learn new pleasures than die." Worse than dying as a diabetic, is living as one, going blind. First a toe gets cut off, then a foot, then whacked off at the knee, then the other leg; it's not pretty. Mom's feet are purple and hurt. The last thing she wants is a lecture. I believe strongly in freedom. The right for us to live our lives as we see fit. Love is accepting that. I eat her cooking. Luckily mom thinks half a cup of food is a filling meal. *At 85 it is!* I'm still active. I can eat half a cup of about anything and be ok. Iris and I go out to eat many of our meals. Mom doesn't have to know. We bring her meals from fast food places she likes, but again, not the sort of meal I can eat.

She wants us gone a lot. She needs her naps.

"At least she is not cranky. You should see my mom, Miles! Always complaining! I like your mom; always sees the bright side to life." Mom is putting together some 'Momma says' stories, as she calls them. Little short stories she remembers from growing up. Well done. Most are funny, or have a moral. Ted is helping her put them in a computer. One day the collection might get printed.

"Maybe I can put one in my book, mom!" This encourages her to write. I'd like to see her have a reason to want to live. She talks as if life is over now, just waiting to die. Mom shows me what she has written and encouraged Ted to get it in the computer.

Mom likes us to go over the family picture albums together. Reminding me over and over who is who in the picture, with a story about each major chapter in the album. This reminds me of the Alaska Native custom. Elders sit around the fire telling long ago stories in the cold winter to the rest of the family, especially the young. So they remember. I will be the only one who knows, so she wants me to have the albums and know who is who and pass on the stories.

"This is the house my grandfather built. He met a woman and wanted to marry her, but she would not live with him without her sister being with them! So he agreed. The house was built with a second story so the sister could live upstairs. After forty years the one he marries dies. Grandpa then married the other one!" This is an interesting arrangement, not how it is with most families. I study the pictures, the expressions, try to figure how life was for them.

Mom fills me in with stories of my childhood. "Here is the picture of the plane my mother took from Maine to Hawaii to see you when you were born!" It is a three deck prop plane - the first transcontinental plane. It tried to duplicate an ocean cruise luxury ship. It had a band playing, and a dining room. My grandmother was a caretaker for a rich family, the Bakers, in Maine. She had her own house on the grounds. She cooked, cleaned, did the gardening. They owned a yacht. Grandma accompanied them on cruises. Here is a picture of this huge ship.

"They were Christian Scientists and did not believe in doctors. Mr. Baker got sick and died of appendicitis. He would have lived if they saw a doctor!" Mom spent her youth in a convent because the Bakers did not want children around. Mom and her two sisters were split up. The nuns beat her. She doesn't talk about it much. It was the depression; work was hard to get. Grandma was a single parent. Her husband could not handle being laid off. Began drinking and became useless. "Dad was drinking all the time. He had to baby sit us kids as mom worked. Women could get domestic work, so had more job opportunities than men." Mom goes on, "My mother came home one day and her husband was drinking with his friends. They were straining wood alcohol through bread to take the poison out and drinking it. He did not know where the children were. So she kicked him out." These were days it was not common for a women to leave their men.

Mom has some fond memories of earlier times out picking blueberries and selling them in the neighborhood. They always had food, clothes, a roof over their head. I study the old-time looking pictures of relatives. Pictures taken in the days when pictures were brown. It is difficult as a senior, seeing these for the first time, to remember. It's not like I have anyone to pass these pictures along to. Mitch might be interested. But I do not expect to ever see him again. I might write on the back of each identifying those in the photo, and let him study them after I am gone; when he is old, and ponders the ways of the world. *Or perhaps his son, if he has one, will inquire.*

We appear to live in an age where families are not close. Tradition is out the window. Our elders are not part of society in a meaningful way as was so even fifty years ago. In Nenana, there is a home for the old. The elders like it quiet, and do not encourage visitors. Many die, and there is no one who wants the belongings. No relatives. Their worldly goods end up in boxes on a table in the senior center. We all sort out the clothes and take home what we can use. *Clothes from the 40s that are coming back in style again!* Take the rest to the dump. So much for the dead. I do not feel bad about this. What goes around, comes around.

There had been a time my father's wife got a message to me. Dad is missing in his sailboat, feared dead, and I should come home. I said, 'no thanks'. If he is missing at sea, how is my being there going to change anything? I'm not interested in the dead. I say it now. If anyone cares, show me while I am alive. I do not care what you do when I am dead. Toss me in a dumpster. Ideally, I'd like to never be found. Die at home, in the wilds someplace. Or, "Put me in my boat, light it on fire, and send it down the river."

Mom smiles, "Like the Vikings?" Yeah, like that. *Or my father, missing at sea.* Mom is much more conventional than I am. Does not seem to know how to deal with my odd notions. It's a struggle. I can see why she and my father had issues.

One of the first memories my mother relates about marriage was how she envisioned her and Dad spending forever in Bathe, Maine. Both working in the mill. "What's wrong with that!" Yes. Normal, what everyone in the area does. What an odd notion to want to go out and discover some other world outside! "It's not the road to peace and happiness Miles!"

I can see the value of being content with your lot in life.

"I want you to have the trailer, Miles. Any money can go to Betsy." *She is the one who came to visit me in prison.* Mom wants to talk over ending times. I am to be the executor of her will. She shows me where all her important stuff is. We had reviewed some of this in the past. She had been concerned what would happen to all she loves; furniture she treasures, her empty box collection and knick knacks. Mom has lived poor and happy all her life. Without sentimental value, all she has is almost worthless to anyone else. There has been tentative talk of Iris and I becoming snow birds. Come here for part of the winter and live in mom's trailer. Do some local art shows and such. We are making friends here. A certain reality presents itself.

Mom lives in a trailer from the 1970s. It might be worth 15 grand, furnished. She does not own the land. This is a trailer park which charges $600 a month rent on the land. There are strict rules - no pets, no kids, no one under 55, no subletting, no long term guests. Literally hundreds of rules, the breaching of which could get you kicked out. If kicked out, difficult to move the trailer. At $600 a month, it does not take long to pay more than the trailer is worth in land rent. It's more than we can afford, and is simply not a good bargain. If selling, the park gets first option to buy. There are not a lot of new arrivals. We think the owners want the park to be empty soon, so they can sell it to developers. It is obvious to me, mom's possessions are her highest priority.

My sister broke a ceramic parrot fifty years ago. Mom still brings it up, and has neither forgotten or forgiven. It's obvious, listening to mom, that parrot was worth more than her daughter. She does not want me having certain things because she feels I will not take proper care of them. A quilt my grandmother made, a grandfather clock my grandmother wanted me to have that I never saw. Now I know why. My view is totally different. When I am dead if you treasure anything and want it, I am glad. Help yourself. It's only stuff. I do a certain amount to protect what I have, but it is not the end of the world if it gets stolen, or goes missing. Loss by flood, fire, accidents from relatives or friends is not worth getting terribly upset over.

Iris and I do not review all of this with mom. Not at first. It is she who figures it out. She seems to accept that when she is gone, so is everything else in her life. Iris and I had hoped we could keep the trailer and mom's things, live here, and have this as memories. Or, have mom believe that until she dies.

"Mom, what you can leave me is not the issue. I do not expect anything. You enjoy your stuff! It is enough you can take care of yourself!" I'm not owed anything! She has her Social Security and some retirement from a past husband. Not a lot, but she has a routine. She knows what it cost, and is happy financially. Not hurting.

We review a lot of this kind of stuff on our visit. We drive the rented car to the Mexican border where I have to wait. Iris has a cab driver she likes, 'Lorenzo,' she can ask for just across the border. She will have her eyes examined. I can drive us back. I have a license, I just do not feel comfortable driving since I do not have experience. I have to wait at McDonalds on the US side. I have my laptop computer to work on my writing while I wait. I go for a walk, find a small museum, and a pawn shop I like. Iris comes back with a patch over one eye. Lorenzo looked out for her.

"Yes, Miles, I got the vanilla extract!" I only smile. Mexico has great vanilla compared to the US.

I drive us back, but do not do a good job. "Miles, you have the high beams on!" I cannot take my eyes off the highway to study where the high beam button is. It's not a huge big deal, it's not dark out yet. At worse I can pull over, stop, study the buttons, and solve the problem. It's not a good idea in my view, to take my eyes off this six lane seventy mile an hour traffic I am not used to. Iris is screaming at me in panic fear, we are all going to die mode. Grab the steering wheel and jerk it mode.

We get home, but she does not want to ever get in the car with me in the driver's seat again. Never. She is absolutely not the person to be in an adventure with. She'd be like my friend, Skip, whose relatives flew him into the ground after grabbing the plane's steering wheel from him. He survived running guns while under machine gun fire, but did not survive his relatives. But we got this major part of the trip done. We used to enjoy going across the border to have a Mexican meal and walk around. There are few things we do that are just fun. It is hard to lose this. Holding hands and walking Mexican streets was very bonding.

We go to the big fossil show. I am not allowed to set up to sell. I say 'hi' to all I know; buy some rocks. It is nice to know I am missed. No one here feels I am a criminal. There are similar stories to mine. The dealer from England is not here. His room empty for the show, because customs found a dead bug in one of his boxes of goods. Held up now a month. Half a million dollars he is not going to make.

"Why not just fumigate, if the issue is to worry about some bugs? Problem solved in an hour!" Few believe the issue is the concern over damaging bugs. The goal, we all feel, is to put him out of business. Another friend has his import permit expire while a shipment was late arriving, and his new permit not in effect yet. His entire shipment of legal mounted 'farm raised' butterflies was burned. He thinks the shipment was deliberately held up until the permit expired.

That's just this year! A common thread weaving through all our lives. I never knew about all this! It's negative stuff I refused to focus on. I assumed there must have been a good reason for our government to deal harshly with those who are up to no good! Until it was me! I miss the show. But in other ways, "Ok not to be here." It's a lot of hard work as I get older. Like the year the wind blew the tent flaps into my shelving and knocked all the gem stones to the gravel. Damaged fossils to the tune of several thousand dollars I had to absorb. While it is fun and exciting, I can dwell on that while I am doing it. When I stop, I can dwell on what a heartache and headache it can be! *The fox and the grapes.*

I had been at a point I was not sure if I need to get a room instead of the tent space! Up my fees by three times, make three times the profit.

"Yet, I was happier when I had a suitcase I set up on a card table by the swimming pool in a relaxed setting for a $100 fee and $1,000 total profit! I could pack my bag and take off all day to shop, visit, and enjoy." As the money increased, so did the stress and work load. Exciting all right! But could not get away to buy, or go visiting. What was it I needed all the money for? I have no pressing bills. "So, no, it is not the end of the world, no more big shows." I had my time in the sun.

There is a knife show I investigated on line. I try my hand at this two day show. I sell some knives, some raw wood. Enough to make it worth my while. Small table, good bunch of vendors; relaxed, fun. Much like the Fossil show used to be. Interestingly, I am smart, good at what I do. It is not beyond my ability to do very well, and often do. I build a business, get innovative, and make good money. Given time if I chose, I could be a dealer to be reckoned with. A mover and a shaker at the top. I simply feel this is not what makes me happy.

"Miles, that show at the mall I told you about is a farmers market, every Wednesday. Rich neighborhood, I think worth checking into!" Yes, we had looked at it one time before, but I got no information.

Foil was supposed to set something up for me as part of our deal helping each other out. I help him in Alaska, and he helps me in Tucson. He just wrote, "Here's the phone number," and that is all the help he offers. I could have done that. I expected him to line up a table, or provide a table, store goods for me, have it all set up, as I had helped him in Alaska a lot! Whatever, not a huge big deal.

Iris and I go down with a few goods. I walk around meeting vendors, asking questions. Getting a feel for the show. I sell some wood knife scales to a knife maker. I see booths set up selling things similar to what I see at the Tanana Fair, and know I could fit right in here. Yes, I see rich customers. The area is crowded with business going on. I know I could communicate with this type of crowd. Many are baby boomers like myself. My Alaska stories would go over well. Tables to set up are not costly. Iris is not as thrilled as I am, she is the driver. We think of showing up one day here during our trip, if it works out. But more like something to think about for the future, like if we spend much of our winters in the area. I'm not sure, being on probation, how this would go over. Mrs. Probation is happier to see me poor, getting on welfare and the like.

A town named Tubac is nearby. An entire art colony for tourists. Nothing but art shops. I sell a few items, but find out shop space is very high end! Still, a possibility if I want to go high end. Or, meet someone to share a building with, or come here for special events. This is a year round, full time deal if interested. It might be nice to be around other artists to bounce ideas off of. I have never lived around other artists.

Mostly just 'potential', dreams, options, choices. A sense of being in the game, holding some cards of life to put down on the table. I'm not between a rock and a hard place. If I had to have some money, here is how I could make it happen. More than one shop is interested in carrying my work on consignment. Two shop owners have heard of me. There is an Alaskan knife maker I heard of around here who might still be around. I did not meet up with him, but vendors tell me he is around. Maybe the potential to share a shop, or get some ideas, if this option is chosen.

"Iris, we still do not know where we might stay!" We know mom is ok with short visits, but needs her space, and would not want us moving in! We can't anyhow, it is not allowed. I add, "Foil promised us a place to stay, his old car, and place to store stuff. Now his trailer is needed by the daughter and new husband! The old car is a necessary second transportation he can't part with!"

"Yes, while you got him a place in Nenana that saved him about $30,000, helped him with his homestead dream, hauled supplies; we took him to town, fed him…" She trails off. I know all that.

"He promised me some work as well, with his landscape business. Saying he could get me to fill in now and then for good money. Talked about money under the table, big cash." Now he says, "So buy a lawn mower and mow some yards." I pause. "Heck of an answer. I'm not sure I could simply buy a mower and open a business without a business license or insurance. Likewise, there is not much money in that - the Mexicans have that kind of work all sewed up at low prices." Foil told me he has a well established high end business, working for the rich who know him by word of mouth. Sometimes he needs help for a day or two, or more.

"Thousands of dollars a day, Miles!" Like it would not be hard to throw a grand my direction for a day's help. "If you help me out in Alaska, Miles! We can look out for each other!" My good buddy, Foil.

Well, we do not have time to get involved in much work right now, this trip. I am on probation and need to be careful.

"Yes, Miles, you can't make over $300 without explaining yourself." No under the table money or big show money. I am not allowed to do shows. I hinted I might do a knife event, a bazaar, or Saturday Market. I got no reply, understanding I might be allowed, but even this is frowned on. If anything could be construed as a show, who knows what might get said? If I came home with ten grand or more? How would I explain myself?

"Oh, this and that, you know," would not work. I could, and I have, made twenty grand during this time period here. $300 is pathetically, 'nothing'. I do not mean to be rude, but I think I have made $300 an hour before. No one believes me, so therefore it didn't happen. *But if it never happened where did I get the photo of me counting sixty grand at one of my shows?* There will be other years.

Near the knife event, there is a Saturday flea market. Nothing like what we see in Alaska. Huge by our standards! In a day you could not visit every vendor. We check it out. I had been here once before with mom years ago, when we brought our cab driver, thanking him for being so nice to me. The event has grown. Mostly Mexicans selling items from across the border. We buy a whole bag of bell peppers for one dollar. Everything is a dollar a bag at this booth. Lots of used stuff, like clothes. A few jewelry vendors. I could see selling knives, my wood, or my low end art, jade, Alaska crystals, and such. An outlet for my more low end items. I am used to that. Know the market and how to sell to it. One huge market for me has always been the other vendors! I could see supplying some of these people with Alaskan items wholesale. I could sell small Alaska crystals for fifty cents if you buy 100, and make money. Eventually scrap mammoth ivory for a dollar a scrap if you buy 100.

There is a guy who wire wraps stones while you wait. I could see trading him some wire wrap work for my raw material. I see the leather belt guy. He is already interested in my custom cast buckles wholesale. One jeweler is interested in my custom necklace claps. I could picture sitting here on Saturdays in the sun, under a palm tree, semi retired. No huge amount of work. I could see an easy $500 a day coming out of here. *Beats working for a living!* Life, and work is not over because I am a felon. I still have about a zillion connections. Connections I do not even recall until I see the vendor. We are at Electric Park, part of the mineral, fossil show. I recognize my fossil dinosaur bone supplier. He trades for jade, and knives at wholesale prices. The opal guy, the Brazilian phantom crystal guy. It's all about 'deals'. I like to think I have a good eye for material I can either resell as is, or add art work and sell.

"Iris, it is an advantage that I hand select all the materials I offer on the web site. I never order by mail, sight unseen. My customers know I hand pick! This means something to them. Likewise, I am selling raw materials I use in my own art, so know something about!"

Our month in Tucson comes to an end. We buy mom a pile of food and store it in her shed so she is ahead on basics if she can't get to the store. She says, "Your friend, Foil, comes by now and then, and brings me gifts and takes me to the store. Such a nice man!"

Iris and I look at each other and say nothing. We did not ask him to check up on her. Mom has her boyfriend, Ted, who takes care of her. But yes, very kind of Foil.

It is time to leave Tucson.

"By next year I should be allowed to go to Mexico to have my teeth and eyes worked on, and we can go together!" I explain to Iris. "The probation officer told me it is normal to let felons off probation early if they are doing well. She sees no reason I will not be off probation by this time next year!" I assume in the same way most inmates get time off their prison sentence for good behavior. It is rare anyone does their full time. Mrs. Probation had said, 'Something to look forward to! You will make more money once you can travel and go to shows!' Iris and I hold hands, while looking forward to once again sharing the Mexico experience.

"MILES, government help got cut back again" 2

"Not surprised. What control do we have on the matter? None. This is one reason I have said it is better not to depend on the government." Often a program looks good when it is begun. Lots of benefits, little investment. Mostly good to see in it. Words beginning,' We are going to help you by...' followed by dependence.

"All the more reason to grow the garden, take care of our own food." We have this kind of discussion often. One view being, "Food stamps are forever and will never end. The government can't just leave us all in the lurch. We are owed. We paid in!" The opposing view being,' Nothing wrong with growing it yourself, knowing where it comes from, being at the source.' The return reply is', But that's a lot of work!'

*Freedom is not free.* We live with a blend. Does the garden really save any money? We try to do the math, keep records and notes, crunch the numbers. "Probably not." My argument can't be won on economics. Everything else is about feelings.

Tax time again. What does food cost us? *Did we have fun? Or was it work?* It's harder to write the garden off when I am not composting animal parts to sell the bones. However, we are planning to sell more transplants, ornamentals, and veggies at the upcoming farmers market being discussed by the WIN group, Wellness in Nenana.

"And pickles and preserves of all kinds." Iris is good with recipes after I grow it. We were surprised when we sold quarts of pickles. It was children buying and eating the whole jar at the bazaar! So who says kids only want junk food and sweets! The goal is still to cover the garden costs by what gets sold. Break even. Free food. Minus the labor. *Minus the fun!*

"Iris, you think I can write off stuff that was confiscated, as 'stolen'? *I wonder what line that goes on, hmmm.* If I'm out of business, you'd think I could write off all the inventory I lost, and equipment I can no longer use. The government has no sense of humor. Bean, my creative accountant and friend has some ideas. The shell game begins. *I wish!* Reality sets in. There's no place to hide. I'm Sylvester the cat, with the canary feather sticking out of his mouth. Has no idea where Tweedy might have flown off to. Iris would prefer I simply retire, declare no business, operate from now on as 'a hobbyist'; collect and live on our Social Security and various programs, whatever handouts we might qualify for. Like the rest of the sheep.

I'd as soon be in the game as long as I can. Not put out to pasture quite yet. With business, comes some write offs. If I am 'in business', there are ways to save the day. If I have no business and make money, I have nowhere to hide. There is no cover story. There is no shell game. There is no discussion if this was a business expense. If I have no business, I let go of any dream of winning the lottery, making the deal of a lifetime that accounts for the feathers in my mouth. I do not need IRS problems. It's better to pay all the fees. Look like a struggling serf. *"I'm trying masta! I really am! I'll do the best I can to scrape together the extortion money, Sir!"* Meanwhile, back at the ranch.

I get an email from one of my long time good shy friends, who I will not mention by name.

### My Twilight Years ~ Clint Eastwood

As I enjoy my twilight years, I am often struck by the inevitability that the party must end. There will be a clear, cold morning when there isn't any 'more'. No more hugs, no more special moments to celebrate together, no more phone calls just to chat.

It seems to me that one of the important things to do before that morning comes, is to let every one of your family and friends know that you care for them by finding simple ways to let them know your heartfelt beliefs and the guiding principles of your life so they can always say, "He was my friend, and I know where he stood." So, just in case I'm gone tomorrow, please know this:

I voted against that incompetent, lying, flip-flopping, insincere, double-talking, radical socialist, terrorist, excusing, bleeding heart, narcissistic, scientific and economic moron currently in the White House! Participating in a gun buy-back program because you think that criminals have too many guns is like having yourself castrated because you think your neighbors have too many kids.

Regards, **Clint Eastwood**

One of my customers writes me:

**Hi Miles**, I'm sure you do not remember me. You had been so kind to allow me to make an order of mammoth bark, and gave me a price break. I am getting close to needing to make an order and thought I would browse your site to see what you had. A bit shocked! So sorry this has happened to you, Miles. Is it really true? No more mammoth? I hope this is not true?

You will always be the mammoth guy in my mind. I have had some health changes in my life these last five years. Had to re think a lot about life, lots of changes, still more to come as things progress. But my wife did say, is there one thing in your life that you are passionate about that you would still love to do? like a bucket list? I have done a lot in my life, much like yourself, cabinetmaker, boat builder, paratrooper, medic, nurse, carver, boat captain, guide, electro toxicologist. I said to her, it would be to come visit you and spend a day in the life of Miles searching for Mammoth. I so hope that one day this is possible...If not I get it, things change, these days, too much change, most bad. Stay you my friend, Wild Man Miles!

**Gordon**

I give a somewhat lengthily reply. Maybe working out my thoughts, coming to terms with where I am at, what to do, etc.

**Hello Gordon,**

Well thanks for words of encouragement. Sorry about your health issues putting you in a position of thinking of the bucket list. I write him a bunch of stuff...

I'm now a felon with fewer, not more rights. **Miles**

I give thought to the words about my fossils not confiscated, and told, "Not a problem." It is possible the agents were actually being nice and doing the least damage they could, considering their orders. In which case it does little good to get all fired up! The agents did not take the cash they found either. If they were crooked and dishonest, wouldn't you think they'd laugh and tell me I'd never see it again and tough luck?

The main interrogator told me, concerning the moose antlers, "Take pictures of this, you might need them to defend yourself." Advice he did not have to give. He had also looked at my shotgun and commented, "And I am sure you have nothing but steel shot in the shells, right?" I nodded yes. We all laughed, knowing no one who gets food for the table uses steel shot! He did not check. He knew I had illegal lead shot. He does not have steel shot in his gun either! The attitude of all the agents was, "What a stupid law!" Nothing was said about all the guns I own. If they had been out to hurt me, you'd think that social button would have been pushed. In the headlines, "Thirty guns found in illegal wildlife search!" I did not get the impression they were out to nail me. Maybe all the Feds needed was some statistics, some numbers. Nothing personal. Even sorry it had to be me included. It's just business. I was not beaten up, threatened, handcuffed, shut up, nor killed.

*Yeah, but they still deliberately mislabeled items they confiscated!* They would not have done that if they were totally honest! Honest would be letting me face any charges I am responsible for, not creating false evidence. What they did was the equivalent of serving a search warrant for drugs, and labeling sugar as heroin in order to make the charges stick. So again, mixed messages. I mean, telling me the problem is I am dishonest and illegal, while themselves being dishonest and illegal. So is it me being dishonest and illegal, that is the real issue? Or is it something else? If it is something else, spell it out. What is the problem? If you can't tell me, how will the problem get fixed? By taking away my rights and ability to do anything at all effectively? I'm not encouraged by this behavior to feel all is above board, for society's or my good.

I get depressed. I sometimes see no hope for a future. Unsure what to do. Options are used up. Too late in life to start all over from scratch and walk away from all I am and stand for. Unwilling to bow down and denounce my lifestyle and all I love. Even to save my life.

### Future Flash

It is not just the government I distrust. I distrust civilization. Part of my rabbit cycle theory of civilization is the feeling we are entering a downslide. An example is an article I read in People magazine while sitting in a dentist's office. A baby is born. The family is waiting for an official qualified physician to arrive. The weather has held him up. The belief being, it is not possible for a child to be born without a doctor present. The nurse orders the pregnant mother to not allow the baby to come out until the doctor arrives. Cross her legs, stop pushing, etc. The baby is 'stuck' and lacks oxygen as a result and is born 'defective', not as bright as a healthy child would be. The child gets older and it is agreed by top doctors in the country to do some cutting edge scientific 'fix the problem' stuff on the teen. A lobotomy. The procedure is described. The teen is in a chair; conscious and asked to talk and answer questions as holes are drilled in either side of her head. Probes root around mashing up parts of the brain as she talks. Soon she goes blank and stops talking.

Problem solved. Now she is no longer functional. She is institutionalized for the rest of her life as a not quite vegetable, but certainly more manageable! Is this some poor person being experimented on? A concentration camp, Jew-Hitler thing? No. This is a member of the Kennedy family. Cutting edge science in modern times, not so very long ago, within my lifetime and memory. Close to home. I think the same thing was done to my sister.

**Future flash ends**

There had been an article about my arrest in the news. Iris knows how to go to the newspaper on line and look at public comments on articles. On my own I would not do that. My arrest did not generate as much comment as my warrant and confiscation initially did. A few had a 'too bad, what a shame, what a waste of my tax dollar' outlook. Others said they knew me, and I got what I deserve. That I have had run ins with the law all along, and it was time I get stopped. A few wrote there should be more rules and regulations to protect the world better from people like me.

One person simply wrote, "bye" and added a smile. There is no way to know who, as everyone can have a secret name not revealing who they are. *We no longer have the right to face our tormentor.* There is a new term I am told for this brave new person, 'Troll'. However, the user name given had a police department symbol, so it looks to me, and I believe it is, a cop, who wanted me to know that. The next day I get an email, unsigned, from an address that looks like this same cop, using the same symbol.

It simply read, "If you need any help choosing door number three, let me know." The message was to let me know that yes, my computer is hacked. Because this 'door number three' reference was deep within the computer, in a password protected personal file. "*Correct, you have zero privacy. I hope you die. Good riddance and you will be doing us all a favor.*" This message actually gave me strength! I need to live. I need to win by living, even being happy! I must endure all there is to endure, and live, unbroken. In this way make the best statement I can. I must meticulously record all that happens. Be it good or bad, this is yet to be seen. With no preconceived outcome of the story. Leave my body and be an outsider, observing myself. In a place where all pain goes away.

Zen. *Like a Zen thing. I stand on one leg, arms out in front in the position of prayer.*

*Stretch out and hold the position, like a sand hill crane. And stare at the sun coming up, in a state of grace. Move slow. As a dance, an opera. Let it not be a soap opera.*

It's deliberate mind games. I know my computer is compromised, everything is. There is no privacy; no safe place. Now I have to face being alone with *these guys*, at least one of who wants me dead. I'm unarmed and helpless, while they are armed, and can do whatever they wish. I am supposed to have trust. They hope I scream and run so I may be shot, like flushing out a pheasant in a cornfield. Some—a few— or all, would find that fun. It is hoped I will crack! They smile, finger twitching on the trigger, waiting for me to say one wrong word, make one fast motion. I believe it happens someplace in the US every day; Rodney King incidents. Winning and survival is to not be afraid; to forgive them, and be at peace. To flush out screaming, and get shot is to play into the game and prove - "See! They can't be trusted, we need even more police to protect you!"

I am human, and sometimes we are not as strong and brave as we wish to be, or think we are! The enemy is a trained professional. *The enemy may not be the entire government and system, only a few hotheads.* I am the guy who crawled on my hands and knees in fifty below snow for five days without food, and lived to tell of it! But, that was a lifetime ago. It is hard to know how it is today. So I sigh, a*nd if I somehow do not make it, disappear, get shot, choose door number three, I hope my friends understand and forgive me. But no, I will not please the Gestapo, scream, turn and run, and be their clay pigeon.* I tell Iris, "The procedure was well described to me years ago by a cop I took on a hunting trip—what's his name—a friend of my ex I took out as a favor to her."

"Yes, Miles, you told me that strange story! Hard to believe!" Yes, who would believe it? How he and his fellow policemen hunt down people on the unprotected list like animals. Tell them to run! Give them a head start! Then track them down in the streets as they scream for help and beg citizens for assistance that never happens. The thrill of killing them after a long chase described to me.

Yes, I understand. Not all cops or government agents are like this! I meet some good cops, as there are good lawyers, doctors, whites, blacks, *even hunters and trappers*! 'Bad' has little to do with occupation, religion, or race. The issue I have is, a cop or government agent has a vast amount of power. One bad agent can do a lot of damage. In the life of freedom I had, I chose a lifestyle carefully, that would ensure I was in charge of my life. No one could put me between a rock and a hard place. If someone tried to hunt me down like a dog, that was amusing. Territorial imperative says when you are on your own turf, your chances of winning are 99%. I depended on no one. I always had the option to walk away. I had no boss; did not have any partners I depended on. It may have something to do with my childhood. I vowed to get out from under 'control' with no way out. I flew, like a released caged bird, as far away as I could get. Found, I was drug back to the cage. *How do you think I feel?*

I think of Orson Wells 1938, War of the Worlds, on the radio. In just one hour he had the entire country in a panic believing we are being invaded by Martians. All Orson had at his deposal was his voice. People smelled the black smoke rolling in and coughed. Saw things, heard things. Believed; made it reality. Orson talked like the president. The country heard the president directing them to take cover. Brainwashing or hypnotism, the power of suggestion at its best. Many things can be made real and possible.

The world is round. If we run far and fast, we end up where we started. Not even Einstein could escape that. Escapes Germany as a pacifist Jew. Wishes to make a contribution to humanity and science. Ends up helping create the biggest bomb in the world. The future repeats itself. "It's never too late to have a second childhood." Words to a 60s rock song. Einstein, always kept a childlike innocence and joy of science to the end.

**Hello Marcia and Foil**

Iris is off on a walk with one of her girlfriends. We had a good visit, especially to get Iris's eye surgery done so she is not blind anymore! It was good to see you and Foil and have the chance to spend a short time. I have been playing with some of the wood I got in Arizona. Unsure if I can develop an interest. I have lots of our diamond willow, poplar, and spalted birch, not as common elsewhere in the world. I have been resin impregnating and dying this. It is usually too soft to use for knife handles. I hope this work I do will be add on value and sell.

My mom seems older, so somewhat sad. Sigh. Foil has some big jobs coming up. It will be getting hot there before too long. It'd be nice Marcia, if you could come along to Alaska and stay here when Foil comes. You and Iris could find lots to do, different than the sorts of things you are used to. Might be a fun change, I would think. Maybe if you and Foil shared some vacation time in a less stressful environment, it would create a level of happiness together.

Anyhow, here are some pictures to show Foil the wood work I am doing, so he has an idea. **Later! Miles**


Foil gave me some orange tree wood, and desert ironwood. As a landscaper, he is asked to remove trees in order to replace them with something more desirable. He specializes in restricted saguaro cactus. Some wood he is asked to remove is hard to acquire commercially, and might be useful to me. I realize I could get into the same problems with wood as I did with animal products. Some wood requires permits, proof, and has restrictions. Foil has told me it is sometimes easier to simply cut a tree up and burn it, rather than risk trying to find a use for it, then finding out he did not have all the selling permits.

When Foil had visited, he told me he and his wife were not getting along and were parting. This Alaska dream project was to be his project without her. The needs of a single man in the wilds is a different set of requirements than for a man and woman. Costs with a woman do not just double. A single guy can take risks he cannot ask someone else to take. Our partnership helping each other, had in mind him being alone and available to help me. His needs increase now, while his ability to pay, trade, or return help goes down. My trip to see mom in Tucson is a blur I have trouble recalling. Foil was supposed to come through for me with a lot of help. He promised to repay me for all my help to him in Alaska. While it is nice he checks on my mother and gives her $100 worth of food, I helped him to the tune of thousands of dollars.

"Who counts favors between friends, Miles!" First, we are not friends. We just know each other. Second, when the difference in favors is 100 times, I notice. This effects future plans.

**Miles!**

Thanks for the email – sorry for the late reply, been a bit underwater with work since the holidays.

Did I tell you that we saw Mitch in SD when we were there a few months ago. Did he tell you? We spent the day at Sea World and really, really enjoyed both it and him. He's really a tremendously bright, nice, interesting guy. You should be very proud. I know dad would be as well. Really glad you found someone, brother. It makes all the difference. You a senior? Gasp. But then again, I'm pushing fifty now

**Love, Avon**

Hmmm. A letter from my step brother. I last saw him at Dad's funeral, whenever that was. I had not heard he and Mitch met up, had a visit. Proud of my son? I shrug my shoulders. *Proud of what?* I had nothing to do with raising him. In fact, a deliberate effort all around to make sure I had no influence. His mother should be proud. As for me, I thought it took both parents to raise a healthy child. But what do I know. *The older I get, the less I know.* Obviously not. I like Mitch well enough. We are strangers. He was not raised how I would like to see a child raised. So this is close to saying, "What a great person! But who knows how he would have turned out if you had raised him!" I have to fight resentment. Few say to me, "I'm sorry you never had a chance to raise your son, Miles." I assumed sadly, there would be a price to pay, and Mitch and the ex would be sorry I was not involved in his upbringing. There would be proof I should have been there. My son being much better off without me is not the fantastic news to me they expect it to be. Sure, I am happy for him; I would not prefer he had a hard time and able to say, "I told you so!" Better he is happy.

There are children I helped raise I am closer to. I can see my influence on their lives, so have something to feel proud of. I at least know that feeling. I do not keep in touch with them either. I shrug my shoulders. My excuse this time is, they are busy, have their own lives. I do not wish to be a bother. They initiate wanting to be close more than I do. I do not get close to people much. I'd like to I think I could. In the case of Joy and May, I am not their real father. I was not married to their mother. The real father took them back. Their mother and I parted. The father did not approve of the lifestyle we lived when together. The children wanted to get to know their real father. He was in a position to take good care of them. Their mother and I were poor. Though their mother saw a benefit from my presence in the children's lives, and we agreed on how to raise them, she did not encourage me to think of them as my children, nor them to view me as, or refer to me as 'Dad', or anyone permanent in their lives.

Once they got older, we each went our separate ways. We did not have as much in common and the bond seemed gone. May might have been closer to me later in life as she loves the wilderness life, with sled dogs and trapping. She asked once, "Let's go on a wilderness trip, I need to get a boat to Lake Minchumina!" It was right after I had back surgery. I was down for a while. May did not approve of the changes in my life. Did not like the new direction of my art. She hoped I would stay more primitive in my art and my life. I think she got stand offish because I let her down; let a way of life down. Possibly when she got older she understood. She struggled to run a wilderness lodge. All the laws, permits, issues. Forced herself to move to town to pay the bills. We have more in common now, two decades later. I have Iris; a life for us. Being bonded and close to an ex-girlfriend's daughter, an adult lover-of-the-wilderness and going on trips together in the wilds, would not work well.

Joy did not take to the wilderness life like her sister May. She got married, has children, lives in town. Joy likes to walk, camp, and do outdoor things, but is very into her family and some of the nicer things in life. I'm not like a relative. I have to love them from far off.

I like to stay in touch with my step brother Avon at least once a year. 'Just because'. I honestly want to know everyone is ok. A certain distance developed with the girls when I did not attend Joy's wedding. I'm not the father. I do not know how to dress. It would be awkward. All the relatives. Who am I? No one. Their mother is hard to figure out, and finds great fault with me. The grandparents are strange enough I do not feel close or comfortable with them. There would be a, "Who is he?" Whisper and an explanation, and then feeling sorry for me. I went through that with my own real relatives. Embarrassment. As with my real son. It's like being a black person at a Klan gathering. It's just better to watch from a distance. Well! I mean my self-worth is just fine! It's just my worth to anyone else is in question! Ha!

None of this was an issue when I lived in the wilds alone. We are all equal in Mother Nature's eyes. My ability to get wood and food and take care of myself is equal to anyone else, regardless of race, religion, etc. I pull the trigger and the bullet does not care who pulled. The duck goes tail feathers over eyeballs out of the sky.

That is the equivalent of 'making a living', where in civilization there is inequality. Putting food on the table is more work for some than others because of race, religion, occupation, etc. Put simply, it would be as if the bullet flew different for you than me with the same skills. I got a duck for dinner and you did not, because God doesn't like you as much. That would be weird, and effect your quality experience in the woods wouldn't it?

"Yeah, that'd be a bit awkward all right, Miles." So here I am speaking of the wilds, one of the best in the world at what I do. King of my domain. In town, a nothing and nobody, with a crosshairs on my back, and open season written across my forehead.

### Hello Becky

Yikes! I wrote 'Gray' down as a last name. Always think of you as a Gray, not a Bell. Sorry about that. It's embarrassing to spin back in time and get stuck, and found out. Or scary. I think of Eileen, permanently stuck and never coming back. Shake my head to clear it.

Becky is a step cousin I knew off and on when young, when the family was in the area. I think Cleveland at the time. She is related to Zane Gray, the famous western writer. I was somewhat influenced by his books and family ties. I fill her in on events. She replies:

**Hey Miles**, good to hear from you. It sounds like things are going well in your neck of the woods.

How have I been? Well, here is a recap of the past year: divorce from Jon final in April, sale of house in June, moved again in July, Jon shot and killed himself in November, I got pretty sick and ended up in the hospital in December, quit my job caring for my grandkids and started collecting Social Security in Jan., have been resting, healing, and working in my studio since then.

I am glad it is spring, it has been a long hard winter. The snow is melting and I have garden plants started on my windowsill. I might even be about done hibernating, and ready to go out a bit.

Last year I was too busy trying to just survive to do much art-making, or keep the newsletter going. I don't have internet access at home, I am at my daughter's house using her computer at the moment. One thing at a time, building a completely new life in a new part of Vermont, as different from my old one as night is from day.

Siberian tomatoes, huh? My sister sent me some seeds from our uncle's family heirloom tomato plant two years ago, but they did not do well in Vermont at all. I guess climate means a lot to a tomato. That is cool that you found one that will grow in your garden.

Thanks for the email. It's good to keep in touch.

**Becky**

Becky is a very good artist, making a living at it. I bought one of her pastels of a moth when she needed to raise money. She loves the outdoors. Lives in Vermont in farming country, with a big spread of land. We exchange pictures of the outdoors, and gardening advice. I subscribed to her monthly blog promoting her lifestyle and art. Now and then I order something. Mostly to help out, but cool stuff. Some of her designs are on tee shirts, coffee mugs. Great idea. I like her idea of a studio with a big picture window overlooking the farm complete with wildlife. Tourists come to this area, I think, all the way from New York city! I recall vaguely, even long ago, that farmers had stands selling corn and apple cider and tourists would come out and buy. Our family was among the buyers. A nice weekend country drive. Maybe stay at an inn overnight along the ocean coast. Becky reminds me of those days when she sends pictures and discusses her life. Family stuff going on. Do all families have stuff to forget?

---

IRIS IS IN TEARS, screaming. We received a notice from Social Security that we still owe $1,204 that was erroneously sent to me while I was in prison. I was not allowed to collect while in. We assumed Social Security would be notified, and did not know it was up to us to tell them. We already paid it back, right away, back in November ! The notice is a threat that we need to pay, 'or else'! There is an 800 number to call. Half an hour of run around. The message machine is full and Iris is disconnected. All the buttons to press, all the automated 'crap'. "I just want to talk to a person!" She keeps yelling in the phone, in tears.

All the automated messages have to do with 'how would like to pay?' Press #1 for credit card, press #2 for check. Nothing about, "I already paid, an error has been made." I do not know any more than Iris does about what to do. "None of the above; please hold for a person" used to be one of the options when 'automated' began. If we simply ignore the notices, could I eventually have my credit ruined; be arrested? We assume, yes. We have heard the horror stories.

"A pregnant woman was drug out of her car through the window; it was in the news in Fairbanks, remember?" She owed the IRS. Government, same people. They are all alike.

"Them" you know. 'Those-Horrible-Evil-Morons.'

"Oh, I thought, 'Them' stood for, Technically Heathen Empty Middlemen."

"Same thing. You know, government, lawyers, doctors, big companies, the rich." Anyone who is not 'us'; not to be trusted; the enemy. I remind Iris that the pregnant lady who was pulled through the window of her car was made real when she sent me some money out of the blue to help me with my fight with the government. She wants to help others now. So the same thing does not happen to them that happened to her.

Iris and I were at the Social Security office in Tucson - one of the things we wanted to accomplish while we had a car rented in the city. I remind Iris, "Getting me signed back up for Social Security."

"The line was around the block, remember?" A hot day. Two hour line.

"Yes, Miles, and there were armed guards!" There was a sign saying, "Do not cause a disturbance, or else!" I forget the exact wording. People were getting irritated. There was only one desk, with one person working it. Many customers were on a lunch hour, and would not get to the front of the line during the only hour break they have. Not today, not tomorrow, not ever. Some are flat out of money, living on the street, and their Social Security is important to them! Cut off. Told they have to come in to fill out a form. But then never get to the desk to get the form. Many act like they believe, on purpose. The government does not want you to get hold of that form you need, so they do not have to pay you. How clever. Conversations about this in the line,

"If they cared, they'd have more than one person and more than one desk!"

The armed guards deal with the irritated. No cell phones or radios allowed. Nothing that might irritate the crowd. No bags, no purses capable of hiding a concealed weapon. Apparently there has been a concern that armed irritated people will start shooting. Iris and I are glad we live in a small laid back village. There are few lines.

Social Security
  In reference to account number 09...30801
  A statement sent 01/16/14
  Concerning an overpayment of Social Security benefits sent to me, Miles Martin. This overpayment was sent because I was in federal prison and not eligible for payment.
  My wife received the notice I was not eligible and immediately returned the money as requested. Our check number 2204 dated 11/26/13, $1,204. So far, it appears this check has not been cashed yet. We have the carbon copy of the check.
  My partner, who wishes to take care of our paperwork, tried to call you to straighten this out. After two hours on the phone, is now in tears. All she gets is automated "press 1, press 2" for nothing relevant to our situation. Sent here, sent there, put on hold again. Never did get a human being on the phone. I decided to write instead.

We are of course concerned if we did something wrong and the payment is not recorded I might end up paying again, or having automatic deductions taken out in the future, with interest, or have my payments held up maybe 'forever.' We are not confident in government agencies being efficient, caring, honest, or even run by humans. So we are both concerned. I'm afraid to depend on my Social Security. But I have no choice. My concern is, the government already spent our social security, is broke, and no longer has it. And giving us the run around as a result, so they never have to pay.

I am in hopes nothing is 'wrong.' That somehow two months later you find the check, and get the payment recorded. That there is simply nothing else we should or can do, but hold our breath and pray. And take more blood pressure pills. We are reluctant to pay again, and yet again. Keeping a record and shall keep an eye out for the check being cashed.

If 'something went wrong' and we need to cancel this check, and send another, or pay by another method, let me know, with a good set of instructions. I'm a senior. Talk slow and use big bold letters. (smile) .

Sincerely,

Miles Martin


I keep in mind, if it is me who spaces out a payment I am a criminal and or pay steep interest charges. I should, just for giggles, demand interest when their payments are late for any reason. If it's fair for the chicken, it should apply to the rooster.

It is always nice to get back to Alaska after Tucson! It's mid March. The sun is up enough to feel the warmth, and know spring is coming (In a couple of months). The Kitty cat is ok. We have a reliable friend we pay to watch the house plants, cat, and furnace, for the month we are gone. Kitty is used to the routine now. She follows Iris around for days not letting Iris out of her sight. I feel inspired by the new art materials, the change, and sunshine we absorbed while there.

Now that I can work in the shop and have that shock collar off, I am excited to put in long hours creating. I look at my prison book notes and cannot seem to get involved in writing yet. I need time away for a while. Anyway, it looks like book four is too long and can be made into two books. So while all my friends are waiting for the book about jail, I have two books to get out first!

"Iris, do we have enough of the three books to make it through the summer?" She is better at remembering and keeping track.

"I think we need more!" That means another printing. I have been doing digital printing through a print shop. There are issues. Cost, shipping fees, and waiting time. There is a number to buy to get enough of a discount to make any money. Minimum $3,000 up front. That is much better than the old offset printing days when I would have needed $20,000 to get a deal. However, I can do even better these days.

I have been investigating Amazon. Where you do it yourself. There are other sites like Lulu, but told Amazon is the leader now. The process looks overwhelmingly complicated. Or, did a decade ago when I investigated. I explore getting help. I explore giving up my rights and having a publisher handle it. I explore just paying someone to do what I need done. I discover a local publisher in Fairbanks in a google search. I have a writer friend who came out with a book. She says she had a local publisher handle it! I recognize his name in my google search. The owner of this one person operation knows me, knows my books. Is interested in working with me. I value the personal interest. I'm excited. We are talking all my books going digital as Kindle downloads, plus print on demand. Once set up, there are no more costs beyond buying my books wholesale to sell, or letting Amazon sell. I could order as few as five books at a time.

I have a nest egg of money saved up I want to invest back in my business. Or more, I need to get various old business interests perked up and running, that were once on the back burner. I explain to Iris, "When I have to invest $3,000 in a book printing, and it takes a year to break even, I am not making as much money as when I could invest the same $3,000 in musk ox horn, moose antler and such. In some cases I could double my money in a month. Why fool around with books? I would 'eventually' have time for books. Now, 'eventually' has arrived. Books could be retirement, once I set it all up. So it is like investing stashed cash that gets no interest, into books, that set me up in retirement income. I can get a deal at $400 a book to format for Amazon. In this way get all books done. No more using a printing service. The Amazon help services all want about $1,000 instead of the $400 from the local publisher, who is willing to get paid simply to digitize and correctly format my books.

Partly, my options are the result of a planned way of life. Lots of options, irons in the fire. The ability to either zig or zag. Not all the eggs in one basket. I was told my ideas are paranoid, pessimistic conspiracy theory stuff. I'm saying, "Well, what if?" I get asked, 'What if what!?' "Oh, global warming messes with the economy, war, government, stuff like that, or unforeseen stuff." I press on, "What if any of us gets sick? Can't do our usual occupation? A fire, flood, wipes us out. We go bankrupt..." I trail off. *No harm in being prepared!* Most people I talk to have less concerns, believing they will get taken care of. Someone else will solve their problem.

One of those unforeseen events happens that I fail to mention!

"What if I get arrested, become a felon, and am not allowed to work my job?" Ta da! Here I am folks! Set back a little, down, but not down and out. There are plans within plans. Survival, and preparedness is leaving an out. If nothing else, it helps me mentally. I'm not beaten. I have hope. Hope is more powerful than an atom bomb. A few people with hope can accomplish more than entire nations can accomplish under suppression.

"Yeah, yeah, Miles, I hear ya. Tired of hearing it actually. Get off the soap box!" With my mouth open to say more, I clamp it shut. *Yes. Of course. Let deeds do the talking. So my book guy is all pumped up.* He's been out of work. This is a good time to come to him. He's down south helping out an aging father trying to hang on to the family farm. He has access to a computer. That's all he needs. I will have to do some of the work myself. Beginning with reformatting to a new template he emails, and getting the text to fit. All pictures need changing. I now need high pixel originals. Separate in a file, numbered, no fancy font changes. I have to choose only two. To do it right, I need to begin with book one. I have to go all the way back to the beginning and 'start over'. While I am at it, edit it better. Kind of a new version fixing the major complaints I hear, and changing more names. I will have five books. Over 2,500 pages. Each reread at least four times.

Hundreds of hours ahead of me. One step at a time. *I'm on probation, can't travel far, need to keep busy, out of trouble. It's a good time to do this.* The web store is slow to comeback with the new changes and me being gone. A little depressing. Do all the 'save the animals' people want to encourage me in a new business with wood and rocks? No, mostly silence, or worse. Many animal rights people come across as, "To hell with humans! My dog has more rights than you do!" The reason given when I ask is, "You are in control of your life and can make decisions, the dog cannot, so the dog is innocent." *But without humans, where would dogs be? I'd think if you were going to save the planet for your dog, you'd have to save the planet for people too.*

Thousands of people, "Oh bummer, miss the wolf claws and mammoth ivory, Miles! Can you suggest anyone else?" It's hard to… what do I call it… get un-brainwashed. Sometimes it is even a physical pain. Part of that is toothaches! Ha! I had hoped to save my teeth in Mexico. The eye doctor here wants $1,000 a visit. Dentist is about as bad. I'm not sure I will have teeth left to save in another year. We'll see, can't dwell on it. No harm in just immersing myself in work. I'm slow to have an interest in my social life. I feel let down. This may have to do with my sense of social status. Or, I may just want to be alone after living in a crowded prison. Spend time with Iris.

Mrs. Probation officer had said, concerning the denial of my trip to Mexico, "You might go down there and kill something" *Kill something? You think my thirst for blood is so strong? I would steal a gun, smuggle it somehow on a plane, sneak it across the border to go kill what? A horny toad. A road runner?* Mrs. Probation and I of course are not equals, so there is no way to have a conversation. My job is to smile, and nod that I understand. *Yes! Good point! I never thought of that! Always good to be vigilant!* My life is in this persons hands. This is what she thinks of me. Pretty scary. I say again, she can at any time simply snap her fingers and point, and I am back with a collar on and put on a dog run for as long as three years. She appears to like her job. She could be one of those just waiting with finger twitching, for me to scream and run. Be the one to collect the reward for bringing me in, dead or alive.

A company keeps calling. Wanting to sell me stuff I am not interested in. "Just a moment, please." I am pleased and excited, instead of getting upset. I grab my small tape recorder and have to find the right spot. *Here* it is. I hit 'play', set it by the phone and walk away. I hear the tape.

"If you would like to talk to Miles, press one. If you want Iris press two. If you need the cat press three." Pause. "I'm sorry, that person is busy. Please hold. Your call is important to us." Pause. "Press four if you would like to leave a message." Pause. "If you would like to leave a message for Miles press five." "Press six to return to the main menu." "Your call is important to us, have a nice day." Ten minutes later the tape is still offering options, and explaining how valuable the caller is to me. After splitting firewood I come back to see if I can hang the phone up. I smile as I tell Iris, "I got the idea from God!"

She smiles. "Yeah, that part about, 'What you shall give, you shall get back tenfold.'"

I smile. "Yeah, once I heard God laughing in the background on the empty line."

"Miles, I like the other message better, how come you did not use it?"

"It's in for repair." Iris likes the one that starts, "I'm glad you believe in selling over the phone. Have a I got a deal for you!" I promote my web site and, "Any order over $100 you get a free batman whistle!" I tell Iris, "I am concerned many of the callers are dropping me from their calling list!" I frown. "I want to add, 'Please do not drop me from your list, and tell other telemarketers to call!' What do you think?" I frown. "I sure wish I could treat government agencies the same way!" Sigh.

"Well, I'd say you did, Miles. I'd say that has a lot to do with the trouble you got into! The government does not like to be made fun of, scammed, or get a dose of its own medicine!"

I smile brightly, "Yeah!"

Spring is around the corner. Time to order garden seeds, and get the dirt trays and lights in order. I make my own seed starter soil mixing last year's soil from the flower pots with worm casings from my worm farm, and compost I set aside for this purpose last summer. Iris has put compost in a couple of five gallon buckets for me. I mix this up in an old steel roasting pan and set it either inside the wood stove on top of logs, or in the oven to sterilize. I tell Iris what I learned in prison horticulture class.

"There are different views on sterilizing starter soil. The mainstream view is, we sterilize to kill weed seeds, bacteria, germs, bad living stuff in the soil so the new seed has a clean pristine environment to thrive in. In the same way we create a sterile environment for new babies or even ourselves, kill all the germs!" Germs are bad! Kill, kill!

I pause remembering something Mushroom told us - 'Everything is connected. There is a necessary balance in the soil of microbes, nematodes and fungus that do a job, and plants need them.' We were shown documentaries showing views under microscopes, results of experiments with fungus and living things in the soil. 'Some tiny creatures clean the microscopic plant filaments off plant roots so they can absorb nutrients. Some breakdown nutrients and deliver it to the plant in a symbiotic relationship, much like bacteria in our own gut.' In fact there is communication going on in the soil. Some fungus roots stretch out for miles across the land and communicate between plants, deliver messages about the environment. Some of this was over my head. Difficult to believe.

"In an experiment, a corn crop was burned in North America; on the other side of the world, a corn crop responded." Hmm. "That was not fungus or bugs. That was pheromones—chemicals plants give off to communicate. These chemicals tell other plants when to produce seeds. I can understand and believe that. But there is evidence the messages go far deeper.

"Around the world, during droughts and fires, plants respond accordingly, getting ready if the change is moving this way." Off subject though. Anyhow, there is a belief a good balanced soil needs 'bugs' in it. Right from the get go. The same argument for people! It turns out, babies and children living in a sterile protected environment get sick and are not as healthy as adults who ate stuff off the floor. Children who crawl on the floor and put disgusting germy things in their mouth, tend to be healthy children.

"Mom told me when I was young, when children in the neighborhood got sick, mothers would bring their children over so they would catch it to, and get over it. Because it is better to get sick when young and build up an immunity. Mom believes children were healthier fifty years ago than they are today. She does not recall many people having allergies. No one even knew what diabetes was. Kids were not out of school much with sniffles." Along this same line, there is a group who believes in balanced natural soil in which healthy seeds do best. I'll do an experiment and label the different soils. For the first time I use just straight compost, worm casings, and old soil, mixed, not sterile. The other group begins with sterile soil.

"Let the best seed win!" I write on little tags made from cut up venetian blinds.

One focus now is art using stones and my metal castings

# CHAPTER SEVEN

## TWO DIE IN JAIL, RIVER TRIP, SUBSISTENCE IN THE NEWS

"Do you recall what needs to be started first?"

"The slow sprouters?" Just testing to see if Iris has been paying attention. The garden is more my thing, but trying to get her interested. "Miles, I recall parsley; let's see… we always do tomatoes early… and cucumbers." That's mostly what we do early.

"I like to start lobelia this early as well, such a small seed, and slow growing plant, but so pretty in the hanging baskets!" We have room for ten flats in the windows and growing area we temporarily set up in the back room with grow lights. "I think I'll order one of these new LED grow lights this year, and get away from the halogen bulbs that use up so much power!" I may need a new sodium bulb which is $80. I can get a new LED system for $100." "Direct from China on Ebay!" Save ten dollars a month on the electric bill.

I try to keep track of what the garden costs. If we sell anything, I need to know if we made a profit! I need to know what our minimum money requirement is, or how we could cut to save money if we need to. I want to know the truth if growing your own food really costs less. If I ever get audited I want accurate records of costs. I pretend to others I am running a shell game on the IRS, because that is what people want to hear.

"Good for you! Sock it to them!"

I want the reality of any investigation to pass inspection. "It's just a malicious rumor Sir! I'm shocked and indignant at the false accusations!"

THE QUICK BOOK program for keeping records and doing taxes I have for the business works well for garden costs. Just have to remember to punch in the numbers. We buy one bag of plant starter mix. I find sprinkling this fine peat over smaller seeds helps get an even covering and gives a good environment when the seed first germinates. I found out the peat holds moisture well. My soil mix takes a little more care. I see weed seeds sprout. I have to know a weed seed from the plant I want! There may be no quick fix that addresses all the issues. Natural is often more work and takes more knowledge. It seems to me, sterile soils get inoculated with bugs and spores of all kinds from the air really fast. By the time the seed comes up, all kinds of other things have made a home in the soil. As long as I have a nutrient rich environment. I can see adding chemicals to sterilize would not be good. Slow soil recovery time.

I began sterilizing the trays and six packs with bleach. For some reason these items collect algae and fungus not best for plants. I wonder if it is the un-natural plastic? Even the sterile soil begins to sprout mushrooms. I'm sure spores are present in my air. Air from under the house, coming up into the room.

Mushroom had said, "It's all good! Plants are happy in a world filled with living things!" I found out how many kinds of living things are in the soil, water, and the air! It's more than there are kinds of animals, fish, and birds. Bad ones are so rare it is an amazingly low ratio. It's the same ratio as Siberian tigers to all mammals in the world.

When I heard this, I realized that, "Sterilizing the world we live in to make it germ free and safe, is like killing all mammals to make sure we do not get eaten by a Siberian tiger!" It was agreed, yes, a good analogy. Imagine a world with no mammals, fish, or birds, because you are afraid of tigers!

Mushroom added, "And just think, a third of our body weight is not ours, but other living things supporting us. Yes, yeasts and stomach stuff digests our food for us." He explained how this is what soil is about. Living things digest food for plants, and feeds it to the plant. The soil digests sunlight, turns it into carbon and sugar, and gives carbon and nitrogen back to the soil that the bugs need. Dead plants give back all kinds of stuff. This is hard to picture. This does not fit the modern ideas taught to us about sterilizing, and chemical fertilization.

It's more than just how it tastes. I'm one to know. I have spent a long time eating wild foods, berries, roots, teas of all kinds, as well as home grown vegetables. I remember Mushroom telling me the nutrients in today's store bought vegetables is about half what it was just fifty years ago. "You need to eat twice as much to get the same nutrients!"

The term 'nutrient dense' is coined. I'm concerned I might begin to sound like a greenie. A vegetarian, bunny snuggling, tree stroking, sprout eating, jogger. Yuck! *I have to keep up my savage image!* Savages did not have to know all this stuff. They just did it! There was no 'store bought'. It is savages who told civilized people, "It's all in balance, a great circle!" How cute. How quaint. How poetic. How sweet. Everything holding hands and dancing. "Next!" Meanwhile the world needs to be fed, so out come tractors, fertilizers, and grateful people. For a generation or two. Enhancing nature might take more skill and knowledge than we have. Or, civilized man thinks he is slick, imitating God, but can't quite pull it off. Or, living like a savage does not take rocket science, nature knows what to do. It's a matter of trust.

I think of these things as I water the trays, watch little green points come up out of the plastic six packs. I put seedlings into four inch pots as soon as I can. Transplant shock is less when done early, I think. Some plants, like cucumber, do not like being transplanted. Tomatoes do better, but there are still secret techniques. Do not grab the plant and pull. It is better to move the soil, loosen it, turn it upside down and slap the pot bottom to get the soil to drop out. Quick is better. Before the plant knows it is upside down and freaks out, it is upright again. I only know that plants that are upside down the longest trying to get them loose, respond the slowest or even die. I'm getting to where I can look at a plant and know what it needs, to some extent. Mushroom is so much better at it! He can say it needs magnesium, or a trace element. He knows what bug might be getting to it. He can look at soil and say what is missing. I did not even know this is possible! Obviously, I am not a farmer! Growing is only one of many things I need to know a little about.

Starting seeds is the biggest event going on for a two week period. I go out with the snow machine to cut firewood and get out to the shop to play with wood and rocks. Plants are a foot tall by the time I get the greenhouse going in early April—about two months ahead of being able to set them outside. We have two Toyo oil stoves in the house to use as backup, even though we mainly heat with wood. One of these is moved to the greenhouse when winter eases up and one Toyo can cover heat needs in an emergency in the house. All the wall fittings are left on the greenhouse so all I have to do is hook up the fuel line and plug it in. The thermostat is set for fifty-five degrees. For the first week the stove runs a lot. This time of year, we expect blue sky and pure sun. During the day, temperature inside the greenhouse get up to eighty degrees even though outdoors it is sixty. At night, it drops below freezing. There are still last year's frozen vegetables and moose meat we are living on.

The boat is looked over. Lower unit grease is changed, the battery put back in and charged, and all is looked over. I move the snow machine tools to the boat, as well as the jack and winch. I will be ready to launch the boat as soon as the ice goes out. With global warming, we expect open water in late April. I have a relatively new engine for the boat. I had been making so much money I did not know what to do with it, but did not want to pay taxes, so kept dumping money back into the business. One investment is a huge 115 horse engine. Huge because my boat is rated for forty horses. I was told the weight of the engine will sink the boat! No. Not if I balance the front with 100 gallons of gas. And beef up the back with welded supports.

I can't open the engine up to full power because I cannot keep it on the water, even fully loaded. The boat is doing thirty miles an hour at 2,800 rpm, which is idle.

"Iris, I was looking at a seventy horse. But for only another $1,000 I can almost double my horsepower." Tired of always feeling slightly underpowered, I decide to be so far over powered that power,'will never be an issue again. Fuel consumption does not change much by adding or taking away 1,000 pounds. I'm burning less fuel than with the sixty horse. "Because with the sixty horse I am running beyond the efficiency power band. With the 115, I am idling."

With experience, I can open the engine up more. It is possible to burn over ten gallons an hour. Yikes! I try to keep it at three gallons an hour. I paid an extra $500 for the full meal deal in gauges. So I can see water pressure and temperature, oil pressure, gas consumption per hour to the tenth of a gallon, RPM, trim, and engine hours. But not speed—I have to use the GPS for that. I think I do not have the most efficient propeller for this engine.

"I'm going to try a twenty-one pitch I think." I will pay $100 for the aluminum one before investing $500 in the stainless. The aluminum will last only one trip though. *"You know what boat stand for, right?"* Yeah, 'Break out another thousand!' Me and I both grin. That is ok with me because it keeps the financially faint of heart off the river. A trip to the homestead cost me $300.

"So I really want to come back with something off the river to help cover that cost! Like wood burls, good rocks, fossils, like that. Or a moose."

**Hey Miles, Seymour here.**

We are finally making good on the talk of winding down the business! This is the last year we keep the survey license. There are a couple of odd jobs to wrap up, but nothing big. The wife and I will handle it. No more employees. Stop by to visit when you can!

So for sure, no more survey work. Those years are over now. I pass the news on to Iris. "I saw Seymour and his wife on the cover of the trappers magazine I showed you this past winter. They looked happy next to the plane and the otter they caught. That has been his big dream. He keeps the plane from the survey years, and uses it to access remote lands he acquired. He goes in to trap and live a more simple life of retirement."

I'm reviewing my options for the summer ahead. I'm only getting $600 a month

Social Security. That amount would have been only $400 if I had not put an extra amount of work and dollars in the last two years, as suggested by my accountant, Bean. Iris gets a lot more, but hated her entire working career. Was it worth it? So far, my business is only breaking even since getting out of the animal parts business. I'm not earning more than the business costs, but I enjoy making knives and casting, so it is like a hobby I can do for free.

I have to report my income. Mrs. Probation encourages me, "You will do well once you are off probation! Once you can travel and do shows you will do better!" What she means is, I might make as much as $500! I smile and nod, that this would indeed be amazing! She is of course encouraging me to keep a good probation record so I can get off early. I think because it makes her look good. A felon going off the deep end on her watch would not be cool. "If all goes well, you will be off probation by the time you go to Tucson next year!" Yes, something to look forward to.

Josh tells me about an article he read in the paper, and asks my opinion. This has been a big topic for subsistence people.

**Monday, March 31, 2014 Katie John Subsistence case**
WASHINGTON - The Supreme Court has turned away an appeal by the state of Alaska in a long-running fight over the control of rivers and the fishing and hunting rights of Alaska Natives.

The court on Monday declined to review a federal appeals court ruling that upheld U.S. Interior Department rules enforcing the fishing and hunting rights on some rivers that otherwise would be under state control.

The state urged the high court to step in to address claims that the Federal Government has improperly asserted control over rivers in more than half of Alaska.

Alaska Natives groups and the Obama administration supported the appellate ruling.

A ruling in the Ninth Circuit court of Appeals gives authority to the Federal Government regarding the use of inland waters for subsistence hunting by Alaska Natives. The Federal Government provides subsistence hunting and fishing priority on navigable waters to Alaska Natives, while the state does not.

"Yes, Josh, it looks to me like the Federal Government is moving in on states jurisdiction over water rights, which affects subsistence hunting and fishing." The Federal Government wants to discriminate by race, showing Native preference over use of waterways. "I heard in the past, the Federal Government has argued the state is not doing an adequate job of managing its lands, as an argument to take over jurisdiction." I'm guessing the state lacks funds, much of which used to be federal grants. If white subsistence people get cut out of their rights, who cares? Or, more state politicians can claim to be working hard on keeping our rights! "It's the Feds fault!"

Once there is federal jurisdiction, all federal laws will probably apply, as Josh points out, "Miles, before long we will have to have running lights, a fog horn on our boats, along with numbers, lifejackets, insurance, registration, and all that other crap." We are already seeing a lot of these requirements resulting in big headlines in the news concerning those who have not complied. Or more, believe the Federal Government does not have jurisdiction, yet. For now, the Feds back the Natives. *Divide and conquer.*

"Yes, Josh, I think that time might arrive when the Feds turn on the Natives. My experience has been that the state is more 'us' than the Feds. The state understands Natives not on a reservation. Many local politicians have commercial fishing and roots that come from the land."

We both agree, Washington is far away, with less understanding of how we live. Much like the issues we faced following English law dictated to us from across the sea. The Feds have bigger issues on their mind than subsistence people picking berries and meeting their needs. I do not think the federal interest in protecting Native rights has to do with respect or understanding of the Native. It may have to do with sucking up while oil and resources are stolen off Native land as well as separating races so they do not stand together to fight. The same technique was used by both the British and French—get the locals savages on your side. Not out of respect, but as unsuspecting allies in a power play. John, from Nenana, is quoted in the news. John is the son of my friend Jack, 'into politics'.

John Coghill says, "We continue to support the state's position. There are guarantees in the Alaska Statehood Act and Alaska Constitution which places Alaska resources, including fish and game, in the state's trust to be managed by Alaskans." This ruling muddles the laws and creates conflict between federal and state subsistence laws. "The Parnell administration's lawsuit was an assault on the people of Alaska who depend on hunting, fishing, and gathering to feed their families."

Josh and I do not see eye to eye on the subsistence issue. Josh believes the white man came in and illegally took over, and claimed Alaska. "The Natives never gave up their rights!" But the tribes did, when they signed the recent ANILCA agreement. They got paid off, plus given land. "If I got paid off Miles, where is that money? I do not have it!"

"No use getting hot at me, Josh. I assume the tribe took charge, and is managing your money for you!"

"Yeah, right!"

None the less, that is not my or the white man's problem. How the Natives divided up the booty is up to them. I believe the Natives are not so different as a race and their politicians are not looking out for their people any more than happens with the white man. Instead of blaming another race of people for all his woes, Josh would be better off blaming a way of selfish thinking, wherever it is found. I believe Josh has allies among all races, the same as enemies within his own race. To make this a racial issue is to not understand what he is up against and has to lose. I refer to information from a web site explaining subsistence laws.

WHAT IS THE SUBSISTENCE PRIORITY

The law states both the state and Feds are, at heart, in agreement. There is no reason based on this law to divide and conquer.

> I quote a friend of mine on the Federal Subsistence Board.
> 
> "A lot of people would like 'subsistence' to go away. Subsistence people are being divided by race and income. Where in truth, it is acknowledged subsistence is about a lifestyle. Yet the word 'Subsistence' begins with 'sub,' meaning 'beneath.' So the very word is about a lifestyle beneath other lifestyles. Thus, erroneously defined by how financially poor and lower class you are."

"You know Frin, from Manley Hot Springs?" This is a respected Native elder Josh knows I am quoting.

I have to review some of the history myself as it gets clouded and confusing. Especially listening to people who only partly understand it. I keep going over this! I can see the expression on the average person's face when I speak. Boredom, politely wishing to be someplace else, looking at the watch, trying to show proper respect for a friend, but really, can't we change the subject? So I do change the subject.

I feel a great part of my problems with the government revolve around these issues of 'the game'. I call it the game of life. Rules of engagement. My arrest warrant had written on top, "Not a Native," and I keep repeating, the Natives involved in the same case who accepted illegal drugs and guns for white ivory they were not supposed to sell, were never arrested.

> Alaska Constitution established that fish and wildlife, "are reserved to the people for common use" and that "no exclusive right or special privilege of fishery shall be created or authorized." [Alaska Constitution, Article VIII ]
> 
> Alaska Native Claims Settlement Act (ANCSA). The act addressed Native land claims that clouded construction of the Trans-Alaska Oil Pipeline. It extinguished aboriginal hunting and fishing rights in Alaska in exchange for almost $1 billion in cash and 44 million acres of land.

*That's got to be at least a million dollars and over 44 acres per native, because there are not more than a million Natives in Alaska!*

ANILCA mandated that the state maintain a subsistence hunting and fishing preference for *rural* residents.

The State of Alaska, which had established its own subsistence law in 1978, took note of the discrepancy between the laws and amended state law in 1986 to match ANILCA by *limiting subsistence uses to rural residents.* The fix, however, didn't last long. In 1989, the state Supreme Court ruled that the rural preference violated Alaska Constitution, including its "common use" provisions regarding use of fish and wildlife.

I pause here and reflect. This is the part Seymour knows and comments on. He feels rural preference is illegal discrimination. The game should be for all of us, equally. "Miles, I work hard, pay taxes. Why should my hard work result in fewer rights?" There is a hint in this, we don't see eye to eye. Seymour accepts I am subsistence, but I wonder if it means to him, "poor and needing help." Hiring me is giving work to a welfare person who needs the job, who is grateful to earn money to pay some bills and not suck off the system and his tax dollar. He has always been worried what will happen to me if he has no work for me some summer. Like now. I get back to this information...

As the state no longer guaranteed a rural preference for subsistence as required by ANILCA, the Federal Government moved to take over management of subsistence on federal public lands. Federal managers took over authority for subsistence on federal lands on July 1, 1990.

Congress also saw a need to protect subsistence uses by non-Native rural residents, many of whom had adopted a subsistence way of living.

**Legally, customary and traditional** is defined as "a long-established, consistent pattern of use, incorporating beliefs and customs which have been transmitted from generation to generation (and) plays an important role in the economy of the community."

It is my view there are many ethnic groups beside Indians who have deep rooted customs connected to the land. In over words, not just Indians respect mother nature.

Initialed in 2000. Areas identified for coordinated actions include but aren't limited to development of regulations, in-season management, research, special action requests, **customary trade and barter, customary and traditional use** determinations and Advisory Committee and Regional Council actions.
Alaska Subsistence

In January 2005, the Federal Subsistence Board approved new restrictions on cash exchange for subsistence-caught salmon. Exchanged for cash to 50 percent or less of a household's annual harvest exchanges between a household in the district and non-rural residents to $500 annually.

*Exchange of fish and other subsistence resources for cash is known as "customary trade," and is recognized by the State of Alaska and U.S. Federal Government as a legitimate subsistence practice.*

I believe most of the activities I was arrested for are covered under the above laws. I note the years in which all these decisions were made. I was out in the wilds, out of touch, assuming I'd get left alone, because I am not bothering anyone or the wildlife. I did not know these changes were made to laws and decisions effecting me.

Josh argues, "Maybe, Miles, but you have been in and out of trouble with the government all along. This was not the first time."

"That would not be my side of the story, Josh!"

Josh rolls his eyes up, ready to hear Miles version of the truth and reality.

"Most of the issues I had over fishing and subsistence I won!"

Changing the subject, but only a little, "Miles, are you headed out this spring to look for mammoth tusks as usual?"

"Is that what I usually do, Josh?" I'm irritated because I make sure I never tell anyone, not Josh, or anyone else, where I am going, or what I am doing. In fact no one knows where I go, not even Iris.

"Everyone knows, Miles, it's just common knowledge." *How is this knowledge acquired I wonder? Not from facts.*

"I have a trip to make to the homestead, Josh. I hope to find diamond willow wood, or nice burls along the river."

"But can you still hunt for fossils?"

"I'm not sure. Fish and Game and the court has no problem they tell me. No fossils were confiscated, not part of my charges." I pause, then add "However," my probation officer says no. She calls it an animal product. I can have it, but not sell it."

"But, Miles, it's not an animal product!"

"Try telling her that! One thing you learn, Josh, is, I am not in a position to argue, contradict, or educate." Eyes down, shuffle feet, and go to the back of the bus, answering, "Yes, Ma'am."

"And you can do that, Miles?!"

"No choice, Josh. Well, there is always a choice. It's just for the best like this, for now. Choose our battles, Josh." I have to go. "Enjoy the rest of the day, Josh!" Josh likes to bait me and upset people in general, it's one of his faults. He knows quite well what prison, probation and the law is all about. His son spent thirty years in prison. For thirty years, I listened to Josh tell me what it is about. His son went to the hole a lot for not taking required anger management classes. He also did his full time, and longer. There is a reason.

I DO my usual computer work, check emails, go to a few web sites. The Blade Forum is useful; I had to pay to join, but have the privilege of selling. So far, I have sold only a few knives and raw materials. There is another Alaskan on the site I know through Tusk and a few others. Sometimes I look on this forum to see what he is up to. My buddy, Knife, belongs to a blacksmith guild and teaches custom knife making and has passed some classes and tests. He represents high end; high tech. I think his products are overpriced. He thinks I'm not a knife maker worth talking to because I don't have any degrees, and my quality is not up to his standards, according to him. I believe my blades will hold up to the same rigorous standards his hold up to in any test given to the steel. My style is more rustic and primitive. We overlook our differences and get along without being close friends. Knife made the insultingly low offer for moose antler to Foil. Trying to take advantage of what he figured was me between and rock and a hard place.

There is a discussion on Blade Forum concerning the use of ivory as knife handle material. There are over 500 posts.

This is what Knife writes.

There is starting to be some misinformation showing up in this thread. Just a couple of things, if the ban is passed as written, it will have far reaching effects. First it puts the onus on the owner of the ivory to prove it is legal. It also makes all elephant ivory illegal to sell unless you can prove with federal documents that it meets certain, very hard to reach, criteria. It makes interstate sales illegal even if you can prove it is pre-ban. There are no provisions for "grandfather rights" in the strategy as written. It could spill over into other kinds of ivory, there is some talk of you having to prove questionable ivory is not elephant ivory with DNA analysis.

A news article is quoted in a post here.

From the Chicago Tribune - Washington Bureau

The administration will ban the resale of elephant ivory across state lines except antiques. Sales within a state will be prohibited unless the seller can demonstrate an item was lawfully imported before 1990 from African elephants and 1975 for Asian elephants. People can still own ivory and pass heirlooms to relatives.

"Because we have an antiquities exemption everything becomes an antique" said a senior administration official. "The biggest change will be that law enforcement will no longer have to prove that ivory it seized was illicitly acquired. Owners will now have the burden of proof to show that they legally acquired it."

I email Knife that I read his comments on the Blade Forum. He replies:

> **Hi Miles**, First, welcome home,
> Next, I do think you down played your illegal activities some, blurred the lines a little bit. But I did not call you to task on that, everyone can make up their own minds about your issues. I will tell you, I try very hard to not break the law, something you did not do. No one was happy to see you go to jail, or out of the ivory business. I have spent quite a bit of time and money on lawyers and time on the phone with different agencies to try and make sure I don't break the law. I know it's possible to make mistakes, but I try very hard. Life is a big enough struggle to bring any of that stuff down on yourself. You would not have gotten into trouble if you had done the same. I wish you the best, **Talk to you later, Knife**

I agree with Knife for the most part. If I had done what he does, I might have been left alone. Only maybe. Knife is not trying to live subsistence. He is among the protected. Of the superior race, lives in town, with traditional job, well plugged in. He has and is near a phone, had electricity all his life, good reliable internet connection and can stop in at the various agencies to chat. I'm not sure everyone's situations can be compared.

I am pretty sure Knife has been deliberately badmouthing me to mutual customers, and privately on the Blade Forum. I can't prove it, but one maker emailed to tell me. Another customer called me on the phone. Foil had a story for me. I'm polite and careful dealing with Knife. I do appreciate his being diligent on the changing laws and direction the ivory business is going. The burden of proof to show legality might be on us now. Yes, that's a serious issue. This could be financially prohibitive as DNA testing is expensive. Customers will likely not want to get involved.

Tusk tells me. "You know yourself, Miles, sometimes paper and pen is harder to come by then mammoth tusks out in the remote fish camps where we do business!" Meaning, how are dealers going to get receipts and proof when they buy? It's an insult to ask for a receipt when remote. "We could carry a receipt book if we know we will be buying. But even so, it puts a damper on the deal; implies we do not trust the seller. People who made the rules are not the ones who have to follow them and see how unworkable they are."

I nod that I understand. "Tusk, in the past I had material stored for a couple of decades, when laws were different. I never had a receipt. It wasn't required. After twenty years of packing, unpacking, sorting, mixing I cannot honestly say where I got it. That should not make the material illegal."

"This DNA test is going to be costly; means shipping a sample out, and waiting for a reply!"

"When it is usually easy to tell the different ivories apart by looking at the cross section and hash marks!" We agree the judge who made the ruling would not know that. Someone, Fish and Wildlife, deliberately pulled the wool over the judge's, or game board's eyes.

"Miles, I think Knife is looking out for himself on this ivory thing he is so into right now." We both notice Knife suggests no one have anything to do with any other ivory but mammoth because the laws are so vague and penalties so high. While he is in the mammoth ivory business. "His following the laws concerning elephant ivory make him look good and legal, as he turns his competitors into the law, and gets their customers to come to him!" I nod, but do not trust Tusk much more than Knife. Information is on a need to know basis.

"So, Miles, you going out this spring getting mammoth tusks like usual?" He's a buyer, and wants to know if I will have any material to show him. I don't answer. *I'm not supposed to be exploring what I can get away with. But accepting what I can't do.*

"I think Knife knows who turned you in. He did not tell me who, but hinted he knew!"

I think Tusk is trying to make like my good buddy. I do not believe *anyone* turned me in! I was being watched for four years. An undercover agent spotted me at the Tucson show and started keeping track. Such an agent is not likely to know about Alaska law, or my Alaska contacts. The biggest issue was my relationship with Jessie. Some early phone conversations were recorded because he was under investigation. Possibly after I was on the radar. The Feds searched out friends on Facebook, and those I do business with to spy on me. By then it was already too late. Someone local may have been approached. Some locals I know found it a good time to clean my clock, proudly thinking they were the main cause of my grief. Collecting favors from those in power to cover their own operations.

I read in the evidence that a California animal rights group worked with Fish and Wildlife with money and gathering evidence. It might even be possible this organization cruises around on the internet looking for sites that sell animal parts, and 'investigates' on their own dime. Then helps set up a bust. At least turn over what they find to the proper authorities. Such groups have a hidden agenda, and money to do something about it. I assume it is legal for a person or organization to spend money investigating the competition or rivals, even set them up. Expose illegal deeds and get a thanks for it from law enforcement, getting the diligent citizen award, even a reward. Government all over the world functions well when citizens turn each other in.

Could the NRA spend money to spy on citizens opposed to guns? Help the Feds financially to put them away for unrelated offenses? What's good for the goose, should be good for the gander. Could the NRA investigate tax issues among its rivals and front the money to prosecute them, or pay to have them audited? Can a candidate running for the Republican party seek out Democrats and earmark them for IRS audits? This has already happened, and been in the news. Bringing up the question, if groups with a hidden agenda can eliminate the competition by investigating them and turning them in? Can anyone with money have anyone else investigated for whatever reason they wish? This appears to be dangerous ground to me. I am reminded of Woman's story in prison.

The agent who interrogated me was offended by a picture of the moose with a big rack I posted on Facebook. He acted like it was a personal slap in the face. For no other reason, I need to be shut down. He came right out and said so. Because? I was not sure why. I got the impression, I am poor, so do not deserve such a nice rack on a moose. I should not be allowed to take such a trophy! As a subsistence person, I only need the meat to eat it, I do not care about the antlers. The argument goes a little like Seymour's. When he and his friends pay big bucks, and work so hard, to try to find such a moose. What right do I have to eat it? This moose is worth a small fortune to a much more deserving rich person than I am. A deserving person is defined as a high tax payer, big consumer, cog in the gears of industry. This agent plans to wipe the smile off my undeserving face. But after interrogating me for seven hours he lightened up. *He got what he wanted?*

Yes! I can imagine a Green Peace person spotting my web site and going ballistic. Making me a person of interest. "What did I expect!" I'll tell everyone what I expect. I expect the law to be followed, that's what I expect. I do not expect agents to label legal wolf claws as illegal eagle claws. Or call ravens migratory birds. Or turn ivory legally gifted to me as collateral, 'conspiracy to commit fraud.' Whatever anyone's personal feelings on the subject, I expected everyone to be legal, including the government. I had dreamed of even more! Integrity, ethics, and morality.

Knife believes what he is saying. I'm an outlaw. Based on my reputation. Not facts. A reputation I created. I am not sure of all the 'reasons why,' since hardly anyone else does that! I have stated, partly to get competitors off my back trail. Partly it got me attention. Partly a lot of people admired talk of doing what I want, how I want, the heck with the government and rules and regulations!

"Right on! Go for it!" Partly, I saw since childhood how hard it was to be me. Short; not a lot of social skills; an artist. I had to work hard at being one of the guys. Macho. Be accepted. To get away with liking to grow flowers, draw pretty birds, write poetry, not liking to fight; I had to come up with a plan. It's hard to question someone who kills bears. It gives me the right, earns me the right, to enjoy the beauty, without being a pussy. Having the image of a care free do what I want and

## SECRETLY WILD

the heck with the law sort, gives me credibility with the people I deal with. The poor, the uneducated, the minorities.

Many suppliers, subsistence sorts, trappers, those who live off the land, are not very literate; not the types who think of the law as their friends; on their side. Somewhat like moonshiners during prohibition. If you wanted to get along with deep woods folks who lived in *them thar hills*, you better not act like a revenuer. There could be no lectures of that still in the holler out back of your place if you wanted to live there and get along. You didn't have to drink, or have a still, but you had to talk the talk and have the respect. To get arrested as 'one of them' means what? To be expected? As if I were really running the still and running roadblocks, carrying a Tommy gun? I assumed all along anyone saying so would need proof before locking me up. Not inventing enough proof to support the rumors. Because a fall guy is needed.

Knife seems to me to imply his poop does not stink and mine does. Tusk and I know 'someone else' we all know. One of the biggest shops at Alaskaland. The same place I parked my houseboat and had Fairbanks adventures in earlier books, a tourist trap. Mr. Alaskaland has been in business since the 70s, knows all of us well. Deals with, and buys from all of us. He told me, "Beware of Tusk? Not me, I have too much on him! He is involved in too many shady deals!" There was mention of Tusk and Knife working together.

THE CENSUS MAN is in my doorway with a laptop computer, ready to take notes and interview me. There had been a note on my door, "Stopped to visit. You were not home. Here for census questions." I have been part of other census taking, that went well enough, just strange questions I recall. Now, a pamphlet, saying among other things, this is mandatory and must be answered! It is illegal not to participate. I did not appreciate the tone. Being ordered to let someone in my home, and answer personal questions. A nasty tone before even meeting me. I wasn't home today, so what? Why get nasty? Questions in the past had been, "Where are the remote cabins on the river? Who lives in them? Tell me about these people. Can you boat me in to meet these people? Are you and the woman you live with married? Where did she come from? Does she work? What is her background? Do you own any guns? Can I come in and look around?" This seems to me far and above a census, a count of how many people there are. It is collecting data, a profile, on everyone. Creating a data base on citizens. [1]

*Unless I am singled out as being investigated, and this is the cover.*

Next day Iris and I see this census guy in the local café. He is staying here; renting a room for days and weeks. Saying to me, "Yes, I know what you mean. I

205

am supposed to find out where empty cabins are, and remote places, and who is using them. I need to go there to ask questions. The people who are my boss have no idea what it is like here, and how hard it will be to do this." Guessing, to him, it is just a job he is getting paid for, not paid to think, and figure out what is being done with the information. He tells me no one yet is willing to cooperate. No one will boat him to the wilderness cabins, or even tell him where such cabins are! What happened to just counting everyone? Years ago I was asked if I was black or Spanish. Then, if I had running water. Nothing that might create hostility, just puzzling.

"These questions tell us..."

Yes. I know what the answers to these questions tell you. I understand why you want to know. Just as I understand why you want to know how many guns I have, and where they are. So now you understand, I do not want you to know the answers. I do understand. If I tell my true feelings, 'Person of interest' will get a check mark. So I joke, and give the guy the run around. Hopefully the box, "A harmless idiot lives here," gets checked.

*"Democracy is two wolves and a lamb voting on what to have for lunch. Liberty is a well-armed lamb contesting the vote." ~ Ben Franklin*

While on the subject of the government...

News Miner April 17th A3=- **"Families seek answers in jail deaths"**

"Two inmates died within a week of each other. Looking for answers to questions not being answered" DOC says deaths under investigation, but does not see how they can be related. Both involve younger people who needed medication. "Mosley's family wants to know why he remained in jail when prosecutors had to dismiss the charge against him more than a week earlier." In an earlier article, when there was only one dead, the family stated they were not allowed a visit on visiting day, and wondered why, when charges had been dismissed, and this person should be getting out and certainly allowed a visit.

I point this out to Iris. We have a routine of going to the senior center each morning for coffee and reading the paper together. On my own, I would not read the news or subscribe to the paper. The reported news is in general depressing. But we got a subscription. This is time for us to do something together. We discuss the news.

"I am not surprised to see this. I told you of my experiences!" I am convinced there is a fly in the soup. This is not the first time strange deaths have been reported coming from prison.

I read the email quote to Iris that I get from a customer. I'm careful what I say, and who I quote. *Repeat after me. The government is my friend! I love my government.*

I often get a hostile, "Darn right!" Proving, it's good to say good things about those with power over your life. Indeed, "Where else is better if you have a complaint! Got a problem? Go to Russia and see how you like it!"

I'm starting to get out and about much more. The sun is higher, spring is here. All of us in the interior blink at the sun, yawn, and leave the house more. I run into Barefoot on a dusty Nenana road on the way to the post office.

"You know, I'm not the only one who talks bad about you. I'm just the only honest one who tells you to your face!" Pause. "A lot of people think you are a rat!"

"And why would anyone think that, Barefoot? What is it you know for a fact that is not an opinion."

"Well, the other guys got twenty years, and you only got six months, so you must have ratted them out."

It does not occur to Barefoot I got six months because that's what I deserved. If I'd been offered more time in a deal, I might have fought and won. It just seems an odd conclusion, that I have to be a rat. Now, it's a fact. I do not argue. I smile, nod, and go on my way. There is a group in town that seeks out bad and likes to gossip; be disruptive; hurt people. There are others who spread good things; have positive news. My accountant friend, Bean, and all those who regularly attend the Wellness meetings I am a part of forward good news. I do need to be aware there are those out gunning for me, waiting for me to slip up; who'd love to see me go back to jail.

I had turned over some of my art to Iris because it contained animal parts. Like knives with antler handles. Tripod days, which celebrates the raising of the Tripod on the ice, was looking for donations, prizes, and are going to the Nenana business people. I want to help out the turkey shoot! I ask Iris if she can donate one of the custom knives I made, since I can't have them or sell them. She does. The prize is gratefully accepted. Worth about $500. Mr. Assembly wins the competition and refused to accept the prize!

"You know Iris, the new guy on the city assembly, what's his name, the military hero ace shooter?"

"Yea, related to Mad Jay?"

"Yes, I am told he badmouthed me, saying I am trying to get others arrested."

"I do not want to go to jail accepting one of Miles illegal items!" He got the other shooters to agree with him.

"Miles is trying to get us all involved as felons!" The $500 knife got given away when five dollar hats and Tee shirts that were handed out to everyone.

I run into one of the Native elders I respect. We sit on the bench by the river to watch the tripod and ice, and chat.

"Are you going to be fishing this spring?"

"Miles, last year Fish and Game told us we had to build our traditional fish wheel differently. The mesh in the baskets has to be special Teflon plastic to help protect the fish. The box has to be lined with special expensive material. We had to change our wheel to meet legal requirements, using acceptable conventional designs, not traditional Native with the curved local wood baskets. We also had to sit and watch the wheel while it was running, so we were away from home for three weeks. It's a hardship, and big change. There are now only two commercial fisherman in Nenana out of six licenses held."

This is an example of what I believe the Feds are up to, divide and conquer. First, get Natives on your side. Then slowly cut them off, too. Demanding unworkable methods of building, a series of permits hard to meet, and unrealistic requirements. They argue. "Oh, yes, we respect and allow fishing by Natives!"

Those who are ignorant of how fishing is done, like politicians in Washington, can glance at the rules, and they look reasonable. Everyone gets a finger in the pie. No one I know openly sells salmon strips anymore. In the past this was commonly used as money for bartering! Now making strips requires an inspection, stainless sink, certified sanitary conditions that cannot be met in the village. So while making fish strips is verbally encouraged, it's impossible to do legally.

I answer this elder. "Yes, I have noticed less fishing going on over the years. As you know, I was stopped from fishing on the Kantishna with nets, and had to get rid of my sled dogs as a result. In the end it cost me a lifestyle."

The elder only nods, he understands. He sees the changes. He doesn't seem angry or upset. "There will always be change, Miles. It's one thing we can count on!"

Yes, this is true. Subsistence people could not count on everything to be the same each year. The entire village might have to pack up and move because the caribou migration changed within this elder's memory! Would getting angry help? You may as well be angry with God! It is good to sit with a wise elder, get some insight into the ways of the world. He tells me, "There are worse things to worry about! The people! These new drugs our kids are into; this meth I hear about!" We agree, if we are healthy, smart, hard working, we will survive. If meth makes us weak and stupid, we cannot be saved! No great fish run will help us.

"The village children at our living center are very vulnerable to the slick city dealers!" I point out. He nods. I ask, "We have elders at the senior center who feel left out and deserted by us. Maybe we can get them to come to the student living center and mentor the children; be a rudder, steer them in good directions as was done in the old days." The elder nods.

This has been thought of before, and discouraged by the school. I'm not sure of all the reasons. I went to the living center to help the village kids because I had a foot in both doors. I understood the village, yet I am a white man, born in the city. I volunteered to teach art. I worked in the evening with kids that volunteered to learn from me. We sometimes talked while we worked and reviewed life choices. There were complaints from the school that I was not a certified teacher, not union, taking a job away from a union teacher. My views did not fit the path the school wished to send the children on.

"The school's goal is to integrate these savages into the civilized culture."

I noticed military recruiters around a lot, giving speeches, showing movies to impressionable children about serving their country, becoming a jet pilot, and such. It looked like propaganda to me, that the children should be aware of. I mean, sure, the military is a good choice for some children and the country needs volunteers. However, there should be choices offered, other careers and options discussed equally. Like what I speak of for example. Nothing wrong with hopes of going back to the village with new knowledge, living in older ways, off the land.

One unhappy native teen told me in art class, her family owns a remote lodge and she hopes to get back to help run it. There are several log cabins, a float plane, several river boats. I do not see what is wrong with this goal and dream. The school did not encourage her. The military donates money to the school. I think the children should be aware of this, and what the implications are. The school has a vested financial interest in getting its children into the military. The school is government subsidized. Teaching is government controlled and standardized tests have to be passed.

I tell Iris, "The children are under age; impressionable. It would be illegal to solicit them with your own interests in mind without parent's consent. It seems wrong then to direct children on a career move without offering choices and without parent's knowledge, in an unsafe direction."

I never brought this up, but my overall outlook was frowned on. Being an artist for a living, running sled dogs, fishing, trapping, growing a garden, is what the school is trying to get the kids away from.

'Being poor.' I gather, 'uneducated' is defined as, 'education acquired outside the school.' My volunteer work was not welcomed the following year.

Elders may represent old, outdated ways to be discouraged. Yet it seems to me, older ways are better than drugs and suicide.[2] Leaping into the future without guidance is not going to work. This old Native elder agrees. He says, "Many of the kids sent here are already problem children. The parents or village can't deal with them, so they get sent away, maybe Nenana can help! This is their last chance."

"True, I see that sometimes, but I also see smart parents who want their children to get the best education possible, and want them to have a life, a job. Adapting to the white man world is a good choice for some." I know many graduating from our school get jobs right away, like down in Anchorage at the hospital. I praise this as an excellent choice for the children who are happy to do so. I heard the statistics at one of the community meetings. We both know many college kids have trouble getting jobs and are burdened for many years with student loans. We also know there are jobs in the village, and many do not require a degree. The law requires they go to high school, but high school does not encourage them to ever go back to the village again!

I head home to deal with emails.

Hi Miles;

All I can say, is WOW! What an enjoyable read. Very informative and very entertaining. Nice insight into the transition to village life. I was wondering how you would achieve, describing the transition and do it in an entertaining manner, and you did it in spades. Definitely different than the prior books. Less stories of survival and more of life in the village; which is what it is advertised as being.

The writing style and stories continue to be entertaining and informative. When I first noticed 465 pages, I thought maybe enough information for book and a half or maybe two books! But after reading, I understand why you left off where you did.

It is often good to get an outsiders viewpoint. My good friend Helm thinks I need to continue with the survival stories, The rest is not interesting. If I continue with survival stories I will have to make it fiction, or tell other people's stories. This would be a radical change from one main purpose, to follow changes through the eyes of one person. So I need a variety of views, to see if the changes in my life will be readable.

Emails are caught up on. I am anxious to get out on the river! I write this in my diary:

Monday, May 26, 2014 **Kantishna trip**

This is my first time back to the Kantishna in over a year. Squirrels got in the cabin. Ate through the spray foam on the edges under the eaves. But less damage than previous years. I'm wore out! There's good and bad in such trips. I'm not physically up to it. Engine broke down, battery went dead. I was stopped for an hour on a sand bar andI did not shut electrical drain off. The refrigerator, ham radio, depth gauge and seat warmer were all draining the battery while the engine was not running. Could not start engine. No way to pull start this many horses. My backup booster jumper was no help. I see now I need more amperage capacity in a jumper. Smokey stopped. He is a guide, taking out bear hunters. I know him just a little.

I got totally wore out climbing over my load, back and forth to the battery, then controls, to the toolbox, to the engine. Smokey invited me to his camp at Tolovana. Tolovana is one place I often stop to eat, and transfer fuel. I am stuck only three miles downstream from the camp. My spare four horse takes me to the Tolovana Roadhouse.

The sun is setting as I arrive and the whole sky is purple. There is no wind and the sky is reflected across the surface of the Tanana River...

I recall the trip well, once my memory gets jogged by my diary notes.

I recall the cool weather and that nice sunset. I was having a good time going slow with the little spare motor. Quiet, able to enjoy scenery. This situation is not an emergency. Lucky I have a spare engine and can go all the way back upstream to Nenana fifty miles if I have to. Such a trip may take two days going slow, but nice weather, lots of food. Mostly, my outlook is born of experience. This is home. I am in my element. So all is well.

I am constantly learning! How was I to know this super duper jumper box will not start my engine when it is advertised to start a car! Later, I read that my engine needs 1,000 cranking amps and the jumper box is only 800 amps. I ran aground for a short time, not seriously, 'a little stuck,' requiring shutting the engine off and using a pry pole to work my way loose. I had expected a minute or two. However, the current is pushing me more onto the sandbar, not washing me off! An inconvenience more than anything! I'm thinking 'rats!' a delay of half an hour!

"What is this stupid sandbar doing here anyhow!" It doesn't belong here! But early in the season is a time sandbars can be unpredictable!

Sometimes an ice jam nearby can cause a temporary blockage and unpredictable river currents in areas not normal. The main current can get diverted behind an island with a narrow channel. As the season progresses, the new sandbars and channels sort themselves out. Rivers bottoms here are very soft and silty. There is a lot of shifting. I am traveling faster with the new engine. Not super fast, but thirty-five miles an hour is ten miles an hour faster than I am used to. I have this area memorized. There is no such thing as memorized. One must always pay attention!

Slightly embarrassing, as another boat comes along and here I am! I'm off the sandbar but floating, trying to get the engine going. Swans fly up at the disturbance of the new boat.

"Need any help? Oh, hi, Miles, what's up?" I explain. He replies, "Well, Dude, camp is just a few miles, I have a generator and battery charger there." He could take my battery, charge it, bring it to me tomorrow.

"No, I can run the spare. I'll be along in an hour. Thanks!" I could go downstream all the way to Manley and get charged if I had to. I'd be there before midnight. But yes, good to have someone nearby, with a camp set up.

I arrive, and there are bear hunters in the cabin, all tired from a day of walking and hunting. Not interested in stories. We hook up my battery to the charger. Everyone is ready for early bed time.

"No, I ate on the boat, thanks!" I have a propane camp stove I can set on the seat, and cook while I travel. I have a twelve volt cooler with everything fresh kept cold.

I'm living good! We all laugh. I could feed them better than they could feed me! There are five hunters, covering 100 miles of hunting area.

The trickle charge on the battery runs all night. The generator runs quietly in a shed out back. I am the first one up. I assume these tired hunters will not be up for a few hours. I quietly install my battery in the boat, and take off before 7:00 am. I had helped this guide out in the past, so he helps me.

There is still floating ice to dodge in the river. Even though we would expect high water in spring, the river is low because the water level depends on glaciers melting at higher elevations that have not thawed yet. We have not had the spring rainy season. The air is still freeze dried from winter. This is duck time! All flying up, competing for nesting grounds. Mating, doing dances and calls. The world is alive with sounds. The morning fog is dense, but pretty as the sun rises red. The fog hides my sounds, smells and sight, so I come across game that would normally avoid me.

The new engine is a sleek beast to behold. I can travel any speed I wish. I have nothing better to do, so as I travel, I play with the gauges, and fine tune my travel. I touch the trim, and see my fuel consumption drop by a tenth of a gallon an hour. I increase speed, watch the speed on the GPS. Increase fuel, and do the math to decide how much gas it takes to go 100 miles at this speed. I spend half an hour 'playing,' to save as much as a gallon an hour, or ten gallons in a long day.

It does not follow that, if I burn twenty-five gallons an hour doing twenty miles an hour I will burn five gallons an hour doing forty miles an hour. The increase in fuel consumption for each few miles an hour gained can be amazing! I am burning three and a half gallons an hour doing twenty-eight miles an hour. Four gallons an hour doing thirty miles an hour. Five gallons an hour has me going thirty-eight miles an hour. Eight gallons an hour has me doing forty miles an hour. All this changes a little depending on trim, wind, how the boat is loaded, total weight and quality of the gas. I can trim the nose down and run four inches less draft, but slow up five miles an hour. About every five gallons burned, I can re trim for less weight, and gain a tenth of a gallon of fuel consumption and part of a mile an hour in speed.

Going upstream I can be in the main channel where it is safe, but run five miles an hour slower bucking the current. I can play the slack water off the main current to go faster. This is where many of the underwater sweepers are that I can snag myself on. I have to be much more vigilant! I can run super shallow and gain more speed, even ride the ground effect for ten miles an hour gain, but have only two inches of water below the propeller.

I watch the depth gauge, which tells me the past. By the time I read it, and realize what it means, I have gone 100 feet past that spot before I can react. I might be running six feet of water in the main channel. Suddenly it shows four feet of water. This might mean I just left the channel and can expect even shallower water ahead, so better change course. However, I can expect a drop in depth in every crossing and shortcut. What I look for is the unexpected. A drop in depth I am not expecting. I then become more alert. Is there a new shortcut, new sandbar, did I miss the crossing? Usually, *Oh yes, the main river goes behind the island now.* I can scoot over to follow the new way. I may not make it the long way around.

I can choose safe and easy, take longer and burn more fuel. I often make this choice if I am tired, the weather is bad, or I have a precious or extra heavy load. I may choose saving time and fuel but being more vigilant. Often simply, 'for something to do.' I am staring at the river sitting in one place for hours on end. I can 'fool' with all the factors and do the math, and save two hours and $20 worth of fuel. It can be the difference between getting to my destination at 9:00 pm, my normal bed time, or getting there in the pitch dark at 11:00 pm bone tired. I can pretend I am a boat racer running the Yukon 800 race. Shaving seconds off my time.

My style boat is not known for being safe, or the fastest. It is known for being economical. The fuel consumption is the equivalent of running a twenty horse engine on a sixteen foot boat, with 500 pounds. Mine is twenty-four feet, 115 horses and 1,500 hundred pounds. It is like driving a semi truck for the fuel economy of a VW bug. But no, not very safe. The sides are only a foot high. When I travel, from shore you can see my prop wash and not my boat. It cannot handle waves higher than two feet. I am not the fastest because higher speed makes more of the boat come out of the water, until there is just a foot of boat in the back touching the water, with no width to support all the weight hanging out front.

I began being happy with twenty miles an hour and great fuel economy. Twenty miles an hour is even better economy! However, if I fight a seven mile an hour current, I am only doing thirteen miles an hour. I'm simply not happy with this speed. I tend to settle for twenty-eight miles an hour which is somewhere around three and a half miles per gallon. All this talk about boat speed, balance, fuel consumption? Remember, no gas stations. Out remote, alone where running out of gas can cost thousands of dollars. Likewise, why come home with lots of gas as payload all the way there and back? Most of my boating life, weight cost a dollar a pound per ten miles. Gas is heavy.

I can roughly calculate how much gas it takes to get to the homestead, and usual places I go, by all the trips I have made. I can take into account load size and weight, weather, wind, water depth, current, etc. I can often calculate to the nearest gallon how much fuel is required to go 700 miles. Like sixty-six gallons. Over 450 pounds of fuel.

I fool with the gauges until the fog burns off. A lynx getting a morning drink of water has not heard or seen me. Not paying attention after a long night of hunting. In one leap he jumps up eight feet to the top of the river bank and lands facing me.

Sitting still, watching me as any cat does. Blending in with the raspberry bushes and new grass.

I arrive at the homestead in the usual four hours from Tolovana. The water is too low to get the boat to the pond where I usually tie up. I relay my supplies in the mud, pull the stashed canoe out, over and through the mud, wearing my back brace, totally tired. Not too tired to enjoy the peace and beauty next day. I boat upriver to look for fossils, burls, Chaga, and rocks. Chaga is a fungus growth on birch trees used for tea in Russia, newly introduced as being healthy, fetching big money. I see it as a passing fad, but may as well make money off it. I am stuck in my slough for two hours winching the boat at the very beginning. Luckily I did not wait yet another day and, that I had a come along with me! It was a chore relaying supplies to the canoe, out of the canoe, then sorting barrels for both my fuel and snap on lid barrels for bear proofing supplies.

It seems no matter what, even uneventful trips involve physical labor. I spot a rare five foot diameter diamond willow. I save a four foot section that weighs a hundred pounds. This will be worth some money when the bark is off and wood polished. Guessing $1,000. Such items may set around for years before connecting with the right buyer. I can gather this and that, at no great cost, and afford to sit on it with space to store things. *Can I prove this did not come off federal land though?* I take a picture of the stump and tree, just in case I have to prove a match, on state land. *But the direction things are headed, there will be no state land anyplace. It will all be federal, or should I say Feudal.* I miss being able to hunt geese. As a felon, no guns allowed.

In the thick alders, I find a lone poplar tree with a big burl and cut it down. Along the river's edge I find a stone I call 'braided river.' It is a black jasper like rock with fine white quartz lines all through it that look like the headwaters of a river all braided. I know from experience, this rock takes a nice polish, and is one of the rocks I can sell as local. I stop at some favorite fishing spots and have a lot of fun catching and releasing pike. If I catch a burbot, whitefish, or grayling, I will keep and eat them. Pike has a lot of bones, and is not as sought after.

A newly arrived Kingfisher chirps, and dips down to the water coming up with a finger size meal. This species is a late arrival, often not until midsummer. They live on this year's hatched fish. I cast my lure over by the Kingfisher sitting on a branch over the water, just to see what he will do. He knows the lure is not a fish! It does not scare him, even as the lure hits the water with a loud 'smack.' While I fish, soup for lunch is heating on the propane stove in the boat.

I check my gas filter sediment bowl for water. There is a thimble full of water to drain, so glad I checked.

I'm making such good travel time, I decide to stop and explore some side creeks and lakes along the way. The map is not accurate. The most updated map is based on an aerial photo taken in 1959. Google Earth has not got this far into the wild yet.

A lot has changed in fifty years. Islands are gone, new ones have appeared. In this age of global warming, arctic areas are changing fastest. Permafrost is melting and not coming back. This is what holds the river in place. Now the river is wandering and cutting the banks faster.

There is a creek on the map that I suspect is almost a river today. Hidden behind a small island, the entrance is hardly visible on the side of the river that boaters would not normally be going. I go slow, watching my depth sounder. I have to use power trim to lift the engine in the shallows. Tall dry sedge grass and cattails hide the entrance behind the island. Once past the hidden rampart of tan colors, the world changes. Deep clear water, and carpet of marsh marigold. This will be pretty in a few weeks when the small yellow flowers are out. For now, I see shiny bright green oval leaves thick enough to walk on, an inch off the ground. Far off in the distance is a line of tall spruce trees. There is a sense of vast empty space. A view few others have ever seen. This is not on the map, and is hidden well.

Lots of moose, bear, wolf, and otter tracks let me know local game has found a paradise away from hunters. A school of large whitefish swims in front of the boat. I estimate sixty fish within sight. This small river wanders around the vast field and swampland for at least several miles. I'm not sure where the river comes from. Over a hundred square miles of swampland might be draining here. Local water, not glacier. Melting permafrost could be making a river. I might build a log cabin here and no one would ever know, see, or bother me. Pilots fly over most of the interior, but usually have a destination in mind. There are so many creeks and braided rivers this will go un noticed. Hunters who use planes to explore, cannot land on this water because it twists too much, so there is no straight stretch to land a float plane on. From the air, the entrance looks blocked. The fact of the matter is, the land is so vast, there is plenty of room and places easier to access. I'm impressed my big engine can get me into such shallow small places! I can motor under power in seven inches of water. If the water gets more shallow I can jump out and pull the boat with a rope.

This is not ideal land to set up camp on, it is too wet. I'm not sure I could build here when I look closer—not even an attractive for an area to camp in. However, I have set my boat up to live on. Many boat campers have built a permanent shelter of wood on their boat hull. I have not done this because the shelter adds a lot of wind drag when traveling. An entire shelter slows up speed by over ten miles an hour. Or increases fuel consumption by two gallons an hour and the cost of travel by six dollars an hour. I fold down my passenger windshield to cut down on drag and save a few tenths of a miles an hour when I can. My main priorities are distance and cost. No one else I know can go the distance I go without refueling.

So my answer to a shelter is a folding canopy called a 'Bimmie.' I designed a light nylon top cut to fit the boat with snaps so I can shelter the whole boat and live under it out of rain and cold. Much like a specially designed tent that folds up and stows away in a tote. My plastic totes are color coded on the edge so I can line them up and have a bed, table, and something to sit on. In this way I do not have to leave the boat when camping. I can camp comfortably in a swamp.

Iris has trouble walking around in a world with no sidewalks and cement. She is a city gal. I have hopes if we do not have to get out of the boat, she might come camping with me sometimes. She likes to fish and see the scenery. She loves the bird life, flowers, sunsets. This spot could be a getaway place away from the maddening crowds. I can't tell anyone else how to get here, or hunters will show up.

I toss a small anchor over the bow to keep my boat in place. There are no trees to tie up to. I get out my sleeping pad, and lie down on the bow of the boat in the hot sun and take a nap. As much to be still, quiet, and enjoy the peace than to get sleep. I hear the Kingfisher in the distance. His chirp is easy to identify. When I awake an hour later I am refreshed, revitalized, and my trip home will be safer, since I am more alert.

The rest of the trip home is uneventful. No one is at Tolovana now. I thought the bear hunters might still be here, but they are gone. I stop anyway to walk around, stretch my legs, check everything, transfer some fuel. The new propeller is still not the perfect pitch. I do not want to spend another $150 dollars to check out another option.

"No one runs more than a twenty-two pitch, Miles, usually nineteen is as steep as anyone goes!" I think no matter what pitch I use I cannot dog the engine down. I may simply reach a point it is impossible to go under ten miles an hour at idle speed and slow speed is needed when docking or fishing. I think my boat has a designed hull speed of about thirty miles an hour. No matter what pitch prop I choose, I will not go faster without expending needless energy.

I have floated in the past, many times. It has cost me thousands of dollars to end up in a remote village, then have to fly to civilization with a broken engine, or get parts in. Cost weeks of time. In those days I could not afford the reliable spare engine, the weight, or the space. One year my main engine was not much bigger than my spare today![3] An overpowered engine is much safer hitting bottom. I am not working the engine hard, so when I hit, and stop the engine, I am not stopping a maxed out engine working at its limit. Big horses means beefed up parts.

**Future flash**

A few years from now I have a heart attack and recover. I knew for several years 'something is wrong'. I know my body. It could be a reaction to medications. It might have been any number of things that can possibly go wrong. Liver failure, kidney problems. I knew I have to be careful going out alone as I like to do! Part of 'careful' is having a lot of backups, and luxuries that make life safer for me and more comfortable. All these heaters, fancy electronics is about a choice between not taking any chances, or not getting out alone at all! I bring along things that take the strain away, and still have my alone time and adventures. I recall my early years when I could and would take off for a week with nothing but a small pack with one meal, a knife, and some matches. I lived off the land and toughed out any emergencies. I could not afford to buy or carry what I do now! Part of getting older is being able to afford some nicer things in life. **Future flash ends**

When I get home I install a car solenoid ordered off E Bay for five dollars including shipping. It is hooked up to the key switch so that when the key is turned off the battery is disconnected from the entire electrical system. There can be no mistakes leaving something electrical on by accident that drains my battery and leaves me dead in the water!

I add a ham radio to the electrical circuit. I passed my ham test and am KL1VC. I can only use seventy cm and two meter. I believed early on, this is all I needed since our Nenana hill has amateur radio repeaters on it that reaches further then cell phones. The barge line, the police and ham operators used it. However, the economy affects life on every level with no funding for this and that. The city refused to pay the $40 a month electric bill to the tower. Big companies put up taller towers and more repeaters on the hill—cell towers and TV towers that create interference with ham signals.

Amateur ham does not have band width priority over other needs. Reliable coverage is getting discouraging. I may have to go for the next level, the general license. *All it takes is money!* The next level radio antenna cost much more! I could have $500 into minimal used equipment.

"One advantage Iris, is once you get the license and radio, the costs end. Talking is free. Unlike the cell phone that cost to talk with a monthly plan. Plus, there is a record of all cell calls that can be retrieved. Cell phones can be tracked. Ham radio is an infinite number of frequencies, unrecorded, untraceable, after the call stops. That increases the chances of having a private conversation. Or at least a conversation the government has not eaves dropped into, or might subpoena later." To avoid what already happened.

"*Do you know this person? If not, why were you at their address for two hours on June 12$^{th}$? Can you explain that!?*" My cell phone was off. Everyplace that cell phone has ever been can be traced, and was. For four years. I read the search warrants for the banks, pay pal, the cell phone company. Every one of them leapt forward. "How may we be of service, Sir! Compromise our customers? No problem, here you go. Let us know if we can be of further service." I read the transcripts. The public gets told how valued we are as customers, how our information is confidential, how we will be defended, they are working for us! Our privacy and security is sacred to us! "Voluntarily help the government bring you down? Not us!" I suspect without even a warrant there is cooperation. Possibly out of fear? But by the grace of God, it might have been them, or can be next time!

Ham is about ordinary people talking to each other with no hidden agenda. Not recording us, keeping track in order to hurt us. All over the world, we can talk to like minded people. Who believe in freedom. Not necessarily 'private' but, just us citizens outside a stored retrievable data base.

"Cell phones are not designed to be long range. They have no big antenna. They depend on being within calling distance of a cell tower, within twenty miles of civilization. Where we are wanted. The older analog bag phones hat could reach a tower fifty miles away were better for remote people." Bag phones are obsolete. Deliberately so. Remote people were flat out told, "There is no way to trace the call. We have to be able to know where you are." A requirement after 911, and national security issues.

I tell Iris, "I was asked by friends, who I thought was involved when the towers were flown into on 911. My first gut feeling was, our own government! Or at least they knew or let it happen. I was asked 'why?' For the same reasons Roosevelt allowed Pearl Harbor to get bombed by the Japanese. It got us in the war, and increased funding for the government." I said at the time, "The proof will be in the future and what happens." Increased security, increased secrecy, government spending in general, and support of recent wars. A total win for the government. Why wouldn't officials be glad, supportive, even the cause? "Why would you think such an evil thing?" The way to know you have the answer with complete confidence, is if you created, and were in control of the problem.

"In the same way I think Norton Antivirus for our computers, creates the viruses it then sells us protection against."I notice the timing. An email from Uncle Norton. "Big new virus infects data bases around the world! Be afraid! You too are at risk!" Followed only a month later with the breaking news "Good news, what a relief! For only $10.99 we have an updated solution that completely fixes your risk of invasion by this deadly bug!" I assume the majority will give a sigh of relief and call Uncle Norton their hero, gladly fork over the funds. "After all, isn't computer security worth it!?"

In exasperation I explain what I see as a big picture. One of the secrets to success with big money and power is control. Control the problem; control the solution. It doesn't take a rocket scientist or business expert to figure that out. It's been used throughout history. Get rid of the buffalo to control food, then offer the solution, government hands out food. I believe the same is being done today with fish and wildlife, seeds and methods of storing food. Create a problem, have sympathy, then offer a solution. Not even 'create' the problem. That's tacky and risky. More like, create an atmosphere in which it is predicted a problem will inevitably present itself in a predictable manner. Deliberately let a weakness exist, and simply wait. Pit two sides against each other. Poke, prod now and then. Show favoritism. Gently steer and orchestrate the news, the flow of energy. Allow or create an unfair situation. When a problem arises as in "Da!" Offer a solution with a hook.

"Do you have any proof of any of this, Miles!?"

"No! And I do not want any proof, either." I do not have to prove it. I grab enough snippets of information from a thousand incidents and events, and piece it together.

**Future Flash**

It is 2016. I have been handed a book by a friend to read and pass around. The WIN group, 'Wellness in Nenana,' sometimes discusses local problems. Among the issues is drugs. We discuss the term 'War on drugs'. We wonder if the war is being won or even a correct tactic. The book I am handed is, "Chasing The Scream" by Johann Hari. The book studies the beginning of the war on drugs. I am only on the first chapter as I edit this 'book 7'. Some of what I write and more firmly believe seems far out to me. I want to deny it. Want to believe I am wrong and paranoid.

"Not my government! It's just rumors, just a few people. Just a few isolated cases! Just me talking when I am feeling down and angry. Someone prove to me it's all in my head!" "I do not want to be a nut case, one of those pessimistic radicals!"

Others notice what I notice, who keep better records, and look stuff up and prove stuff, quote important people.

"This is hard for us to believe today, but the position of every official in the U.S. law enforcement until the 1960s from J. Edgar Hoover on down was that the mafia was a preposterous conspiracy theory, no more real than the Loch Ness Monster."

I remember the late 50s and 60s and recall this line of thinking, so believe it. A guy named Harry Anslinger was obsessed with the mafia. To sum it up he becomes head of a new department, 'Drug and Alcohol'. The department was not big. In 1914 cocaine and heroin were outlawed. There were not a lot of addicts. Harry wanted his department to be bigger. He began noticing isolated news events like a New York Times article, "Mexican Family Goes Insane" A widow and her four children have been driven insane by eating the Marihuana plant."

Until now, Harry had dismissed cannabis as non-addictive; not related to violent crimes. But almost overnight he began arguing the opposite. He argues the two most feared groups in the country; Mexicans and the Africans were taking this drug more than white people. Harry presented a nightmarish version of where this could lead to the House Committee on Appropriations. He wrote thirty scientific experts asking a series of questions concerning marijuana. Twenty nine wrote back saying it would be wrong to ban it, and marijuana was falsely represented in the press. Anslinger decided to ignore them and quoted the single expert who believed it was a great evil that had to be eradicated. "Marijuana turns man into a wild beast!"

The end result being Harry got the funding he was seeking to move forward with ambitious plans. Various cases were recorded of the evils of drugs. Not the truth. I recall the 60s and the stories my friends and I heard about the evils of weed. We knew people who smoked and most smoked themselves, so these stories told by scientists and the government seemed odd. I'm sure it lead to major distrust among my peers of the government in general.

"Where are they getting their facts?" Followed by, "But how could they be wrong? After all, it's the government and top scientists!"

His advice on drug raids was always kill first. It was not only scientists he had to silence. He had the famous jazz musician Billie Holiday killed, the book gives believable hard evidence. Harry Aslinger was told that there were also white women just as famous as Billie who had drug problems, but he responded to them quite differently. Judy Garland was a heroin addict. Harry had a friendly chat and let her go. 'Because it would destroy the unblemished reputation of one of the nation's most honored families.'

The argument we hear today for the drug war is that we must protect teenagers from drugs, and prevent addiction in general. We assume this is why the war was started. But it is not. The main reason given for banning drugs was that the blacks, Mexicans, and Chinese were using these chemicals, forgetting their place, and menacing white people. Harry told the public that "the increase in drug addiction is practically 100% among negro people." The Harrison act was passed.

A typical New York Times headline of the time reads "Negro Cocaine Fiends New Southern Menace" A police chief was informed a previously inoffensive negro with whom he was acquainted was running amuck. In a cocaine frenzy he attacked the chief and the chief shot him point blank in the heart, and the negro did not die, did not even stagger the man! Cocaine is turning blacks into superhuman hulks who could take a bullet in the heart without flinching. Getting rid of the white powder would render black Americans docile and on their knees again. The man who killed Billie Holliday said, "Where else but in the Bureau of Narcotics could a red blooded American boy lie, kill, cheat, steal, rape, and pillage, with the sanction and blessing of the All-highest."

This covers just the first chapter. Quoted because I believe it. I am a product of this era. I recall the news articles, the attitude. I had mostly forgotten, and did not want to recall. I tip toe out of 'all that' to go live in peace with bears and wolves. Many of the conclusions I am coming to on my own are mirrored in these words. My observation is, other agencies, other policies, both government and large companies that run the world, are woven from the same thread. Not much has changed today in more modern times. **Future flash ends**

The proof is in predictability. Like the twin towers. I said at the time, "Watch and wait. I think I know what the future holds." Detectives say, 'Follow the money.' Or, 'Who has the most to gain, that's our first suspect. And, 'Usually someone you know, a family member. Rarely is the guilty some total stranger you never heard of, who does not know you. In many cases, look for an inside job.

"So, Miles, we have digressed. What does all this have to do with ham radio!"

"Connect the dots," is all I say. I laugh. *A Morse code dit, dit, dot joke.*

Survival is keeping as much control as possible over that which is a requirement for life. Communication is one of the requirements of life for social animals like man. Right up there with food, fire, water, and air.

If you want to control people you need to control any one of four needs and you own the world. Power = money. Freedom is Food = knowing what it is, where it comes from, how to get it yourself. Fire = how to keep warm, be in control of how to stay warm. Shelter = owning it. Water and air = having a good source you are in control of. Communication = how to reach like minded people without a lot of outside help. Communication is knowledge. Knowledge is power. Isolation is a form of control. It's about being in a position to say, "No thank you, not interested," in deals and compromises you are not comfortable with. It's about not being between a rock and a hard place; not being in a position to be extorted.

This to me is the essence of freedom. *No one can run our life as well as we can, because no one cares as much about it, or knows as much concerning what we want and what is best for us.*

BY THE END of May the greenhouse is running seriously, with some plants four feet tall. There are about 100 tomato plants started from our own heirloom seeds, now five generations old.

"What are you working on now, Miles?"

I hate to even begin explaining. I decide to keep it simple. "Modifying a temperature control switch." I get an, 'Oh', and that's the end of that.

My old switch got water in it; corroded bad enough it stopped working after fifteen years of service. I buy a simple in line cord temperature switch that turns on heat tape for electrical pipes to stop them from freezing. They cost four dollars. I take this apart, and flip the bimetal strip around, bend it and play with it. Now, instead of turning on at low temperature it turns on at high temperature. I bend it until it turns on at eighty degrees. Off at seventy degrees. A big fan is put in this line. Louvers cover the fan, the window closed when cold. When the fan comes on at eighty degrees, the louvers open as the fan blows hot air out of the greenhouse. Until the temperature drops back down to 70 and shuts off, louvers close, and all is well with the plants.

The old watering timer still works - the mercury tilt switch on a balance rod with a sponge on one end. When the sponge dry, so is the soil; weights get moved to adjust balance. Sponge gets wet like the soil. Sponge gets heavy, weight moves, tilts switch, switch shuts off. It might happen five times a day, or once a week, depending on the soil needs.

All this only helps, and is not perfect. I have several hundred plants. It would take a while to manually take care of watering each plant. By my methods, there might be a few plants that get too wet, or too much air by the fan. I have to move a few plants. I have to hand water a handful. No more than fifteen minutes a day. I can leave them alone for a week or more with no great loss. I'm constantly fooling with drippers, misters and timers. My system is not as efficient as a commercial system. I'd expect a 20% loss if I left it on its own for several weeks. Iris would rather come in spending hours a day to take care of the plants manually. I see the logic in that. It's relaxing, nice to fool in the greenhouse. If that was my only hobby.

More than just growing our own food, I am making knives, running the river, writing, attending city meetings, and just doing a lot of things. The compromise is, not any one project gets my full attention all the time. The main priority with the garden is simply having it available and functioning. We could, in theory, live all year on what we grow, along with what we harvest from the wild. We do not, but it is nice to know how, have the ability, the space, everything in working order. If store food, or funds, suddenly were not available, I could be taking care of those needs within a week. The simple joy of it all is secondary, though a nice secondary benefit. Another advantage, is being able to have lots of hanging baskets of flowers around the yard. We could not afford to buy them! We set out at least fifty baskets! We also plant flowers directly into the yard here and there along the various paths. Flowers attract insects that pollinate our vegetables. The neighbor's honey bees come here for example.

"Miles, have you got those nice black prince tomatoes? I got the starts from you last year and the tomatoes had so much flavor! I need more!" I sell a few four inch pots of tomatoes, cucumber, and vegetable starts. A total of $35. I rarely make much more per customer. The goal is to reach $300 a season, which is what I figure are my costs. This might be the year to do that. Over time, the locals have been happy with my plants that were started right here in the village with our local soil.

"That's bound to be an improvement over starter plants from big outside companies selling cheaper plants, imported from Mexico using chemicals to keep them looking good." Those are however, cheaper. I often say, "Do you want cheap, dead plants or healthy live ones for a little more money?" I try to play the "Buy local" card. I commonly hear, 'Well, yes, my Walmart plants all died last year, but it must have been my fault.' It could not possibly be Walmart's fault, they are a huge reputable company, and, after all, who am I? That's hard to argue with.

Not as many people buy my flowers as I would like. I tend to prefer wild flower mixes, not the usual domestic kinds. My arrangements are not as spectacular, but often more hardy for our cool weather, and they bloom longer. The big stores want their flower baskets to look best the day you buy them. What happens after that is not their problem. There are plant drugs they can jack them up with.

The plants are not often adjusted to our weather, but raised in a greenhouse, imported from a nicer climate. I sprinkle new seeds on top of the soil after transplanting flowers in the basket. So about the time the blooming plants wind down, the seeds sprout adding greenery, and in a month take over with flowers. My baskets are actually prettier in a month than when you buy them. Few understand this concept, it's not normal customer buying-thinking.

"Miles, I like the strawberry plant in the middle of the basket. Good idea! I can walk by and grab something to eat among the decorative flowers!" I do that on purpose of course. Sometimes there is a cherry tomato plant in with the flowers.

"It's just that locals tend not to want to pay much!" We notice. *It's local, so it must be cheap. It's someone I know so I do not have to pay as much, I can rip off local and get away with it.* A majority would rather go to Fairbanks for all their needs. Rather discouraging for all locals in every line of business. Local business is also at fault. A few of our business people take advantage of the good will of locals, and make profits off local donated time and energy. To the extent there is lack of trust, commitment, and loyalty. This effects all of us.

Nenana no longer has a Chamber of Commerce. When I was head of the Chamber, one of my goals was to police ourselves and maintain a minimum standard of ethics, that gains back the trust of the citizens. The community struggles as an entity. This may be the price we pay for improved roads and being now a suburb of a bigger place. We just commute. We do not depend on each other as we used to do. I do not see us as being a happier community for it. A couple of the largest business in Nenana have a monopoly, control the community, and do not allow the equality some of us strive to create. Those of us who compete, cannot do so in our community. The internet and shows outside the community now must support me, not my trusted community.

Cart of plants get hardened in. I roll cart in the house at night till night temperatures are above freezing.

Photo Section

My great grandmother holding my mother.

My father in Hawaii in 1951 the year I was born.

My sister as I remember her - happy, with long blonde hair.

Me and my sister before our parents got divorced.

Baby peregrine falcons in a nest that fell off a cliff down to the water's edge. The mother seems to be raising them here just fine. I was three feet away taking the picture, and left them undisturbed.

Moose antler natural sheds piled on a barge. Acquired in a remote village.

I arrive at my homestead with load of supplies to spend some time fishing.

The Russian gal mentioned who had an interest in me, as a fossil hunting partner arrangement.

I get my moose with a bow. As a felon I can't have a firearm. I depend on moose for my year's supply of meat.

One of my custom chef knives.

Salvaging my boat after it sinks.

My great grandfather Erving on my mother's side, in Maine. He had to take both sisters on when he married one.

I do not drive, so I pick up my mail with a snow machine.

Me with a nice pike. I'm sort of retired now.

Only Indians are allowed to ride in this community van. I joke I should label a van 'White Council' for Whites only. Truthfully, I do not like discrimination.

My only picture in uniform. I'm eighteen in the navy.

Foil and I move shed.

When I travel the rivers I stop at places like this looking for rocks for my art work.

Trumpeter swans are common along rivers I travel.

Tolovana lodge mentioned a lot as a favorite stopping place. Locals have use of it when traveling.

SECRETLY WILD

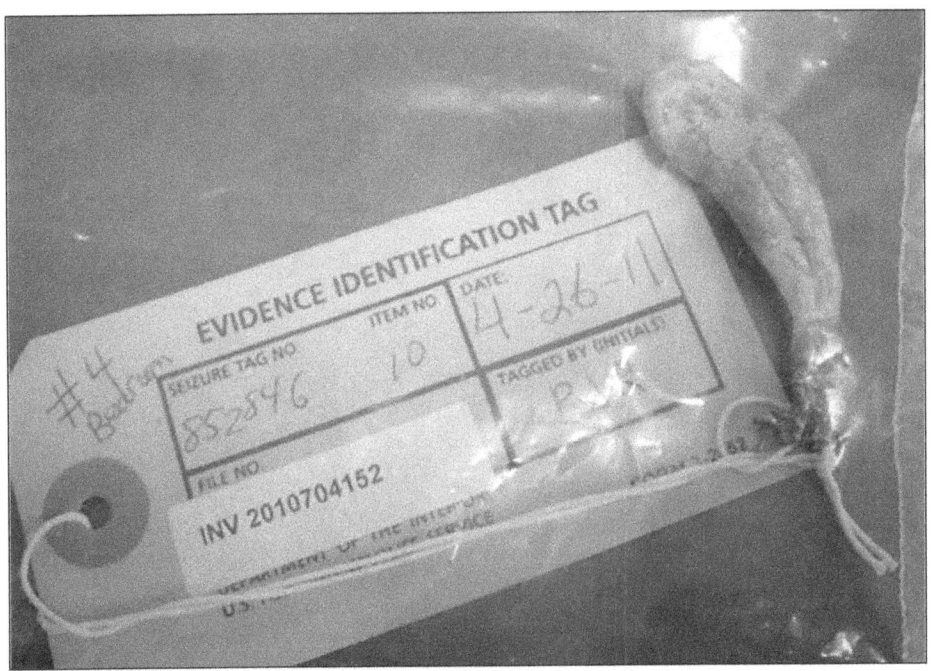

This tooth is clearly an old legal fossil. Marked as an illegally killed bear worth ten years in prison.

Slicing local birch root into sellable slabs.

SECRETLY WILD

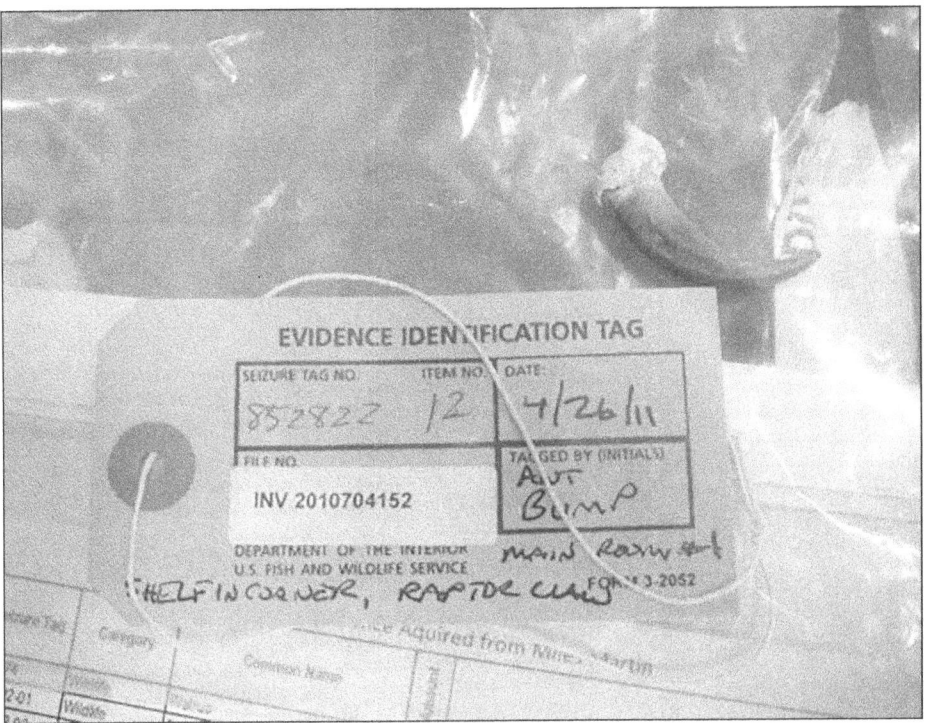

Many confiscated items such as this were mislabeled. This is clearly a wolf claw. Labeled as an illegal raptor (eagle) claw, worth a $250,000 fine and ten years in prison. In my plea agreement in order to get 'only' six months jail time, and minimal fine, I had to admit this is an illegal eagle claw.

**City of Nenana**
PO Box 70, Nenana, Alaska 99760
907-832-5501, 907-832-5503-fax
http://www.nenana.org

To Whom It May Concern:

I have been asked to relate an experience that occurred while attempting to obtain information and permits relative to the possession, purchase and sale of possibly regulated animal parts that are encountered during the course of business of operating a gift shop.

We have had in the past opportunities to acquire items from around Alaska to be placed either in a gallery setting or for resale as Native Alaskan artwork.

Prior to acquisition, research was done in order to ensure that all the pertinent laws, rules and regulations were known and abided by.

Research in one instance indicated that a federal permit may be needed for the acquisition of a specific item. Contact was made to both State and Federal authorities. The State of Alaska indicated that it was possible the acquisition may be illegal however they were not sure and recommended calling the Federal agency responsible for enforcing the regulations. Upon contact with the Federal agency, the immediate response was one of suspicion with a query of why I needed a permit and what object had I purchased. The conversation continued with an accusatory tone and did not result in any assistance toward furthering permit information.

My point with this letter is not to cast a negative outlook on the agencies responsible for enforcing the law but to bring to light the points of the extreme difficulty in obtaining information regarding the regulation, permits and the process as well as the overtly suspicious attitude of those that were contacted for assistance.

It would be very advantageous to all if a central database was available for reference as well as a checklist of documents needed for trade items.

Thank you,
Jason P. Mayrand

Letter of support for me from the Nenana Mayor. Mayor relates an incident he was involved in showing how hard it is to know what is legal concerning wildlife parts.

This letter concerns the mayor trying to find out if it is legal to offer certain wildlife art in the Nenana Cultural Center museum either for sale or simply display. I have been an official buyer for this museum with the authority to acquire objects of cultural or economic interest for the community. Museums have specific exemptions when an item is for public display and scientific historical interest.

>This letter reads in part:
>Prior to acquisition, research was done in order to insure all pertinent laws rules and regulations were known and abided by....

The State indicated that it was possible the acquisition may be illegal, however they were not sure. The federal agency's response was one of suspicion, with a query of why I needed a permit, and what object had I purchased. The conversation continued with an accusatory tone, and did not result in any assistance toward furthering permit information.

The mayor just wanted to point out how difficult is it to get information and know what is legal and what permits might be needed. As an authorized buyer for the museum I have been put in the same position. Since there was no trial after being charged, the subject never came up, as to whether any items I had were for the museum. Items were confiscated from my bedroom, and a drawer in a locked room clearly marked "Not for sale." The plea bargain was not a discussion as expected. I was handed in writing, an ultimatum.

Take what is offered or go to trial.

# CHAPTER EIGHT

## A PARTNER NOT WORKING OUT, MOVE A SHED

"Miles! Joe Miller is coming to Nenana to campaign!" I'm interested because we met and talked a while back. He was doing a commercial and wanted to use my moose antlers in the background. A woodland setting, while he spoke of saving wildlife and what an outdoorsman he is. He wants the village vote. But what is really the agenda? We had a chance to talk one on one while taking the pictures. Joe shows up at the park across the street with a picnic and free food. I show up, and eventually get him aside. He wants to promote his ideas, so is willing to talk to locals. I ask him about his outdoor interests, and express concern for the future of subsistence. We speak of the Native preference issue differences between the State and Federal Governments.

Joe tells me, "Yes, I was told in the past not to give the Natives any trouble! No natives will be arrested for fish and wildlife violations." He goes on later, "Rest assured... Bla, bla."

I did not hear what he promised. Whatever I wanted to hear, I think. On his cheat sheet of places and things, 'Nenana' would be listed as a traditional Native subsistence village. His advisors may have suggested, 'Stand up for the Indian here.' Because I used the key-in word, 'subsistence', I think he assumed I am Native. I do have a dark tan from being outdoors a lot, am short, could pass for Athabaskan. I note his admission, there is an effort to specifically protect the Native, who is outside the law on fish and wildlife matters.

Though he might tell an Anchorage crowd, "Rest assured, I am here to protect trophy hunting and I belong to the NRA!" Rah rah rah!

Iris points out, "Joe did not seem pleased when he said he is told to leave the

Indians alone. Nor did he say he supported that, only that he has orders from above." Politics is about reading between the lies. I rather enjoy politics if the truth be known. I'm an expert at playing with words.

OUR FRIEND from Tucson shows up as expected. He wants an Alaska vacation. Good to see Foil! Joe Miller is off my mind. Foil needs to get to Fairbanks to shop for food and supplies. He is staying with us until he gets settled in someplace. We are not sure how this will go. He wants to go to the homestead. I assume I will take him there and leave him for a while as he wishes.

"Miles, the first stop is Walmart, so I can get food and other supplies."

"Foil! Usually Walmart is the last place I go, after seeing if local shops have what I need." Usually when I bring visitors to Fairbanks to shop, they are grateful for the ride, and get food and supplies where I do, at the same time I do, without demanding special stops.

"Well sure, ok, but I am used to Walmart, and know how they are set up, that's all. Anyhow, we cannot stop progress and the way things are. It is true, as you say, Walmart is just cheap, and in return for the good price we lose local shops, small time sellers, even American made. I am with you, and want to support local crafts, local made, and keep local jobs intact."

What I hear from Foil is, the bottom line is price and convenience. The bottom line for me is, Foil is our guest. Iris and I bring Foil to town to tag along, to get what he needs at places we stop. We are not his taxi. He is not paying us. We are politely saying we do not shop at Walmart. End of conversation. *You want to argue, you can get out of the car. Iris is still uncomfortable driving in Fairbanks on roads and going places she is not familiar with. It is not necessary to bring up personal issues with someone not close to us.*

"What difference does it make, Miles? All the products in all the stores come from the same source, China. No matter where you shop, you support China!" I understand many, even most big companies have moved overseas.

The sign on the lavatory at Freddie's says 'Men.' It's not written in Spanish for the convenience of Spanish speaking people. I feel like I am in America. The employees are local hire. Not clerks with accents I can't understand. I spot food bought locally with 'Alaska grown' symbols. Fred Meyers is smaller, so I get more personal service. I know Charles, the produce manager. He points out the most fresh, the best price, hands me items he is about to throw out, and discounts them. In return, I shop exclusively here for produce. I believe in loyalty. My heart is with small communities where everyone knows each other. Again, not an issue I wish to defend and argue. I let it go.

We stop where Foil wants. I'm more resentful when Foil takes his time. Judging from the crowds, the whole world likes Walmart, too. Support local and American made are just empty slogans to chant. I agree there are some items that have the reputation of being a better product, and I do seek them from overseas. Large ticket items like Honda and Yamaha outboard engines. Though I ended up with an American Mercury outboard.

Foil has asked me to teach him my secrets, how to live subsistence. All about my lifestyle. It starts here. Where to shop.

'Know who you buy from. Trust your supplier.' Possibly I pay a little more. Maybe not. I know Charles, so he points out the deals. Knowing who you bought from can be important if there is a problem with a product and it needs to be returned. Iris says to Charles, "We got avocados a few weeks ago and we were disappointed, they were black inside. Maybe they were frozen and thawed before getting put out?"

"No, that should not have happened. Sorry to hear that. Here are some fresh ones." A replacement, because Charles knows us as regulars. Would Walmart treat you like that? "Si Senior, no receiptio? No ablo can helpio." Service is especially important when you are both poor, and out remote depending on the supplies you have. When you trust your supplier, you have more trust in the product. This leads to more confidence in the wilds. You can depend on things your life depends on. It is normal for ordinary warranties to be void because of how we live. We cannot return the item in a timely manner. We used the item for something not listed on the package. A reliable local who knows you, trusts you, as you trust them, is more likely to cover honest product failures, and perform repairs with care. A local deals with other locals and has a feel for how this product works in your environment and will tell you. These are reasons to support specific places you like and trust.

"Foil, I got a chainsaw at Rods, he handed me a spare plastic part. He says, 'This part on the saw has not been holding up well in our extreme Alaska weather. A lot of customers have reported this plastic breaking. It's not critical but is the rewind you need. It's easy to put in if it breaks.' He knows 'easy and cheap' is not the point if you live remote and depend on this saw. Rod is honest, knows and cares that I am a repeat customer, so treats me right. Walmart would have some kid at the counter who does not know what a chainsaw is, nor care. If you asked about it's reliability in the cold he would roll his eyes up. How would he know. How would he find out? His boss would label you a problem person. It's under warranty; you have no worries! Till it fails you 500 miles in the wilds. With Rod, you got that spare part in the toolbox." I can tell by his expression Foil does not get it, is not listening; has his own way to shop.

"It's time to renew the boat registration, Dear. The notice arrived in the mail." I go through the roof ranting and raving. Nothing irks me more than permits. "It's no big deal, Honey, just pay it." The fee is low and good for three years. It comes across as no big deal. Unless or until it is denied. It's a form of control. It's a form of having information. Where I am, where my boat is, how to find me and my boat. Who owns the boat? "Why is that a big deal, Miles?"

"It may not be the government's business if I own a boat or not. What if I want to own something and not have the government know? What if I want to build a boat and the government will not register it because a government inspector did not approve it? My boat is rated for forty horses, and I have 115 horses. What if the government realizes this, and considers this illegal? It's unsafe, can't be registered! It's illegal to have a boat with a 700 mile cruising range because the government may not know where I am."

I think I'd have trouble getting my houseboat registered if I built one today. I built it in the 70s and had a conversation at a boatyard over its engine parts. 'How did you get it approved?' I had laughed, "I am from Alaska! We do not need anyone's approval!"

I have no choice. I write out a check and renew the boat registration and wonder if there is a place on the planet one might have a boat with no numbers on it; that never got inspected. Some free place that matches my dreams.

"It's not the money, Iris; it's not about the money." If I could hand over $10,000 to be left alone I would. "Here's the money. In return you do not get my name. Go away, leave me in peace." I hear there are countries like this. You simply pay the local official and he leaves you alone. No records are kept. *Grumble, grumble; permits! Humph!*

"And, Miles, you haven't changed the numbers on your boat. I reminded you they are the wrong size!" I had put 'numbers' on my town list. I saw a package of numbers that had a picture of a boat on it. I therefore assumed these are boat numbers. How big a deal can this be? No. The numbers have to be three inches tall. These are only two. I'd like a little flapper, that when I pull the string, changes the numbers or blocks them out. Because I want to get away with something and not get caught? Not especially. I suppose for the same reasons I would not want the mark of the beast tattooed to my forehead. Half the boats on the river have no numbers at all. Most are Native. Natives are exempt. *For now.* Their time of gloating shall end.

"A time will come, Iris, when the rivers will be like the roads. There will be a camera up and all traffic will be known. Every time a boat goes by, there is the number on the screen. That number is fed into a computer and recorded, so a pattern of behavior is charted. Did this boat go by the day before moose season opened? 'Look, I do not see lifejackets on all the passengers!' An automatic ticket will be generated and sent by a robot.

I point out that already, in town, a camera catches your car number and the fact you were speeding. A computer automatically sends out a ticket. We pay on line, a computer accepts the money and another computer spends it. No human was involved in the process. Who would you complain to, or contest the ticket with? The computer?

Working with Foil. It seems like no big deal when spring arrives, and here is Foil. He wants me to boat him up to the homestead. He has arrived early in spring. Sadly, spring is late. Still ice. *No can go to the homestead.*

"I need a storage place here in Nenana, Miles. You know, a place to keep a truck, boat, a few supplies locked up. Can you help me find some cheap lot here in Nenana?" I know of such a lot a few blocks from me. Gravel pad, small log cabin tucked in the woods no one pays attention to. Owner has been gone twenty years. Might be for sale.

The owner knows me! So is willing to do a killer deal. $3,500. It's worth $35,000. This seller has money. He forgot about his Nenana property. It's only $62 a year for taxes. Foil only offers $3,300 and 'whatever'.

Foil is excited and says, "Miles, this can be both of ours as part of our deal! Now you have a place to store stuff you need to get off your property! See, we can help each other!" He tells me he is leaving his wife. It will be just him here. Tired of her. She's a money drain, lazy, etc. I wouldn't know. Foil implies I need to leave my woman. She doesn't treat me right. "Miles, you need to be partnered up with me, back out in the wilds where you belong! Get back to the life you really love, Miles!" He thinks it is because of my woman I seem so irritable. "You are not a good listener, Miles. I told you what I was doing, but you chose not to pay attention so I am not going to bother to tell you again."

"It's not that I was not listening, Foil. I have never done this before, and did not understand what you were saying." We are trying to work together to move a small building with hardly any equipment. The professionals said they would not, could not, do the job. In my opinion that means the job will be difficult for non professionals. We should expect the job to go slow, and have challenging obstacles. It appears to me, while I may not be a good listener, Foil is an equally bad teacher. We are both used to being the boss or working alone. Except Foil tells me he owns and runs a landscape business with employees. He says it is a very successful business. I assume then, he knows how to work with people.

"G=-";/.- and Da*[']\\/.,! Miles! You F*&==! How can you be so ignorant! Do I have to do everything!" Foil is telling me how much I have screwed up this job and made it so much harder for him.

I calmly reply, "Yelling isn't going to help teach me, get me to work harder, make me smarter, care about the job more, or help get the job done better, faster, or more safely. If you do this sort of job all the time, you know more than I do about it. Where I know more about the lifestyle you want me to teach you, out in the wilds."

We are using a 1984 four wheel drive truck I just acquired, so do not know much about it. I do not drive. All I use the truck for is launching my boat and I have done so only three times. The truck has a ball hitch on the back to hook the boat trailer to. The job is moving two sheds. Moving the first shed requires unhooking the boat trailer, and hooking up a small cart that was given to me. I have never used it before except with the four-wheeler to haul wood once.

It had been my idea to use the cart to move the sheds we got killer deals on when buying. Previously I had used a handyman jack to get both sheds a foot up off the ground in preparation for what we both thought would be a big fork lift that we'd pay to come in and move them. Power lines are in the way! There is a mowed lawn to consider. The big equipment would seriously tear up the lawn. The property is being rented, and neither the renters or landlord would want a ruined lawn. It is even possible the killer deal we got buying them, had to do with the fact they might not be able to be moved.

Foil's argument is to work as fast as we can because it is dangerous. "We need to keep the time of danger down to a minimum!" I agree there are some critical times when speed is important. I do not agree on basic principal, that fast is safe. There are less critical 'stopping points' where we can rest, step back, reassess the job, make adjustments or modifications to the process as we go. But we will do it Foil's way because the first shed to move is his, and because I assume he has more experience.

"G*&/?* Da*&.>! You can't put that block down first! That will never hold the rest! I thought you knew better. I can't be two places at once!"

I get an idea what type of personality Foil has when working under stress. We have never really worked together on a hard job. Foil has helped me at the Tucson show selling art, providing rides, doing favors. I assumed at first, he is just a nice guy who likes to help others. I have been getting more streetwise as I spend time in civilization. A time came I wondered why this guy is being so helpful so often. I suspected a hidden agenda. I suspected, because I saw Foil around others, and Foil does not seem to be a likable, or good, kind person. He yells at his wife, I'd say to the point of being abusive.

The hitch on the cart we are using is not the same size as the ball on the truck. The sheds are blocked up and the cart is under, and suddenly we cannot hook the trailer up to the truck. In my mind, the shed is successfully up on blocks, with the trailer under it if the blocks wobble and the shed slips. The shed will fall two inches onto the cart. Not the end of the world. This situation is not good, but not critical. I have the right size ball in the shop. We simply need to switch balls out. This requires finding the ball, and dealing with the rusted one on the truck. This may take time.

Foil goes ballistic, "*&^%$#@ Miles! Do I have to do everything! I told you to get prepared! You were supposed to look over everything and get what we need! Well, hurry up G*&^%D*&^%$ it! I haven't got all day! I trusted you to take care of this."

Implying of course that he did his part so this is my fault; he is smart and on the ball while I am stupid and lazy. I recognize this behavior. Once again, yelling and being insulting is not helping the job get done better. My outlook is, no one goofed or is responsible. One step at a time. This is a difficult undertaking with challenges. This is not what we do for a living, so we learn as we go. This is not a learning experience that is dangerous and costly, so why sweat the small stuff? If this step took an hour or even a day, there is time.

"God *&^%$# it, Miles, don't you know anything! That blade in the saw is not going to work! It's the wrong blade for steel!"

Here he goes all over again yelling and insulting me. Ok, I did not know. I got what was sold as a universal blade. I have cut small bolts with it and been happy. I never tried cutting anything major. I do not work with big steel objects. I do not cut and weld in my normal line of work. I do know a little bit about a great many things. There would be a polite kind way of informing me I might try another specialty blade for such projects, let me know such blades exist. I'm only thinking, I do not yell at Foil when he does not understand how to read the river, or use a GPS, or how to know a good edible mushroom from a poisonous one. I politely teach him. How would he know? I understand I am not going to be working with Foil again. I will politely have other things to do. We manage to get the sheds moved in, blocked up where we want them.

It is clean up time back where we got the sheds. Foil had disconnected the satellite dish cable supports on site so we could lay it on the ground and drive over it instead of trying to fit under it. We now have to hook it back up as an after job clean up. There had been an issue taking it down.

"Miles, the home is occupied. The landlord told me the renters were not going to be here for another two weeks, but here they are anyhow two weeks early! So screw them!" Adding, "Some foreigners of some kind, the hell with them."

I wonder what the confrontation was. I wasn't there. The lady renter is watching me out the window. I unhook the cable and she comes out. Asks me if I unhooked her cable TV. Well, Dah! She just watched me. I wonder what Foil said exactly. Apparently the woman wanted Foil to talk to her husband on the phone. Foil had told her he does not need to talk to the husband, forget it. We are doing a job that is none of her business. She has not lost her precious cable TV connection. We have just lowered the line. But she does not know that. She's a new renter and a stranger in a strange land. I wonder, if I should even now, go talk to the family and explain what is going on. But Foil assures me he is used to dealing with people on their property in his line of work. He knows best how to handle these kinds of situations.

"Hurry up God *&^%$it, we don't have all day, crank on that winch so I can hook this up!"

We have to winch on the dish cable, so it can be fastened to the hook on the house. The tension is getting great. I want to stop and figure out why we have to get it so tight. But Foil is in a hurry. "I can't hold this all day, pull God*&&^%$ it!" More cussing, no discussion. I feel something give, not a good thing.

I tell Foil, "Look at the other end, I can't get a view from here, is everything at the other end ok?" I'm up on a ladder facing the wrong direction.

"F*&^% the other end, God*&&^%^%$it, let's get this done, quite stalling. There is nothing else we can do, we need the tension to hook it up and there is nothing to discuss!"

I can't win. He had yelled and screamed earlier in the job because I had not told him an issue was developing under our eyes he needed to be aware of. I had not told him because he knew it all, wanted no help, was the boss, and if he wanted an opinion, he'd ask for it. I was not sure there was any problem of danger. What did I know? I'm stupid, lazy, and ignorant. Seek and ye shall find. So Foil is the boss here.

He screams and yells for me to crank, "God *&&^%$ It!"

So I crank. There is a pop, and the cable gets pulled right out of the connection box at the other end. It isn't two seconds and the foreign renter comes out to tell us we just cut off her important connection, like she knew we would. She was in the middle of communicating with her relatives overseas, conducting business and we cut her internet off. What are we going to do about it? Yes, she in fact had every reason to be concerned when she saw us coming. Now Foil is polite. We will contact the land lord and have it fixed. I know that might take a week. I suggest she can use free internet at either the library or senior center a few blocks away if there are important things to get done.

"Yeah, right. I have three babies here. I can't leave the house." I feel for her. More, I understand what happened was preventable. Foil must have to go under lines and cables all the time on his regular landscape job. He says he moves huge cactus, then plants them for people. I assume that involves a lot of getting under lines of all kinds. Oh, well. We did get the sheds moved. Foil is all buddy, buddy with me. My best friend now.

The cable fix fee comes to us, $600. It requires a call out from Fairbanks for the cable company. Foil feels I alone should pay, as it was my fault, I'm the one who cranked on the winch that broke the cable. I get him to agree to split the cost. Foil feels I am ripping him off and scamming him.

"Who is this Foil guy, Miles?" Josh wants to know why he is here.

"He is just someone I met." Not worth mentioning. I knew him no better than dozens of others I never mention in my life. I forget when or how we met. "He was a customer in Tucson who showed up regularly during the fossil show. Now and then he'd see something he wants to buy. He began hanging out, talking to me." This is normal. He helps me out in return for deals on things he wants. This as well is normal. Nothing is standing out as more than normal. In 2012, Foil wants to pick us up at the airport when we arrive because he does not live that far away. That would be kind. But normal. He has got deals to the tune of saving a couple of thousand dollars by now. He is only returning the favor. Again, there are a dozen customers who would make such an offer, and have. Ruby is still around, for example.

As Foil hangs around the show more, we chat about Alaska, our lives, our dreams, and such things as is normal. I can mention four to five others I have the same relationship with. One of these other people is, 'What's his name' who helps with the booth each year. The kid. You know.

Iris reminds me, "Andre."

Yeah. The one the cops beat up. Sleeps in the booth. Trades. Good kid. Kind. He's opening the booth, closing it for us.

Foil gets into an argument with the kid over War Veterans. Serving your country. Andre is a war protester, man of peace. But also slightly mentally retarded. I'm sure the military would not accept him.

"And my tax dollars support low life leeches like you!" Foil yells at him; insults the kid, has him in tears, threatens him. Andre leaves and does not come back. Foil is 'helpful,' but has now run off our hired help. So Foil is only 'ok'. He has a lot of baggage. His view is what a great help to us he is. I'm not paying attention. My focus is on the show. I have a one track mind.

The subject of Alaska comes up. "Miles, I dream of Alaska and has been my life dream to see it. I suppose I never will. It is so great to talk to you about it. Your words brings me right there!"

"Well Foil, why not just come up for a visit! I can help you out. I have a homestead I hardly use. I could take you out, drop you off for a week or two, or a month and pick you up. Bring your own food and help with the gas cost, have your life dream."

He is saying he cannot afford what such a trip would cost if he paid for it. Thousands of dollars! I have done this before many times. It has been the highlight of most visitors entire life that they never forget. I'm glad to be able to offer that. A little effort on my part is a huge help to someone else. In hindsight I should have invited Andre! Now my friend Josh wants to know why I invited such a mean person to our happy community. I don't have an answer.

"I suppose Josh, I assumed I was not going to have a lot to do with Foil. The plan was to have him come up, drop him off at the homestead, pick him up and that's it."

Foil takes me up on my offer. In 2012, Foil flies to Alaska at the end of April. We have this brief time together In Nenana somewhat like a past experience with Lye

Lye, weather does not cooperate, late break up. I eventually boat Foil to the homestead.

The homestead has most everything one might need to live a month. It will not cost me much. I have tools and supplies in duplicate. I like to share, help out, and flattery works with me. I like attention, appreciation; like to look smart, have fans. We have an uneventful trip. I show Foil where the canoe is. The smaller cabin is more of a shed that replaces the nice log cabin I lost to a forest fire. I show Foil where the big cabin used to be. Overgrown now with new birch trees. Not much evidence of the fire.

There are fish and the slough, ducks and swans all around, moose and bear tracks. This is a real wilderness Alaska experience he says is his life dream.

"So here is it! Enjoy it, I'll be back in a month!" Life goes on, I forget about Foil, I have a life to live.

FOIL SPENDS HIS MONTH. I pick him up. I get the usual response.

"It was the experience of a lifetime, Miles I am so grateful! Thanks!" Foil covers half my gas cost, and I'm happy enough. Until Foil says, "I liked the experience so much I have been thinking about it. I'd like to buy it!" My mouth hangs open in shock. I do not mind sharing my dream. But it's not for sale! How could Foil afford to buy the homestead, when he can't afford to pay to come here to see it? I had to donate his vacation. because he could not afford it.

"Foil, I was offered forty grand for this homestead, and turned it down." I assume that would shut him up. While I am out here, I may as well enjoy a few days! So Foil and I run further upriver. We fish. I show him some good camping spots, good fishing holes. He helps me haul some heavy wood burls.

I show him a place to fossil hunt. We find a mammoth tusk! Foil does the dangerous climbing. It is an experience of a lifetime for him. He expects half cut on what the ancient tusk should sell for because, "Miles, we are partners!"

"No. You are my guest. Lucky just to be here. You did not front any expenses, skills, nor offer anything to a partnership." The tusk is worth ten grand minimum, as is, wet. No way buddy Foil gets five grand up front even before I have it sold. There is no guarantee what I can get for it. I turn down offers of people who will pay me big bucks to take them on a fossil hunt, just for the experience.

"But Miles! Think about it! I am younger. I can do all the grunt work. I can build a nice cabin on your land, cut trails for you, do heavy lifting." I'm not looking to be partners with anyone. I once looked for one. If I had a partner, it would be some young teenage cutie pie, fit female. Cook, clean, run up the cliff, keep the sleeping bag warm. In return for all expenses paid, and the adventurous summer vacation she can't otherwise afford. That is when I was younger. Now I have Iris, the only partner I need.

Foil is only five years younger than I am. How much 'youth' can he offer me? I'm not interested. I later give him $1,000 for his time and effort for a couple of hours of work on the cliff fetching the mammoth tusk. I get no thanks. As far as he sees it, I owe him $4,000 for his half. We had agreed ahead of time, he is along just for the ride, the experience, the adventure. My trip, my money. I could have left him at the homestead, told him I have business upriver further. I did not need him.

It is true, the tusk was up a hard to access cliff, and Foil was a help. So in my view, if I pay him for that few hours that would be more then fair. $1,000 is a lot of money for a few hours work. I'll get the $4,000. That's life. This is my occupation. How much of a cut of his occupation would Foil give me if I was on vacation in Tucson on his dime? Even if I helped him landscape for a few hours, I'd say, "Glad I could help, I appreciate this vacation you give me."

Foil is fun to be with, mostly. Full of energy, excitement, and wanting to know everything. Asking a lot of questions, often filled with flattery. "You know so much! I envy you! I wish I had your life!" Sadly, flattery works on me. More talk about my homestead. "You said you might need money for your court case, lawyer fees, and being out of business! I can do you a favor and give you some money! Cash"

"Foil, I can't sell my dream, then what would I have?" I have had this place for ages. I was here raising kids. The kids slide I made is still here, even after the fire. I admit, "Not the same anymore though, Foil. No kids, no woman out here, and the forest fire changed it all. I will never trap here again. Much of the shine is gone now." I admit it is hard to portage everything over the beaver damn and into the canoe as I get older.

"Miles, I could do all that hard stuff!"

"What good is it all if it is not mine, Foil?" I'm in a depressed mood right now. The wind is out of my sails temporarily.

"How about I pay you, and it is still yours, Miles!" Foil wants to build a cabin - a lifetime dream.

I told him to, "Go ahead! Be my guest! Build a cabin, stay whenever you want!" I'm picturing a week or two every couple of years on a vacation. Foil tells me how many hours he has to work to pay bills. He'll be lucky to get away at all! I would not even be here when he is. I canoe in, use my own cabin, while his cabin is 'over there', out of sight. There is 1,500 feet of water frontage. My little place is at one edge. Foil could build over at the other edge. I picture, I lock my place, he locks his. Nothing about a partnership. He can do me some favors in return if he wants. No real obligation.

"Miles, the cabin I build can be ours to share! You can have a nice place here!" Implying I do not have a nice place here already. I'm happy with what I have. I do not want a new cabin. Foil gives the impression my shack is of no interest to him whatever. Not up to his standards. "I am just worried if it is your land, that something might happen to you; if I have a cabin here, then what?" I can sympathize.

"I can help you find a nice piece of land of your own. It can be all yours to build on, if you wish to buy."

"No. I want yours!" He tries another tactic. "Miles, what is the difference if we are friends, if you own it, and I am the guest, or I own it, and you are the guest? You know I respect the heck out of you. I have proven that. No way I would want to hurt you, deprive you of your dream. You come here and stay, and treat it as yours, plus you have the money for it!"

I begin to wavier, mostly because he will not let go and wears me down. I do not like to argue. *That's one major reason why I moved to the wilds to live alone in the first place!*

"Of course I'd expect a deal, Miles. After all, I am helping you in Tucson." He reminds me I was considering being a snow bird. Partly for Iris's sake, who seems to like being away from the cold and dark. I could be closer to mom, and have a getaway place when I get old, and winters are harsher on me in Alaska. Partly in the beginning, mom told me she wants me to have her home! That plan sounded good at first. So I toyed with what life might be like with a home in Tucson. Near the fossil show. A seed was planted. Foil sees the gears turning, and jumps on this notion.

"Miles, I have an empty trailer you can have! Think of it as yours! I have a car we do not need, just sitting around. Why rent a car! Consider it yours!" After a pause. "Think of me as your Tucson connection, taking care of things at that end, as you help me out here in Alaska!" "Because we are buddies! How long have we known each other now? A long time. I do not have many friends, but you are my one true friend, Miles!" So I go along with the plan. I want my friend to be happy.

SPEAKING OF HAPPY, I have customers to please. I keep working on a game plan, business strategy. I focus on rocks again, since I found some rocks on this last boat trip.

I run the idea past Iris. "Local rocks that are unknown worldwide, cut rough, both sides polished to be displayed on both sides with custom cast caps." This should be unique enough to stand out. Those who like and want this, will have only one source—me.

"Alaska wood not in the mainstream market, hand selected, custom cut sizes, triple dyed, stabilized." My competition has well known types of wood, commercially dyed one color, traditional sizes. Double dye is twice as expensive. Triple dye is not found. I discovered more than one method to triple dye without triple baking. My cost and time is way down. I can offer fairly exotic looking patterns not offered by mainstream markets. Unique enough if you want it, I'm the source. My style might be a narrow interest. There seems to be fewer like minded people in the world outside the box. Fewer customers want something unique. *Or have I changed?*

It seems more customers go for name brands, with what everyone else gets—the fad, normal, standardized items. That's what is advertised. I noticed years ago, the public in general would rather get a reprint of something we all know by a famous artist than something original and exciting by an unknown artist, even if they like the work. Are people less daring than in older times? We fight less for individual freedom as we get accustomed to standardization. I see a gazillion prints of Van Gogh's 'Starry Night'. I get discouraged making originals that take time and are not selling. Even my copied items like castings, have a lot of handmade work and personal touch to them. It is difficult to compete with huge mass production and slave labor overseas.

I'd simply be challenged if I were younger. I'm looking for semi -retirement, finding something fun, interesting, challenging enough to keep my mind occupied but secure enough not to rack my brain much selling. I think back over the prison time. Iris fills me in more on what happened while I was gone.

"Iris, how did Tucson go, did Foil help?" Since I now question Foil's loyalties I want to know if he was of help to Iris.

"Foil and his wife were good to me, Miles. I stayed with your mom, but Foil invited me to visit at his place. I watched the dogs while they went to work. He gave me a ride to the Mexican border so I could see the dentist and eye doctor."

Foil takes her to the Mexican border so she can take care of doctor stuff. He takes her to his home to give my mom a break. Iris tells me what a great time it has been. What good people Foil and his wife are. I'm not in favor of hanging around someone else's home like that. I'm slow to exchange favors. I'm more likely to 'give' than 'ask for'. I'm careful about obligations. I offered Foil a chance to stay at my homestead because it is there and empty. It should not put me out much if someone stays there. It means a lot to Foil, to experience his lifelong dream. Someone does not have to be my friend for me to extend such an offer.

I did not give this offer a lot of thought at the time.

Iris reminds me, "I paid Igor the $5,000 we owed on fossils." Igor had extended me unlimited credit, no interest, after ten years of getting to know each other. I wanted to be sure I was good to my word and got him paid. I made a good profit from fossil material Igor fronts me. This is very kind to do so, at no interest. Iris had the hard job of sorting all the art and materials we forwarded down for the show that we could not set up at, thirty five boxes.

"Foil let me store some of the fossils and animal products at his place. A lot got put under the house at your mothers. Mostly tables and show stuff is under the house at mom's."

I recall in past years we removed the tin skirting off one side of the trailer and scooted totes of show goods on the cement pad under her house. I screwed the tin back on and out of sight, off our mind. I'm not sure what all is there now, or what Foil has. Much of what he and mom has is fossil materials I can have, but not sell. I might be able to sell fossils some day. Much is material I have to make a decision as to whether it is a fossil or not, or even what the material is. Only I would know. I recall some plastic teeth and claws. There are some fossil looking rocks that are not fossils. Some art has black bog wood that looks like whale baleen. Only I will know the difference, and have to do the sorting. Mom does not want to get involved in anything questionable. It would be a shame to get in her life to help her in her old age, only to have her involved in a crime of some kind. The plan was to have Foil take care of anything questionable.

I was not happy about the situation, but sometimes life has to involve other people. I forgot, I sent some of the boxes to Foil instead of my mother. Mom had taken care of packages in the past, having her boyfriend bring them in the house. But he is old, and Foil had offered. Not like I owe him more for the favor. Foil had oohed and ahed over my art and materials, followed by, "Can I have this?" Some he paid for dirt cheap, other times I gave it as trade for help he offered. No one was keeping track. The trades were in the few hundred dollar range; nothing to get excited about. I'm reviewing in my mind the sequence of events to see if I can figure out at what point I should have spotted a sociopath! [1]

Iris picks up on his attitude. Now a rift begins between the two of them. Foil has already been ordering her around. "I need to go to town!" At first Iris was taking him whenever he wished to go. He's been flattering her as well as me. I am upset because I think Iris would as soon live in Fairbanks and hates Nenana, and uses every excuse to get away. It's me paying, not her. For gas, the car, car upkeep. Foil is not even offering gas money.

Iris ignores her chores at home. "Oh! Foil needs me today!" I begin to frown.

At first I heard a lot of, "What a nice guy buddy Foil is!"

"What a good cook!" He'd say. She invites him over for dinner every day. Feeds him food I grew or hunted. Not completely hers to offer. Foil is not offering to pay or contribute. He seems to give just enough to keep things smooth. He seems to study what that minimum might be.

After a while, Foil tells Iris how to drive. At first he is trying to be funny. "Go faster! Pass that truck!" She refuses, and he goads her, challenges her, intimidates her.

At first she laughs, "Stop it!" halfheartedly. Soon Iris is not interested in giving him free rides to town whenever he wants, or free meals. He has a place of his own now and can eat there. The small cabin he told me is just a storage place is now his home. He's beginning to request certain foods cooked a certain way. We let him use our refrigerator. He needs tools. I let him use my shop and borrow tools.

Iris and he (I technically can't help) move 'her' animal stuff over to 'his' property. It's a big help I admit. $200,000 worth of legal animal parts and gun reloading equipment and what not. This, that and the other. It's not mine; it's not on my land. Upstairs in what Foil once called 'our' cabin, he now only calls it 'his' cabin. I do not mind as I am not interested in sharing anything with this guy. For the sake of all the 'stuff' that used to be mine, it is best the land be referred to as 'his' with no suggestion we are joint owners. Foil is just looking out for me. My original thought on the Kantishna homestead remains. He has his cabin, and I have mine.

I forget the time line on all the various happenings. I am not writing it all down. Partly, I do not want a record of where animal parts and guns went to. Partly, I tend not to record negative things. At first just annoying, *Whatever, it will soon be over I'm not putting up with this Foil guy! Next!*

A YEAR GOES BY, Foil shows up for his summer vacation. He is upset his whole vacation time was passing. He had not had the chance to get to his Kantishna cabin building project, due to late breakup of the ice. I'm supposed to care and be part of his concerns. He has four walls up from his trip last year. I honestly forget when he got that done. I do not consider it any part of my concern. He had said he expected the project to take just one season. He is going to use all natural materials for little cost. Now he wants plywood sheets, nails, store bought picture windows, roof tin. I want to know how he is getting it all out there?

"Well, I can cover some of the gas cost and you bring it!" *Buddy Miles!*

I'm thinking the free party time is over. I donated a free vacation. I donated another trip. At some point he needs to kick in and pay.

"All the things I do for you, Miles, you want this to be about money?" I have learned that when someone talks like that about money not mattering between friends this person is usually the one who gets ninety percent of the free stuff.

"Foil, Kantishna trips cost me $300. That's breaking even. I might consider making trips and breaking even. $500 would be fair. It's two days of my time. If you pay someone who is not a friend, just hire someone for what it is worth, it costs $1,500 a trip." Foil has been paying $100. Now complaining when I might need $300. He is getting ripped off, and will not stand for it. Now is threatening me. *Fine, ask around. Pay the $1,500 if you feel I am ripping you off. Bye. Have a nice trip.*

One thing that does not work with me is threats. I can often be conned, flattered, used. But my real button is threats. Now Foil wants me to help him get a deal on a boat and motor of his own. This is the guy who could not afford to pay for a vacation. I get hints he can't pay the interest on his credit card. Both he and his wife work. What he says he does for a living is not matching his expenses. Iris overheard he and the wife talking. I try to show Foil how to save money. He is not interested.

I find Foil a deal on a boat engine. "You need a really good engine. You can sacrifice on a cheap boat." We can come up with a boat about anywhere. The main thing is, we got a great engine lined up! This is advice from over forty years experience. Someone who asked me to show him the ropes. Foil commits and arranges delivery of the engine. I see him a few days later.

"Miles, I bought that boat and engine with trailer from Dalia's brother. You know, the boat we saw in the yard!" Yes, I know. The package I suggested he not buy. The boat is not big enough, and the price is too high. "I only paid $7,000!" I had a nice big engine with controls lined up for $500. I'm sure we could have found a boat for another $500 and a trailer for $300. For under $1,500 I could have gotten him better.

I'm shocked. "Did you tell my friend you made the deal with on the fifty horse?"

"No, Miles, you can tell him, or better, you buy the engine! It sounds like a good engine. But I needed a boat too, so I got this package deal!" I had also suggested he not make friends with Dalia or the brother Ollie. A couple others in town as well. Foil can choose his friends of course.

I explained why. "These are people I do not trust, who come across as wanting to see me back in prison. I do not trust them with information you might inadvertently pass on due to our friendship."

I had this conversation because Foil already had a long conversation with Dalia who suggested to him I am crooked and not to trust me. In my opinion, making trouble. Rumors are already getting passed on and distorted based on information Foil is feeding these people. My purpose is not to badmouth or attack any of them in retaliation, making myself like them. My tactic is to simply avoid such people. Smile, nod, say hello, keep it simple, without offering any information.

Almost to defy me, Foil deliberately makes these people I mention I am having issues with, his best friends. Tells me about it and laughs.

I am now concerned Foil has the key to my shop, run of my house, knows all about my life, what I am up to, and is passing this information on. In his own words, "People who want to see you go to jail, Miles. So be careful!" I interpret that as a threat. *If you aren't nice to me and do as I want, I can at any time pass on information to your enemies.*

Foil needs all kinds of tools out at the homestead. I had said earlier when I wanted to look out for him, " I have all that out there. No use you buying and hauling in the same stuff. Just use mine and we'll work something out." This has somehow got interpreted to all the tools come with the property as his. I had meant it to mean I am helping him out for now and down the road he can make it right, as a friend. Like replace tools with new ones later on, or help me in Tucson. I assume he'd treat the situation as I would. If it was him in Tucson letting me use all his tools so I could repair a home I bought there, I would treat the tools with respect. Fix any that broke, clean them, eventually buy new ones for him as a rental payment; thank you.

Foil is wearing out my tools, and not fixing or replacing them. At first I assumed if we are friends, he will make up for it in Tucson! *I'm getting a trailer and car he promised!*

Time passes. "Oh, no, Miles, my daughter just got married and we gave her the trailer. You understand! But hey. I meet a lot of rich people while landscaping who have places to sell, or who owe me, and I am sure I can get a killer deal on property and a place for you, just wait. Be patient!" Next, "Car? Well, gee, it is our only spare! Of course, if anything happens to it, you will be responsible, that's only fair!"

Iris and I decide spending $500 for a car rental is safer. His used car could blow up! He could say we owe him some inflated value for it. I have now received almost zero help from Foil in Tucson. For a short time I think he may make up for it later.

Until I hear, "But, Miles, you stay with your mother! You do not need a house in Tucson!" Now I know he is not looking, feels I do not need a house, a car, or help, and has decided what is best for me. I have now saved him about $50,000. I received $1,000 worth of help if I had to pay for it. But have spent about $3,000 out of my pocket helping him.

"By the way, Miles, I need your things removed from my cabin. The wife and I need the space now, so you have to move everything this week."

It's not my stuff, and he should not be referring to it as such. It's sort of his, sort of Iris's, sort of in limbo. It needs to get sorted one day. Some can be mine again. Some art I might reclaim. I am not trusting Foil enough now to have him follow my thinking. If he sells it all, or simply claims it, there is not much I can do. I agree we are not getting along well enough to have that held over me. The next step is, he will tell me it has all disappeared. What did I expect?

That is how the idea of getting a shed comes in. Store the shed on his land. His suggestion. I am not interested, but Iris is mad at me. Telling me what a disgrace my buildings are, how cheap I am and why not invest in something nice, like a real shed for once! Talk of how I need to trust my friends who are trying to help me.

Foil adds, "It's a big lot, I only need the cabin, there is room for another shed here, no big deal." His cabin in Nenana was, in the beginning, 'ours.' Much like the Kantishna homestead. He has moved into 'my' little cabin on the Kantishna he previously insulted.

"I need it only until my big cabin is built, Miles." Surely I understand? Who knows how long that will take him. Years, it looks like. At first, he said, "One to two years max. I want it done so I can move in!" I assumed he'd live in a tent in the meantime, as I did. "Can't do that, Miles! Bears around!"

He has re-arranged my small cabin to suit his needs. Put a different bed in to accommodate him and his wife. Moved all the food, moved the shelving. I can't find my things when I visit in the fall.

Dalia and her friends have all kinds of gossip about me from Foil to spread around town. "Yeah, he will fix his outboard with baling wire and duct tape like before ha, ha!" "I can't wait to catch him with an illegal tusk and turn him in!" "I wonder where all his illegal stuff is hidden!"

Foil hints sometimes, I need to go along with the program because he has something on me. He has me by the short hairs. I'm not going to argue that he doesn't. I want to see where he wants to go with this. Let him think I'm afraid. Not show my cards. "Miles, you can't legally charge me for boat trips! You are not licensed in that business."

Knowing I am on probation, I take that to mean he could turn me in if he wants. His words sound like Dalia and her little group talks. Beginning with, "Well I happen to know...!" Which could lead to doing one's civic duty by calling the proper authorities. It is legal for me to ask for costs taking friends out on the river. I do not argue.

I learned in the past this is what Dalia is baiting people for. Engagement in a conversation. The joys of arguing. *Let us eventually end up in a screaming match.* I think Foil is a fool to dismiss my boat trips. He will find out his boat will not work. I now have a good excuse not to have him in my boat. I do not have insurance. I'm not licensed as he himself points out. In fact, for similar reasons he should not be on my property. I have no insurance if he trips and falls. Only trusted friends should be on my property. Or, certainly not people who have already hinted they might be in the mood to sue me for anything they can.

"The idea of this boat, Miles, is that I will never have to haul heavy loads. I will live a simple life out there, and go back and forth cheap and light."

His speech is smug, he is smart and has it all figured out. Foil does not know that is every homesteaders dream and intention! He now needs a big door, big windows, roofing tin, flooring, plywood. None of these things can be hauled well with his boat. I told him that a year ago. There is no spare engine if he breaks down. I told him that a year ago, also. He needs gas tanks, fuel hoses, float coat, rope, controls, seat, and more. He can easily spend another $5,000, if he does not know what he is doing. Especially when he does not like anything used, but requires everything new. All those things also take knowledge. I mentioned all this last year.

My take on his position is, he feels he has it all under control now and does not need me or my advice anymore. He no longer needs to smooze me or flatter me. Since Foil does not need me, he has no reason to continue to be nice. Life in his world is about suckers and the suckees. It's my tough luck if I do not know how to protect myself. The joke is on me. I'm both a fool and an idiot, so deserve to be scammed. Survival of the fittest. The bush law. Whoever can take the bone gets to chew on it.

I try to smile and am partly curious if what he says works! Let us see! In ten years let's re-visit this. Find out who is ahead of who, and who has what. Who is happy, and who has regrets. I have dealt with other tough guys in my life. I would not trade places with them. It might be this is what many people think I represent, when hearing me referred to as a mountain man, wilderness guy, with the nick name 'Wild Miles'. A tough cookie, with a kill or be killed mentality. Like a gun slinger, Foil decides I'm not so tough after all and he's smarter, faster, and will eventually call me out.

"Miles, I know all about boats. I have owned boats before! I just need a little guidance here and there, a few tips. You told me you learned it all the hard way over a long period of time. I do not have that time. I need to know it now, with a few tips from you." We are not singing from the same sheet of music here. I hear background fiddle music to a song called 'Foil.'

Foil is upset the river ice has not gone out early as it did last year. He spends his time fixing up the Nenana log cabin that was meant to be just a storage shed. The cabin is run down, un-lived in for at least twenty years. The logs are sound, roof does not leak, floor not warped, so there is a good beginning shell. He needs a bed, windows, stove. So of course he needs to borrow all my tools, pieces of spare plywood, extra windows I may have.

"I'd do the same for you, Miles!"

I'm reluctant to leave him in the lurch. I just see a different situation now. Foil wants this cabin to become a nice vacation home, and he has little money. He says, it is nice to dream and work towards that, but not on my dime. He asked me to help him find a cheap storage shed, not a livable cabin. What he wants is not matching what he told me he wanted. If he had told the truth up front, I would have politely told him I can't help him and good luck. I had decided not to help people with dreams I do not believe in. I will not interfere, but neither will I help unless I believe the dream is reachable. Anyone's dream may well be possible! Go for it! But not with my help. I do not owe anyone help. Help is voluntary. My choice. In this way, I might be what civilization views as 'tough.'

I may have done the same as Foil when I got started, but I did it all myself, and it took years, even a lifetime. Wanting it all in just a few years is a big undertaking!

I tell Iris, "I do not think it is a good idea to leap into such a dream and not be able to afford it, then put the burden on someone else. We have our own dream and list of priorities. We can take care of ourselves, and do not need hand outs or be a burden on anyone else. Foil needs to be able to take care of himself, pay his own bills."

I feel sorry he does not have all his tools with him. "They are all in Tucson, Miles!" That is not my fault. I can lend things out to friends if needed. I am simply not the sort who either borrows or lends in general. I have friends who can take care of themselves, and rarely if ever need to borrow. A shed to store things as he first told me does not require tools he left behind, nor seeking out my spare pile of goodies he needs.

This situation is looking one sided. I offer all the help. Foil has little to offer. He is not paying. He offers no skills I can use, and if he has skills, he is very busy. I offer to show him how to save money so he has money to pay for tools or fix mine that he wears out. No, he feels he needs good quality, so gets the best, gets it new, and does not have time to go look for second hand items. He is living a lifestyle far above mine financially, then telling me he is broke and can't pay me.

"We are friends, Miles, friends help each other out!" I decide we are not friends, but have no polite way to let Foil know.

Foil's vacation is over. He has to get back to Tucson to the heat and grind of his physically hard work. Foil brags about what a hard worker he is, showing his hands to anyone he meets. "These are the hands of a working man! See all the calluses! No one I hire can keep up with me! I learned when young how to work hard. That's the problem today, no one knows how to work!"

I see a flaw in this outlook on life. It is sometimes smart to work with your head and not your brawn. Especially as we get older. The outlook Foil has is one I may have had when twenty, not the outlook of someone fifty. What will he do when his back gives out? I see the flaw as well in the one job we did together moving the shed. Brawn, brute force. "Pull, by God, pull!"

That cost us an extra $600. The shed I bought was only $400. He tells me proudly how every log to his new cabin was carried on his shoulder. I did that as well when I was twenty-five. I built a dozen cabins since then. I made a simple rope between trees over the cabin site and used a come-along on a pulley to lift, then run the log on the pulley down the rope to set it in place. This lifestyle may well break Foil, before he breaks the lifestyle. I already see a huge slow down in his original plan of 'done in one year.' No more, "Use moss between the logs, poles for the roof, split wood for the floor." Now he wants it all pre-made from town. Why? I think the work wore him out and he will not admit it.

"That costs, Foil, have you got the money?" Two dollars for every pound you haul to the Kantishna, just as a freight, your cost if you do it yourself." Foil does not believe me. This sounds impossible. Actually this is the cheap way, using used stuff and doing as much yourself as possible, under ideal conditions. Two dollars a pound hauling can become ten dollars a pound and more, much more. Even thousands of dollars and not even get it there. It's possible if you do not have knowledge, to lose your entire load along the way. Many homesteaders never got to where they were headed. *The famous Donner Pass story for example.*

Foil has gone out with me, and I have made it look so easy. My take on this is, Foil cannot accept I can do it, and have the knowledge, and he does not. Whatever I can do, he can do too, even better. Part of that civilization mentality. How can I possibly know anything without a degree, dressed as I am, with my income and station in life? I'm a subsistence person, by definition, poor and stupid, needing help. [2]

Foil and I manage to get out on the river before he leaves, just as the ice goes out. I take off with him into the ice jams. Foil is terrified! That was not my intention! I have been doing this all my life. I know how to do this. Foil will need to learn how to boat under a variety of conditions if he wishes to walk in my shoes.

I want to teach him about his new GPS. This is a very important tool when you do not know where you are. "Oh it's simple, Miles. I'll read the directions later."

"Maybe, but while we are out here, let's just get it out and check to make sure you have a river map in it." I am also concerned for him, because these new tools are nice once you get them set up. There are things to know. One important thing to know is what map system you want or need to be in. As a land surveyor, I know there are several common systems. 'NAD 27' I think is the one to look for; contour maps we usually use are there. If the GPS is not set up right, the coordinates on the GPS and the intersection on the field map can be fifty miles wrong. You need to know how to set up waypoints, routes, and how to save and access them later. It's not that simple. (This does get more simple and easy in later years. Right now, GPS is new and not as user friendly)

I am not going to make anyone learn anything. There is very little I order anyone to do or even tell them. If you wish to explore another way, have at it. Good luck. I am told I am not a good listener. My 'excuse' is, I believe I listen to those I decide know what they are talking about. You need to be very, very good before you get my attention. Otherwise, you may not know any more than I know. I had no problem listening or taking orders from my survey boss and friend Seymour for example. I decided he is very gifted at what he does. I listen to Josh when it comes to sled dogs. He won the Iditarod. I feel I am good at most everything I set my mind to learning. Not always the best, but better than average. I may well have an inflated opinion of myself. If so who does that hurt besides me? *If you don't like it, walk away, change the subject. I'm not going to apologize.*

It is not me going to Foil telling him I know a lot and he needs to listen. Foil came to me asking for help and advice. I am willing to download GPS data out of my machine into his. So he has my map, routes and marked points.

"No, Miles, I will make my own routes." I shrug. I think he is going to get stuck on every sandbar he comes across, based on his knowledge. But what do I know? No use interfering with a man and his destiny. It is not my place to pop his balloon.

"Go forth young man!" It is hard to know for sure what Foil thinks. He tells the community what a fool I am running out into the ice. Negative gossipers who accomplish nothing, laugh, "We told you what to expect from Miles, the idiot! Ha ha!" From people who do not own boats and never will, but offering advice from a bar stool on how to best do it.

"Well, see you in Tucson this winter, have a good trip, Foil." We bring him to the airport. Iris and I do not even bother asking for gas money. It's over $100 if he has to take a cab. It's 100 miles round trip. Let him figure it out. I'm thinking on the way home. How I lost confidence once, and asked a local native about the river, if everything looked ok downriver where he came from a week ago.

"You are a river man, Miles, and know as much as I do. There is no need to seek advice," said in a calm kind way. Not flattery, not conning me. Just telling me his opinion. He is right. Whatever the river was a week ago is not relevant now. The river can change by the hour, certainly by the day. It's like asking the city person how was traffic here yesterday, I'm headed that way. I assume five o'clock rush hour is somewhat predictable, if there was an accident it would be in the news. You simply have to sally forth and greet the world, and see for yourself. If it's a highway you have taken for twenty years, it would be an odd question, "How is the traffic?"

As for buddy Foil?

"Honey, I do not like to argue or fight. I prefer to be optimistic, give people the benefit of the doubt. I offer as many chances as I can afford to before writing someone off. It will be Foil's loss more than mine if I disconnect from him entirely. I'm giving him all the chances to 'see the light' and repent, so to speak. If he does not, then I may not have the right to decide what he should do and what is best for him. But I can decide what is best for me and act accordingly."

"Miles, he is using you and this happens all the time, is all I am saying!"

"Maybe! But where is he and any others you feel have wronged me? Where am I? Who is better off? Has any such person really gotten ahead in life by ripping me off? I think not!" It was also Iris who was part of connecting with Foil in the first place, implying we owe him because he took such good care of her in Tucson. Her own advice at the time was what a good guy he is and how I need to trust people. If she had said with her street smarts, "I think he's a con artist, I'd stay away from him, Miles." None of his would be happening. I'd have taken her advice. I do not blame her, but she must be like me, not so good at spotting con artist. I remind Iris, "I spent twenty-five years alone in the wilds. I learned things many would never learn. However, the price has been not spending a lot of time getting to understand people and civilized situations."

## MILES MARTIN

THE GARDEN NEEDS TENDING. We are harvesting a few things now. Lettuce, radishes, greenery that grows fast. Everything is in the soil. Many plants I put in five gallon buckets so they can be moved around, or brought into the greenhouse at the end of the season to finish them off. There are a few green tomatoes and small cucumbers. By the fourth of July I usually expect the first ripe tomatoes and cucumbers.

"Did you send in your probation information?"

"Yes, thanks for reminding me." I had to go to my bank account on line, print off my statement, then forward that with my probation papers. I print my quick book business records.

"How is business going?" Iris asks since I have just done a monthly summary.

"I have a visitor counter on most of the 65 web pages now."

The stats just came in the email. 474 people have visited the homepage. 88 in the past week. Eight of those were looking at knives. I'm surprised only one went to the art sorted by price, but five went to my main art selling page or art by subject. So maybe no one cares about price? One possibility is, people are only looking to get ideas as craft people. Or to download pictures for their own use.

I know with the old web site, ¾ who visited bought something. I got comments like, "Been looking for twenty years for this sort of stuff and finally found you! Wow, how exciting!" I'm now selling rocks, wood, custom knives. Ho hum. There are 500 other sites just like mine, selling the same thing. People can look, and might be back, and might not, and who cares? I do, but not them. I do not need to be found again. It's a buyer's market. A search for 'stones' or 'wood' brings up a gazillion choices. A search for teeth and claws had me in the top five in the world, among only a dozen listed. Big difference. A customer in Iceland puts 'teeth, claws' into their search engine and I am the first to come up. I made a his and her wolf matched pedant set for newlyweds. I had created a seller's market.

"You want it? I'm the man! The source!"

That is not as likely to happen in the rock business. I'm challenged by how to make this work! My basic outlook has been to find a pie no one else has discovered, and control it. By control I do not imply, 'with a fist' through intimidation, negative energy. I'm a negotiator, wheeler dealer, word jouster. Control is having a unique art form no one else can easily copy, combined with materials hard for ordinary people to get. I planned it this way on purpose. It took a lot of work. Words like 'control', 'unique', and 'hard to get' are key ins for law enforcement. As a felon, these words should not be in my vocabulary. I am to use advertising words more in line with words sheep know. 'Standing in line words' like bargain, today only, deal, free shipping. Phrases like, 'I am here for you!' 'The customer is always right!' Your servant. Back of the bus words. So now what? I'm not interested in normal sales pitches, one sheep addressing another. I think I have some ideas. They just take time. I am a senior now with less energy. If I were twenty, I could pull this off better.

"Miles, what is so funny!" Iris wonders. I admire Einstein. We saw a Nova special on him. Einstein did not do well in school; he was a problem child, a trouble maker. He could not get into college, was not even good with numbers and his math. He was an idea man who could not get a job. He was poor. Nothing about him stands out in a biography of his early years. He had a flunky job at a patent office, was married, about to be evicted from his apartment for being unable to pay rent. He was simply lucky some high up respected scientist said, "Hey, I think you have an idea I want to know more about." It would have been easy for him, his life, and contributions, to be brushed aside, never to come forth. For a decade and more, no one was interested in what he had to say, about splitting atoms, and time being relative.

My concern is summed up by a commercial I saw using the term 'outside the box.' Selling cars. Outside the box was a cup holder that holds soda cans. How cool is that! No. I mean 'unique,' as in a car you look at and can't figure out how to get in it. There is no engine. There are no wheels. Not 'leader of the pack' but a whole new pack. Not 'lone wolf,' but a whole new species. Where God breaks the mold, after creating just one. Not one in a hundred, but one in ten million.

"If you want one, come see me." If only a hundred in the world would be interested, let that hundred find me. Like that. Or it starts like that. The financial goal would be to start a fad. There are other goals. Like a small knit group of very satisfied like minded people who appreciate me. A hundred people telling me I'm the cat's meow, giving me steady income, is equal to 'thousands' I can't remember, stopping to buy. Ho hum, maybe yes, maybe no, let's see how high you can jump for me first. It's not entirely fun having to start from where I am at my age, at a time I was looking forward to coasting in to the final slide at home base. Iris reminds me of what I know.

"It's worse for many others! This worldwide economic situation is affecting a lot of people!" I see it in the news. Lost jobs, factories closing, lost homes. Whole neighborhoods out of service. While I feel bad, I can pull myself together.

I am not in the greatest of moods today. My casting kiln goes tits up.

I hear, "That figures," from Iris who lets me know something is always going wrong! I do not agree! I have had this kiln trouble free for twenty-one years. The kiln has done thousands of jobs, made me thousands of dollars. Now an error code informs me my kiln needs a thermo coupler. They wear out, I assume. I do not believe the problem is neglect or misuse. I look up replacing the entire kiln. The model I have cost me $550 when I bought it. Now costs over $2,000 to replace. This reminds me how long I have had it, that the price has gone up this much. A web search turns up a thermo coupler for $111. Yes, a bit of money. If I cannot change it out myself, or there is more wrong, or I break something else trying to install it, that would indeed increase the bummer factor.

"More than bummer, Miles, just have a professional fix it! Buy a new one!" A comment from the peanut gallery, someone who has no stake in the decision, and is not paying the bill. I may not value the opinion as much as the person speaking wishes me to. When anyone has been running a successful business or had a successful life, I listen better. Even then. I have habits, a personality type, way of doing things, not likely to change. It works for me. It does little good apologizing, feeling guilty or bad, or trying to be someone I am not. I have already tried those options. Most important would be, to be around like minded people.

I keep repeating myself. This is just one example of fixing stuff myself. Maybe it works, and maybe it fails. A sore spot to me. I cannot recall anyone who was important to me, saying, 'Go for it!' So I have given up. I must settle for getting made fun of, reprimanded, made to feel guilty, weird and worse. From my parents, relatives, my own woman. That's just life. I learn to overcome. On some level, everyone is my enemy. Does not want me to succeed on the terms I wish. I shall be an over comer then. I will say though, anyone who claims to admire my accomplishments and asks me to teach them, anyone who wishes to walk in my shoes, must for a certainty have the mind set of fixing things yourself. Daring to fail.

The thermo coupler arrives in the mail from China with no instructions. I take the kiln apart, down to almost every part to get at this coupler that needs replacing. Without instructions, or knowing what to look for, I have taken more parts off than I needed to! The new coupler goes in. A lot of time is spent remembering how the kiln goes back together. Some parts do not want to go back as easily as they came out. I finally think the kiln is back together and ready to test. I have a few screws left over I toss out. The kiln will not even turn on now. No power. *Dang!*

I have some slight knowledge, because I have taken a lot of things apart in my life. In cases involving electrical items, if there is zero power, the issue is most often with the power supply, cord or fuse. Usually something simple and basic. The power supply checks out. I change the kiln fuse just in case, but no change. I may have to take it all apart again. *Groan.* I learned when taking it apart, there is a way to get just the electrical main parts out, with just a few screws. I access this compartment and pull the tray out. I look for loose main wires from the supply side.

There is a loose wire at the fuse. I plug this in. Everything works. The insides have been cleaned. Now I feel this kiln could last another twenty years. In my opinion, I saved over $2,000 by wisely investing some time and $111 for a part. I enjoyed the work, learned something, and feel good about myself. This success goes unnoticed by others. If I had not gotten the kiln going again, that would be remembered and added to a long list of failures. *Is my list of success, longer than your list of failures?* My guess is, those interested in the list of failures, would be no more interested in my list of successes, then I am interested in their list proving my stupidity and incompetence.

I think from the 1950's, as far back as I can remember, up until about the millennium, it was cool to know how to fix things. This was almost a definition of the male role. 'Mr Fix it'. I recall many 'How to' books - books on wiring, plumbing, making toys for children, and just 'Handy Man' books. Many things; most things, arrived in a box with instructions to put it together, in English. There were Heath Kits, Tandy Leather, Erector and chemistry sets. These shops, out of business now. Most teen boys knew how to fix and tinker with cars. Many built go carts. I remember almost every kid had a pocket knife and learned how to whittle. We made spoons, whistles, toys, faces for dolls the girls sewed clothes for. Mothers repaired our clothes, darned socks, sewed buttons and zippers into clothing that failed. Likewise, women cooked from scratch. Today 'made it myself' means added water and put it in the oven. Even that is rare. When my mother says, 'made the pie myself', she grew and picked the apples, hand rolled the crust. When I say I handmade a necklace it means I founds the rocks, cut and made the beads, hand carved the clasp and cast it myself. Those days and ways seem to be gone. Lifestyles have changed. The modern words of 'handmade' means 'I bought a necklace, then added a store bought pendant.'

"Take it to your dealer," is the line of the day. Fixing it yourself is a sign of being dirt poor, not very bright, or weird. I am reluctant to even tell anyone I fixed something. If the kiln fails again, I will hear, 'Ah yes, you should have taken it to the dealer as I suggested.

I hear, "That's fine. But you aren't touching any of my stuff!" Even when I succeed. Because,' You broke something five years ago and I remember!' Implied is, 'Mr. Baling Wire and Duct Tape! How embarrassing!'

It's amazing to the world that anyone puts up with me! How lucky I am that someone does! Indeed. I live in a world of my own, with only me in it. I may as well be in the wilderness. Not much different. Foil could be right - "Only happier!" As I state all the way back in book one when I first arrive in the wilds. How wonderful it was not to have anyone looking over my shoulder commenting on what I do and how I do it. I am filled only with the joy of playing with stuff! It's like heaven.

"What did you break now!" is never heard in the wilds. Only God saying with a smile, "What will you try next?" Out of curiosity. Well. Of course God knows what I will do next! But wants to know if I know! Wants to verify I have not called it quits yet! God is amused! So I am too!

As part of my probation conditions, I have to fill out papers now and then. This arrives in the mail.

### PCRA Offender Section

Directions: The following items, if answered honestly, are designed to help you better understand your thinking and behavior. Please take time to complete each of eighty items on this inventory using the four-point scale defined below. 4=strongly agree, 3=agree, 2=uncertain, 1=disagree.

I glance at the questions before beginning. This addresses 'the offender,' as if there was only one offender in the plea bargain. Did Fish and Wildlife get such a questioner with eighty questions as an offender?

*#8 I have found myself blaming the victims of some of my crimes by saying things like 'They deserved what they got.' Or, 'They should have known better.'*

What victims? My crime, according to the judge, had no victims. There is no place for "I do not understand this question; question does not apply." This is a, "How often do you beat your wife" question.

*#13 The more I got away with crime, the more I thought there was no way the police or authorities would ever catch up with me.*
*#15 I have helped out friends and family with money acquired illegally.*
*#22 Even when I got caught for a crime I would convince myself that there was no way they would convict me or send me to prison.*
*#53 I have rationalized my irresponsible actions with….*

*There is an assumption I have been both irrational and irresponsible. There is an assumption all crimes are. I feel many crimes can be a difference in views. Your view rules supreme not because the rules are just, right or correct, but because you have a big stick. Some crimes are a rational smart choice. Like bank scams, Ponzi schemes, make a move get rich, get out. Getting caught is a calculated risk.*

*#56 The way I look at it is, I'm not really a criminal because I never intended to hurt anyone.*
*#59 Looking back over my life I can see now that I lacked direction or consistency.*

There is only one right answer to this, and all these questions. *"Yes! I see the error of my ways now. I am a changed man. Thank you! I have been rehabilitated by my positive prison experience and fine! I had a horrible life until I met you! Bless you for the kindness you have shown in helping me to find a better way, the path of the honest citizen! I feel so much better now!*
I am not going to answer like that of course! I'd be right back in prison as not rehabilitated yet. The system is not looking for sarcasm. Luckily this is multiple choice.

Even in an ultimatum, by definition, I am agreeing to a lie because I am between a rock and a hard place. So now what is all this crap about looking back over my poor depraved life and realizing I needed direction? How about looking back over my life and realizing I was such a sucker to believe in my government. I actually volunteered to fight for my country and what it stands for. I have been brainwashed. I feel like vomiting from shame. It's one reason I think the military likes the young and impressionable.

"Miles, it's just words! What is the big deal, really!" Hmmm. Just words. Yes.

"Well. I am a writer. Writers paint with and play with words."

"Not really, Miles. You do not use big fancy, eloquent words."

"No. You are right. I think simple words work fine. I like to examine the simple and understand it. Words like money, law, moral, ultimatum and what not." I have to pause and think. "An artist with paint mixes colors; blends; uses a variety of strokes for light effects. The shimmer and glamour is a blend of four basic colors. A painter does not have to create fancy colors with pretty names. It is possible to tell a great story with paint, using only blue, for example. Or even black and white." I do not agree a good writer has to use high faluting words few of us know the meaning of. I contend few of us know the meaning of the most simple words. A very long debate could be engaged in defining what the most simple word, 'I' means. *Just who is I anyhow? For that matter, who are you? Entire books are written on just you and I. Some of the greatest writers in history wrote in simple words for the common person. Like Shakespeare.*

"Honey, did you see this article?" Iris likes to point out articles of interest in case I missed them. She hands me the paper. Interesting. An article about a plane that crashed. The pilot was relying on his maps. It is pointed out how inaccurate maps of the wilderness are in Alaska.

"Mountains can be miles away from where they are marked on the map."

There has never been enough money to accurately map the state. There are vast stretches, even today, where no civilized person has ever set foot. We do not know what is there. Iris adds, "But if you did go? You'd have a telephone; book of rules you better bring with you!"

It is a 'going to town' day. Headed in to the big city for groceries. At the end of the day, the last stop is at Fred Meyers to get groceries. A last ritual. This store is on the highway, the edge of town, on the way back home to Nenana. They sell gas. We can use our built up Freddy points to get a discount. We'll gas up and head home when done.

In Freddy's, I often run into people I know. This trip, I see a teen with a T-shirt that has, 'I am a Peters' written on it.

Out of the blue, I ask, "Are you one of the Peters, related to Emit from Ruby?"

He says, "Yes, I am Emit Junior."

The Native next to him says he knows me, reminds me. Arnold Marks from Huslia, who helped me in a storm in the early 1970s. I have not met this guy since then. It is like the early days when for years in a row I'd run into Will when I needed a ride. Here I am, meeting them right when I am working on this part of my life in the book.

"That was a bad storm. I still remember it, friends lost their boats in that storm!"

Arnold nods as he recalls. He had the first big engine in the interior of Alaska - 80 horses! He yanked my stuck houseboat off a sandbar. I did not know he would know the Peter family. Emit is the first Native to win the Iditarod! He knows Josh, one of my best friends. I stopped in Ruby along the Yukon with the houseboat many times and always looked up Emit. Very knowledgeable about sled dogs. Someone I am proud to know, I look up to.

I tell Emit Jr. this. I put my hand out, "Proud to meet you, tell your father, Hi!"

A lot of village people prefer to shop at Fred Meyers as I do. This store has a 'bush service'. Orders are call in or sent by mail. A store employee shops for you; items are boxed and taken to the airport to be flown to your remote village. You can request a catalog. I never used this service, and am sure it is costly, but it costs less than flying to town to shop yourself. Mostly the service shows me the store caters to, cares about, the savages in the state, like myself and the Peters family. I wish to support and be loyal to such a store. I do not want to see such a store go under to the bigger worldwide monopolies set up in malls. I do not agree with Foil, that it all comes from China and all made of ticky tacky; all just the same. I think it matters where we shop and what we support. It could be just an illusion, fooling myself. Meeting these two Natives helps confirm another reason why I shop here. Like-minded people shop here and I meet them. It's like where my tribe hangs out.

Emit says, "Your name comes up in Ruby all the time, Miles. You are one of our respected elders."

Arnold adds, "Same in Huslia and Galena, Miles."

I nod my thanks. This means a lot to me. Inspires me to be the best person I can, live up to what these good people expect of me.

Iris does not understand. "Who were they? You always know people here!" As if she is not totally happy about it. She does not want to be known by anyone. Wants more low profile. Being an inspiration to others is nothing but trouble.

"Look where it got you, Miles!"

*What is wrong with where I have gotten to,* I wonder. She is just trying to look out for me. "Do not talk to anyone, what is the word of the day?" I know the word of the day, "No!"

"That's right, Miles, you need to learn to say, 'No', 'Go away!'"

"Skip?"

In one of the isles in Freddy's. Yes, it is Skip! He turns and smiles. He was just an eighteen year old when we met. A kid who owned his own plane; a bunch of planes. He flew for me to Hansen Lake in trade for art.

"I lost that necklace, Miles! Everyone loved it, the whale on jade. I still miss it."

"Skip, you still live up Chena Ridge Road?"

Yes, he is still there, but not flying anymore. I heard that; we met a decade ago on the street and he told me that he had an accident, health issues; has never been the same. I note a large box on his belt.

"My heart, Miles. It is a battery pack for a pump that replaces my heart. I have no pulse, just a constant blood pressure from a turbine pump. A lot of people do not survive the adjustment. Their body has to have that pulse. I'm lucky, my body can take it." Skip looks fairly healthy and happy, alert, walking fast. I'm amazed he has no heart. I'm surprised he is still alive. I recall now a visiting relative grabbed the airplane controls and flew them into the ground when he took them up to see the city.

Running into Skip out of the blue as I am editing the part about him in my book, reminds me again of 'always' running into Will when I came to town in the early days. Spooky. *How do we do that?* As if, this is beyond the laws of coincidence. If not coincidence, then what is it? And little Emit and Arnold. I have not seen these guys since the 1970s and they show up just as their name comes up writing my book.

Before parting Skip says, "F*&^%K the Feds." He has obviously heard I am now a felon. "If you deserve to be a felon, Miles, everyone does!" He mumbles, "It's time for a revolution. I've about had it with the government." He does not elaborate. He must be in his fifties now. Only eighteen when he flew for me. Had a story about running guns in South America, making a year's wages for a few hours of flying. Owned half a million dollars' worth of airplanes when he was eighteen. *I bet he has some stories to tell! But no. Nothing specific that would be printable.*

"I can make you another pendant, Skip, give it to you, how do I get hold of you?" He gives me his card. *Imagine not having a heart, having a turbine pump instead, on your belt.*

"Yeah, Iris, long ago friend!" I proceed to tell her some Skip stories. "All that money." Someone else we know joins in the conversation about the distribution of wealth in our country and such subjects. This is a common topic I review with lawyers, politicians, business people. I have a long background invested in a variety of opinions. I still keep asking. "We agree the government has a great deal of money.

What I do not understand is, where it comes from. If the government is extracting money from the people, and the people are poor, this is not making sense."

"Miles, the government just prints it!" I review what this means. This is possible. I do know nothing is backing our money anymore. However, gold and silver backed the dollar for a very long time. For the past thirty years or so, nothing backs it. In most countries where nothing backs the money, people are not stupid, and simply do not trust the money. The money quickly becomes useless. I believe money is the symbol that stands for some trade value, like an IOU. It can represent man hours. If I have a $100, that means I earned that at the going rate of maybe ten dollars an hour. This $100 means I worked ten hours. When I present that at a store, I am saying, "I am trading ten hours of my work for groceries." The value of the groceries is set by man hours spent along the way and added up, to grow, transport, market, and get the groceries into my hands. The buyer and seller are agreeing on the value of the man hours involved in the deal on both sides, and calling it fair. Money then is a symbol of a trade taking place.

I make a custom knife. Instead of carrying that knife around trying to trade it, I trade it for money, an IOU that says I am owed for five man hours of work. Whatever the work was does not matter, it's recognized when I cash it in. I hand this small piece of paper to the grocer and it means, "I made a knife and sold it. This piece of paper is the substitute. You can take this paper and redeem it for a knife if you want one." Or, he may see me at the fair and hand me the same $100 saying, "I traded groceries for this piece of paper. Now I hand this paper to you for one of your knives, because I don't feel like carrying groceries to trade at the fair." That $100 represents so many items of groceries. I can go to his or any other store that recognizes this IOU called 'money' and exchange it for other goods. We agree on what this piece of paper represents. This is my understanding of what money is. Gold used to back money so we could take our dollars and redeem it for gold. If we chose, we could stockpile the gold. Why bother? Instead I can redeem my dollars for goods, food, commodities, services, and luxuries. I prefer not to hang on to too much money because a time could come when this form of IOU is no longer honored. I do not wish to get stuck with a pile of useless IOU's! So I redeem them for 'stuff' I can use on a regular basis. I lose the interest? No. My stuff increases in value faster than interest in the bank.

If you are saying the government steps in and interjects an extra hundred dollars into the system that no one earned, believing it boosts the economy, this is workable on a small scale. But who gets that 'free' $100? Me? The grocer? Interjected into the economy through who? Perhaps the banks? Someone, somewhere has $100 no one earned with man hours. Since we could fool some of the people some of the time, but not everyone forever, it makes me think this is not the correct answer to where all the money comes from. I consider the stock market backs up the dollar. I think the stock market is a Ponzi scheme. That's what backs our economy?

I no longer believe money comes from the rich. We both agree, the rich avoid taxes to a great degree by keeping money overseas. The government favors the rich. It is therefore hard to imagine the rich are fronting all this money that supports all of the growing poor majority of the population. The rich are not about to voluntarily hand over their hard earned money for free. The government in my observation wants people to be poor; creates poverty, then supports the poor. Time and again on more than one level I see free enterprise stifled. Why would that be to anyone's advantage? I kind of grasp the Feudal System as I read about it, and why the lords did not want commerce and trade. Does that really apply now?

I have a theory, that it is cheaper for big companies to buy from the competition, than to have us compete. It's cheaper to pay you $20,000 a year through various programs than to deal with the same $20,000 loss due to competition. Cheaper to pay 1/3 of the population to not work. Get out of the game. Leave the game to those of us who run it. Cheaper than going to court over rights to compete. There is an advantage in creating a work force of slaves. Those between a rock and a hard place begging for a job, any job. *Have the rich got a job for you!* I am not sure how this saved money gets from the hands of big companies into the hands of government. A method not out in the open or above board, but universal. Election contributions? Lobby money? Kickbacks? Instead of paying taxes, companies in some way pay to get things done. Is it some system related to paying off the mafia? Someone named Bugsy comes around with a baseball bat and collects it? Or, are there really trillions of dollars paid in taxes?

I used to think government money was our tax dollars. Then came to the conclusion there is way more money than we all pay in taxes. The Enron scandal happened, huge bank rip offs to the tune of a trillion dollars. That is $50,000 per man, woman, and child in the country, I'm told. Whose money was that? That is not tax dollars. The average person is not contributing that kind of money in taxes. That is the baby boomers retirement money; Social Security they paid in, interest paid on homes, cars. But, how does that trillion dollars end up in the hands of the government? From the hands of bank officials if that's where it is generated? Do they keep a few million or a billion, and pass the rest off to the government to grease the wheels? How did that trillion get spent; where did it go? Is it an ongoing unlimited supply? I see the next generation after the baby boomers not being such suckers to be workaholics. Banks deal in debt. I am not clear on how debt gets converted to dollars unless debt equals future expected dollars. Debt and loans are connected. That's a Ponzi scheme. Such schemes eventually fail. It's just a matter of when. That's supposed to be a crime and illegal. Would we all buy into such a scheme knowing it is going to fail, and is illegal? That would be odd.

The upcoming generation is much less trusting of either banks or the government. They have no choice? They simply do not work as hard. As our society gets more socialist or communist where we are all guaranteed a certain level of living, where does the influx of prosperity come from? Is some other country being exploited? I have trouble following the money. Will we run out of countries to exploit? I wonder. I'm just a peasant. A simple person wishing to survive living a simple life. It would take someone higher up the food chain to explain. I see the next generation with the hand out claiming they are owed. Gimme, gimme! It all should be free! So! How is it all going to get paid for? Who is handing out all the free stuff, and who paid for it? Why aren't more people wondering? I don't get it. If a stranger stops me on the street and hands me anything for free, at least I wonder if the gift is stolen, or what this stranger is up to. What is it I am being part of. Maybe the stranger is just kind, and wants me to have this gift. But often times not, they want something not asked up front. I have trouble believing my government gives free stuff out of kindness.

My good friend Norman Vaughn, the rich explorer, tried to explain it to me. He understood. His money originated from old money in England long ago.

I had told him I believed in cash. "Norman, save the money, buy what you want with the cash."

He had snorted how stupid that is. "It's all about credit, Miles."

Credit is like a shell game. Somewhere along the credit line, money simply disappears. He tried to explain how banking works; interest rates, stock, loans, credit. Coghill taught me how it works as well. I suppose I was beginning to get the hang of it on a small scale.

Norman tries to introduce the concept of money to me. "Miles, to get rich you have to understand money does not represent something you earned, or deserve, is backed by something, or can be redeemed for anything." He gives some examples. Money is numbers being shuffled across a screen. Power points, a shell game, a scam, movement in the direction of bigger numbers, by betting, bluffing, flexing. Sometimes the privilege of a bloodline. The rich depend on a population of worker bees, who think money means something they earned, backed by something tangible to be redeemed. The lure of it motivates the working class to get things done. "The poor, working class, and semi rich, get to keep some small amount. The truly rich lend it, borrow it, have credit lines."

The bottom line might be, how much does the government really have? Is it unlimited? On the one hand, 'we are broke' and cannot afford road signs, better police pay, the VA, fire trucks, or toilet paper for prisoners. 'Broke' we are told. So far in debt we can't pay our interest to China. Yet plenty of money to go to war, explore outer space, or track a criminal down. It's all very puzzling. I wonder if it is the stock market backing our money. Isn't the stock market a sucker's game, no different than bingo, or the lottery? Our economy is based on Powerball? Isn't that scary? Especially when we find out it is rigged? The stock market is rigged. Meaning, for one person to get rich, thousands have to lose. I doubt very much it's purely random. Likewise, I doubt very much the average investor is among those privy to inside information. Are there enough who think it is not rigged? Or are the majority addicted to gambling and do not care?

What is wrong with simply being in as much control of what is required for my survival as possible? It's hard to bet into a game when you do not know who is holding what cards. That's gambling. I do not believe in gambling. *If my life depends on gambling, I'm going to load the dice.* I did not make the rules. I do not like the rules. But I am going to survive. There is no way to bet into another man's game and come out ahead. Norman told me getting rich is all about your credit limit. Buying power. The more you spend, the better the deal. He thinks saving and paying cash is a suckers game. You pay full price. You go broke. As Norman explains it, someone somewhere along the line gets caught holding the bag; the pig in a poke.

"The object, Miles, is not to let it be you!" Norman tells me my view of what money is, is flawed. The rich define money differently. He repeats again, "It is not an IOU, it is units of power. Grains of powder in a weapon. Power that in itself can demand services and goods, without spending it." He goes on, "If you have a billion dollars, you do not spend it. People give you stuff, do things for you because you just might help them some day. Banks lend you even more money at even better interest so they can use your numbers as collateral. Your numbers go in a portfolio, a bundled package, that is shown to another bank, and used to get an even bigger loan, at even better interest, with perks thrown in on the side. I never see the paper, Miles. I swipe a card, and goods pop up in front of me. It's magic."

"MILES, I got a notice in the mail, my food stamps got cut by $20 a month." A friend laments.

I reply, "So what are you going to do about it?"

"There is nothing I can do, Miles."

"Exactly." Once you depend on it, it can be any amount down to nothing. "It did not start out at nothing though did it! Oh, you were promised all kinds of things when you got sucked in, right?"

"It is the same if you grow a garden, Miles! Weather can ruin your entire crop!"

I do not agree it is the same. "There are things I can do about it ahead of time and afterwards." I can grow a variety of produce that can withstand different weather conditions, plant ten times what I need. I can handle the little I have more efficiently. Save carrot, turnip, and beet tops. I can move five gallon buckets into the greenhouse to grow there mid-season. I can give more personal care to the garden, like cover it in the cold, protect it from rain, bugs, and drought. I am not helpless. I am not sitting with an eye full of tears, and a rejection notice in my hand. There are lights on in my eyes, a smile on my face, a cockiness to my walk. How do you protect your food stamps? I think the rich say exactly the same about their hedge funds and investments as I say about the weather and my garden. There are ways to protect your future, just not so many options for those in the middle. Does the money then come from the 99 percent of the population on the edge who are serfs to the rich? Someone explain it to me please.

I believe in cash. Here I am counting just the $100 bills at a show.

# CHAPTER NINE

## AUTHENTIC INDIAN ART, TRUE PUBLIC SENTIMENT, PROBATION ISSUES, REALITY TV IS INTERESTED

I pass a news article over to Iris to read. Kind of a related subject. One of our necessities of life, health care, right up there with food.

Sunday, November 16, 2014 **Obama Care**
    News Miner Nov. 16th opinion page
    **The Gruber confession**
    Gruber is a major participant in the formation of Obama Care, and admits in order to get it passed, the laws were deliberately made obscure and deceptive. "If you had a law which made this explicit, that healthy people pay in, and sick people get money, it would not have passed."
    "It's not unconstitutional to lie."

Mandatory government health care. Iris tells me, "Yes, I inquired. Under the plan, my monthly payments would be $750. Nothing I can do about it. All I could do is opt out and pay the penalty. That's more than half my income." *That's what happens when we bet into other people's games.* "Aren't you going to face the same thing, Miles?! We all face it!"

"Not really, I hardly worked for wages in my life. I set it up that way on purpose." I explain, I did not pay much in, there is not much to take out, get stolen, or owed me. I'm one of those poor people mentioned, one who is handed money - if I choose to put my hand out. For now, I prefer to go to Mexico and pay cash for health care as I need it. I do not use ordinary methods to measure and record my worth. Much of my wealth is not in dollars. A majority of what I have in dollars, is cash that can't be automatically deducted with nothing I can do about it. *You want it? Come and get it. Good luck! Put another way, to get sugar from the beet, you have to find the beet to squeeze. No findy, no takee.*

A discussion goes in the direction of being 'legal' later on with Josh. He is Native American, and does not understand the white man's sense of justice, taxes, and various laws, including money. He is in many ways 'exempt' by the fact of being Native. We discuss how the handcrafts of his people are protected.

"Miles, you do art that may as well be Native! You live more Native than most Natives I know! You use authentic materials, have knowledge, live the life." Josh still thinks it is ok I can't get the same money or sell it in the same way as his Native son, the artist, can. Because the white man screwed his people. So his people are owed. I only nod. We have discussed his views over the past 30 years. His latest bit of information, "Look up the sale of Alaska between the Russians and the whites. It says right there in the deed that the land belongs to the Natives."

We all know what long ago treaties with the Indians means right? Diddly squat. I can only say, "Well Josh, in the lower states anyhow, the Natives and whites went to war and the Natives lost. But the Natives for the most part tried to win. If they had won, it is my opinion they would have wiped every white man from the land. There would be no reservations for us. We'd have all been killed. Conquered people anywhere on the planet do not have it so good. It's the short end of the stick. Bummer. In most places, guess what happens when the conquered complain!" I add, "But, Josh, I am on your side. I am treated like one of the minorities; one of the conquered people; because I chose to live like this." I look up laws concerning native art after talking to Josh about his Native crafts.

## INDIAN ART AUTHENTICITY

The Indian Arts and Crafts Act of 1990 (P.L. 101-644) is a truth-in-advertising law that prohibits misrepresentation in marketing of Indian arts. It is illegal to offer or display for sale, or sell any art or craft product in a manner that falsely suggests it is Indian produced. Penalties up to a $250,000 fine or five years in prison. The Act broadly applies to the marketing of arts and crafts by any person in the United States. Some traditional items frequently copied by non-Indians include Indian-style jewelry, pottery, baskets, carved stone fetishes, woven rugs, kachina dolls, and clothing.

    DEPARTMENT OF THE INTERIOR
        Indian Arts and Crafts Board

25 CFR Part 309
RIN 1090-AA45
Protection for Products of Indian Art and Craftsmanship
American Indian and Alaska Native arts and crafts, improving the economic status of members of federally recognized tribes, and helping to develop and expand marketing opportunities for arts and crafts produced by American Indians and Alaska Natives. Phrases that refer to the 'style' of a particular Indian tribe when the items are not made by artisans of that tribe, but imitate the work of that tribe is allowed.

Hmmm. Ok. I go to eBay rules to see what internet selling accepts. I use Pay Pal that is owned by eBay, so even my own web site must follow eBay rules if I expect to use Pay Pal.

Not allowed on eBay: Describing items in the following terms because they make it hard for buyers to find authentic versions:
Alaska Native style
American Indian style
Native American style

Other descriptions that may suggest the item was made by a Native American. Items not made by Native Americans can't be listed in Native American categories. Not allowed on eBay, items listed in the Non-Native American Crafts category described.

**What is allowed**
Non-Native American items in the style of Native American art or crafts have to be listed in the Collectibles > Cultures & Ethnicities > Native American: US > Non-Native American Crafts category only.
You should describe items as Non-Native American Crafts if they weren't made by Native Americans or if they are reproductions.

Ok. I take in all of the above. On the surface it makes sense, with good intentions. In general, anyone can alter anything by 10% and call it their work to include written books, music, visual art, patents, trademarks, drugs, scientific discoveries, inventions, etc. Stealing and mislabeling anyone's craft is a bummer. Look at all the knock offs coming in from overseas! Taking advantage of other people's discoveries is a way of life. Look at the computer age and what is going on! Why would Indians be specifically protected with added wording. Rare coins get copied, furs, fossils Viking art, war relics, antiques in general, famous artists, famous musicians. Some are of more value and interest than 'Indian art'. All unmentioned. Similar to the prison rule, only Indians get special clothing privileges for religious reasons. Christians cannot wear crosses, Jews cannot wear head cap.

At one time, seventy percent of all native crafts were not authentically made by a native. That sucks. It's wrong. I agree. I did something about it in the past. I tried hard to help create rules that would help validate Native crafts, connected with the native ID card number in a data base.

Ninety percent of all crafts made by Native Americans are not authentic. For example, Natives can buy a Barbie doll, alter it by the legal ten percent and call it an 'authentic native made doll' with no legal problems.

Natives can—and do—buy my art, alter it ten percent and resell it as their own personal traditional handcraft, and get twice the money I can get. There is no penalty for that. I have seen natives get dolls, rings, Mandela's and various crafts from China for a few dollars, add a do-dad and sell it on an exclusive market they have a corner on, that no one can compete with, for top dollar. Some Alaska Native ivory carvers send their ivory to 3$^{rd}$ world country carvers, have the ivory carved by slaves, and sent back, to be sold as authentic Eskimo art.

I know this because my friend, Jay, in Tucson has his Bali workers do the carving for the Eskimo. He works for communities, through Alaska Native corporations. Part of his payment is in finished carvings made from Eskimo ivory, exempt from restrictions for resale. Tucson vendors buy these in large wholesale amounts, including myself. I often made a rubber mold and made copies in wax, altered them, made a new mold and made bronze replicas for caps on my crystals. None of us *in any industry* can compete with slave labor at twenty-five cents an hour.

I have, in the past, tried to sell authentic raw materials to natives to use in their traditional manner. There are few buyers. I offered real sinew from moose; leg bones, natural dyes, teeth, claws, feathers - all naturally handled with no chemicals.

"No, I have a source in China." I see these natives bless the product, sing a native song over it, hand it to a tourist with reverence, for 'top dollar.' Given by someone who has zero connection to the land or the real materials, or even the spiritual aspect of a lifestyle that many Indians lost long ago. Many natives have no clue how their ancestors lived. They were raised on Big Macs. This seems common, as my friend, Bean, tells me his stories of shiploads of copies of about anything you want getting shipped from 3$^{rd}$ world countries with fake labels.

Prison showed me this. Not one Native American was interested in fresh produce from the garden. None were interested in gardening. None had a connection to the land. None appeared to be interested in getting back to the land by joining in such discussions. None believed in subsistence, or being self-sufficient.

I live in the old way; authentic, understanding the land; the lifestyle that these Native artists I meet, only talk of. I cannot sell my product as authentic. I have to call it a replica. "You see the eBay rules!" I can't get the money or the validity; nor deal with companies through selling outlets like eBay, that bow to the Indian.

Yes, I sound miffed; personally insulted, jealous; feel spiteful. Ok, there is that. After all, I started out worshiping everything Indian. I've lived in the old way as Indians did more so than most Indians. More connected to the land. The authentic is labeled fake, while the fake gets the authentic label.

But let's set my personal feeling aside. There is a great deal of hanky-panky going on selling art in the world. Few offenses come with such a penalty as imitating Indian Art. There are all kinds of ethnic art. It's all being exchanged worldwide in a free for all.

Part of my market in the past was 'Mountain man art,' or 'reenactment,' or 'Goth.' None of these categories exist on eBay. They are tiny niche markets in search engines.

"MILES, did you get an email yet from Dr. Stephaney?" Iris wants to know if I heard from the Mexican eye doctor. Once again I am trying to get permission from the probation officer to go see both my dentist and eye doctor in Mexico. I already lost teeth I did not have to lose. I wish to save the rest if possible! Prison food and treatment was not good for my health. Mrs. Probation still wants some proof I have an appointment and legitimate reason to go to Mexico. This is reasonable. She is doing her job and wants to be sure I am not scamming her and going to Mexico to buy drugs or something else illegal. I do not mind having the eye doctor or dentist contacting Mrs. Probation. Or better, give the contact information to Mrs. Probation, let her do a checkup! After all, she called my mother to talk to her for verification I have a mother, and my mother really wants to see me.

"No. You have the dentist contact me." Ok. "No, email is not a good enough method. Emails can be faked." Ok. But I have to contact the eye doctor by email with a request she call the US legal system. I do not hear from the eye doctor after three tries. We do not have long distance on our phone. No international on the cell phone.

"Miles, let's ask our friend Valarie at the seniors if we can use her phone!" She is in charge there and helps out seniors like us with a variety of senior issues that come up.

We reach the eye doctor's office in Mexico on the phone, but it is the secretary. She cannot speak English. All we can really do is ask the doctor to email us. The doctor cannot come to the phone, she is performing surgery right now.

"Iris, maybe we can use the seniors computer and email from here!" Iris does not know why it would make a difference whose computer is used! Partly I am not trusting my computer. I am not confident I am the administrator. Summed up, I may not be in charge of my computer. Worth a try. We send out an email.

The next day we have a reply at the senior computer. We read the rely, and the copy of what we sent to the doctor. The date is the same, but the email copy we sent is exactly one year old. The email was sent by the doctors phone. It is unlikely she would still have a message from us in her phone a year old! This is the only message she gets that she is replying to, even though we sent three others from home. She thinks it is our new message. It seems unlikely the server would get mixed up by exactly a year.

Valerie says, "It looks to me like all messages you try to send addressed outside the country are being monitored, intercepted, read and possibly resent, and possibly not. The ones from your home computer were blocked. The email from this computer got intercepted, and those who held it and read it accidentally forwarded the one they kept in the file from a year ago." I admit it is odd to get an email outdated by a year.

"Miles? Yes, this is Mrs. Probation. I did try the phone number you gave me and got New York." I confirm I gave her the right number for the Mexican doctor. I do not believe Mrs. Probation. If she does not want me to go to Mexico, just say so. Let me get on with my life, make other arrangements.

December comes around. I have been keeping busy with art to take to Tucson to the knife event I signed up for. There should be a Green Valley Saturday Market, Foil is supposed to line up for me.

At the senior center one of the new helpers and I talk. Helper tells me he finally got a temporary job working for Fish and Game doing a survey in Healy to get opinions on the impact of the gas exploration going on across the river in Nenana. We both wonder what that has to do with Fish and Game. Then we both wonder why people outside the affected area are being asked how it impacts them, but not those inside the area.

"It goes much further than that Miles. This is random, and I am given a map that is hardly usable. A photo of a photo that had pins in it, marking where people who are to be interviewed live. None were in a subsistence areas. Yet the questions have to do with subsistence activities, getting berries, cutting firewood, hunting moose, fishing, etc. A lot of money is being spent for this survey. Not much useful information will come from it. Whatever information is received will be very biased in the direction the gas people want."

Yes, I see how it goes. The gas company will say, "Extensive research was done and money invested to get the opinion of the locals before proceeding to the next level. We care about the locals and what affect we have on them." Any survey should be Nenana people. Subsistence people should be involved. The ones out trapping; using the area where the gas exploration is going on. Helper gives me details of how much money is getting spent to accomplish nothing. To fulfill a legal requirement to have local input. Healy, thirty miles away meets the legal federal, 'local' definition. In the same way the new moose hunting policy in Nenana was discussed at a meeting in Healy.

"The gas people suspect they will get questions asked they can't answer, Miles."

I repeat my own wish. "Put a power plant in the area where the gas is. Make power, then transport the power down the new power grid intertie. Rather than building a gas pipeline. A lot cheaper. A power plant would employ some locals with permanent full time work."

There is little use protesting gas exploration. We need it, it will be gotten. I'm not against it. I am against our need for it. The solution I believe in is, all of us as a society cutting back on our power needs. Stop being so wasteful.

"Not going to happen, Miles." I know. "But you set a good example for others to follow, Miles."

"I used to. Not so much anymore. Where has it gotten me?"

"Miles, it seems to me everyone who used to live remote subsistence in your area on the Kantishna was run off. In the same exact area where the gas exploration is going on. Is that just a coincidence?"

A bit of a loaded question. There would be no way to know the answer. I'd rather not think so. I hear from others like me around the interior having issues. Parks are expanding, Native claims get involved. I sense and over all dislike for citizens anyplace a camera cannot be on them tracking their whereabouts. A tractable cell phone should be in all our hands, ideally turned on. We are not going to discuss why.

Iris goes to the post office to check our mail while I stay and chat at the seniors. The latest Alaska Trapper magazine comes in. I am lifetime member #47 and get the magazine each month during the winter. Iris points to a section of the magazine for me to read. According to the Fur Information Council of America (FICA), U.S. fur sales were a staggering $1.39 billion in 2013. The market created more than 32,000 full time jobs and an additional 155,000 part time jobs for seasonal workers.

I nod after reading. "I did not realize trapping is still a big industry in the country. At one time, trapping was the single biggest business in the country. "Iris, Alaska was most valuable to the Russians because of the Pribilof fur seals. Before gold, timber, fish, and other resources, it was furs."

"The country seems ashamed of that now, huh?"

What can I say? My public defender told me, "You chose an illegal profession to get into!" Not illegal activities within the profession. The entire profession is held in suspect as, 'Only criminals trap furs'.

"It is hard to get a handle on true public sentiment, Iris." Certainly this note in the trapper magazine is good bait for the brain to snap up and hold on to. I do not even know if 1.39 billion is a lot of money, compared to other occupations. It might represent the amount of money made by the sale of Hershey kisses in the past week. "Once I get past counting all my fingers and toes, it's all Greek to me." We both laugh.

At home I am dealing with customers and emails. I get customers asking a lot of what I feel are un-necessary questions, wasting my time over a four dollar product. I cut and paste a standard reply to one, a month after my time was wasted.

> "Hello Dear valued customer, did your package arrive? I'd like to verify. Could you give me the check number you paid with, the time it arrived, tracking number, name of the postmaster who delivered it, the exact shipping cost charged, and, the condition of the package? I do not need the information, I was just wondering. Thanks!"

I sigh and grumble. I do not send the email. I just feel better pretending I did, to give the customer a taste of their own medicine.

Iris is back to a conversation about numbers. How we can visualize a certain number of something. "I could imagine ninety-nine bottles of beer on the wall."

I say, "I can visualize a flock of a thousand geese." And add. "I'd know the difference between a thousand and two thousand."

"A thousand cupcakes on a bakers shelf." Could we comprehend a million? Say, 'No, that is two million?' We doubt it. At some point numbers become meaningless in terms of understanding them.

"Except money!" We agree.

"We know how to count zeroes."

"Speaking of counting, how many Christmas cards should I paint this year?" I missed Christmas the past two years. Many people in my address book will have moved. I lost touch with them. My sister for one. I'm not quite sure where my son is. He is supposed to be in Hawaii going to school. His mother says he got an apartment and not in the dorm anymore. Mitch never wrote and said. Even the letter to the ex had to be forwarded. I'm not sure where Karen, May, or Joy are these days either. I heard Joy moved into the house her father had when I met her, some potato farm out of town. I thought her father gave it to her. I think though it had gotten sold and the owners wanted to resell and Joy and her husband bought it. She has children now, more than one. Older than she was when I met her. Geez.

I have kept in touch with Helm, my German friend. Will writes he is living outside these days. Alaskans refer to anywhere not here as 'outside'. There is 'us', and then the rest of the world I guess. Will has MS. Trouble getting around. Not dirt poor though. He has enough money to have a house and care. He last wrote that the weather here gets to him, and the high prices. We remind each other of the early days when we were both greenhorns, living in tents and in his car. Being short, I could stretch out and sleep sound across the front seat. He would have to listen to me happily snore while he was all scrunched up in the back seat.

He joined me one winter, for a short time in the furnace room of an apartment complex. The Rampart building. I explain to Iris. I discovered the furnace room unlocked roaming around as a street person. I bought a lock, and put it on. Found a mattress alongside the road and moved into that furnace room. Others saw me come and go sometimes, but assumed I had one of the other apartments. As long as the furnace ran, there was no reason for the land lord or a maintenance man to enter.

I was that maintenance man. "Yup, yup all is fine, go back to your room. I just need to grease some bearings; make sure everything is working!" People were happy to see me making sure they kept warm. That's me. Will rolled around on the floor laughing. He thought that was so funny. "No need to live in your car, Will. Come on over to my place and warm up for a few days!" It was fifty below outside. I smile at those long ago days.

I usually print up sixty to eighty Christmas cards. That's about how many people I know well enough to say hi and wish well. A few are long term customers. There is Simon, who I helped out on a hunting trip thirty years ago. He has never forgotten. He lives in Michigan. Every year sends pictures with the deer he got, or turkey, or fish. He now hunts with his girls. The girls have kids now, who hunt with them. There had been a hard time a bunch of years ago. Car crash. Killed his wife and threw him for a loop for a few years. Never seemed to get over the loss of his wife. Raising two girls by himself. Always cheerful when showing off pictures of him and his buddies and girls at deer camp!

I have memories of others I know.

**Past flash**

I'm in the newly opened Riverfront Café in Nenana along the river. I stop in to check out the food since it is next door to the cultural center where I sell my art. The waitress looks familiar. I ask her, "Is your last name Isberg?"

She blinks like, 'how would I know that?' She nods. Yes, I was correct.

I say, "I know your mother. You look just like her."

The waitress says, "I do not know my mother. She died when I was two years old. How would you know her?"

I'm sorry to hear of the loss.

"Nancy and I used to go dancing at the Howling Dog Saloon in Fox, back in the

70s. I suppose she was like a girlfriend for a while. We both loved to dance. But she fell in love with the drummer of the band. I was gone a lot in the wilderness trapping."

The waitress nods, "This sounds about right. My father was in a band that played at the Howling Dog. He strangled my mother."

Forks in the road, playing 'what if.' Nancy had wanted me to stay in town and be with her. The musician was her next guy. She was ready to settle down. If I had stayed with her, she might be alive. This child might be mine, and she'd have both parents.

**Past flash ends**

I have kept in touch with many long ago girlfriends. I think of this when putting together a Christmas list and who to track down. Not so much now that I am with Iris. I rarely parted on bad terms with women. Only once in fact. There was that gal I met through Mother Earth magazine, Palace, from Georgia. She lied about her age; started writing me when she was sixteen. Said she was eighteen, I was twenty-five. She did not take well to being remote. Ran off with Joe. Hard to recall now. Involved in the Silka killings so long ago when a tenth of the population of Manley Hot Springs was shot. Made national news. She took a dislike to me; I was not 'outlaw' enough for her. Told me I was not a survivor; too nice. She met an outlaw all right. Years later he's dead, for the very reason of being too quick to make threats, use intimidation, pull a gun. She assumed this is what being Wild Miles, was about. *No. Wild is more kind. It is civilization filled with cruelty.*

Maggie was my first love at fourteen years old. We still write after losing touch for twenty-two years. Heidi, Karen, Nancy, Sue, are the main ones. I think of Becky from hippie hill when the houseboat was being built all those years ago. What fun we had on the snow machine exploring the wilds together. She was temporarily with another guy, so I lost touch. We were always just friends, with that 'what if' factor hanging unspoken. She got a pipeline job. I heard she got involved in women's rights and sued the pipeline company for discrimination. That was the latest cool thing for women to do back then. I can understand getting the short end of the stick because you are a woman. This needs to be fixed. But when you are being paid $30 an hour when normal wages is five dollars an hour. Shut up. She had said, "Yeah, everything is fine. But why turn down the chance to get a million dollars when you can?" I was not interested in her after that. I felt if she had that outlook on a job, she'd do the same to her man. No thanks.

I'm lucky. All the women I have known have been fairly descent, good women. Issues were over lifestyle mostly. If a personality clash, it was nothing we fought about; just recognized it isn't going to work. We can still be friends. Two women wanted to have children and used me to do so, without being honest with me. I decide instincts can be strong, and capable of running our lives. That does not make them monsters. It just put me in a precarious situation at the time. One time, heartbroken because I thought it was love. The other time angry, because we had a deal. Who of these do I wish a Merry Christmas?

There are guys too! I never forget Maul, the friend and pilot who flew for me and had me over for Thanksgiving, took me in as part of the family. The schoolteacher in Manley and her pilot husband are dear friends. Piper, who flew me out my first year is still alive, but I never kept in touch with. He's the one who told his wife, "We'll never see him alive again."

Bill Underhill from the Diamond Willow shop at Alaskaland is still alive but his wife passed on. He is still a preacher in his old home state of Tennessee. I hear he is elderly and not in good health though. My old neighbors on the Kantishna, Tom and Forest are not close friends. They are animal rights people. We got along, but maybe only because we had to, as neighbors. I did not see it that way, but maybe they did.

I never forget Crafty, Tim, Seymour, even Tusk. I hardly see Moonshine and Wren, but write them. They still live on the river near the mouth of the Kantishna. Over the years their lives have changed. They have a sail boat in the Canary Islands and go sailing in winter. Moonshine does not race sled dogs anymore, but fishes and keeps dogs! These two are a good example of what a subsistence life left alone can be like. It can still be done. Proving it is me who has issues unique to me, or maybe a majority of subsistence people.

A lot of this comes up every Christmas when reviewing who I know. Who to be grateful to. It's good to take time to remember and think about the past. At least once a year. Count our blessings. For someone who likes to be alone and doesn't like visitors, I seem to know a lot of people.

---

It's winter. The dark, cold time of the year. Wind, snow swirls around the 1916 log cabin. Northern lights flicker overhead at least half the nights. The walk to the shop across the yard becomes an adventure. Most mornings, I venture out about 5:00 am, head to the shop by moonlight. I'm making next summer's art and knife inventory. Prison is becoming a lost memory of long ago. I enjoy those creative hours in my cave. Winter is a laid back time in the village. Meeting times mean, give or take half an hour. Common notes on business doors say, 'Back tomorrow,' 'Call me at Sue's,' 'see me at the café.' No one is upset. Even the city office may or may not be open today. The mail may or may not arrive today. The paper might be two hours late. There is always tomorrow.

There are a variety of happenings for those with hobbies. We have a book reading club. There are clubs for those who sew, cook, and exercise-yoga. Guys may get together for a shooting event, and talk guns. There are outdoor activates like trapping, snow machine rides, skiing, and dog mushing. Outdoor photography works as a hobby or a way to make some spare change. Winter is often computer time. I feel the things to do are endless! I'm puzzled by, 'There is nothing to do!' There aren't enough hours in the day to do everything! In the evening Iris and I usually watch TV. There are a few free channels put on by the university. Hardly any commercials. Usually educational programs. We like Nova. We look forward to Antiques Road Show, Red Green, Masterpiece Theatre, Globe Trekker, and Cashing In. Some of these shows might be local and few outsiders ever hear of them.

I abandoned my dish network. I decided I was being scammed. The attitude of the service was a grin and, 'What are you going to do about it, you have an investment!' I replied, "How about walk away from it!" And I did. I can rent movies and save money. But mostly we get movies at the library, garage sales, thrift stores, and the dumps transfer station. "That's what I can do about it."

At the end of summer, the owners of the RV park across the street give us their box of movies they offer to summer customers. We return the box of fifty movies in the spring when they open, with a few new ones added by way of a thank you.

I get tired in the middle of the day, and usually take a nap for an hour. It is nice to be able to rest when I am tired. Many people do not have that luxury! I feel the cold more than I did when young. I have hardly any wilderness adventure stories to tell of these days. Usually an adventure involves making a mistake. I have been at this so long, I seem not to make a lot of mistakes anymore. What could be an adventure, is just a routine, solved by having the right tool, and knowledge.

When young, going on a 700 miles trip into the wilds was guaranteed to be worth half a book. Now it's, "I went. I came back." There is no more to tell than the civilized person saying they made a trip to the store, "Oh yes, I ran into Ted." I work on a Christmas letter since I have been out of touch for so long. "Iris, I write up a standard letter I can cut and paste, but then add something personal to each person I send to." This letter goes with a hand painted card, that doubles as a small gift that can be hung up. "I visit people, and it is common to see years of my watercolors all lined up on a wall proudly being shown. Some of my Manley Hot Springs friends I visit have fifteen to twenty cards out!"

"That's nice, Miles, that you can do something that others appreciate like that, bring a little joy and beauty into their life."

So even though I could never afford lots of financial gifts, I have something to give from the heart.

I hear from my buddy Will who I have known and shared some adventures with since '73.

Glad ya made it through all that. I still feel you was wronged. I'm fine, been out of hospital since 14 Nov. I just can't walk. Got electric power scooter, don't look good for going back to Alaska, or my old life. I really don't know where this is taking me, it's hereditary perhaps, just drew a wrong straw. I love to hear what you got to say about your ordeal. Probably cannot talk on phone, huh, three years' probation must suck. I'm doing therapy, if I get much worse they are going to put me in assisted living. When it rains it pours. Is this what getting old is about? Love to hear about your ordeal, keep me posted! Will

I hear from people I do not recall! Many find me on the internet.

**Hi Miles**

Hope you can remember me and my family from the past of your childhood. I finally made it to Alaska to do some fishing on the Kenai River, and thought I should drop you a line. My brother Paul is the only family member left, do you ever talk to Eileen.

I still have, (or inherited the old wooden rocking chair) you managed to carve a notch into the arm rest. Hope you are doing well because life is getting shorter, and the bucket list is getting longer !!!

Your old friend and neighbor, **Dave Kratky**

No, I do not recall. My mind is not on people as much as others wish, or might think. I've told friends, "Folks who are close to others do not take off and be alone in the wilderness for most of their lives. Usually they have social problems of some kind." I'm glad our friendship meant something to this person, and they have good memories.

I AM NOW REPORTING for my probation contact by computer. There are some terms to review and agree to. I cannot have access to any 'dangerous weapon'. This is defined in the agreement I sign and understand.

*The term 'dangerous weapon' is defined in Federal Statute (18 U.S.C. § 930 (g)(2). This section states, in part, "[d] dangerous weapon" means a weapon, device, instrument, material, or substance, animate or inanimate, that is used for, or is readily capable of, causing death or serious bodily injury.*

I am once again puzzled. I have a machete, an ax and a chainsaw to get firewood. If these are not dangerous I do not know what is. I am allowed to make custom knives. How can I make them without having access to them. Propane, acetylene, oxygen, gasoline, Clorox, Drano - just off the top of my head are fairly deadly. I could level all of Nenana with these items. How much more 'weaponry' can you get? I am supposed to understand what is meant, but I do not. I am not being sarcastic or flippant, I'm honestly puzzled. Even if I got rid of 'all that', I have access to it every time I go in someone's home or a store. How do you get away from gasoline? Not dangerous? Say that after someone tosses some on you, followed by a match. It is not these items that are dangerous, it is the criminal mind desiring to do damage.

My understanding is, at any time I can get picked up and arrested for violating these conditions impossible to meet. I keep mentioning that. It's on my mind.

In order to maintain a law-abiding lifestyle, you will have to stay away from places and situations where illegal activity is going on.

YOU SHALL NOT ASSOCIATE WITH ANY PERSONS ENGAGED IN CRIMINAL ACTIVITY AND SHALL NOT ASSOCIATE WITH ANY PERSON CONVICTED OF A FELONY UNLESS GRANTED PERMISSION TO DO SO BY THE PROBATION OFFICER.

Association is defined as any planned, prolonged, or repeated, personal, telephonic, or written contact with a person having a felony record, or engaging in criminal activity, and/or if you had knowledge of, or should have had knowledge of his or her felony conviction or the criminal activity in which they were engaged during the times of your association. Incidental contact is not considered association. In the event you have casual contact with a person having a felony record, you will have to report this on your Monthly Supervision Report. If you are sought out or specifically approached by a known felon, immediately contact your Probation Officer. Incidental contact on a job site is not considered criminal association.

Permission for criminal association cannot be after the fact. You must have permission prior to the association. This permission will only be granted in exceptional situations.

This condition above seems impossible to meet. How do I know who is a felon? It is not tattooed on everyone's forehead. I do not ask everyone if they are a felon or not. A person may not tell me the truth. It states above, or engaging in criminal activity. *Well, Mrs. Probation officer, the most criminal people I have ever knowingly associated with in my life were running the prison. They are not felons, but it says 'or' criminal activity. Not 'and'. I take that to mean 'do not be around anyone who is engaging in criminal activity'. Frankly, that's everyone, including you. Can we be a little more clear on this?*

> NOTE: According to 18 U.S.C. § 1001, false statements on a written monthly report are considered law violations and not technical violations. Any false statements may result in revocation of probation, supervised release or parole, in addition to five years imprisonment, a $250,000 fine or both.

I take this to mean that I am agreeing to impossible rules and a violation of them can mean five years in prison. I take this to mean at any time Mrs. Probation could be upset about my book, my political or spiritual beliefs. The fact I eat meat, how I dress, my lifestyle, was an animal trapper, anything whatever. All she has to say is, "You broke the rules! You read them, and agreed! You were in possession of an ax. I consider that a weapon don't you?" Headlines in the news. I can see it. "Felon has ax waiting by door as officers approach." There is only one answer. No matter what she says, "Thank you!" smile, bow, whatever she wants. I've never been that kind of person before. I went through a lot of effort in my life to live in a way so as not to have to do it anyone else's way. Or be under anyone else's thumb doing their bidding. I do not like blackmail, intimidation, threats, extortion.

NENANA HAS a Christmas bazaar each year. I recognize one of the Huntington family members from when I lived in Galena in the 1970s. I greet him fondly and ask how life is with him.

"Miles, I had a hard time from the flood. Twelve feet of water in my yard. Even though the house was up on stilts, water was to the top of the windows." He explained how FEMA arrived, and offered to pay him $250,000 to move, suggesting Fairbanks. "What would I do there, Miles? My life is here, in the village." I remember when he built wood river boats, I had acquired one there many years ago. I know how much he loves subsistence and the great outdoors. This is his whole life. His father has been on the Federal Subsistence Board.

I say, "Yes, we dealt with FEMA here in Nenana when we had the flood. It was an odd experience."

"It is interesting, Miles. When I said, 'no thanks' to FEMA, I was told they could not help me. I got zero money for anything. I am trying to rebuild. I ran out of nails and scrounged some bent ones at the dump. But it is hard." Most residents took the money and moved to higher ground.

Josh has been hanging around my table and adds a comment. "There must be something under your land they want! Gold or oil! They want you to move so they can get it!"

I doubt that myself. Someone else adds, "The government prefers we all live in larger areas and not out remote. It is harder to keep an eye on us when we are so spread out."

It is hard to know what is going on. The only fact seems to be, lots of money was offered to move, no money to stay and rebuild. This appears to be 'help' steering someone in a specific direction. Anyhow, it is good to see someone from so long ago. Nice to get caught up on the news from Galena. My buddy, John Stam, is still there! He is the one who traded for one of my first boats, and helped me when my engine quit in a storm crossing the river. Larry, who gave me permission to use his trapline up Jack slough, is still there

TUCSON TIME ROLLS AROUND, as the annual event to look forward to every winter. Iris and I use our Alaska oil permanent fund money we each get to buy our tickets early. Deals this time of year are about half price. Quite a few customers remember me, and inquire by email, asking where I was last year, the year before, and will they see me?

Wednesday, January 07, 2015

**Hello Miles**, this is Ted Champine. Hey, I was wondering if you going to rock show? Nina and I are going Feb. 3rd thru 14th. How's everything else going there? Sorry so slow sending email. Hope to see you in Arizona. later bro **Ted**

**Hello Ted!**
I will be there in Tucson to see my mother during the show but do not set up there anymore. Hope to see you there! **Miles**

Iris sees an article in the news she thinks is of interest.

Wednesday, News Miner January 07, 2015

**Slaves freed from salt farms** living in grim shelters, some want to go back. In South Korea slaves working on salt farms were turned free. They ended up in shelters and did not know how to take care of themselves. What little they acquired was stolen. They were beaten up, without food. Ultimately some wished to return to the salt mines as slaves. The farm owner says, "It would be extremely difficult to run a salt farm without slaves. Normal people would not work at salt farms even if we begged them." "Doing society a favor, taking in the homeless, the disabled, the uneducated, and those who cannot get jobs doing anything else."

Iris and I discuss this. "Honey, this reminds me of my experience with the Cambodian mushroom pickers!" I got the impression they would not know how to be free and may not like it. There is something to be said for being taken care of, even if you have to work hard. Heck, many people have to struggle to the same extent slaves do working for someone else; for minimum wage or just enough money to get by. If you struggle you might come up with rent for this month, junk food, and the internet bill. Not everyone wants the responsibilities of being free!

Free can mean free to die, starve to death, get sick with no help. Slaves get some minimal level of everything required to survive. It is not likely you will be left to die any more than one lets their plow horse die. I believe people easily talk of freedom. As hard as it is for me to comprehend, some will not fight for it, struggle for it, give it the time, work or energy it requires. Freedom is filled with heartache and failure.

I like to study options; ways people live; choices; the various ways basic problems of life get solved. How we find food, shelter, the necessities of life. One option others choose, or prefer, or suits their personality, is have someone else do it all, and to be the boss's slave. Such a person can dream about a life such as mine for entertainment, as I read about their life for fun.

Iris comments: "I find it interesting such a story makes it in the news. That itself is interesting. There were decades when a story like this would not get printed. Possibly not allowed. Stories of people preferring slavery would go against government agenda. We were fighting communism and control. We were told only democracy works." It would be interesting if choosing this story has anything to do with preparing us all for a new agenda. Starting with, 'Actually, some people choose slavery voluntarily; maybe it's not that bad. Think about it.'"

A seed is planted.

**Hello Miles**, My wife has given me two of your handmade knives. I love my knives and was hoping you would be in town for our gem show. Please let me know if you are attending and where you will be located.

Thanks, **John Powers**

I add a note later, to remind me when reviewing my orders. (see reply after return from Tucson)

**From:** stevenwrigley@windfallfilms.com
**To:** miles@milesofalaska.net
**Subject:** Railroad Alaska

Hi Miles, Steven here, one of the producers on Railroad Alaska, I came across your website whilst researching Nenana and will be in the area tomorrow and Saturday—would be good to meet up if you're around as you may know someone in the area or you yourself might be interested in appearing on the show.

Let me know when a good time would be.

Thanks,
**Steven.**

I reply

My wife and I eat breakfast every Saturday at Roughwoods between 8 and 10. I assume this is where you would be staying so meeting there might work out. Or meet there and head on over to my house. **Miles**

We go back and forth a time or two.

Perfect let's meet for breakfast at 0930 on Saturday... Look forward to meeting you, give me a call when you arrive.
    S.

**Love your deal**. I go backcountry with mules and horses. Make Deer Jerky. Live on it and natural water. Process all my own meat.
    I want to make knives. For now, use blanks like yours and Edvanhoy. One day I will play with my own steel.

I make a note this guy buys a knife—pay pal $386
He wants to be friends. We begin discussing knives.

**Question**. I sharpen on a steel rod or diamond. Flat from. AG.Russel. How do you sharpen your knives that are hard enough to shave bronze or copper?

I explain how to sharpen a knife and how to put a guard on a knife.

Very good information. Good stuff on hard or tuff. Understand. May have to work at those guards on straight tangs. Your plan sounds great.
    Thanks. Miles.
    **Jeff**.

Also. I made a complete order. Then went back and ordered again to get some blades. If I'm charged the $60 twice. Just pick me out 4 more guards @ $15 EACH.
    I WILL be using whitetail horns for my handles. Thank you.
    **Jeff**.

Jeff wants to pick my brain, walk him through each step as his personal teacher. I save questions and answers in a file in case I ever put together some 'how to' instructions or books. My publisher friend suggests starting a blog. I think I am too busy to spend my time sitting at a computer chatting. While I get in and out and tend my web site, I am not interested in Facebook, Twitter, Live chat, Tweet or Blogging. All that has come along since I began business, and has gone beyond what I understand or enjoy. I'm shocked how much information we put out about ourselves on the internet. At heart, I am a 'back to basics' person; simple life, not complicated. I prefer 'one on one' contacts. Iris notices unhappily that I'd much prefer to find someone and talk rather than call.

In the same way, I prefer to deal with real people when I order items, one on one, in person is best. I prefer smaller business, Mom and Pop type suppliers. I'm willing to pay as much as a third more, to support this small business. I'm not looking to increase the volume of friends through the internet. I do not believe in privacy, but believe it is a necessity because the world is not open minded and accepting of anything different. Some people go so far as to be hostile.

All this is at the bottom of guys like Jeff, who thinks he wants to be like me, and thinks we have a great deal in common. It takes me time to open up and let anyone know me. I tell Jeff : "There is a secret or trick to getting a hard edge and soft back. I only heat the edge of the blade using a torch."

"Miles, this is a shock! I thought you knew what you were doing! Every master I ever read soaks the entire steal ten minutes for every quarter inch of steel at exactly 1450 degrees before quenching in 120 degree special oil!"

What can I say? My reply is often evasive and short. "Its magic!" People hear that and smile, and remain buddy.

"How do you do that, Miles!"

"Talent!"

"No! I mean I want to walk in your shoes, duplicate what you do, tell me how!"

I often say, "I could tell you the basics in ten minutes. I'd ask you to come back for your second lesson in twenty years. Or after making 10,000 items, whichever comes first." I am not trying to keep secrets. There is a 99 percent probability based on past experience you will come unglued at what I tell you. Worse, you may decide how I do it is illegal and or dangerous and I need to be stopped. I'd love to have someone say, 'I get it! How clever! Yes, I'd love to put the time in and do work like yours!' Not going to happen. So at some point I have to suddenly be busy. "Next!"

I think if I had more real relations and social interaction it would affect my fun. I'd feel guilty for how I do it. My confidence would waver. *How could I be right, and the rest of the world be wrong?* It's a choice, to simply not know how you do it, nor care. Press on! I am on my path as you are on yours. What I'm doing works for me. I hope what you do works for you. I really can't judge that. I'm sorry if your way is not working. Proven by the fact you are over here looking over my shoulder wondering how I do it. Yet, oddly when you find out how I do it, tell me, 'You can't! You shouldn't! I'll stop you!' How much sense does that make?

I take a break to do my emails. I have customers looking over my book writing before I'm calling it a done deal.

**Miles,**

I did a review, and ordered Book 3. Can you autograph it for me? Is Iris still in Alaska?

Hope all is well and you like the review.

**Thanks, Harold**

The next email involves a new customer overseas who wants a large amount of my stabilized wood! A big deal to me because I have been making a lot of product and not selling much. I'm convinced I have a good product so keep at it, but I need some sales!

**Ray**

I am waiting now to hear from 'some government agency' I was referred to on the subject of sending wood outside the country as you request. Like you, I believed this overseas shipping is not an issue. No problem, no permit needed.

I reflect on my progress.

I now get the impression that the government is in the mood to come unglued.

"What! Send wood! How can we protect the planet if you cut wood!" Is the attitude so far. "Of course, you might, if you pay us." I think comes next. This web site for the permitting process is less about getting a permit, more about protection.

The first paragraphs to come up on the site are instructions on how to turn people in and report offenses. Nothing about how to conduct or encourage legal business. Due to this, I am concerned. This should be a 'how to' site. Instructions on how to conduct business.

I expect "Welcome!" Welcome to the wonderful world of woodworking!

Gibson guitar was shut down for a while over a shipment of laminated wood. It is difficult to know where the rules come from or why. I have trouble believing it has to do with saving the environment. I pass on to my customer what I find out.

eBay now offers a service where a company handles all the permits. Items are sent to a US company that resends the material under their paperwork. I do not know what this added shipping fee is, or if such a service might be available outside eBay. I will inquire if I have time. This could solve a lot of headaches. **Miles**

Beyond the automated reply, I hear nothing from a human. The toll free number does not work in Alaska. It is common for us in Alaska to be treated as a foreign country. We get used to it. I get a run around. I never get an answer to my inquiry. Much like I went through over animal products. I feel treated like an enemy. I am concerned I am now on the 'person of interest' list, for no other reason then I made an inquiry that perhaps sparked an investigation. No one else I know is using any permit, or even asking if sending wood out of the country is a problem.

"Better to beg for forgiveness than ask for permission, Miles!" That is fine, until some official decides differently. Friends in small 'corrupt' countries laugh and tell me, "We pay off the local official. No problem. He has to eat too. He tells us exactly how much he wants. We pay him. He is our friend. We like each other. He eats dinner in our home. His children go to school with my children. As a friend he warns me if there is an inspection coming, or change in the rules, or officials from higher up arriving. We, together, keep it all in order. This helps both of us. It might cost me $500 a year. I know how much, pay, and there are no concerns, stress, anything to wonder about. Stamp, stamp, stamp. I have all my proper papers." He adds, "God bless the Czar and keep him far away!"

**Future Flash**

I'm reading a book in 2016, 'The Five Stages of Collapse' by Dmitry Orlov. I was attracted to it because of the cover words, 'Survivor's Tool Kit.' There would be a lot to quote to explain what I am observing.

One topic chapter is, **"Money corrupts."** I had noticed in the past that locally, the gal who dominates and has a monopoly on tourism in the community, Eagle, made a cool million in her life here. She donates flowers for the community flower pots, and $100 gift certificates for community events. A majority of the citizens praise how generous she is. There are a lot of words in the book discussing gifting, trades and barter. Talk of how well this works as life gets harder in a failing economy. The book reviews history and the process of collapse as it happened in other countries, thus not just an opinion, perhaps a lesson.

"Keeping the line between work and play purposely blurred," Rings a bell that resonates. People end up having to find things; make-do. "This state of affairs gives rise to widespread reliance on personal favors." Followed by, "Central banks become black holes." And, "You can learn how to opt out of the world of consumer gadgets. Create closed cycle systems for food production, shelter, maintenance, transportation, and so on." Further along, "forced to resort to illegal forms of commerce. The focus on illegality is in some sense inevitable." "A weak government can impose a ban but not enforce it." "The business of private protection consists of producing a substitute for trust in a market economy." "Extortionists would only take away their riches, the authorities will take your riches and your freedom." Speaking of local mafia control, "There is an oral culture, with minimal reliance on documents."

In Russian there were bandits after the collapse of the government. "In 1992 protection rackets were more or less legalized." "Business owners preferred to deal with racketeers rather than the police, the tax collector, or the courts. Seeing the legal process itself as a form of punishment." "Businesses avoided contact with the state in order to avoid having to pay taxes, fees, fines, as well as the need to file paperwork." "The most distrusted institutions are city hall and the police." "Mid-level criminals started to work for the government." "Financial and commercial collapse tend to be hard on those who fail to prepare." This refers to other countries that fell apart such as Greece, Russia, past societies throughout history that collapsed.

There is talk of what the early stages look like. Where and how collapse begins. It is considered very workable and realistic to pay for local protection to a mafia type organization that, 'takes care of things.' The very definition in Russia is, "smoothes things over." The book is filled with examples, details, but this sums up what is on my mind. These concepts support a lot of what I see and conclude on my own. Not that I feel it is a best solution, or even that I'd prefer this myself. Only that the idea crosses my mind and I study it. Like, "Pay this mafia guy his asking protection price, and actually receive protection. No more fees, permits, hidden costs, denials, courts, lawyers, delays, grey areas, maybe yes, maybe no. I could see that being a relief."

**Future flash ends**.

My friend What's His Name, says, "I come to the US and discover the one I pay is not my friend. This official does not tell me how much I owe. I must discover this on my own, with no help! If I pay the wrong amount, I go to jail! What help am I to this official then? I now pay him nothing! I am out of business! I'm hurting, he's hurting, the public pays for my prison time. A lose, lose, and lose all around situation. Does this make sense?"

I honestly say, "No it does not." I do not understand forms of government and how they work well enough to have an intelligent answer, based on facts.

"Information on other countries is as suppressed in the US as any other country. The difference is, we know it and you do not. As for permits, Miles, it appears to me your permitting process is simply paying organized crime for protection."

**Miles**. Ray here.

What is going on! I order from others and the wood arrives. No permit, no question! Are you in business or not! Have you heard anything yet and how much is this permit I never heard of? I cannot wait on this order forever, I have customers waiting! I'm willing to begin with a first offer of 100 blocks for knives at a wholesale to me of $35 each. If I like it, I have a need for another thousand at the same price.

**Hello Ray**

Sorry for the delay. The government appears to be antagonistic rather than helpful. It appears a permit is needed, but none has ever been issued. My hands are tied. There is no way to do so that the government does not know about.

I am on probation with fewer rights than the ordinary citizen. It is better to lose this order and not end up in trouble. I do not know how to get the permit I'm told is required. If you are dealing with others who avoid this permit, I suggest you deal with them. sorry! **Miles**

I am out many thousands of dollars in future sales here. I recognized the issues long ago. I ask Iris if she recalls.

"It was before my time Miles."

I just nod. I ask a judge as part of a plea agreement, to assign me an official who will be responsible for me having all my proper permits! So I may be legal! I wished to be in a position of saying, "Stack em up, where do I sign, how much do I owe!" Let me pay and leave me alone. If it's $1,000, fine! Because I am losing thousands of dollars in business not knowing what to do, turning away business. Let there be someone with a name I can point to and say, "Why didn't you give me all the permits I needed and collect all the money there is to collect?"

The person I was assigned, asked me first, to name all my contacts and sources that we may begin investigating them, and prosecuting more criminals.

Bean explains it to me as he sees it. "Tell everyone they need a permit. Do not supply the permit. The public hears the simple permit is only a few dollars!" Reasonable, so the public buys into it. Try doing business without this permit! Now you are avoiding paying your fair share! Angers the public!" I get it. The argument now goes, "Imagine! Your taxes are high because this selfish criminal will try to avoid his small $100 permit!" The public is outraged!

"Teach this criminal a lesson!" An indignant public screams.

"We need more strong government!" Not having this permit that is not available, is worth ten years in prison and a $200,000 fine.

"Now, Miles, look at where the big bucks come in!" I nod. He goes on, "So now, you did not pay $100 because there was no one to accept it. You now owe $200,000! You go to jail for ten years." The prison system gets $80,000 a year for ten years. And when you get out, you have been disarmed and cannot vote. "People who ask questions and complain are thereby neutralized."

The $100 is just the bait and jiggle. The yank and reel is not being able to pay the $100 because no one can issue you the permit! How slick is that! Ingenious I say!

"What a racket!" I see; the effort is not to have us obtain this $100 permit. The effort is setting you up for the fall. *Yet how would this work? It's odd. Doesn't the government want us working?*

"It gets even better than that, Miles!" I wonder how it gets any better than that. Now no one has all the correct papers. Even if they think they do. What that means is, anyone, at any time, can be brought in for questioning. Threatened, controlled, brought in line.

Bean gives the punchline. "Those selected to take the fall, are not randomly selected."

I pause and explain to Bean how this may have happened right here in Nenana! Nenana ran into this issue. Our mayor wanted Nenana to own and control a bridge across the Nenana River. Access to gas, oil, farmland, timber, and other resources. Nenana got the go ahead. Got as far as the pilings in the river and bridge parts delivered. This was financially difficult for our community. Unexpectedly, all is held up.

Being told, "Wait! You do not have a Federal Coast Guard permit!" It's free, but needs to be applied for and approved. The state says it is not necessary to have, and not federal jurisdiction. Information was supplied by Nenana four years ago. The Coast Guard has not had time to respond, may in fact never have time to respond. The work done and entire project is now 'illegal,' and halted. The free permit is absolutely a form of powerful control. The official reply is, "The form was not submitted in the correct computer format that we can read." Moving forward without this permit was deemed illegal.

Nenana lost ownership of the bridge. Millions of dollars. It is now under the control of the oil company doing exploration across the river. Nenana will not be able to collect a toll fee as a form of local income from the oil company. The bridge could end up gated. Nenana could end up without access to land we control across the river, due to homeland security risks to oil equipment.

Maybe worse than this, few in the community understand what happened. They blame the mayor for operating without a permit, and for this and other reasons, move to impeach him. A person who does what he is told is now in charge. There are no longer any bright ideas about how Nenana might get ahead.

I can see reasons big business that runs government would do better without small time competition. Free-lance private enterprise, or small communities may interfere with the big gears turning smoothly. What big enterprise is up to does not bother me as much as how the public buys into it. Like a mayor impeached by his own people.

If what Bean explains is true, this affects any interest people have as free thinkers, self-sufficiency and such ideas. Some may well get left alone. This depends on what? *Something not in our control.*

I remind Bean again, "My objective is not to get anyone in trouble. My objective is to live a simple legal life, left alone in peace. Pay off whoever needs to be paid off, and everyone remain happy."

"Well, Miles, you told me once about how organized crime handles things in other countries. I have had my own experiences along those lines. I told you of working in the high end hotel business overseas." We both agree there can be downsides! Organized crime can get rough! Increase the amount of their cut, extort us, burn our business down and such things as we hear about in the news. I had a little experience with this.

"I may have told you, Bean? About the local drug lord?" He does not recall. So I sum it up. I had some of my art stolen and the local cop was not interested in solving the crime. He is too busy and overworked. I worked things out with the local drug lord running the theft ring. It was easier than dealing with the cops, and got better, faster results.

Bean reminds me of a story he told me before about ordering any label for any item from India. Fake labels a lot of companies order, including his company.

"Mostly clothing and furniture since I was in the hotel business."

**Hello John**

I am just back from Tucson. Going over all my emails. I was not set up in Tucson. I was there more as a buyer this year. Think I emailed and gave my cell number, maybe my mother's number? But I also know we had some glitches with the phone. I should be attending again next year. Emailing me is better, I check my emails even at the show. Talk to you later then. **Miles**

**Miles**,

Welcome home my friend. I hope the Arizona sun did you well, and that you are getting on with your life. Two years ago we met your girlfriend at the Tucson show. She filled us in on the nasty little details of your situation. This was wrong from so many stand points, but now it's water under the bridge so to speak.

What really makes us mad is that Kurt Trump of Ivory Items in Anchorage has been caught with his second offense of dealing in restricted items this past fall. Then there is this link, which has been removed from the internet, but still has a foot print left.

www.pantagraph.com/news/world/asia/report-africa-ivory-smuggled-on...

Nov. 6, 2014 Chinese officials used a state trip by Chinese President Xi Jinping and others.

It was reported that they paid as high as $65,000 per pound for tusk. However this was the Presidents plane... The little guy doesn't stand a chance.

I smile. One of my long term customers, suppliers, friends. I hate to get into radical discussions. I try hard not to get upset over things I have no control over. This adds to the overall feeling all the regulations have little to do with saving animals. It's about control and power.

**Hey Martin**, oh my god this can't be fu+_)+* real.

I'm still in shock! I can't believe I quite randomly picked out the person who probably is as close to McCandless as can be by searching on the internet. I am not religious at all, but what I believe in is karma. And now I obviously got proof it exists. Thanks a lot for the immediate answer by the way.

Second thing I hardly can realize is, that you even would be able to pick a nice stone out of the river for me and document that with photos. Thank you so much! This is awesome!

I smile after looking at this customer's file. Young kid, engaged to get married. His lady is in love with Alaska, the wilds, and survival stuff. She read, 'Into the Wild' about the kid who went in the wilds and died. He is her hero. I am just like him! Now I can supply matching rocks from Alaska for the wedding rings. Not far from where this (*Idiot*) guy died. I mean how cool is that! I'm the man! Guess what I happen to have! Just for you!

I ask Iris, "What should I charge for such a rare item that would be fair?" The German couple is young and has little money. They occupied three hours of my time. I emailed pictures of where the rock (could have) come from.

"Well, within fifty miles." The view her hero might have seen as he was starving to death.

I put on my Wizard of Oz hat. *Do not pay attention to that man behind the curtain! I am Oz!* And I bestowed upon them with ceremony, in two part harmony, two local pretty stones with all the certificates of authenticity one might wish for, along with a story and pictures, to cherish and pass on to the next generation. I charge $30 for two stones sold to local children for fifty cents.

"Plus three hours of your time, Miles!"

This accident did not make the news for over a week. There was the potential of a fuel spill. The gas exploration company would have reason to not want that news out. People like myself spending a lot of time and living in the area, even depending on the area for subsistence could represent a huge problem for gas and oil interests. I see a lot, know a lot, even record a lot.

# CHAPTER TEN

## TEASING MILES, THEY UNDERSTAND TEASING!

Bean told me stories from overseas as hotel manager. I retell it to Iris.
"He'd order bed sheets, lamps, clothes, from his supplier. He'd get asked what label he wanted. What papers, what port of origin would look good.

"Lamps by Tiffany from New York, clothes from designers in England." Royal symbols, certificates signed by presidents. All knock offs from India arriving in huge numbers by ocean liner. "Bean said guests who got cheap vacation packages routinely stole lamps with 'Tiffany' written on them and smuggled them in luggage.

"Who was the real sucker, and who got ripped off here?" Bean laughs hilariously. "Musical chairs of goods of the world, where they stop no one knows."

I do not like it. I heard the same thing from the street people I lived with in the 70s. *The guy that stole the leather jackets at the fair and gave me one, remember?* But, as I always say, "Life is that train zooming by at high speed. There is only one question. Will I be on it or not?" Give me the ticket, I'm on. Count me in. I'm a player.

Who am I kidding. Who says crime doesn't pay. There was the game warden who had locals killing bears and selling him the gall and raw salmon eggs. I wanted no part of their illegal crap. Got told I'd be the one arrested! None of those neighbors got arrested, just as the warden promised. Well, I admit, the warden himself went to prison! Oddly enough, had nothing to do with Fish and Wildlife. He went to prison for molesting his daughter. Life is filled with irony.

*As a felon, how well did I do?* "Next subject!"

I have trouble shaking that subject. I notice I have an attitude problem I never had before. I had always looked at the positive, bright side; focused on the good. Forgot the bad. Pushed out negativity, did not want to hear about problems, only overcoming. No complaints, only solutions, and what to be grateful for! Being a felon and under restrictions is affecting me. Or, when I was on top of my game and doing well, who cared how anyone else was doing? I could sympathize, suggest the other person focus on the bright side. Suggest their own attitude can change things around. If others had more rights, got legal favors, that is them and has nothing to do with me. I'm still on the inside track, with a game plan, an in.

Now? My entire retirement investment of raw materials has been denied me. A lifetime of careful planning, work, and a strategy has been removed. The one who hates paperwork now has more paperwork than the average citizen. Possibly my issues are nothing but age and hormone changes, less testosterone, something like that. Physical, not mental. Would I have overcome all this when I was younger? *This is just a lesson, education, a test.*

"Miles, do you think there could be an issue over the rocks getting sent without a permit?"

"Yes," I reply, "Nothing can come off land you do not own, and get sold. Not a leaf, branch, shed antler, piece of dirt, or rock. The burden of proof is now on us, the sellers. Can we prove an item of any kind did not come off someone else's property?"

"Where did those rocks come from?" Can be questioned. Do I have a permit? I am in fact thinking of staking a mine claim for rocks. The mine office told me this is legal. I just have to show I find the rocks on the claim, cut and sell them for profit. That is how to be legal. Unless the rocks come from a mine claim, or off your own land, or you have written permission to get them, it is not legal to sell them. Even then, how do you prove it all in a way that would hold up in court?

If you pick up pine cones off the forest floor and sell wreaths you make at the Xmas bazaar, you could be arrested and be a felon if the cones crossed state lines or were sent in the mail.[1]

"Next!" *I am trying to change the subject. Didn't you notice?* We do not talk to people about the joys of our life, and get into details. I never know when a conversation is being recorded by a smiling face, nodding encouragement, with words of respect.

**Hi Miles,**

I just left you a voicemail but I thought it prudent to send you an email as well.

I work for an award winning British documentary company called Arrow Media and we are developing a documentary about mammoth tusk hunters in Alaska.

I'm casting for the series and I'm trying to find passionate Americans with an interest in this area who could be willing to be involved. Filming could even include the possibility of traveling to Siberia to search for mammoth tusks there.

Is this something that could interest you? Please do get in touch if it is. Let me know when it's best convenient for you and I'll give you a call. You can reach me on 207-489-6243 or please send me an email so you don't have to pay for an international call.

I look forward to hearing from you.

Best,

**Christian**

I have always believed fossil hunting would be something exciting for TV reality, or a documentary. 'Raising the Mammoth' was very popular. Christian and I meet. He is on another assignment and is able to stop by to discuss his pet project.

"Yes, Miles, I agree! Amateur fossil hunting would get the public's imagination going. Much like treasure hunting. The opportunity to make thousands of dollars for a small investment has appeal. Also finding something with an ancient story!"

"Christian, the biggest issue I see is the legality; getting this recorded legally. Most areas are restricted or off limits. The people who own land where it is legal to get fossils, are concerned their property will get confiscated as an archeological site. Is there a way to be vague about exactly where we are, and even state the reason?"

"Maybe, Miles, but people want details. It's like a fishing magazine with an article and good pictures, but adding, 'I'm not telling where!'"

"Yes, I see your point. The people I deal with though, would not want to get overrun with fossil hunters, or risk being an archeological site. Also though legal, the government frowns on it, and finds the activity unacceptable."

I begin to get suspicious of the drift of the conversation, seeking out exact locations, names, dates, the desire to get film footage in specific places that might be illegal.

Iris frowns. "Remember what I keep telling you! Learn to say 'No!'" She thinks this is a set up. An undercover agent trying to set me up for something illegal.

"If you are predisposed to commit such a crime it is not entrapment." *What exactly does that mean?* I take it to mean, if you were inclined to pick up a ten dollar bill off the sidewalk that was not yours, and keep it, then you are predisposed to being a thief. If you ever got a speeding ticket you are predisposed to speed, so there can be no entrapment. If you got caught smoking pot once, there can be no drug entrapment.

"Miles, we really need this kind of footage to make the show work. There are not many people like yourself with the knowledge. We'd pay you well, and the story is so exciting it needs to be shared and enjoyed!"

"Well, we have not addressed the legal part I asked about."

"Don't worry about that! We have it covered."

"I'll think about it." *I'm not seeing this in writing.*

I contact Tusk and ask if he has ever heard of these people in our line of work.

Tusk has worked off and on with film crews doing documentaries. He is in a better position than I am, being in Fairbanks and easy to get hold of.

"Arrow? Seems like that is the name of the outfit used to set up Victor a few years ago. Remember him?" We agree, it is hard to make a solid case against fossil hunters without documented proof. Film footage and witnesses work well.

"Tusk, this Chinese guy keeps calling me, asking for tusks, offering to buy all I have at good prices. Calls himself Peter. Has he contacted you?"

"Yeah, Miles, he is for sure working for the Feds. I usually do not deal with anyone who comes to me. I seek out people. I'm careful how we meet. I turn the radio up loud when we talk."

"Why bother, Tusk? You conduct legal business pretty much, nothing worth getting excited about!"

"Legal doesn't matter, Miles. The Feds want to control the land, all resources, and sources of all money." We can't discuss this sort of thing over the phone so I end the conversation.

"Repeat after me, Tusk. 'I love my government, it is the greatest.'" On that note, we hang up.

**Hello Miles,**

Very sorry to hear of your misfortune. I am assuming you're in trouble for your lifestyle as much as anything.

I am having a bit of trouble with the USA Parks and Wildlife people myself. I sent a Sperm Whale tooth that I legally owned, to a friend in the USA, only to have it confiscated, (despite the fact that I filled out a Customs Declaration and showed the item to the Postal Service). I have been charged with dealing in endangered species.

On another subject, I want to use the knife and have it be beautiful as well. I like your idea of the D2 steel and will go with that. I like the one on your web site with the Dall sheep etch. Could you use that blade and make a handle for me from the spalted birch? **Dave**

**Hi Miles!** You are spectacular!!! Thank you so much for all the wonderful work finding these crystals and giving me the information about them. I want #2 from the four crystals. It is beautiful. This is sooo cool because you said that there was a stone statue where they were found and in my dream there was a stone statue in connection with the crystal. Please tell me how I can go about ordering it! You are truly excellent at what you do : ) **Melissa**

**Hi Miles,**

I just ordered the dragon guard. When May comes around I'll contact you about

the custom wax piece. I'm ok with ordering 5 or more. Any suggestions on a complementary wood for the piece? Thanks!
    **Heidi**

The internet business is starting to get better. The local Nenana tripod days is upon us - the yearly event celebrating the raising of the tripod. Bets are placed on when the tripod goes out with the ice. I enjoy talking to people I have not seen in a long time.

"Miles, how is the Kantishna these days?"

"Not sure. I have not been there in a couple of years."

"But I thought you lived there." He opens his arms and adds, "I thought all this," encompassing all I offer at the fair, "Is about selling a lifestyle you profess to live. Now you do not live it and are a has been?"

"Well, that is one viewpoint."

"Ha! What other viewpoint is there? You are either scamming or you are not."

"I think we need to hit rewind here, back up, and define some of your terms. I sell a lifestyle, and that is still so. I spent thirty years in the wilds. I still have the knowledge, the materials, access to more materials. I still have all the connections in the wild for raw materials direct from the land from people I personally know. I still do get out in the wild to visit."

I try a new approach. "Every decision, or lifestyle involves some compromises and adjustments. It will never be exactly as we want all the time. About five factors affected moving to the village and accepting a village life instead of a wilderness one. Women, the law, my health, money, getting wiser, and a forest fire."

"That's six excuses not five."

I ignore the comment about excuses instead of reasons. "Not one of those things would have caused the change. Maybe not any two." But all six had me reconsider my life's goals and how I can be most effective in being happy and having what I want. "I might point out that you appear to be booing the bull rider, having never rode the bull yourself, or been in the ring. If what I do and have done affects you so much, means so much, maybe you can do it better?"

"You are so full of dung, Miles, it's coming out your mouth. I used to respect you, and thought you were for real!"

I only smile and reply "Hmmm," and let it pass. I learned that no matter what we do, someone will object. I'm uncertain what it is this person wants or expects. *I'm sorry! I will immediately go live in the wilds again so you are happy. Or, I shall disqualify myself from selling outdoor products, since I am now unworthy.* "If my products no longer interest you, I suggest you do not buy them." In general I get compliments, and sell enough to make it worth being here.

Iris brings up the fact we have things for a dollar, for the kids. "It's amazing how much we make on the dollar items!" Each year I try to have a different hot new item with the children in mind. "The small shark teeth were poplar one year." Iris does well selling to the children, they like her. This year it's the dollar crystals. When we are at the thrift store, we grab up deals on junk jewelry. Necklaces, charms, earrings, lots of flash at low prices that we can offer to five-year-olds for a dollar. We make $140 just on the dollar items.

Another customer wants to get in a discussion about my past, my lifestyle, and being a criminal now. "Miles, if you did not operate on the fringes of the law you would not be in so much trouble. You bring it on yourself. Just stay away from the gray area completely! I've never once been in trouble, been investigated, or been to court!"

"I understand your view. It makes sense from your perspective." I leave it at that. I'm not likely to change this person's mind. This person is telling me something, not asking anything. *I heard you, thanks for your perspective, have a nice day. Next!*

Iris has been reading an Alaska Magazine during slow spells on the last day of our bazaar.

**Alaska Magazine "Smarter Than You Think"** Ravens proving their ability to talk.

An article about ravens. Bernd Heinrich is quoted. This is the famous raven expert who asked me for raven stories, then used the stories as an example of foolish nonsense. Quoted now as saying about ravens:

"These abilities appear to be on par with or exceed, those of the great apes."

The article describes sophisticated high level communication and behavior, very similar to what I spoke of in my stories a good decade ago.

Heinrich concludes:

"Considering how many stories describe the mystical, mischievous, qualities of ravens, I'd say it's wise to pay attention to anything they say or do."

"Iris, I said about the same thing ten years ago, remember?"

"Yes, that's why I point out the article." Between the two of us, and our neighbors, we have racked up quite a few amazing raven stories we have been witness to.

"Just this morning, I heard a raven trying to imitate the church bells as they loudly bonged out a tune." Each time he tried, he got a little better as the church tune repeated itself. The raven tried again to imitate it. "Iris, remember when you asked the raven how he was doing? He flies over to the ball field, lands on home plate, and yells, 'Safe, Safe!' while opening his wings?"

"Miles! It was not quite like that! I just said "Hello."

"Close enough!" She agrees we watched several ravens slide down a metal roof laughing, falling in the snow at the bottom, and going back to get in line to do it again.

"Who would believe us, Miles?"

"I think no one, but who cares, we are not trying to prove anything to anyone. It is something fun we saw and share together." Prove it? Geez, I could not prove I had a good time, much less a raven. This is still the days before phones with video, or any kind of reliable cheap video cameras.

One time Iris and I heard dogs barking like feeding time, but there were no dogs around to be fed, so we walked over and looked around! *Who is feeding sled dogs over here?* It was five ravens imitating the sound of dogs at feeding time. They saw us looking around, jumped up and down laughing, and flew off still laughing. I have imitated a bunch of excited ravens, got the ravens all excited, then come around the house to show myself. Laughing. *Do animals understand a good joke?* I have pulled jokes on my sled dogs and cat, and had them play the same joke back on me. So I think so.

"Teasing, Miles, they understand teasing!"

"Well, isn't teasing a form of a practical joke?" There are many incidents of ravens figuring out how to get food, get water, steal from sled dogs, etc.

"I saw several ravens on the edge of a heavy, full trashcan rocking the can back and forth in unison until it fell over, spilling the garbage for them to sort. Our friend at the seniors said she saw a raven get in her shed, open a bag of dog food, and shove pieces of the dog food one piece at a time under the door to the other waiting ravens outside." I know ravens in general do not like to get into confined places. Someone has to be a lookout. It is often one brave raven who does something, while the others nervously watch and wait.

Another tripod weekend ends. We usually have a good time. The events for the children are fun. Pie eating is the most fun! "Yeah, and they win a dollar, that's why we have stuff for a dollar, and encourage them to run over and pick something out."

"The kids remember too! They tell me they still have the shark tooth from last year, or the gold chain from the year before!"

Tax time comes and goes. Iris is still not used to money that comes and goes erratically.

"This is part of subsistence, Honey, feast or famine." She nods, but I know she does not understand, or simply does not agree it is either safe or workable. The only money that really registers is Social Security in the form of a number in the bank account that shows up regularly. Everything else is just me fooling around. Income and expenses as recorded, show a tiny bit of income generated by the business. Enough to call it a legitimate business that has write offs and expenses. I repeat again, "Just about everything I do is business." Like what? "Well fuel oil, wood hauling costs, the car, truck, boat, and their fuel." What is clearly not business? "Some clothes, most food, movies we buy, half the main utilities."

"I added that up, Miles, and it comes to $400 a month." I glance at my own records and, "Yes, that's about right." The business cost $21,000, and I brought in $25,000. I like how the numbers look. It's not out of line. It's not tons of money, but looks promising. I'm appropriately excited and hanging in there! Just any old time now business could be booming. My web site has had a total of 58,000 visits this year. About 160 a day. As many as any store might expect. I do not know why this has not resulted in more sales. With allowed credits and this and that I end up owing zero taxes.

"Wow, what a coincidence! How lucky, huh!!" *What a bummer for the government.*

I used to average a sale for every fourth visitor. But I used to sell fairly exclusive items with few competitors. I used to be in the top five in the world at what I sold. It's still hard to step so far down. Many of my heroes were captured by the enemy and, or, had lulls and setbacks in their careers. They were over-comers. Some of the most famous artists in the world died in poverty and or could not sell their work. Considering my situation, these numbers are what I want the records to reflect.

Mrs. Probation encourages me, "Look how much better you might do when you can do shows and travel again!" Indeed! I nod my head with a proper smile that shows I never thought of that, and am properly cheered up! Cheered enough to struggle, and reach for this goal, and not give anyone any trouble. *Good dog!* I'm concentrating on getting the books done and out there without thinking of advertising or promoting a lot. Deal with that later. Right now I want to show lots of costs. Not much coming in. In this way, I like to think I am more in control of my life than it looks or that I let on. Other people think this is just an illusion that makes me happy. There are legal sources of income I have not tapped. I need to bide my time.

One issue I come across with the taxes is health care costs, matching VA funds, and my co-pay. The subject comes up with my friend Witty. "Witty, I got a medical bill from imaging at the hospital when they took an x-ray. I was sent there by the VA who approved it. Imaging said the VA has not paid two bills for my last exams. I am liable, and need to pay these bills. I wrote and explained it is the VA they need to be talking to. Imaging asked me to go to the VA and get them to pay. I thought, "This is strange." I call my buddy John at the VA. He says one of two things is going on. Imaging did not submit its bill in a timely fashion and is out of luck, or the VA is simply behind. The usual wait right now is sixty to ninety days.

Witty, if I was this late paying my bills I'd be in jail. My power would get cut off,

I'd get evicted. What's up that the government can be this late? Pay no interest or late fees I might add."

"Miles, that is just the tip of the iceberg. I'm in charge at Mental Health, and we submit bills as most of our funding is government money. A year goes by and we do not get paid. Sometimes we do not get paid at all. We even have to borrow money and pay interest to make payroll because the government has not paid us. Someone decides what bills will get paid, and which ones will not get paid, and we never know."

"What about payroll for employees? Getting your own departments bills paid?" The subject seemed to be changed.

"Miles, in Russia…" Witty explains how there was a time during the collapse, when the government could not pay its bills. Workers showed up anyway without pay! Why? "The workers got a free meal, there was running water at work where they could wash; do laundry. There were various perks that helped them stay alive." I wonder how this works. Witty tells me, "Well, as one Russian told me, "They pretend to pay us, and we pretend to work."

I wonder if the subject of our conversation had changed or not. I'm still puzzled. "Then how does the government come up with a million dollars to find out what Wild Miles is up to? That kind of money could put in the new water treatment plant our community so desperately needs."

We both agree the government will not let us take care of ourselves on top of the other issues going on. So what is the governments objective and plan we wonder. Facts match our conversation. I just ask what is the gain, what is it about this that gets anyone ahead? If there is a scam, wouldn't you think the scammer is gaining something? Would I run my car into the ground until it quit and then have to buy another? Would a farmer run his horse to near death and call that being a successful farmer? Isn't it smarter to feed the plow horse well? Do we want it to run away when we turn our back? Kick us as soon as it gets the opportunity? "Witty, we the people, are the golden goose laying the eggs." *No people, no money. No work, no money.*

Still, I see bosses do not always treat their employees well, which is similar. Other money issues are on my mind as this tax season comes around and I once again wonder how to define my life in terms of money! How do I deal with trades, barter, exchanged services, gifts, donations?

This reminds me, "Witty, what are you growing this coming season? I have extra room for seed starts if you want me to start some seeds for you."

"Sure, Miles, thanks for the offer. I have some special cucumber and cabbage seeds I have never tried, and do not have room. I can share them with you if you start them for me!"

I have room under grow lights. It does not make sense to have a greenhouse half full when I open it. The time and costs are about the same full or half full. I have room for about thirty flats. Around ten six packs per flat, is over 1,000 plants. So if I wish to be legal and honest with the IRS, how does a deal like this get translated into income and expense? Its promises backed up with favors owed. We have not put a money value on, but defines our existence and wealth. I have room for extra plants when they are seedlings, but not room when they grow in four inch pots.

"So, we sell some Iris!"

"I know, you told me, so we can maybe break even on our $500 costs!"

She at least has my goals memorized, even if she does not share them. Among the things I have traded are four inch pots of plants for gas, fish, firewood, yogurt, fresh milk, tools, tires. Hardly any cash. But 1,000 plants allows me to high-grade and get rid of some that are not as healthy. Some even get eaten as sprouts, like lettuce and radish. I often get rid of a surplus I can't put a value on. I give away stunted ones. Yet may collect a favor a year later in return with no direct connection. That favor as well, may have non-monetary value put on it. If I report to the IRS I only made $1,000 this year, the question of suspicion and cause of an audit might well be, "That's impossible, how did you live! We don't believe you!" Being on probation, the implication is, I am up to something, probably selling drugs. My phone gets tapped again.

"It's about time for Foil to come up from Arizona isn't it, Miles?"

Iris is right. He should be here! He has not called or written. Foil arrives and wants us to pick him up at the airport in Fairbanks. If we say we are too busy, it is $200 cab fare. We hate to see him have to pay $200, so we go pick him up. We assume he appreciates this. We stop at the store to get groceries, so something else is accomplished by a trip, in that we usually only go grocery shopping every two weeks. Iris says, "Foil! Aren't you going to get any food?"

"Oh, I'll just come in another day." She looks at me and rolls her eyes, thinking the same thing I am. He will ask us to bring him to town to get groceries. He may offer to cover half the gas for compensation. He has so far, not even offered gas money for this trip to come get him. Thirty dollars out of our pocket in gas, not that this is a fortune, but it adds up. We'd think he would get food.

When I get a ride to town with a friend I usually pay $20 to help out. Iris and I never come to town without a list, and always buy food, otherwise can not justify traveling 100 miles round trip.

What is he expecting to eat until he gets into Fairbanks again? Does he assume he is eating free with us? He says, "I have not put together a grocery list yet." By way of explanation.

Iris forces him to get some basics, telling him flat out we are not coming in again so he can shop. It is possible his wife does all the food shopping. He seems clueless what to get.

"The basics, Foil! A loaf of bread, some sandwich materials, potatoes, rice, carrots, onions, stuff that keeps for a while - maybe some soups of some kind." He does not get much of what we suggest, and grabs up junk food—chips and soda. Can he really live on this? Teenagers can, but when we get in our 50s? I wonder if that still works?

Foil wants to buy my truck.

"I got someone local willing to give me $1,500, Foil, it blue-books for over $2,000."

"Miles, you told me last fall you'd take $800!"

"Then you should have taken the deal! Last fall is a long time ago, Foil." I can't hardly ask less now than what I'm being offered by someone else. *It would be different if we were friends.* "You did not commit to the deal last fall. You said you'd think about it. Ya snooze, ya lose!" *Can you see a truck on sale at the dealers in town, and a year later demand the same price*?

"Miles, I thought we were friends! You know it is worth only $800! I'll need new tires, new battery. It's old. It burns oil! It's a 1986!"

"It blue-books over $2,000. It runs good, runs in the cold, never a problem starting. First crank and it's up and running. Reliable, never has quit on us. The oil pressure is good. There is an oil leak around the lifter cover, not worth fixing. It takes a quart every 500 miles. We do not know the true engine miles as the engine has been rebuilt."

"I need transportation, Miles! $800 is all I can afford!"

Well, whatever. I'm not going to argue. It's not like I'm desperate for money. So I take the $800, and Foil and I are best buddies again. Not that I fall for that, but he's Mr. Nice Guy for a short time. His wife will join him in a month. She only gets two weeks off on her job. I am not understanding the change, after telling me he is fed up with his wife and getting another woman, or being alone.

The change does matter. There is a huge difference between helping someone live alone in the wilds, very different to do so with a city wife. Two people more than doubles the issues. Twice the weight in the boat for supplies triples the boat, engine, and travel costs. A one room cabin in Nenana with no electric or water is more complicated with two.

Foil does not say anything when we never invite him over for dinner. I write up a contract of sorts spelling out what he will pay for the Kantishna land, to my next of kin, with an agreement he can build on my land so he feels covered in the event I die. I write it up for him more than me. I was not thinking much about my protection. I do not live in the world of lawyers.

I bought my own Nenana home, an agreement written out in pencil on a piece of notebook paper. Cars, trucks, boats, engines, all paid for in cash.

Foil wants to know when we are headed to town next so he can hitch a ride.

"I thought that's why you got the truck from me, Foil."

"It is fine to go in with you; you know where to get all the things I need at the best prices! I can learn from you, Miles." He has had two years to learn where the stores he needs are. He is not a good listener and it is frustrating telling him my opinion. We appear to not have the same goals. We, in fact, do not shop at the same places. He is not interested in second hand stores, used stuff, garage sales. He wants it all new. I also recognize his flattering me to get me to do something he wants.

"Miles, so it works! I'm not into buying junk!" *Great, but then do not tell me you are too broke to buy my truck for what it's worth. Go get a new one.* I am not interested in an argument. I notice he has not said, "I am headed for town in the truck, would you like to come along or do you need anything?" Others have told me he has been bragging what a killer deal he got on this cool truck. He has had over a dozen free trips to town with us. I do not hear, 'Now it's on me!' out of him. Another issue is, Iris and I enjoy what we consider quality time together going into town. It is something we do together. Foil interferes with this when he harasses Iris, gets us to argue. He is not quietly riding alone, being grateful for a ride. He treats her like a cab driver, orders her around, tells her how to drive. Iris is a nervous driver when pushed. Her mother got her in an accident long ago. I notice she gets lost and confused easily and the way for the ride to go smooth is to let her go the route she understands in her own way. Friends understand. She is in fact a good driver with a spotless record.

"Miles, when are you headed for the homestead? I need some stuff hauled in." Again, that is why he bought a boat and motor. To make his own trips. I told him I think he bought a boat too small and an engine without enough power.

He told me. "I want to take light loads, cheap, and fast, Miles!" *So go for it!* I think. "Miles, you owe me. The contract you signed says you will help me."

We may each define 'help' differently. Enabling someone is not helping. The agreement reads, "Help with some advice." The plan had been to teach him and help him be independent with a little advice here and there as we have spoken of. Verbally, "To help you get started for the first year." Not, "Your free teacher for life." Foil should know how to run the river and boat by now, I cannot accompany him on all his trips anymore.

Foil is angry again. "You promised! Now you put me in a bind, Miles! That is not being a friend or living up to our agreement!" I know I will go when I feel like it. I will not be a free freight hauler. "Miles, I can offer $100 for gas like last time!"

Last time was last time. I had offered a token fee to help out, not what it cost me. It had been $100 when he had promised to do the same for me in Tucson. I had needed to make a trip, felt healthy, weather was good, I was in a good mood, Foil was my buddy. We are trading.

We never traded, and looks like never will. Welcome to the full meal deal of full price Buddy. One hundred dollars is not even worth discussing. He obviously did not appreciate the deal on $300 trips. *No problem, let him ask around.* Let him use his new forty-five horse engine to move his heavy loads. It will work. It will take two days one way, and 100 gallons of gas round trip. It will cost him $500. Been there, done that... when I was twenty. I am not interested in doing that anymore. I can tell him almost to the dollar what it will coast. This is what I mean by advice and knowledge offered.

"Well, come with me, follow me, show me the way, Miles! It will be an adventure!"

I do not buy into other people's adventures, nor is anyone else in charge of my adventure, nor offering advice how to do it who has Foil's zero qualifications. The equivalent would be someone coming to his world who chooses to buy a small sports car against his advice when they need a semi-truck then want more advice and help hauling building materials. Again, no use getting into an argument telling him my opinion. I already know Foil has an explosive temper. He appears to be switching strategies trying to find what works with me now.

Foil shows me the load piled in his yard and wants me to pack five sheets of plywood on the front of my boat deck space. That could possibly sink the boat, or, at least create a very dangerous hazard if I had to come to a sudden stop. My boat is efficient and fast. But is not safe. I have my homesteads, so my-y main objective is to no longer haul huge loads of building supplies. I can haul a few thousand pounds balanced - usually in the bottom of the boat for low center of gravity. I need to go at my pace, my way, not with someone who is not getting their boat on step doing five to ten miles an hour. I plow water at that slow speed. I need to power up and get my load well out of the water - flying on top hydroplaning with the entire boat out the water. I'm not sure Foil knows what hydroplane means. To hydroplane overloaded, is extremely dangerous. More than dangerous—foolish. The equivalent of driving in city traffic with no brakes. Some say it's impossible—it's not. You have to know well in advance what everyone else is doing, and if things are not working, pull over. I know, because I have done it. Drove the truck Foil now has fifty miles thorough the hills to Fairbanks with no brakes in order to buy brake parts. I would not do it for anyone else for less than a grand.

I'm very vague about my plans, to avoid a confrontation. Foil needs to learn to be on his own. If he admires me like he says, he admires independence. If he admires me and my ways, he knows I'm a strong believer in paying for our mistakes as a way to learn. Not blame anyone else or ask for a bail out.

He did not learn how to use his GPS as I suggested. He is not interested in loading my river map into his machine. "I know the way Miles!" Foil does not want to take his new boat and engine for a test run to determine how it handles, or what the fuel consumption will be when computing his fuel load. Foil has no fuel tanks. I have extra. I feel sorry for him.

"You can borrow my extra tanks, Foil, get them back to me later on when you can afford your own." They cost $100 to $200 each. I have accumulated a dozen over the years from garage sales. I pay ten to twenty dollars each when they are offered. What looks like a junkyard to some is 'stuff' like spare fuel tanks.

"Keep your eye out for me, Miles!"

*Why?* Foil has a truck. He can go to garage sales. He has had two years to get stuff I suggested he needs. What others consider camping gear is one of the first categories of items people with money troubles dump. Outdoor gear is common at low prices at garage sales. Foil says he never shops at garage sales.

"Foil, your engine is not the same brand as mine. You will need different hose connections. These connections are critical, get the right ones!" I tell him who sells them, and hand him one connector to bring in.

"Hand Mr. Reed this and tell him you need these!" I'm using a 1950s fuel tank in my boat. All my tanks use the same outdated fittings - so outdated that many dealers do not know what they are. One side advantage is, it is less likely anyone will steal my fuel tanks on the river in the villages if they cannot connect to anything they own. All newer tanks I have get the old style fittings. I smile at Foil and quote the song words, "What's the matter with the car I'm driving, cant you see it's out of style?" Something about white wall tires and the miracle mile. *It's still rock and roll to me.* I can tell buddy Foil is not impressed. *Then stop telling me you admire me. Go forth young man, and find a better way! But do not ask me to pay.*

I am there on his launch day. Foil cannot get his engine started. I take a quick look and right off see he has the wrong fuel line connector. What he bought, snaps on but does not actually connect inside. I ask how that happened. He says, "I went to Walmart, and the guy there told me this is what I need, Miles!" He trusts some punk kid fresh from another country who can't speak English to hand him the right gas hose connector, instead of my advice. What a slap in the face! To happily use the word 'Walmart' when he knows how I feel, is a second insult. This is so far beyond an insult, it is like being five years old, or being retarded. He needs pity.

I give Foil a connector. Now he can get started. I doubt he would have ever figured it out on his own. This is the first time he has started his engine. Fully loaded, headed out on a month trip into the wilds. He may well die. I smile and wave. He is not taking me down his rabbit hole. His load is not balanced right. He'd come unglued if I said anything. He will learn… or not.

"And he has his brother with him, Miles!" Yes, I forgot to mention that. "Miles, I think he called his brother to join him to get free labor!"

Hard to know. His brother knows less than Foil. In my opinion, just two people and their survival gear and gas would overload this boat. I'm guessing the boat and engine is rated for about 500 pounds. Foil has over 2,000 pounds on board. There is no way I want to be part of this adventure. My last parting advice, "You are way overloaded and will not be able to get on step, do not even try. Back way off the throttle and just steer the first eighty miles downstream to the Kantishna. Use the gas to go upstream." If he does it right, he may use only ten gallons going the eighty miles downstream and twenty-five gallons going the next forty miles upstream. He has sixty gallons. The return trip should be within the 500 pound limit and he can get on step. On step happens about fifteen miles an hour. Once on step, there is less drag in the water and he can back way off the throttle and the fuel consumption becomes acceptable. His sixty gallons might be enough... if he knows what he is doing. He has little choice unless the trip is only gas. It's a catch 22. If it were me, I'd check my fuel consumption at a few checkpoints like Minto and Tolovana to see how I was doing. Not having enough gas can cost thousands of dollars. It's a great way to learn. *Like the price of a college course!*

Foil has a cell phone. Manley Hot Springs is downriver, so I do not feel he is really in a life threatening situation. If he has to float to Manley, he will find out, as I did, how high the cost for a trip can get. It has cost me a year's wages to break down and end up in Manley.[2] His trip can easily cost $1,000. Let him discover he would save money paying me $300. Foil is off my mind. I'm a bit tired of him borrowing tools, helping himself to sheets of my plywood, doors, chain, nails, tape and on and on.

Foil asked me to keep an eye out for things I think he needs. Iris and I suspected he was helping himself 'by accident' to our food. He had a key to my shop because I had found a refrigerator at a garage sale I thought he might like. I put it in shop for him to use, so his food and ours could be separated. It could run off solar panels and an inverter, if Foil set that up. I show him this cool compact refrigerator I got for $50, almost new. He does not want to buy it. "I do not need it." I'm out $50, and he is borrowing it. Using my electric. His new home has no water or electricity.

Foil told me when looking for a place that it was only for storage. His objective was to be out at the homestead, and only storing belongings at the Nenana place. What I found for him meets these needs. Turning a storage building into a home was not the plan I agreed to help him with. He now needs windows, furniture, insulation and much more cost to keep two homes in Alaska. This is not what I teach, and is out of the realm of my knowledge.

Now I am not so sure I want him having access to my shop with his own key so he can borrow my stuff without asking, or even stealing my stuff. I say 'steal' because Iris told him about some boat fuel tanks our neighbor owns next door that it looks like they rarely use. "Ask if you can buy them cheap, Foil!"

"Thanks! If I just take them, they will never miss them!"

Two tanks end up missing the next day. I notice Foil did not offer to return my borrowed ones. If, "No one will miss them," is a reason to steal, he may feel the same about much of my stuff just sitting around. I do not even know what I have half the time, until I need something and go look. Foil does in fact say later, "You are not using it, you do not even know what you have. Someone else can use it, so they should be able to, Miles."

I hear this argument often about sharing goods. How it is not right for some people to have… and others not. That in fact, if someone has something you need to survive and you are not using it, they have the right to take it. On a large scale the government feels the same way. A farmer can have surplus food because he thought ahead and used good growing practices when no one else did. Now, those who did not plan ahead are starving, while another farmer has a surplus. I could picture the government deciding to take the surplus food and giving it free to the poor. The government would not say, "You did not think ahead, it might cost you your life. Bummer." The farmer with the surplus is willing to sell, but the starving have no money to buy. The one with the surplus saw this situation coming and warned the public. The public said, "Who cares! No one will let us starve, we will get fed, so don't worry about it!"

Partly I do not want to talk open and honestly with Foil about what is going on with me. I no longer trust him. This is more than just stealing from my neighbor. He has been befriending all the people I suggest he not do business with. People with a community reputation of taking advantage, charging too much, and using people are pointed out. I told Foil I do not like to reveal the details of my life, then have him turn and tell the gossiping town trouble makers! There was almost a perverse pleasure in intentionally doing what I do not want, that gets his rocks off. I hope Foil does not have that personality type, of getting joy out of others discomfort.

I understand that we cannot dictate to anyone, even our friends, who to do business with or be friends with! However, if someone raped your daughter and you have a friend with a young daughter, we might suggest, "It is not a good idea to leave this person alone with your daughter." And their response is to go out of their way to invite this person around, what should the reaction be? My response is, "Do not come crying to me when your daughter gets raped." I suppose in civilization such a person who rapes goes to jail. In a community like ours there is no jail and there are no police and no one in a far off community cares. Here, people who do not behave are ignored by those who care. If enough people care, a thief, rapist, etc. can no longer live in the community. No one will sell them gas, food, firewood. They leave. Let a big community with police deal with them. If things get out of hand, a serious criminal disappears and no one knows anything. If you plan on living here, this is what you should learn.

"Iris, remember that new school teacher and the dog story?" Related to this issue. A new school teacher is in the city office when I am there visiting the mayor who is dressed in jeans with a shotgun on the wall. The new teacher is practically in tears, 'I got a new piece of property out the road. I had my dog tied up in the yard. The neighbor let their dog run loose! Their dog came over and tore up my little dog on his chain!'

Both the mayor and I go, "Uh, huh." Wondering what the point is.

Teacher expected us to care. "Well, what you are gong to do!"

"Us? Do? Nothing. I suggest if the dog comes in your yard again, you shoot it."

Look of total shock. The sort who stutters, "Ga... ga... gun?" I feel sorry for her. She does not belong here. She does not even live within city limits and thus not paying taxes. There are advantages and disadvantages in living with nature. She cries, "The neighbor told me their dog has the right to be free!"

My reply—if it were me—would be, "Yes, and as such, your free dog will learn what freedom cost when you screw up." The bottom line for our community I realized at the time is, "What kind of teachers will we attract for our children? They have to be certified and as such will have spent time in civilization where they are taught not to have an interest in firearms, know all about protection provided by the government. In not so long ago days, within my memory, we hired teachers with no other qualification than being local parents and adults.

I recognize an even more important issue! *I guess related to the Foil situation. I'm reminded anyhow.* It would have been wise of our mayor to at least act concerned, and sympathize with the school teacher. I say to Iris, "Her dog has more rights than all the people in our community."

"So civilization would say." Iris understands. Word gets out that Nenana allowed a loose dog to kill your little Fifi and suggests you be armed and blast away at your neighbors dog.

"Yes, I could picture the government spending millions of dollars, whatever it takes to clean our clock." Our entire way of doing things forced to change. A protected member of society will have her rights defended. When one of the sheep bleats, the shepherd shows up.

Our mayor was born and raised in Nenana. Has no clue. I was born in the protected class, so have the advantage of understanding how it works. Someone like Dalai could cry to the right people about the right stuff going on and people would go to jail, or worse. An excuse to disarm our entire community would fit the government's agenda for example. If a situation looked like discrimination against a minority - women, a Black person, a Native. Millions would be invested into bringing Nenana down.

Iris points out, "A black robber was shot by the police and the family was just awarded 28 million dollars... it's in the news, Miles." The public felt the man was shot because he was black, not because he was a thief. Do white thieves get shot? I do not know. So many changes have taken place since I have been gone. It does seem odd to me, people of minority races can, have and do insult me and mistreat me all the time for being white, and that's ok. It was explained to me there can be no such thing as discrimination unless you are a minority. Oh. So there are people who are among the untouchable. We need to be very careful who we complain about... and why. Foil is one who knows how the system works and knows how to play it. I am not one of the protected sheep. Foil knows it.

I TELL Iris another issue trusting Foil is him keeping the friends he does. "One truth is, my health concerns me." My diabetes acts up. I get dizzy, disorientated, cannot think, make poor decisions, often need to sleep or cannot accomplish anything that requires hard work, thinking, or that is important. Consequently I have not been able to get my boat as ready as it needs to be to launch into the new season.[3] There are people in town, who, if they knew this, would laugh, spread the word, and it might affect my business in town. Or the local thieves could get wind and see me as vulnerable... an easy target. It should be no one else's business how fast or slow I am running my life these days.

If I get close to anyone as a friend, it needs to be someone who helps others in their time of need, not looks for weakness to exploit.

I finally got the boat engine oil changed; the lower unit is greased. Still thinking of things to pack in the boat to keep at all times. I want to get the fishing poles ready with this new spider wire. I have canned food to keep on board. The ham radio needs testing. There is boat trailer work to complete.

I'd like my first planned trip to be a fossil hunt. I for sure do not want anyone, not even Foil to know when I am going, or where I am going. He would be one to follow me, and take over the good areas I know about.

"I saw Miles get gas!" One of the gossips does 'drive-bys' now. Several times a day Mad Jay drives by very slow, and stares to see if he can figure out what I am doing, or will do, so he has some gossip to spread, hopefully something illegal or nasty. Mad Jay and Dalia are two in particular I like to stay away from. Both would like to see me go back to jail.

Dalia had said, "I saw Miles go to the post office! He is on probation! I should have turned him in, but I'm too nice for that. But someone will turn him in and he deserves it!"

There is no use telling her the terms of my probation, and being allowed certain times to do things away from the house during the time I wore the shock collar. I do not owe her an explanation. She is not looking for answers, but ways to hurt people.

Sadly we used to be friends. I knew Dalia when she first arrived in Nenana and helped her get established.

Iris said, "Let her call the probation officer then! See what an ass she can make of herself!"

The last thing I need is Foil passing information to her. *And it is not true that Dalia would look like an Ass.* I'd go back to jail.

Mrs. Probation could have the outlook of the prison system. It does not matter whose fault anything is. "If there are problems, misunderstandings, conflict, complaints, you are responsible." Everyone involved goes to the hole. I'm the felon, so the assumption is I'm to blame. I'm the one with zero rights, less rights than your dog. "You upset Dalia, a responsible citizen, so you are going back to jail!" Is the kind of thinking I expect.

There is talk along the lines of, "Ha! Miles used duct tape and baling wire to fix his boat trailer! Everyone knows that is not going to work! How come he doesn't fix it right! What an idiot!" I had not taken Foil's advice on how to fix my boat trailer. He suggested I have a professional weld it for $500. Instead I drilled and bolted on guide posts to guide the boat onto the trailer. Not life threatening if it fails. This is not something I want to spend $500 on right now.[4] It should be no one else's business. In my opinion, a friend would not bad mouth how I do things. I understand this is a temporary fix. *If you feel I am incompetent ok, but do not tell me how much you admire my decisions.*

Witty stops by, "We got some pork back from the butcher, thought you could use some!" and hands me some packages of fresh pork. She laments she cannot butcher it herself. Too much liability, not legal to offer to others. Has to be processed by a professional. That's a 100 mile round trip. Now the meat costs twice as much. "When we know how to butcher!" Now it is 'safe.'

I chuckle, "I trust you to butcher more than I trust a big outfit." Talk is, the big butcher mixes everyone's meat, then hands the proper weight back to each customer. The meat may or may not be what you brought in. It may not be the range fed you started with. It may not be fresh. The butcher in theory, could high grade, and sell your better meat to discreet high end customers. The meat he hands you must legally meet minimum standards. The meat you brought could be way above those standards.

It was my survey boss Seymour who told me about the butcher Witty goes to. The same one that made burger from his moose. Only when Seymour got it back, it had sand in it. His moose was shot in the tundra... no sand. I met someone else who told me when they have bad moose they bring it to the butcher for burger. The meat is mixed with everyone else's and the average grade is better than the quality they brought in. Bad can be cutting scent glands, getting guts and piss on the meat, sand, hair, leaves.

I had been a little interested in buying a whole pig on the hoof from Witty, and walking it home three blocks. Butcher it like I do moose. That's legal. A whole pig on the hoof cost more than Iris wants us to pay. We sort of have enough moose meat left from two years ago to last a while, depending how often we eat it. The best is gone.

"Thanks for fresh pork ,Witty!" I had not asked for it, just an act of kindness.

"We have all the cow and pig manure you want, Miles, just come get it!" She has piles that are now two years old, good for garden mix. Her garden always looks so good. I confess; better than mine. With less work! It must all be about the soil. "Miles, it is the farm! The chickens, pigs, and cows! In the old days country people had both animals and gardens that worked hand in hand!"

I agree. This is one of the secrets to an older lifestyle society once enjoyed. Country people provided the produce for the city. Country people had a mini eco system. Garden surplus fed the animals. Aanimals fertilized the garden. Not much had to be acquired outside the local system.

"Now, Miles, in the age of specialization we have separated the animals from the vegetables, and both from the compost. What animals give the garden now we consider a problem to be paid to dispose of. The garden surplus that used to feed animals is now a waste product we pay to have hauled to a dump." We both study a little on how people lived in the past. We buy processed grains and commercial feeds that are almost required by law to feed animals for human consumption. We now buy chemical fertilizers to grow our crops, required by law to sell produce to the public.

"You think, Witty, the old way spread disease?" It is hard to get a handle on the truth that can be trusted. *Who is doing the study and what answers would they like to get?* Do commercial interests distort statistics to suit their profits? Were people ages ago less healthy than we are today? Witty must leave. We are not going to solve the problems of the world today.

"Have a good day!" We will see each other on Tuesday, at the weekly WIN meeting. The health fair is over. All I did was put up the flyers announcing the event our group puts on each season. Inexpensive blood work is offered, free hearing tests, health geared towards educating children, such as balanced meals. I wish we were involved in more aspects of our community than we are, but at least the group is about positive things, offering solutions, and doing something, not just talking.

Win promotes the community garden. I put new plastic on the greenhouse. A dozen locals have garden boxes. The Native Council supplies free seeds. Sometimes we can manage some new soil. Volunteers weed, cut the grass. One of the churches offers water for the garden with a hose to use any time. Even though I have a garden and greenhouse at home, I have a box and spot in the community greenhouse.

"Josh, I like to try a different location with different light and different soil. Then note the differences in how it goes at my place." Josh's wife loves growing things and has a plot here. She and Dalia are friends. So I am on polite speaking terms with Dalia. Iris is on livid tension terms. I learned that anything I say to Dalia gets twisted and commented on in a negative way.

'Who does he think he is, does he think I'm poor, or his stuff is better than mine!' comes from."Would you like to try some of my seeds Dalia?" Offered free for the sake of sharing. I go to the community plot early in the morning when hardly anyone else would be around. It's right across the street from the post office! Dalia sees me at the post office.

"Miles, I am thinking of not growing anything this year. Last year someone stole one of my cucumbers!" I make no comment. It is true, now and then someone steals some produce. I do not dwell on it. I still learned something about this type of soil and what it produces. This soil tends to be mostly peat. We use commercial fertilizers at the community garden. I notice a difference in taste between commercial fertilizer and compost grown. Compost soil makes for tastier, healthier produce while commercial fertilizer makes it bigger, more uniform, better looking. I notice no difference with lettuce. Flowers grow about the same.

"Yeah, Iris, I ran into Dalia. She mentioned the theft of her cucumber."

" Miles, I recall the sign she put up demanding the return of her cucumber!"

"And I recall putting a pile of dog do do where the cucumber was."

"With a 'thanks!' sign." I do not think she saw any humor in that. I have had a cabbage or two stolen, a tomato or two. Not the end of the world. I promote the garden whenever I can.

"You do not have a space? We have room in the community garden! See Mrs. Assembly for free seeds and getting your name on a plot!" I add, "Free! What a great community we have, huh! What other community would give you a free garden plot and free seeds!" I offer free rototilling for your garden plot. It takes me five minutes while I am there doing my own plot. I often teach children about gardens at the community garden.

I got the librarian to get a plot. She has a big family. They live in a swamp area with a lot of shade, so not much grows where they live.

"I do not have time Miles!"

"But it is right across from the post office. You come by every day checking mail!" The potatoes she grew helped the family a lot. Now Mrs. Librarian and I hardly talk due to the borough investigation fiasco. Oh well.

FOIL IS off to the homestead. My life is back on normal, so no interest from Mad Jay in where I am anymore. I can disappear on a trip, and this would not be noticed. I still have one or two things to deal with on the boat. I put some engine oil in after changing it, but have not checked the level with the engine in the full down position because I have to be in the water. 'Full down' is on the ground.

A call from Foil. He has to climb a tree to get cell phone reception. He comes in broken.

"Miles, I am in trouble, come help!" I am unsure what is going on, the phone is scratchy, batteries low maybe. I only know someone is in emergency mode and needs rescuing. Part of village life is to drop everything and show up when there is a life-threatening emergency. We do not call in an emergency unless we are dying. I make out, "Need gas." Within an hour, I am in the water. Not sure I have enough gas, have not checked my engine oil. Sounded like Foil is down by Moonshine's camp. This is odd, as this is past the Kantishna River. He must be floating with a down engine. I assume I will find out what is going on when I get there. The important thing is to rescue Foil and his brother. For all I know he lost his boat and supplies, and is soaking wet on a sandbar someplace where every hour counts. This is the sort of event it would take to be considered needing a rescue to local people.

If he is ok, he can just float down to Manley and the road system. Fly back to town, whatever needs to be done. Foil says he needs gas, so the assumption is, he still has a boat.

I load 115 gallons of gas which will give Foil at least eighty gallons. This is the maximum I think he can burn under the worst conditions. I worry what is going on, so go fast, take shortcuts, and chances to get there sooner. Weather is fine. I open the throttle beyond what is really safe speed. Only the back foot of the 24 foot boat touches the water. The sound of the water on the hull is louder than the engine. At these speeds I can just about steer the boat by leaning. I fly by my checkpoints looking at my time, checking my gauges, looking at my fuel consumption, my GPS speed. My depth sounder is not working well. This is another of the reasons I take my time getting ready for trips, to fine tune all the gadgets and tools. The sensing unit angle for the depth sounder is sensitive and critical. Air bubbles going over the unit cause erratic readings. A stick, or hitting bottom can move this sensor out of alignment. A nut and bolt fixes it, but the boat has to be out of the water. I have to be more careful not having an accurate depth reading.

The engine siren goes off. I am not sure of all the codes of the beeps. I usually just slow up, pull over, and if I cannot decipher the problem, get the book out. I usually begin cycling through all the readings from the digital monitor screen. I have to push a button to cycle through water pressure, water temperature, oil pressure, trim, engine hours, gallons an hour. I notice low oil pressure. This happened once before, and it was too late to save the engine. I had fried it. My heart skips a beat as I take the engine cowling off to see what the trouble is. *This is not good.* I have the spare four horse engine, best for steering downstream. Heading upstream is days of travel to get back home. Not good if Foil's life is in danger downstream waiting for me.

I check the oil level, and see I am down two quarts. That seems like a lot, but have had little experience for what it takes to keep the engine safe. I am not sure why I am low. Did the engine leak, burn it or blow a gasket of some kind? I have only one extra quart with me. This is one of the little things I would have caught if I had more time to be fully ready for a long trip. Normally, a single quart for emergency use is enough. I add the oil, but see I am still low. I turn the key to start the engine with trepidation. Sometimes if the engine is fried, the engine seizes up when turned off and not even turn over when the key is engaged. The engine starts like no problem even existed. All gauges look good. Temperature, pressures, all within normal. I am puzzled by the low oil reading and alarm. I can only hope it was some anomaly and not an issue. Usually that is wishful thinking.

I travel fast, but no longer at warp speed. 'Subsonic' I call it. It is evening when I pass the mouth of the Kantishna. Foil and his brother are at the old Burke cabin, once owned by my buddy, Weedz, who was killed by Silka in the Manley Hot Springs massacre years ago. *He was supposed to wait for me here at ice break up so we could go to town together. I was an hour late. He went in and got shot out of his boat. I would have been with him. Only a high Jesus factor saved me.* This is getting to be the time of year the sun is out late. I am puzzled when I pull in. Foil has a cabin fire going. He looks well rested and fine; so does the boat. I see at least thirty gallons of gas in my tanks he borrowed. Enough gas to get back to Nenana or go down to Manley.

"What's the emergency Foil?"

"Miles, I do not think I have enough gas!" I expect more to follow. But that's it. Low on gas is not an emergency. *So boat down to Manley and get more gas. Why are you bothering me?* While transferring gas into his empty stolen containers, he tells me, "I must have missed the mouth of the Kantishna, Miles! How could I miss it? I got all the way to Manley and turned around and came back."

"Why didn't you get gas there, if you need more gas?"

My situation is this. If Foil had a real emergency like he said when he called, and I replied I am not interested and hung up, that is a problem. If he died, and his phone was checked and that conversation heard, I'd be in prison for negligence or murder. If Foil make a false emergency call to me, no one cares. Complain to who? Prove it. Foil should have called 911 if this is a real emergency. I was not thinking. My mistake. *Maybe he could not get through.*

"They sell gas in Manley?"

*Is he really this naive?* Hard to believe Foil thinks there is a community on the road system with no gas. I do not say anything to insult him. I just nod. He has his gas, and is ready to take off. He noses his boat downstream.

"Foil, aren't you headed for the Kantishna River homestead?"
"Yeah!" and begins to head downstream.
"Foil, it's the other direction!"
"Well, I wasn't sure."
"Why aren't you using the GPS, so you can be sure?"
"What good is a GPS if you do not know where you are?"
"If you do not know how to use it, learn how, it's an important tool you will find to be handy." I am guessing he looks at the GPS map of the river and there is nothing on it he recognizes. But he can zoom out until he sees a name like Kantishna River. He can start to zoom the map in as he gets closer. Or, if he thinks he is close, turn the GPS on and the river name should show up on the map if he is near it. Like now. Foil is just three miles from the mouth. *He may not know how to zoom.*

"Miles, as long as you are here, why not run this load up to the cabin for me?"
"Because you do not want to pay me, Foil."
"But you owe me. You said in our contract you would help me, and teach me."
"I am helping Foil. This is how you learn, because you do not want to listen."
"But it would be easy for you Miles, just a few hours! Anyhow, you are retired now, not doing anything important. You can do what you want."

This could be true. I mostly do not like his attitude saying I have nothing worthwhile to do, that I am obligated, and must help. No. Help is appreciated when given, not demanded. He is correct about the part where he said 'Want.'

"Foil, when we discussed this, you told me you already know a lot about boats and life in the wilds. You told me all you needed was a few pointers. You need way more than a few pointers. You need more then I can offer for free." Iris is already upset at how much my help offered to Foil is costing me— us—financially. "It's money out of our household budget. Iris now contributes more than I do. Her Social Security is greater." I am not going to tell Foil I have 'other income' and doing 'ok' financially. Mad Jay would love to hear that! It's just better if it looks like I am struggling. I feel bad Foil has no clue where the Kantishna River is. *Three miles.. may as well take him and show him.* "Let me give you a ride in my boat to the mouth where we can tie a ribbon and I can bring you back. We will be gone fifteen minutes."

"Miles, it's late, why not spend the night with us and I can follow you in the morning!" I do not want to spend the night with these two. I'm livid and speechless with anger.

"No, I want to stop and do some fishing at one of my favorite spots, good place to spend a night."

I take Foil and his brother to the mouth of the Kantishna. We tie a ribbon.

"Miles, I must have missed that bluff I was looking for! It's all the way on the other side of the river! I do not remember that when you brought me."

"The river reads different in the fall than in the spring. The channel is over here this time of year." He will learn this in time, but I think he'd be smarter to pay me to haul his freight. The way this looks, he is going to spend a great deal more money doing it himself. He may in fact, not even be able to. He's already burned fifty gallons of gas going down stream. He must have had the throttle wide open. He did not idle down as I suggested. He could, and should, have burned ten gallons. This rescue is not going to be cheap.

"Thanks; Miles, I owe you one!"

*Owe me one? Referring to a beer when we run into each other again?* Again his words just rub me the wrong way. "This is going to cost, Foil. I almost lost my engine leaving before doing a good check over."

"Oh come on, Miles, your engine looks just fine! Well, anyhow, see ya. I should be at the cabin in three hours, so will head out in the morning." I do not bother to tell him he will be lucky if he gets there in a fifteen hour day. He is not getting on step. He will be going three miles an hour. *Been there, done that.* He is not asking for advice, but telling me how it will be. When a wilderness three year old knows more than Foil about running the river.

I ask if he is replacing the wood he burns at the cabin and leaving a note. Foil is using someone else's cabin. Burning their wood, eating their food.

"No, these cabins are here to use, Miles!"

*I'll remember that when I go past your house next winter in Tucson.* I want no part of this. *Again, telling me how it is, not asking for advice.* The owners will be outraged, for good reason. Foil is not having an emergency by accepted local standards. The owner will hold me responsible for bringing an idiot into the country. I feel ashamed. I suggest, "You would burn less gas and it would take less time to haul a partial load to the homestead. Leave half your load here. Come back for it." It's all about getting the boat on step. If he can get half his load on step and go fifteen miles an hour and burn five gallons an hour, this is a lot more efficient than five miles an hour not on step burning ten gallons an hour. If he does the math he will see it is faster and cost less to make two trips. Plus a lot safer. He can leave his brother there and come back. Make two round trips in a day.

Foil has the right to believe he knows better than me. I am not someone to make anyone listen or do it my way. Good luck. Smile. Leave. I stop at a favorite fishing spot. I hardly ever spend the night here, so it is nice to spend quality time at this very magical spot on the river. I'm as comfortable as I would be in the cabin. My dome tent sets up on the bow of the boat in ten minutes. My propane stove cooks a meal of moose stew as I fish. I have a book to read into the late evening. A couple of big pike are caught and released. The sun sets red about midnight. The happy quacks of contented ducks lull me to sleep. I am up about 5:00 a.m. as usual, and on my way after a hot breakfast by 6:00. After a lifetime, I am still awed by the beauty of morning fog drifting over cattails, and a pair of trumpeter swans coming out of the mist. I'm sure Foil is upset I did not spend a night with them. I'm sure he wanted more time to talk me into offering more help, especially hauling his load to the homestead for free.

I puzzle over why he called me in the first place? He had enough gas to go all the way downstream to Manley, or possibly back to Nenana. From his behavior, I suspect he found out gas in Manley is over six dollars a gallon! Twice the price of Nenana gas. He was outraged! Gas cost that much? I bet he tells his brother, 'I can just call my buddy. Miles, he'll bring me gas for nothing!' I notice Foil did not even offer to pay for the gas he asked me to bring. I had to buy it out of my own pocket. No. I will not let myself get scammed if this is what is going on.

He could have been too scared of the river or his ability to go back to Manley. Or, was lost and had no clue where either Manley or the Kantishna was. *Where did fifty gallons of gas get burned? Where did he go?* On that amount of gas I could go 300 miles. Foil is only eighty miles from where he started. I think he is not being up front and telling me everything.

He needs to learn that when you make a mistake it is going to cost. If he refuses to pay, he'll never step in my boat again. He will lose a great deal more than I lose. He has already asked around for someone to haul his freight cheap. The locals are being polite. So far, no one coming through with help. Foil has said, "Sure, come on, it will be a fun trip! Get out on the river away from here! I'll cover half the gas!" No takers.

I keep an eye on the engine gauges. There is no engine glitch, no alarm. I have water in my gas though. Luckily, I have a top of the line filter with sediment bowl that catches a cup of water. I just check on it through a clear housing, and open a drain on the bottom before the water gets sucked into the engine. I now suspect the alarm I heard on the way down was a low gas alarm due to water in the filer and fuel pump struggling. I just happened to notice low oil that was not the issue. I notice oil pressure changes as engine warms up. Not critical, but being low on volume might mean the oil gets warmer. Or, the oil foams when the suction can't pull oil fast enough. Foam does not pump as well. I do know if I lost my engine, Foil would not be there to buy me another one.

Nice warm day, smooth water. I have trouble staying awake. This is also part of a diabetic issue, blood sugar too high makes me fall asleep. I have nodded off now and then running the boat and woke when the next turn comes up. Falling asleep at the wheel is probably not a good thing. It's not anything I want to talk about. Once again, a reason I want to be in control of when I take boat trips, without having to explain myself.

"I'm not healthy enough today," is not going to cut it. I'm not interested in people feeling sorry for me, or thinking I need help. *If you trip and fall, people like Foil show up to kick you and steal your wallet.*

On previous trips, I have stopped and taken a nap when I felt like it. Part of my routine at home is an afternoon nap for an hour. A 'power nap' as it might be called. *Why not! I get up at 5:00 a.m.? Wouldn't it be normal after eight hours of work to feel rejuvenated by a rest!?* Humph! The good news is, I get home, just a routine trip of 300 miles with nothing to talk about. I recall the days the trip would be a Foil adventure worth a chapter in a book. And was, back in my early books. I recall not knowing where Minto was, getting all the way to the Yukon and being unsure if I had passed Minto yet.

I got lost on the Kantishna too! Made a wrong turn up the McKinley River and went all the way to the canyon, ran out of gas and had to wait a month for anyone to notice. Tore up my engine and needed a new one as a result of this one trip. I may have gone a hundred miles out of my way, 'lost'.

I recall when I did not understand how a compass worked, much less a GPS. The needle points north. How does that help? North of what? It's true. You have to have a point of reference. Something on the map has to make sense.

I had met an old trapper at Lake Minchumina, Kenny, who watched my sled dogs. We talked about trapping, but I think this old guy could not read a map, and did not want to admit it. I'd get a map out and begin showing him where various trails are. He could not show me where he is, where his cabins are, where his trails are. He had his trails all in his head and had never seen a map before. Trapped back during the depression in the 30s. Perhaps people did not need maps back then.

I forgot what it was like looking at my first map. Everything on a map now is obvious. Even Seymour, my survey boss could not look at a map, look up at the land, and visually translate the map into terrain we are traveling across. I look at a map, and, "This is the hill over there, that is the swamp, even if a different shape, and there is a new creek, but you can see the low spot and predict from the map this could be a creek one day and yup, it is, see?"

"If you say so!"

After cutting 200 miles of trail over a twenty year period crossing four maps that cover the ceiling, I can only guess I learned something not just everyone knows. I feel for Foil. I was there, too, once. He is not stupid; just out of his element. Little Joy was three years old, telling me the Latin names for the edible plants in the area. Plants I could not recognize. Foil has a lot to learn and as I said, no time to learn it, and not the money to pay for his education, nor nothing he offers in trade. I'd like to help.

On the other hand, I cannot cover Foil's mistakes financially. I cannot be responsible for him, rescue him every time he gets scared. Because this could go on for ten years. This could cost more money than I have. Foil needs at least ten times more help from me then I need from him.

"Iris, I would be glad to work for him and have a job. I could use the money. He could use my skills. It would be a bargain for him. Foil does not know enough to see that." I think about it and add, "I bet I have invested several hundred thousand dollars in my lifestyle learning what I know and recovering from mistakes I had to learn from. I have bought at least five boats and engines at ten grand each. Dozens of saws, half a dozen generators, solar panels, paid for a million miles of flying…" I trail off. "A lot of stuff!"

"What does Foil have in mind, Miles? He thinks he can plug into your lifestyle for a few thousand dollars?"

"It is true, I started out pretty poor. It does not take money at first. But if not money, then blood, sweat, tears, and time. You have to have endless time on your hands. Time Foil does not have, and it takes youth. He's on vacation, his time is limited."

"Well, do not support him, Miles, he's a user! Disconnect!"

Not so easy when we are in this land deal together; sharing the homestead. *How is that going to work out? If anyone needs to walk away, it should be him!* My thought is, that at some point Foil will figure out that it is cheaper to pay me. I think right now if he pays me I can get along well enough to work for him. For $500 I haul his load by myself to the homestead and drop it off. Once he realizes I know what I am doing, he may value me. Perhaps help me as he promises in Tucson; help cut trails, do stuff he says he can.

I AM HEADED for the boat landing to check on my boat. An older couple that look like tourists are standing around looking lost. At first I think they are off the beaten path and took a wrong turn someplace.

"Do you know where Jade is? He said he might give us a ride with his sled dogs!?"

"No." I reply. "I am looking for him, too. He said he could use a boat ride to get fish wheel poles. Are you having a good time in Alaska?"

"Oh yes! We went to Denali, but it is so crowded! There should not be so many people allowed in a park!"

"The park is a big money maker for the state. The tourist season is short. All those people are buying things." I pause and suggest, "If you want less people and a more quality experience, there are guides and situations to pay for with fewer people."

"Oh, no! We can't afford that!"

So instead, they look for nice Alaskans, willing to give of their time for free, and get the experience they want without paying. Great for them, not for us Alaskans. Likewise, if Alaska was to limit how many can go in the park, this couple should be in the category banned. Users, only thinking of what they want, not what is good for all of us. I cannot help but wonder if I was in their world and said, "I could use a cheap place to stay, can you help me out? I can't afford a meal, but have one dollar, can I eat with you at your house?" Thinking and adding, "I'd like to see a museum, the zoo, an art gallery, have a quality personal tour of some kind, avoid the crowds, can you give me a free tour? Maybe I'll slip you a five if you do a good job!" I wonder what they would say. I already know. They'd call the police.

However, I was in this position, and my friend Helm and his wife invited me to Frankfurt, Germany. They put me up, fed me, took time to take me places. I could not afford to pay much. They were very kind. I still give them art and take them on boat trips every year, but it does not make up for all they did for me. Deciding to help people is not a simple yes or no issue.

Jade is the young kid Josh has sold his dogs and holdings at $10^{th}$ Street. Josh is not handling it well. He swore he'd die on the runners of a dog sled. Been saying that for sixty years. Now that time has arrived. He cannot stand on the runners anymore. Jade respects Josh. Josh found a good person to take over the old guard, pick up the reins. Jade is a go getter who wants to dog race, and is serious about the subsistence lifestyle. Sometimes he takes tourists out for rides.

I guess I used to do that more when young. I'd hang out at the café and take out the tourists, give them an experience to remember... cheap. That is how I got involved with Foil!

"Come stay at my cabin for free!" Sometimes, even most times, it works out. I am getting cynical in my old age. This concerns me. *What happened to being kind and forgiving, just being happy!* Partly, I just do not feel well. Partly, civilization itself is getting to be more like an agitated bee hive. More people expect free help as their due, and are not truly grateful.

---

SOMEONE I KNOW a little stops to visit me. We have known each other off and on for thirty years. I hear about him through others, as he hears of me. I do not get many visitors. This visit is welcome because we have things in common, both living a subsistence lifestyle and connected close to the outdoors.

He has been in, I think he said, the forty mile country. "Miles, the government burned me and my neighbors out. Burned our main cabins and trapline cabins to get rid of us."

I'd only heard of this; never met anyone who had it happen. I tell him, "Oh, yes, way back in the 70s by Delta Junction. The government burned hippie hill to the ground. Remember that cabin?"

Axford had visited my cabin I. "Axford! You knew Becky who lived there?"

That was back in the 70s. He tells me she left the state after her pipeline job and getting rich. I knew she left the guy she was with when we met. He confirms she could not keep up with the payments on the lifestyle she bought into when the money was good. "Miles, worse off than if she had never made the money at all!"

We both know others this happened to. Those who made several hundred grand, the pipeline ends and these people are back at the poverty level again. Local hire does not mean you are qualified for much. I never understood until recently what was going on back then! It meant, in this case, a legal obligation was being met to hire local. Demanded by the state. Get the job done fast, pay whatever it takes. Pay ten times the going rate for people to answer the phone, wash dishes, make beds. I think most young people I knew who got such jobs ended up with an inflated opinion of their worth. It's hard to get back to reality after making such hourly wages at ten times the going rate. Josh had such a job. He got hired because he is an Indian! This looks good, even required.

"Hire Indians!" Josh told me he was told to go sit out of the way... for $30 an hour. Becky was a minority woman. Many workers we know got into rich man's drugs. Cocaine was the drug of choice during this time, I'm told. We get back to the hippie hill cabin.

The locals complained. Various scruffy riff-raff were living off and on for free in this not so remote cabin. The issue came to a head when 'someone' was dynamiting remote legal recreational cabins. Some idiot with problems who had access to miner's dynamite, but did not live on hippie hill! The excuse worked to burn hippie hill down. I did not pay much attention at the time.

"Miles, I feel half the state has become government land of one kind or other. Parks have expanded and such."

We both agree that when Alaska became a state, one of the agreements was that the Federal Government would transfer a high percentage of land into the state's hands, and then into private hands. This part of the agreement has not been lived up to. My mind wanders a little bit on this subject as Axford goes out to his truck to bring me some Alaska jade he heard I buy.

The whole statehood issue seems interesting to me. Some historical date has arrived having to do with statehood, and the 100 year anniversary. Old timers tell stories in the news about the wonderful world of statehood. How the state was hurting and how wonderful a day it was when the Feds agreed to accept us as a state. Making us all free, etc. Just 'bla, bla' sound in the background as I do my chores. All I really pick up on is happy sounds. Puzzling, because I had talked to old timers who said life was good before statehood. Alaskans had voted two to three times and turned down wanting to be a state. Why? Is it even true? *How many of my views are based on inaccurate information?*

Old timers expressed this same sentiment. "We had the resources the Feds wanted. We could sell resources to support the state and control the money ourselves. Why just give management to the Feds?" Oil, gas, timber, fish and gold. "We are a rich state, not needing the Federal Government." This made sense to me. I'm also told by quite a few people, Alaska was illegally taken as a state because the last time statehood was voted on, the Feds gave the right to vote to temporary military in Alaska who were not legal residents, so not qualified voters. This illegal vote got statehood passed. The Feds wanted our resources, and stole them.

In fact, the head of the Independent party, Joe Vogler, had a case going before the world court, arguing for Alaska seceding from the Union based on the state being illegally taken. He mysteriously disappears, and is found murdered just before the hearing date. A lot of people, including his campaign manager, who is a friend of mine, and has inside information, believes the government killed him. This whole story is so crazy and preposterous sounding it's just, "Ya, ya right," news that goes in one ear and out the other. Spoken by out to lunch radicals who totally make up stuff.

The same group of people who tell me to be careful because aliens have taken over the Earth. The sky is falling, the end is near. Bla, bla. Yet the person I am close to who has inside information is sober, sound of mind, trustable and not known for exaggerating. In fact, tells a very factual, dry, boring story with no embellishment. Backing up the talk that Vogler was assassinated by the Federal Government. *Oh good heavens!* I do not want the facts! Do not want the sort of information that is dangerous to have. It's all water washing out the bridge. There is no way in hell Alaska is going to be free of the United States! But curious, and at odds with news stories about what a great time it was for Alaska when statehood came. Somebody is seriously lying. Either the Vogler people, or the rah, rah statehood people.

Axford comes back. "One thing I wonder, Miles, is maybe there were factions in the state. It may have been those like us—trappers, homesteaders—lovers of the wild who did well; liked an independent Alaska. Maybe a lot of city business people thought federal management was good for business. Maybe a lot of government jobs were created. More federal subsidies, loans and such."

I think there was more military presence as well, like the DEW line going in. Alaska was in a strategic place during the Cold War. Russia is only fifty miles away.

"Axford, do you think the government wanted to force you out of a lifestyle and out of the wilds on purpose?"

"Absolutely! No doubt in my mind. A dozen of us were burned out." The question is still, "Why?" Were all of you on someone else's land?"

"That is the reason given, yes." Axford explains it is not that simple. "I am not sure of the others, but I had a trapping cabin permit from the state I paid for. I had a registered trapline."

We both wonder, registered with who? The state does not recognize traplines and unofficially allows trappers to cut trails and use the land, but trappers do not own it. Anyone can use the public trails we cut. The state is happy to collect a user fee for what they call a 'trapper cabin'; and trappers and fur dealers pay taxes that are gladly collected.

"The Federal Government did not honor the state's permit." So sounds like, came in heavy handed, no warning, and burned them out.

"All my belongings were in the cabin. There was no warning. I was in town working."

I'd heard in the past, a notice would be put on the cabin door to be replied to. A notice of eviction, with the reason stated that could be contested; a procedure was followed. The process takes a minimum of a year. I saw the notice on the hippie hill cabin. The cabin was empty and unoccupied at the time. If I recall, the argument was the cabin is unsafe, condemned, and the land owner—the state—did not want the liability. Regrettable, but understandable. I did not think this was the real reason, but, oh well. No skin off my nose. I wondered at the time why the state did not fix the cabin up, require a lease payment, or have it as a recreational remote cabin for the public to enjoy since the cabin has lake frontage. The response is to destroy. I found that confusing, sad, but, again, oh well!

I do a partial trade, on the jade from Axford, and thank him for stopping by. He leaves with some moose meat, jewelry for his wife and gas money. Yes, he is doing fine. Just like me, unable to live in the wilds anymore and misses the old life. *So I am not the only one who feels like I was deliberately run out of my lifestyle.* I hate to think this. I do not care for people putting the blame for their own woes on someone else.

"It's not my fault the world is out to get me!" My attitude has always been, "You are in charge of your life! Seize the reins!" And, "What does it matter?What matters is what you do about it! If you are not happy, do something, change things, create situations you can be happy in!" I've always been known for being optimistic and cheerful. Lifting others when they are down. Where has all that gone? Maybe I have simply lost the enthusiasm for life that youth has?

When I was in the wilds I only had to be myself, there was no guilt. Now I struggle to be like my heroes. Others have expectations of me.

Wilderness cabins get destroyed by BLM.

# CHAPTER ELEVEN

## FISHING WASTE, LAND DISPUTE, GOVERNMENT ISSUES

I have art put together to bring to the community culture center. "I'm glad to see the cultural center begin another season!"

The mayor replies, "Yes, I'm not sure who is going to run it though."

I had already heard Alley is not going to be in charge. He quit... or so I heard. Though at the end of each season, Alley had said he was quitting, so I am not sure if this time it is for real. Alley is the Native who gave me the dead raven that ended up being part of the charges against me.

"Yeah, Miles, he does a good job all right, and is the one who got the center going with Princess Tours. But he demanded the city pay year round medical benefits at a cost of $40,000 a year for his seasonal job. This is about the total summer profit for the cultural center. Alley is already covered under his Native tribal program."

I do not hear any more details than this. I can understand from the city's perspective, if this is how it is. I'd like to know the other side of the story, but the main thing is, no Alley!

"Miles, you would be good for the job." I had been involved in the culture center right from the beginning. Heck, I knew Wolf when he got the grant to build it. I was on the board of directors and the first art buyer for the museum.

"To much politics over there." Mayor understands.

The whole time I was there, I kept asking, "Is this is an Indian only center?" I was adamantly told, 'No!' By law it cannot be. The center was built on a federal grant, not Indian money. This was never intended to be owned by the tribe, but was a grant to the city for all of us. The grant set very specific uses this center must live up to or we have to return the grant money. Though Native culture is important, we have railroad history, radio history, trappers, homestead, Denali Park affiliation, gold mine history. All this is also interesting. The shop sells other local art that is not Native. Mine for example! The sad truth is that there are not enough dedicated local Natives who produce enough crafts for the shop to have a local 'Native only' gift shop. No other shop I can think of, has even 'just local' or even 'Alaska only'. Some claim to, but it's not so.

The Natives took over and ran the culture center for years after I left. The mayor says, "Because more money comes to the tribe than the city."

A separate Native grant was acquired to hire employees. I was not brought back even though I was a volunteer. They imported Native crafts from outside, including Canadia, to support 'Indian only' rather than keeping the art local. Much of the art labeled 'Native' is not native made - just native style created by factories as far away as China, but with good profit mark ups when signed by a local Native. Much is acquired from my buddy Crafty. I think because he makes it easy. He shows up with boxes of goods.

I worked for Crafty for years, helping out in the busy summer season. One of his suppliers is a company called Indian Crafts. I understood the advantages to the Nenana Culture Center. For a short time, I accepted Crafty's deliveries at the gift shop as the shop's buyer. One receipt, one transaction, maybe payments and credit. No mess, no fuss, no keeping track of each artist. It's a sweet deal financially, not a sweet deal for the tourists who get scammed, or for local nonnative artists like myself. Not even for local Natives trying to sell their own crafts for more than slave labor. However, the profits help the city and the tribe.

There has been outright antagonism against helping out local white artists. There has been a desire among some of the Natives in charge, to deliberately put a monkey wrench in the white artist gears. I hear, "Yeah, you white people mistreated us Natives! Now it's payback time! We will run all of you out! We will go back to the old way that worked!" Even Alley is hard to work with. He gives different deals to different people, favoring his relatives and other Natives. I stopped putting my art in his shop. Alley asked me to pay five percent more for protection that is not asked from the Natives.

"Your work is not guaranteed against theft. If you give us 30% instead of 25% this covers protection. If anything is stolen, we can cover it if you pay extra to help with the loss."

There has been a problem in the past with employee theft. This new policy sounds like, if I did not pay, then it is open season on my art. If any workers like my art they can help themselves; sell it someplace else, or take it to put a monkey wrench in my gears.

The mayor is saying, "I am looking over the inventory, and it is hard to know for sure what was going on. We have work not checked in and art that is not legal for us to sell, like white walrus ivory and bear claws, feathers of all kinds." We assume, bought from Alley's relatives who needed money, using city money. But then, sold to who? Something going on under the table not recorded or reported? We do not know. There is simply no paperwork anyplace. The shop can't legally sell it. This is not necessarily something not approved, or criminal, but means it is taking time to sort out what belongs to the shop, and what has not been paid for, or is owed.

"Miles, Alley is advising his friends to pull all their art from the center, saying it is not going to open this season!" Oh great. I admire Alley for all the hard work he has done. He is single handedly responsible for the tour buses finally coming and stopping after fifteen years of trying to convince them! The Chamber of Commerce could not pull it off in all my time in charge. For Alley to do so single handedly is truly amazing. Partly the tour bus can announce, 'Operated by a real Indian, selling Indian art. Shopping here supports local culture!' Will all that be lost? I have to wait now to see if the cultural center will even open this season.

IN FRED MEYERS, someone greets me with a hearty "Hello!" Since they call me by name, I assume I must know this person. I have no recollection whatever who this is. As usual, I smile, and give a warm hello back. "Miles, how did your ordeal end up?" I'm sure they refer to my legal matters.

"I'm fine. I got off easily enough." I mention the cost a lawyer wanted up front. I'm trying to get past this and not talk about it. This is old tired news now. This is also not the kind of attention I want to be getting. Through the conversation I understand this is a pilot. He could have been a firefighter I met through my BLM job long ago.

"I ended up working for the government. I have flown Tony Knolls and many politicians and overheard many conversations. You'd be surprised how the world works." He says, "The fire that burned your Kantishna place was deliberately set. I was flying when I saw a military helicopter dropping flares to start the fire."

I'm puzzled. "Why would the government deliberately set a forest fire?"

"To run people off the land." A pause. "The government does not want anyone in the wilderness, including Natives. Mostly get subsistence people out who might request compensation for loss."

*Loss for what?*

This is a pretty strong statement to be making. I have heard this several times before though; even direct from wildlife officers. I assumed these were rouge ideas held by only a few. I sometimes repeat this as a truth, but more of 'they wish'. Not like this is war. Not like the government would burn people's homes, as if the US soil was Viet Nam. This seems such an impossible truth. Deliberately running people off the land by fire? I refuse to buy into that. One possibility is that the government was trying to do a controlled burn or back burn as land management conservation effort and the fire got out of hand.

The pilot goes on, "I also overhead conversations concerning specifics for how to get rid of people by setting them up and arresting them." Somewhere in the conversation, he mentions oil and gas being under the land I live and trap on. "There are a lot of people wanting to do something about it."

I reply, "Well I'm a writer. I suppose I fulfill my role by recording events, trying not to do so with emotion. Simply report what I hear and see."

I am not interested in any active group against the government. In my opinion, people who talk this way will disappear. I do not even recall this guy. Who the heck is he to me that I might trust him if I had any negative thoughts? For all I know he is an undercover government agent looking for dissent among the population. Making a list of those who need to be watched or shut up. I did not rise to the bait. I would not be surprised if a year from now someone says, 'Did you hear what happened to your pilot friend? His plane crashed a month ago.' Pilot error, big investigation, no more news on the subject. What would he expect? You can't bite the hand that feeds you and think there will not be consequences. What did I do when one of my sled dogs decides to go on strike or badmouth me? Shot him and got a replacement.

My mind wanders. In this day and age, the government does not have to take you out back and shoot you, or send you to a concentration camp. That's costly and bad for the public image. Someone at a desk hits a 'delete' button and there goes your bank account, credit, ID, passport, driver license, right to vote, right to work, have a gun, or permit of any kind. How effective are you now? You may as well be dead. All it took was the drop of a finger on a keyboard.

"Bla, bla the government, bla, bla do something, bla, bla. So what do you think, Miles?"

"I'm fine. Retired now. Collect Social Security. Go fishing, fool with the garden..." I trail off with a happy smile. *Life is good.* I'm puzzled and concerned there is so much negativism going around. Conspiracy theories! Doom and gloom! *Geez people! Get a life!* I also think the government wants me to spread doom and gloom and do their work. Have me be an example. *I've said it before, I repeat myself so much these days.* Feel sorry for me. Let the world know what can happen to you as well if you decide to circumvent the system and upset the apple cart. I hear it.

"Well, because of what happened to you I will never pick up a feather off the sidewalk, that's for sure!" Not touch, or help a wounded animal, or wear a wolf claw. Fear controls them, and it would be nice if I set an example and spread the word to give up! Like in India, when they cut the hand off a thief. Such a person goes around as an invalid, begging; slowly dying in the street. Beats paid advertising. A testimonial reaching hundreds, maybe thousands of people, who make the sign of the cross and swear to be good.

"MILES, I am running the culture center this summer, so stop by, we need your art!" Garden is talking to me on the front steps of the post office as we both come by to get our mail. I look puzzled. Garden is a white haired elder with a couple of missing front teeth and a lot of energy. His personality often makes me wonder if someone knocked them out. He is not mean, but has views not accepted well by the majority. He believes in UFO's and Sasquatch. I think the leading expert on these subjects in the state, quoted in the news. "Mayor asked me if I'd do it as I once ran a gift shop on an Indian reservation, so know a little about it."

Yes, I think Garden would be a good person to have in charge. He happens to be white, which does not matter. He has a business background; university education; has been in charge before, is honest, sober, dedicated at what he does, and fair. He understands the Native culture, so might get along with the tribe. I have worked with him in the past.

I was a boat operator on a university project looking for invasive weeds along remote river banks. The university wants to spend thousands of dollars to find out where dandelions are growing. *Cool! I'll run the boat!* While looking for invasive weeds, we dip fishing poles into a remote lake. It is interesting how invasive weeds are mostly at places where people come ashore, like fish camps, and hunting spots. Garden is proving weed seeds must arrive on shoes, cloths; bottoms of boats. The fascinating part is, while I get paid $300 to run the boat, there is not enough money to study people. Whatever, I'm adaptable. My hand goes out with a smile, getting paid to take Garden and his youths out fishing.

"I have some youth workers under a grant to help out. We need inventory, Miles!" He has the original concept I think works for our community. To carry only local art, no imports or fakes. Garden has his own ideas, but in general wants all local art, as I'd like to see. I'm excited to get my art back in! One summer I made $6,000 here. I believed I was the best seller in the shop. I was not the buyer, and not an employee. I had no special influence with Alley. We got along though, for a while. He allowed Iris and I to come in and set up our own display using our own materials from home. We made our own tags, and brought our own cases; had our own shelf in the shop. It was not a prominent shelf, but we arranged it ourselves. Anyone else could do the same thing with their art, but were unwilling to spend the time.

"That's the shop's job!" True, but what matters whose job it is? I'm sure there was some resentment.

"How come Miles makes so much money? Whose hinny is he kissing?" was a comment from Dalia who also has art here. Few other artists could keep up with inventory. I do not know why. I do not watch to see how others work. All I know is, at any given time I have 500 finished pieces on hand. I do not find that hard to do. I can create thirty pieces at a time. I could produce twice as much if it was selling and I wished to.

A WEEK LATER: At the post office again. Garden stops me, "I'd watch my stuff at the center if I were you. I just quit." I look puzzled. He responds. "Same issues you spoke of. Native issues."

Ah, yes, bummer. Garden tells me he has Native youth workers who can't add and subtract, run a register, or do much of anything with their 3rd grade level education. More than this, unwilling to learn the job. An attitude they are owed. "More than this, we suspect theft. Part of why Alley had expected extra money for protection." *What did he do for the 10% more? Pay the thieves off to say this stuff is off limits for stealing?* This does not sound like Alley as I know him. He might be sticking to his tribe, not liking what he is seeing, but going along with it. Garden is hinting at the same issues. He is not naming names. Apparently the tribe in backing the Natives, saying,

"Our grant money pays the youth workers. We own and run the shop!" In fact the city owns it, as the building grant demanded. But the city is in financial trouble and cannot reply, 'No problem, we will pay the workers.' The city ends up between a rock and a hard place with the tribe taking advantage. The tribe seems not to care about the community as a whole, but only its own people. However, many whites have done the same, so the pot is calling the kettle black here. Why aren't the Native kids more educated? Who graduated them? And why? In the long haul we will all lose due to the racial issues.

In the past, when the tribe ran the cultural center, it was run on Indian time. Open when they felt like it, not the hours posted. The visitors center stopped sending people over, and buses would not stop. It had been Alley who brought the change. He was a perfect choice to bridge relations between cultures, between tribal laws and city government. I stand up for him as a good person for the job. The best. Even if my work is not there. It's best for the community. At least one of the employees is stealing art, taking it to Fairbanks and pawning it. They got caught. Garden does not want to be involved if he cannot stop this due to Native politics.

"Garden, I was in the cultural center the other day and some of my inventory was in the office, and not out for sale." I asked what's her name in charge that day. She told me it got pulled because it is illegal to sell.

"Only Natives can sell mammoth ivory." There is sometimes a misconception, a rumor, talk, that this is so. "But Crafty Tim has his mammoth ivory products still out for sale in our gift shop. He is not Native. She told me, "The mayor ordered it."

This seems odd, as I get along with Mayor just fine. He would have explained, and given a reason or warning before he just pulled my art. I go and talk to Mayor. He is livid, and gets on the phone right there in front of me. The family name of the gal who did this is a name I remember from twenty years ago, related to trapline disputes. "I never said anything of the sort! You put his art back out right now. I do not want to hear of this again!"

I assume some of the Native artists are jealous my work and material sells well. Some Native crafts sell really well of course! Quality work. Other artists are not producing quality, and asking too much money. Not just Natives! It's just the Natives working there feel they own the place, and can run it as owners.

I tell Garden, "The plot thickens! Stay tuned to this channel!" I laugh and he chuckles. This is not worth getting upset over. I have other outlets. The city is losing revenue if the shop is not open or not doing well. It's possible the tribe is not so interested in profits as much money is given to the Native and is not earned, beyond feeling owed by the white man. I'm not convinced free money is helping the Natives. I care, and many Native leaders agree.

News Miner Sat June 6th 2015
    Cutting back on Wanton Waste

"Miles, did you see this article?" I glance and see it is a subject brought up many times over the past forty years. I have been following it. In all that time, I see little change. The article explains as if it's a new topic and the public has forgotten.

I glance at the highlights.

> "By-catch is a term used in the commercial fishing industry referring to the fish caught by accident while fishing for another species. The amount of fish caught as bycatch is staggering. Estimated 82 million pounds of halibut in the past decade have been dumped while fishing for yellow sole. A whopping 93 percent of halibut caught are brought aboard as bycatch and dumped to rot, with only 7 percent caught by the local commercial halibut fleet. Public outcry has been abundant. Despite well moneyed interests in Seattle opposing reductions, Alaska citizens and lawmakers have weighed loudly in favor of mandating less waste."

It's been the same story in the salmon industry. Subsistence fisherman like myself were blamed and shut down. The public is in an outrage over the news of how many fish sled dogs eat. Now interior commercial fisherman, including Natives are part of the problem. This accidental ocean bycatch for salmon thrown away, is greater than what is allotted for the entire interior for commercial subsistence and sport combined. The public gets sold the idea we have a limited resource we need to protect, so more restrictions are required to save the planet. But who is being restricted? Who is not? I was a lot happier in the wilds not knowing, not being involved in all this. Ignorance is bliss. With knowledge comes responsibility. Not long after, Iris points out another article in the news related to wasted wildlife.

Friday, June 19, 2015
    Ton of ivory crushed in Times Square to highlight poaching
    By KAREN MATTHEWS
    Associated Press-- Actress Kristen Davis, a longtime advocate for elephants known for her role in the HBO show 'Sex and the City', said at the event no one should ever buy ivory even if a dealer says it's an antique.
    Officials said they are committed to fighting the ivory trade, not just to protect elephants, but to combat terrorists who profit from elephant poaching.
    "Animal trafficking, we now know, is funding those dangerous groups out there," said U.S. Rep. Steve Israel, a Long Island Democrat." "It is a source of revenue for terrorist groups around the world."

I run into Seymour in Fred Meyers, which seems to be a meeting place for people I know. I have not seen him in a while. and miss our surveying years! I ask how he is, and mention the article I just read. Seymour likes to hunt and is a strong outdoor advocate, a member of the NRA, and believes in our constitution, and the rights of the individual. I have trouble understanding exactly what his views are though. When we talk, we quickly reach a point where we are not agreeing. I do not know why. I know his source of information is different from mine, and he looks down on my sources as not reliable. I do not feel I have any particular source. I talk to people mostly. People I think should know something. Lawyers, judges, politicians. I ask people what is going on in their chosen field; many are layman working class people. Fisherman, trappers, secretaries, close to the issue we discuss.

I get the impression Seymour knows people even higher up in the government then I do, and or feels he talks to people who are smarter or know more than people I talk to. Seymour is of the formally educated and smart class of people. I admire his opinion a lot. He asks me, "Do you think our country is collapsing, coming apart at the seams?"

I do not think we are safe discussing such a question honestly. "Before I give a yes or no answer I can tell you what I believe." I explain how I consider it a fact, no civilization has lasted forever. Every high society in history has collapsed in time. Some lasted thousands of years though! I consider my country is only 200 years old! A drop in the bucket of time! Yet in our short history, there have been some serious flaws, glitches, disasters, instability. We have in 200 years consumed major natural resources that made us big. We now depend on resources from outside our boundaries. There is less strength in that, in my opinion. We made our power and economic base on the backs of slavery. We still do. I saw in the news just today that workers in India are earning sixty cents a day producing coffee for US markets. We have acquired wealth in a very wasteful manner. We wiped out the buffalo, stripped most of the land of its nutrients. The list is long of all we have devastated in a mere two generations. "It is difficult to picture a graph on a timeline without being concerned."

My business cannot compete well with slave labor overseas. Most of the industry in our country has moved overseas for cheap labor. I am not saying we are, or will, come apart at the seams now, or even soon. I am saying there is no harm in considering the possibility, and being prepared with a plan.

Seymour could be in a different situation than I am. His back up plans would not resemble mine. He has his life savings in a bank, has paid a fortune into retirement, unemployment, workman's compensation and government backed money plans, filled with promises, and guarantees. If the system as we know it collapses, Seymour would be left with the pig in the poke. If Seymour agrees with me, I do not know what his backup plan looks like. He seems to be counting on a lifetime of medical coverage, and banks being solvent. He told me years ago that he had 200 grand in the bank and hoped to get to 400 grand and live off the interest.

I have never agreed a couple of percent interest banks pay is anything to get excited about. My opinion is, that interest paid does not even keep up with inflation. Nor do I like the fact banks gamble with money I deposit.

In terms of survival, Seymour seems more interested in gun rights. He thinks voting for the right person will make a difference. "All we need Miles, is to get that bozo out, and the other party back in!" He looks at his watch. "Well, the wife is waiting back home Miles, got to get all these groceries over to the airstrip and fly home; getting the plane loaded up. Want to fly home before dark." We wave good bye. My buddy with his own private plane.

"PHONE FOR YOU, Miles! I think it's Foil, I can hardly understand him." I grab the phone and assume he has arrived at the homestead, is getting work done, and just checking in.

"Miles! I'm broke down! I need your help!" He sounds desperate. I am not sure what is going on.

"My engine runs only in reverse!" He is at Tolovana Roadhouse about fifty miles downriver. Less than two hours run for me, but a forever walk for him. I feel more ready for a trip now than a week ago when I rescued Foil. Whatever. I'm going to charge him.

Iris is trying to talk to me at the same time, "You charge him, Miles! No more doing Foil favors! He takes advantage of you because you are nice and naive! He is nice when he gets his way. You try asking for what is fair and I guarantee you will see another side of him!"

"I'll make it right for you Miles, whatever it cost!" *Yeah, right.* But if he is paying, I am not so concerned with why he feels he needs a rescue. *Pay me and I am at your service, how many trips do you want? When do you need to go? I'd love making money with my boat.* I made $200 a day profit boating for the mushroom pickers. My friend Josh has a commercial license and bigger boat than I do, and makes $800 a day boating fire fighters.

So, I head on downriver next day, early. I stop and catch a big pike on the way while transferring fuel. I am there in three hours. Foil has plenty of gas, like forty gallons. He is all ready to load everything into my boat.

Foil yells at his brother, "Hurry up "G*& Da^$it! We do not have all day. I always say, if you can't talk and work at the same time shut up!" Foil is treating his brother the same as he did me. Foil turns to me for support, expecting me to agree we need to shut up and work, and reprimand, beat up on the brother together.

I interrupt. "I'm not taking off right away, Foil. I just got here, it's been a hard trip. I want to walk around and rest at least a few minutes." Meaning they can take their time to load up, there is no rush. Foil has planned to abandon his boat here, to come back for it with another rescue operation. He appears to be in panic mode, making poor decisions. I suggested it might be possible to tow the boat empty behind mine. He is concerned we might have to hide his boat and come back later.

"If not Foil, run the boat empty, using your eight horse spare, get it on step and get the boat into Nenana in a day. It would be an advantage to have me just ahead of you."

I used to run a ten horse, not so different from his eight horse, as my main and only engine to haul all my supplies. It was slow all right! But I did it as routine. I am not understanding the issue here. Did Foil even try his eight horse spare? I think he could have come on home with it, even though the trip would take two days. I suspect more is going on. Foil might think he will get lost, or stuck, or break down. He may be out of food. He may not have a tent and sleeping bag with him to stay overnight.

The first rescue trip was not just about the gas he ran out of. He was lost.

Without my help, he most likely would not have found the Kantishna, and thus never got to the homestead we are sharing. He was ready to head the wrong direction. He would have gotten to Manley Hot Springs a second time, and probably given up.

We load up and are able to pull his boat at fifteen miles an hour. I calculate we will be home by 5:00 p.m. Foil at least turns his GPS on to save the track we are running. He now has the track for the main channel... for this part of his journey anyway. We chat on the trip home. The engine runs nice and quiet, not even working hard. There is a little glitch in the engine sound and hesitation. Foil panics. I am thinking he does not have the personality type to pull this lifestyle off. Foil wants me to start pulling hoses, to stop and begin tearing the engine down to look for problems. Do a rebuild here in an open boat with a crescent wrench. Foil thinks the sound is internal, so pistons need to come out. He is not interested in learning from me about how to deal with such situations. He is not asking me what I think is wrong.

I have learned to trust my equipment over the years. My first guess is not that the engine failed, but likely something I did. "Let me check the oil level just in case." Something quick and easy to do. Oil looks good. Next guess is a gas issue. I check for water in the gas filter. No water.

"I have an old 1950s fuel tank. Now and then the pick up tube acts up. As if there is a rag floating around inside that blocks off the suction now and then." We switch tanks. That is most likely the problem. But I think of something else. I re-trim the boat. I think as I have been burning fuel the boat has less weight in the front.

"The propeller is starting to cavitate." We are not sure, but have no other issues. Cavitation would normally not be a problem, but I have raised my propeller about two inches higher than the bottom of the boat. The usual level to set the propeller is even with the bottom. I've tweaked it out of tolerance. At the price of needing to be careful of my trim. A whale fin was bolted onto the cavitation plate to stop the propeller from sucking surface air. *There are other factors, but this is the basics. Why explain to Foil who doesn't even know what 'cavitation' means.* The advantages are, less drag in the water, two inches less draft, a tad more speed and better fuel economy. The price being more sensitive to trim adjustment, and needing to be sure my cooling water pick up stays primed. I can lose water pick up prime if I turn sharply at high speed.

Foil's brother says, "One of your fuel tanks that we stashed was bitten by a bear and leaks. We lost a few gallons of fuel."

Foil says, "Thanks a lot big mouth! I was just going to fix it and not say anything!" Nothing will make the tank new again. Seal-All glue he suggests, might work for a while. Or Bondo. That for sure will not work. The tank is compromised, and is now a messed up tank that can never be trusted again. I can't afford to lose gas. It's a fire hazard, and I may seriously need the gas or need to stash the tank and can't lose the fuel.

*Foil was not going to tell me?*

He changes the subject a little. "We stashed two barrels of gas in the shed at Tolovana. I'll have gas when I come back."

"Foil, did you leave a note?"

"No, Miles, what for?"

"Because Foil, this is someone else's property. You put barrels and gas in their shed. They may assume someone gave it to them, and it is their barrels and their gas. They may think their partners left it, or some grateful person they helped. If you found this in your garage at home what would you think? Would you think someone you never met is storing their gas in your shed?" I do not care, except these are my gas tanks he is being so free with. I assumed he'd take care of them and give them back to me when he bought his own—in the same condition he got them in. But if not, at least acknowledging they are damaged.

Now I am low on barrels, and maybe having to use a fifty-five gallon drum to keep gas on my boat. Kind of a pain, as it is hard to move around if I need to adjust weight traveling. Foil is also, in local resident minds, under my care. I am responsible for his behavior since he is my friend and guest. I invited him here. The argument being, "Miles, he doesn't know any better, he's a city slicker. You know better. It is your responsibility to watch out for him and us!"

We tell fishing, hunting stories, gun stories, and exchange good conversation on the way home. I point out the village of Old Minto as we go by. "Another thirty-five miles to go. If you had to, you could get help here. This is the alcohol rehab camp. There are at least a couple of people here all the time throughout the summer."

"What about the road, Miles, where is the road?"

"There is a road to New Minto, a long ways off. This is the old village that once depended on the river, never a road system. The village moved to be near a road and to have a runway. It would be hard to put a runway in here, as it is all swamp."

***

We arrive in Nenana about five, as I predicted. Foil gets the truck that he bought from me, loads his boat and is gone. I tie up my boat to deal with later, grab a few needed items, and head home with the four wheeler. Foil later wants to know what he owes me. I have been putting the subject off because I am sure Foil does not know what it cost to run a boat, and he believes paying for half the gas will be enough.

"Because we are buddies looking out for each other."

I add up the costs and here we go, the bomb shell is dropped. "$500 a trip, times two trips plus eighty gallons of gas is $1,500, Foil."

"That is way out of line, Miles, and you know it! You are trying to take advantage of me and my predicament. If the situation were reversed, I'd come rescue you for free! It's all about money with you! I will never ask a favor of you again, you can be sure of that!" I think that's good. I do not ask favors of others very often. I do not expect anyone to depend on me.

"Foil, if you called a licensed legal professional, these trips would be $2,000, each, a total of $4,000." I also find his offer to rescue me rather empty. With what boat? He can't help himself, how can he help me? I also suspect the river scares him.

"Yeah, you cannot legally charge me, Miles. You are not in business and are on probation." I view this as a threat. In truth no one should even step into my boat. I have no insurance. I am technically not operating legally. To be legal I need a life jacket for each passenger, a fog horn, a fire extinguisher, running lights, and insurance. To charge anyone, I need a commercial license, business license, a contract, liability insurance, pay taxes on it. This is not realistic, so locals help each other out for reasonable amounts of money. Friends, relatives, locals, people we know, and trust. We do not take out strangers, or those who would wish to turn us in or sue us. *We are living in the end times. The big question in this situation is this. Do you want to make a deal between the two of us as friends for $1,500? Or, would you like the same trip with nothing different except we pay a third party for protection, as a business trip, for a total of $4,000?*

Knowing how Foil feels, I will never take him out in my boat again. Let him call one of his new found friends like Mad Jay, or our friend Josh. I suggest Foil ask around about what these trips and rescue cost. If word gets around that Foil is concerned about the legality, no one will take him but a professional, at business prices.

"If it is all about money with you, Miles, I ask you to pay rent on your shed on my land. It has been here a year, I think $360 is fair, $360 a year." The shed is only worth $400. If he wants to go back in time and we each pay the other what is fairly owed, this is not someplace it is wise for him to go. A months use of a remote furnished vacation cabin is an amount Foil would not want to hear. I think Foil is trying to be penny wise, while being dollar foolish. I could ask him to take it off my boat bill. Instead I hand him the cash.

"Foil, I'd appreciate a month or so time to remove the shed off your land."

"You have nowhere to put it, Miles!" Now I get the impression he thinks he has me between a rock and a hard place. Not the game to play with me. I do not trust him enough to tell him my various options. I believe I now know the true nature of my friend. It is more his loss than mine. He can be on his own now. No particular hard feelings. I blame myself for not knowing this guy better. I accept the price of that. Mistakes cost money. This guy appears to me to have a similar personality as Gene Gram who ended up burning my house down. Being right or winning an argument is not that important. Foil can be right. I can back off, and in my view, let him hang himself. He will have a hard time without my help, or help from others. In fact, I predict he will not have enough money to see his dream through.

Foil's engine trouble is something simple. His shifter connector came loose. Just a screw. *This time.* I think he cannot keep overworking an engine running way overloaded without something failing. Been there, done that. No, I am not going to be critical. None of my business. I smile and wish him well as much as I can. Good weather, good cheer.

I notice Josh is in Foil's yard visiting, so I stop to say hi to Josh. They are becoming buddies. Josh bursts out, "I'm ashamed of you, Miles! You should know better!" I'm guessing what this is all about. I'm not going to get in an argument. I stopped to offer good cheer and friendly chat. I feel hurt my friend of thirty years will so easily be swayed by his new friend of a week, without asking for my side of what is going on.

I have always known this about Josh though. I think Josh and Foil will not last as friends. If Foil pulls on Josh what he did on me, Josh will kill him. Josh is not kind in such matters, or willing to back down. There is a hint Josh is going to haul freight for Foil for free. Foil gives a look my way of, "See how true friends should be, Miles? Take a lesson here." I nod appropriately chagrined, like I have learned a good lesson. My bad. But do not follow up with an apology, or move to make it all right. *Gene was like this*. Your best buddy when he got his way. Your worst nightmare when he felt slighted. A little bit like the cycle of an abusive violent relationship.

Foil volunteers around the community as 'Mr. Nice Guy.' He mows lawns for elders, runs errands. It is me who is evil. I let it go. Again, all tends to be known with the passage of time. I suck it up. Foil tells me to take what he owes off his bill for the homestead payment. Saying he is broke, can't pay.

Our neighbors at the RV park are the first ones to tell me they think Foil is a con artist. "I hired him to paint a building because he said he could use some work. We agree on a high price of $400 because he needs the money. I supply the paint. It's a one day job." Turns out Foil talks his wife into paying $500, with a sob story.

"Where is Foil? I need my lawn mowed again! I need wood cut. I need my sidewalk fixed!" Word is out Foil loves to work for free. We should all be more like him.

"What a good friend you have, Miles!" I smile and nod. No one wants to hear bad mouthing negativism about someone who volunteers to mow lawns for free. *Will these people come back to me angry I did not warn them?* I decide, 'No' because they are not asking my opinion. They are telling me all about how great Foil is. In truth, who am I to judge? It is possible Foil and I simply have a personality conflict and its personal. It is not for me to tell others I am the good guy and Foil is the bad guy.

Iris shows me an article in the news related to a previous one having to do with other kinds of fish. Again, an ongoing story repeated every few years with no solution followed up.

### Alaska groups seek cut in salmon caught by pollock industry

Tribal organizations and fishing groups in Alaska are urging federal fishery managers to drastically reduce the number of king salmon allowed to be inadvertently caught by commercial Pollock trawlers. Each year... Scores of Alaska Native subsistence fisherman are forced to go without.

The very next day another article.

### Cutting waste, Juneau processors grind fish byproduct for pet food

"The Alaska Department of Fisheries estimates each year about 13 million gallons of fish oil goes unused from waste by products. In another part it is stated, "On average about 25% of a fish like cod is for human consumption."

So 75% is wasted.

I repeat once again to Iris, "Fishing issues and subsistence are in the news on a regular basis, often a repeat of the same issues. It is not worth mentioning anymore." Once again, it is hard to believe all this talk of needing to do something has to do with saving the fish, or a subsistence lifestyle. Is it talk to calm the Natives down?

"Yes, we'll get right on it, this is an outrage!" Repeated a few times a year, for forty years I know of. Who is really slapping the commercial fisherman or arresting them? It's just interesting to notice. *Like the war on drugs.*

Another article of interest.

### State House passes potentially unconstitutional bill

Juneau- In a legislative session highlighted by battles in the ongoing fight between Alaska and the federal government over resource development... House bill 115.

I glance over the article and pick up the gist of what this particular battle is about. Alaska wants the Federal Government to turn revert management of 100 million acres to state control, as was promised Alaska at statehood and never complied with. In this bill the Feds maintain control over federal parks and military land only. The Federal Government argues this is unconstitutional and illegal. One big issue is the cost of a court battle that the state cannot afford.

"There is a legal weakness to the bill, but it is supported because it is standing up for unkept promises. Land selections were supposed to be turned over to the state within thirty years, the government has not acted in good faith." "It's never unconstitutional to fight for what is rightfully yours." The bill passes 27 to 11. The state passes the bill but there is no money to go to court. The state has the same issues the individual has.

Mayor and I talk a lot. "Miles, we lost control of our airport. We are one of the few communities in the country that owns its own airport!" I know this. I know what happened as well. We were happy with our airport. It worked for us, a small community. We have a float pond. Locals can land and take off free. "The Feds came up with regulations saying our airport no longer meets federal standards. To get the runway up to federal standards we need new lights, new pavement. To help us, the Feds will pay for it and have it done."

"Yes, and once they paid, they owned us." I can picture the state being in the same kind of bind. There is a certain reality we must face.

I understand my lifelong outlook may not work. "Focus on the positive. Forget the bad stuff. That's bad energy. Move forward in a good direction. Do not let the negative hold you back!" For evil to win, everyone must do nothing about it. I go into the wilds so I am not part of civilized problems, but they find me in the wilderness and drag me back to town. I focus on the bright side, and make the best of it. Find a new game, new goals, new rewards, and ways to be happy. I did not play my part as demanded.

A headline in the News Miner gets my attention. On the opinion page big headlines.

**'Civility not too much to ask'**

Subheading, 'Comments are a forum for discussion of issues, not abuse and threats.'

"There is room for legitimate disagreement." This catches my eye because it is unusual when the editor has to step in as moderator, and reprimand the public for submitting opinions. Apparently the paper's forum was swamped with threats, hateful words, abusive language against a woman, and the article that was printed about her. The woman is in fear of her life. I recall the article. I find it in the pile of fire starter.

A week ago there was a story of a local woman who went to Canada and shot a polar bear—legally—with a guide. This dream hunt cost a small fortune. The story was covered in a positive way. She shot the bear with a bow and arrow. Pictures are included. I wondered at the time if this would be a button for many readers! The main point I make is 'legal'.

I do not trophy hunt. I do not believe in it. I respect that others do. I recognize in most cases the huge cost paid for the permit helps support Fish and Wildlife efforts to do studies and deal with environmental issues. In theory, this offsets the loss of the animal. I have met and have gotten to know ethical guides whose family is supported on just a handful of game harvested each year in their area. Possibly the same number of animals that could be expected to die naturally each harsh winter. Harvesting and making more room allows the remaining to have room to live. Not everyone who pays goes home with a trophy. In many cases, the big trophy animals are past their prime; no longer breeding. I have seen such animals with worn out teeth having a hard life, facing tough winters. Shunned by their own kind. No longer breeding, no longer leading their kind with wisdom. Such animals will not survive long and can be suffering.

In a perfect world these get harvested, and has no negative biological effect on the population. I know 'ideally' is not always happening! Dream on! But when is perfect the only part of any equation, in any endeavor? We can strive to reach the best compromise. It is a fact! More money from hunting fees goes into helping wildlife than animal rights funds. Habitat enhancement is 90% acquired with hunting fees. Studies are paid for with hunting fees. Locally, hunters fees paid for and maintain Creamers field, a migratory bird sanctuary in downtown Fairbanks. While 90% environmental groups money pays for neutering cats and dogs. Unless I have my facts wrong. Hunters I talk to may misrepresent the facts.

Hunting is a multimillion dollar business for the state. It's not going away. Fishing is also about killing living wild beings, which we seem to have no negative feelings about. This is a hot, controversial topic, constantly being debated. I was glad to see 'the other side' to trophy hunting, showing something good coming of a hunt. Instead of doom and gloom.[1]

Apparently, the paper was swamped with hate mail following this article. It is not the hunters I am afraid of! The fear is of terrorists with lynch ropes in their hand, yelling, screaming, foaming at the mouth, environmentalists. It is difficult to believe their anger has to do with saving animals. I am suspicious of any group that is not willing to sit and discuss their view in a sane reasonable fashion. I am suspicious of anyone in any group that foams at the mouth and goes ballistic. I am distrustful of any group that breaks the law with threats, violence and anger. Hunters tell me the opposite side refuses to attend any public debates. The reason hunters give is, 'Because environmentalists know they will lose any debate based on reason and sound biology. It's all about emotional anger and hate with them!' I do not meet hunters filled with hate, just confusion, not understanding where these people's heads are, and what drives them. Fear. I meet a great many environmentalists who make threats as the main way to get their way. Environmentalists I meet are not in physical fear of hunters. This is my personal experience.

Way way back when I was a child of the early 60s and meeting the new flower children I took notice. I heard Peace, Love, saw handing out of flowers, when the first vegetarians came out. This group was the first group to get nasty if your bell bottoms were not cool enough. At the time I wore a dress jacket and tie to school. I never met crueler people then angry flower children. Charles Manson's followers were flower children.

"Save the flowers, kill the people."

---

"Miles, I heard you sold your Kantishna homestead! I never thought I'd see the day!" Crafty addresses me. Word is spreading all around. Crafty has met Foil.

"Well, that might be his side of the story, Crafty!"

"Well you either sold it or you did not, Miles!"

"No. There is an in between Crafty. The plan is for us to be partners, joint owners so to speak. He builds on the property, and in return helps me out as I get older. He is making payments toward owning, but with the understanding I have use of the land as long as I live." In our verbal talk Foil was my buddy helping me out. Filled with promises. I had not wanted to sell, or even share. I gave Foil a vacation, a visit, that's it. "No you can't buy it!" Geez! "Foil you can build over there... away from my cabin. Come visit as my guest... no problem. We will probably never be here at the same time anyhow." As friends, we'd respect each other's privacy. Foil had talked like he understood my concerns, and these concerns were shared and respected. His bottom line had been, "What is the difference if you own it, and I am your guest, or I own it, and you are my guest? As long as we are friends sharing the land. The only difference is, I want you to have the money! You need it, being out of work now! Let me help you out!" That's a little complicated to explain to Crafty.

Crafty only wants to know, "Who holds the title, Miles?"

The simplest answer is, "I do, Crafty."

We discuss the tourist business. Crafty gets a dozen of my books for the store.

"Gulliver's sells them regularly, Crafty. Wish I was doing better with them though. Not spending any time marketing yet."

Crafty does not handle as much of my art as he used to. He doesn't pay enough. His deal was all right when it was all I had going. Before I knew better, or is it that my priorities changed?

"Miles, do you have any new outlets for this year?"

"Yes! Iris and I took a short sales trip to Denali Park. We like the area and the nice drive. Figured we'd bring some art to show the shops in Glitter Gulch. That has worked out fine. One shop in particular wants to carry a lot of my work!" I do not elaborate. Mostly my custom knives. It's not a great deal. The usual high percent to the shop on consignment. I might get forty percent of the suggested retail after it sells—if I'm lucky. No choice. That's the deal artists get. Take it or leave it. The line is long of starving artists needing to get bills paid, ready to sell at any price. The good news is, it is not called Glitter Gulch for nothing. Tourists pay ten times the market value at Denali Park shops on many items. So 40 percent of $500 is more money than 90 percent of $100. Crafty knows better than I do how the pie gets divided up.

"Yeah, Crafty, Princess gets the biggest wad. I think the shop owner told me the tour company that owns the building wants $1,000 a day in rent." Crafty nods that this sounds about right. He supplies most of the Princess owned shops. Crafty makes his money because he handles such huge volume. A million dollars worth of inventory a year. His cut is $200,000. Most of that goes back into the business.

I look back at Crafty. He is busy with a customer. His shop has not changed. Looks like a bomb went off in a flea market. Good prices, but you have to find the deals. Customers sit on the floor and sort boxes of junk. Only it is not junk, it is just displayed as if it is. I am a bit like this, but over the years, less like Crafty. I improved my displays, and Iris helps me keep it clean. Not as good as a gallery, but better than Crafty does, or so I like to think. Crafty has his market. He sells. Prices are way lower because he has no high end employees, displays, bright lights, someone to dust it every day. He may not have insurance. His building should be condemned, All that keeps his costs way down, so he can sell way cheaper than the gallery. I have the same line of thought. With Crafty an item may be $50, a block away in the gallery, the same item is $200. Glitter Gulch it's $400. It's all about location, display and perception. Crafty even supplies the galleries and Glitter Gulch! Same exact product by the same artists. I see customers cry the blues about their income and the economy, yet spend $400 on a $50 item.

Some smart rich buyers seek out Crafty for their fine art. They like to shop closer to the source. These high end customers tend to be collectors of antiques and artifacts. As a seller I have had to make a choice. I can get $50, or $300. Each market has its reward and price to pay. Does the owner of the gallery walk home with more money in his pocket than Crafty? My guess is, 'No.' Glitter Gulch, move em in, move em out. Rawhide. Crack the whip and the mule train moves. Busloads of tourists by the thousands every day. A year's wages for shops in a three month season. All winter off. It's an interesting life.

"But not for me, Crafty!" Glitter Gulch shop owners may not make yearly wages that exceed Crafty. Crafty knows I hate permits, taxes, unemployment insurance, paperwork, and records. He gives me a look like he knows, and the proof is, I'm a felon now.

After I leave Crafty, I am stuck for a while on the whole felon issue again. The truth is, Crafty sells the same exact items I got in trouble over. He forgets that. From the same sources. He and I would buy, trade, the same products back and forth. I think he has no reason to be so smug, thinking what happened to me could never happen to him. I look around at the same wolf claws, feathers, ivory I was arrested for, right here on Crafty's shelves. Advertised in the paper. Go figure. *So is it just about saving animals?*

Iris and I meet the shop owner in Glitter Gulch and over lunch discuss how to handle my art. The subject of Foil and my Kantishna land comes up. Mr. Glitter says, "My son is working with me. We are just getting together and knowing each other. His mother raised him. I'd love to give him a wilderness experience." There is a hint in this for me to offer such a trip as part of a deal we may work out. I'm usually up to trades, partial trades, I do this, you do that. Some amount of favors involved in lieu of cash. Cut the bank, middle man, and IRS out of it.

"It helps keep the bookwork cloudy, Miles." I make no comment, but understand his drift. *Cloudy does not necessarily mean illegal.* He is also a lawyer of sorts. "This homestead agreement is not in your favor. Once this Foil guy pays, everything on the homestead is his, including all the tools and everything you consider yours. As it is right now, it is jointly owned by the two of you." This was not the verbal agreement or intent. The contract is not clear. "It looks like he knew what he was doing, and knows what this contract means." After looking it over. " If there is a breach of contract. You two are not, and cannot not work together anymore. The contract stated 'working as partners'. There was no specified time line to pay this off. It looks like you are both the seller and the bank." I'm not sure what that means in legal terms, and how it has an effect on anything.

Essentially Foil will own the land, everything on it, and everything related to it, once he has paid, and can kick me off. I would be trespassing to go on the property. I'm sure in my heart this was not Foil's intention. However, I look how this has already come about for the Nenana land. I'm not welcome to visit. Foil wants my shed removed or I owe rent. Mr. Glitter reviews my legal options.

"First, send a breach of contract notice. Followed later by a foreclosure notice, with full payment due within 90 days. Leave it up to him to respond." There are more exact details about filing public notice, have a public auction, and what not. Iris is ready to jump on this option right now. I'm told, "If Foil pays more than half the money it will be harder to claim breach of contract."

"If Foil makes the full payment you are out of luck and lost it. I suggest sometime soon, remove all your goods from the property while they are still jointly owned. Once he owns it, removing these items is theft." I have a lot of things stored at Kantishna. Many survival type tools. More than one good wood stove. Iris's guns, generator, ham radio, propane tanks, spare boat engine, and just 'stuff.' More than I can easily remove. No place to put it.

"How will Foil handle this? He might burn me out."

"That would be illegal, Miles." Like the law means anything? I've already been illegally burned out, and who cared? No money, no time. Tough luck. For now, this is the plan. File for breach of contract. *The plot thickens, let the games begin!* Mr. Glitter will be my legal advisor if I need this. *I'm sure for a price.* Mr. Glitter is much like my buddy, Crafty. Anything to get out of parting with money.

We get to the art part of the visit.

"Miles, I am lacking inventory and have two shops here. My shipment got held up overseas. I need some Alaskan product to meet the Princess contract agreement. I do not have any other art but my own. If you leave me substantial inventory, it will only be your work and mine in the shop." I have some questions in my mind. Like how someone makes a contract first at $1,000 a day per shop, without having inventory confirmed first. His references seem vague. Like how he got here! I know in general what the talk and walk should look like. I see some of his inventory, and am convinced it is neither made by him nor Alaskan. He may need my work to make his other inventory look legitimate. Iris seems confident this is ok. I trust her to be street wise. We can always pull the inventory if it is not working out, I own it.

Ok, Mr. Glitter is willing to drive down on the weekend to my Nenana home and look over the inventory. He needs raw rocks and wood, as well as the art. His answer to the situation he is in is, "Miles, I am having trouble finding artists who understand the tourist market and the shop split."

I understand what he means. I have been a buyer at the Nenana Culture Center. I have worked with Crafty. I talk to artists at shows and we discuss splits and who gets how much and why. I am in more of a bind than in the past. I can't do shows, I can't travel. I can't make more than $300 without paperwork. I might not get paid in this deal until after I am off probation. I need not report 'consignment'. That is only potential. It is not a done deal until I get paid. I have not spent any of Foils payments because in my mind I might still return all his money and call the deal off. Iris says, "No way, Miles, he deserves nothing!" If I gave all the money back, I'd have a partially built cabin that would make up for all the aggravation he has caused. I'd feel like we were even.

I feel in my heart, there is no way Foil will walk away from the work he put in the cabin. He'd take his money back and tell me I owe him for the cabin he built. Mr. Glitter agrees with Iris. Summed up, "This is the oldest land scam in the book, Miles. I have seen it many times. Partner up with an elder, make improvements together, then the deal goes south. Ask for more than the elder has for a buyout."

Iris and I drive home in good spirits. It is a lovely drive. The view out to the park is a view of the mountains getting closer. Snow capped Denali is a sight to behold. The two lane road twists through some awesome country back to Nenana. This is a drive tourists pay to see, and take postcard pictures of.

"For us, a business trip, a write off Iris!" I'm trying to help her see how great our life is. How others envy it. She does like to drive. There is a nice place to eat along the way. We look forward to trips back and forth now, checking on our goods, and collecting checks.

---

Mr. Glitter and his teen son show up in Nenana. We make piles of goods and inventory it with prices I need to get when it sells. It's not the greatest deal for me. Its prices I should get cash for wholesale, only this situation is, wait to get paid and lose over 60 percent. I agree with Iris, I need to move inventory. I think I will be inspired to create more when inventory I am tired of looking at is gone.

Meanwhile, the Nenana Culture Center has my work. None seems to have been stolen. My work is selling well. I begin to get a few checks. The percent is a lot better than at Glitter Gulch. I only lose twenty percent. *I can show where money is coming from if I need to spend any of my previously stashed cash.* I decide I should go on a long boat trip. I can either go to the homestead and gather up some of my valuables in anticipation of a war with Foil, or go make money fossil hunting, or both.

Foil said he left some gas hidden at Tolovana, but did not show me where. Stored in my gas tanks. I'm upset that without my spare gas tanks I am running off a fifty-five gallon drum. *It should be Foil stuck with a drum not me.* I now keep an eye out at garage sales for gas tanks, as I assume I will never see mine back.

As luck has it, a yard sale in Nenana has two cool matching 1950s tanks that match the one I have! Eighteen gallon tanks I can lift when full, at 125 pounds, so I can move them around the boat, or stash someplace if I need to. Being steel, they are more bear proof than the plastic ones Foil has.

> **Diary** Friday, June 20, 2015
>
> Use new twenty-one pitch prop. Keep track of mileage and time. Do really well. Go faster.
>
> Night at Fish Creek. Fish biting every cast. I get about ten and let them all go. A huge twenty pound pike. Rock gathering spot next day, lots of smoke and fires from lightening. Can hardly see to travel. Find nice jasper, jade, quartz mix, good bubbly jade, spotted jade. A tusk seen last year in same spot, just look at. Next day two tusks on top of each other I get pictures. Lots of small material. About $4,000 retail value in rocks.
>
> Foil's gas and my barrels appear to be missing from Tolovana. Dog musher with kids needed gas for Manley run, says he found Jerry cans. Unsure if Foil told me the truth about where he put his gas. Stopped to visit in Manley. Got home without incident.

I am concerned Foil will think I took his gas.

"I hid it someplace else." Very vague, as he trails off in the telling. *He does not want me to know where his gas is. Never did from the beginning want me to know.* More proof of 'breach of contract'. We are not friends, sharing, working together as partners. If he hides his gas from me, in my fuel tanks, he borrows and needs to return, obviously we are not friends. I am having trouble writing a simple letter summing up a breach of contract. It always goes into too much detail and gets overly complicated. I make a dozen attempts or so. I often have issues determining what is important, relevant; a provable fact that is wroth recording. No one will read a hundred page document.

I have raw materials from my boat trip to sort. I smile, thinking of some of the fossils. I stopped in to visit Moonshine and Wren. Their new baby is walking around now. Cider seems to enjoy life on the river. Wren said, "It is good to have people stop and talk to her a little, Miles." I get the impression she is a concerned mother who thinks her child could be overly isolated and lack social skills. Karen and I had the same issues with her girls when we lived remote.

"Cider seems ok to me, Wren. Remember things could be worse in civilization, with drugs and crime all around." I take time to talk to Cider. She is interested in my fossils in the boat. I try to explain how old they are in terms she may understand. She just laughs and makes drawings in the sand, of extinct animal. I draw next to her. Explain I am an artist! All I have to show is the belt buckle I cast of a grizzly bear.

"This metal used to be a propeller like the one over by your father's boat, bronze!" She sees the colors are the same. I give her a small fossil bone to start a fossil collection.

"Whenever I come by from fossil digging I can give you something to add to your collection!"

She is excited. "I can look for fossil at fish camp!" A cheerful happy child. She says as I get in my boat "Is your boat engine too big?" *She already knows what is normal and what is not.*

I smile and reply, "Yes it is! I'm little like you, so I want a huge engine!"

"I like big stuff too!" We all laugh.

Moonshine reminds me. "You started out with a ten horse, come a long way huh!" He remembers those days, and how slow I traveled, always overloaded.

BACK IN NENANA, Josh stops by to chat. "Yeah, I know what you mean now about Foil, Miles. He came with me to help two other guys to COD Lake. I think he stole an important part for my generator when we got into an argument!" Apparently

Foil did not want to do a job the way Josh wanted it done. "Foil said he was a welder, but I could see right off he has no experience, Miles!"

I did not need any details and did not comment much. I am not out to badmouth anyone. I did not reply. Josh says, "Miles, I think if Foil is simply left alone, he will end up going home and leaving Nenana for good. He has not got what it takes to make it here. He will run out of both money and time. He does not have enough knowledge to get out to your homestead on his own regularly. He has the wrong boat. Just leave him alone. He'll never get the cabin built. He will not want the land. If he pays for the land, he will never be able to pay to be there. He will have no cabin to live in. Your shack will not be good enough to keep him happy. He is a city kid. He needs room, a nice bed, good food."

When I think about it, I agree. If I simply do nothing, my 'problem' may well go away on its own. I do not need to make it a confrontation, or say no. I can say, "Like to help! Busy right now!" "No money for gas! Boat not running good right now, got obligations, maybe later!" He can believe me or not, but this avoids a direct antagonism between us. *No court costs, legal fees, posted notices, and all that!*

**Diary** Friday, August 07, 2015
Boat trip

Gone four days. Got some fish. Hooked King salmon that got away due to taking barbs off hook. Got some more nice rocks to sell. Anticipated some repel work at Burke's land, but reason to cliff dive was already gone. Cliff falls and quarter mile away at camp the wave is three ft high. Another section falls ahead of me and I put boat in reverse and back away faster than wave approaches. I might have been under it fifteen seconds later.

Saw Peregrine falcons. Very fast. Stop at Moonshine and Wren's to give them old photo albums from shed they told me I could have. Old pictures of Moonshine's Dad and children when young. Their garden does well, got some crooked neck squash. Moonshine says is the only squash worth eating! Camp at Zits River.

I make another boat trip later in the summer. Forest fires along the river systems all summer made for interesting travel. The three mammoth tusks I saw last trip might still be there. An investment is made in more advanced repelling equipment to go off the top of a cliff. I learn about ascenders, descenders, grabbers and newer technology. I considered a drone with fishing line. I thought about a remote twelve volt winch to lift me up and down the rope. Two tusks are gone, one remains. The top of the cliff is in flames from forest fires, so no way to repel off the top. Many locals think this is part of major weather changes related to global warming. The entire river for four days is engulfed in thick smoke. I had concerns about finding enough fresh air to breath when I spent one night. *How much would suffocate a person?* Smoke is that thick.

I manage to get to the top of the cliff, but am unsure where the tusk section is. I am not seeing the landmark I spotted from below. I walk past flames and still burning trees, careful to avoid hot ashes. I cannot see the sun, and the air is hot. I may be able to tie to a small tree I think will not be in the flames. This ten foot tall tree is only three inches in diameter.

I set the bag down that contains all my climbing gear. I cannot carry the heavy 'certified for climbing' rope and settled for half the diameter at half the weight. The rope is rated for 900 pounds , but since I am not going over any rocks decide this can work. However, the hardware is designed for the larger rope so adds a slight complication. I am going to use only one rope. Two are usually used.

I practiced a little, well… twice, off the roof of the house. I sort of understand how this stuff works. The harness itself is a big help, and lets me set comfortable and rest, being held by the grabber that slides one direction on the rope. Going downs is not so hard, getting back up is what takes talent. There is an aluminum gizmo the rope goes in and around that creates friction for going down. I can let up on it and control a slow trip down or lock it up and completely stop for a short time till I engage the grabber.

I go off the top and down just ten feet. I look around and still cannot figure out where I am or where the tusk is. I hang here—comfortable—thinking. *Too many factors are against me.* Smoke, fire moving towards the tree I am tied to and I cannot see where the tusk is; lack of suggested equipment combined with lack of experience with choices not suggested. This is still good practice, so not a total loss.

Getting back up is complicated. I have ascenders on my feet and grabbers I can move and hold on to for my hands. As well as a grabber for my harness. It is a slow process but should be relatively safe. I move my feet up, slide my hands further up and lock my harness. I gain one foot at a time. It takes a minute to move each foot up. I am not in a hurry. However when I wish to move my feet up the rope, the rope moves up with me more readily than my foot ascender sliding up the rope. I am thinking next time I'd need to have some kind of weight tied to the end of the rope to hold it down. This is one reason I only go down ten feet. If this was going better and I went down and up ten feet I could have more confidence starting again and go down further. Since going down just ten feet is an issue, I am glad just to get back up!

I decide I do not have enough practice to try this again right now under these conditions. I like to think I am willing to take risks, but am not stupid. I give thought to how I could do this better. *I can have a twelve volt winch on the boat, run with a remote switch.*

I envision how to work this. I climb to the top from an easier route and tie off a pulley, then run a light rope through the pulley and send both ends down to the boat. Usually within 200 feet. So need as much as 400 feet of rope. I climb back down the way I came up. In the boat I hook the winch to one end of the rope and me to the other end. In theory, I push the buttons for up and down and move accordingly. I'd need at least 200 feet of cable on the winch spool. Not possible. However, there is a new product out that is a small diameter rope stronger than steel. It is expensive but rated for 1,500 pounds, and 200 feet should wind up on the spool. Cutting edge technology applied to old concepts. If I have a problem, coming back down to the boat can be done manually with my prussic gizmo.

There may also be a way to design a marker bullet for the gun. I can shoot this to the top so when I get up, I know where I am. Most likely the shotgun, that can handle a two ounce load, at slower speeds. Same idea as a paint ball gun? Hard wax with dye that splatters if it hits anything? Wads of coiled colored string? I can play with designs and come up with something. Obviously nothing on the market. I already know I need slow burning blue dot powder with a three inch magnum wad. An overshot card rather than a crimp is a given. As long as I weigh my payload, it is not dangerous. Probably illegal. Especially as I am a felon. As I boat home, I think about a place to store stuff.

MOONSHINE GAVE *me a cabin he has no use for.* The reason? It is insulated with asbestos! Moonshine acquired it years ago and had no clear title or papers, just a hand shake from a person now dead. He lived in the cabin a short time. He also had and recovered from lung cancer.

This cabin or shed is on the property line Foil bought. He claims no interest in the shed, and the owner who sold the land, says it is not his to offer. Being on an easement line it is in 'no man's land' in terms of being on anyone's property. Now abandoned on a vague easement. I understand some day the cabin could present environmental issues, and I would lose it. "No problem, Moonshine." Keep the ownership vague. The more people who could conceivably own it the better. There is zero paper trail.

Moonshine and I discuss the legal issues of claiming ownership and getting a cleanup cost. It is understood, Moonshine does not own it and neither do I. No one really owns it. However, I may be able to move it. Mayor, who would rather the city not be liable for an asbestos problem down the road, said he'd use city equipment.

I have moved goods into this shed and put a lock on the door. I can store Kantishna supplies and Iris can store 'her stuff' as required, "off my property." I do not let Moonshine know I only need it for a short time. I am not going in and out often enough to worry about asbestoses. This shed solves a short term need I have. I am not between a rock and a hard place over the shed Foil wants off his land, *that has things in it I cannot have on my own property.*

I find a buyer for the shed. The shed is empty when sold. I get my costs for it back. The shed is off Foil's land. The disconnect from Foil continues. Foil is gone, back in Tucson. I do not want him to have anything over me. Nothing he can threaten me with, charge me for, badmouth me about. Kind, polite, sympathetic, and distant. Will that work? How do I handle people like this? Killing him is not polite. The real issue is, how sure can I be I am right, and he is wrong? All I have to go by, is my opinion. Based on that, I can decide to not be part of his life, without causing him or wishing him harm.

"Isn't it fair time, Miles? Your favorite time of year?"

"Sure, Iris, it used to be. I suppose I look forward to going. But not setting up." I could probably get away with it with the probation officer, as it is not a show.

"Why aren't you happy about fair time, Miles?"

We talked about it before I went to prison. I was at a turning point. Abandon the fair altogether, or expand and get two spaces. I was standing still or going backwards with one space. I believed the answer was more selection. I believe this is because my buyers are more discriminating now, and have more choices on the internet for supplies and gifts. Possibly being loyal is not the factor it once was. A lot of that may have to do with the fair changing over time. It used to be a friendly happy event; filled with local flavor.

We used to have Alaska bands play music. A local magic man did tricks. Car racers put on events. Crafters sold art. Natives came in from the villages to offer beadwork. There were contests for locals to compete in. Local 4-H kids came with a prized goose they raised to show us! We cheered and encouraged them. It was all about having fun! If a fair is not fun, what is it for? Why attend? Why sell?

"For money, Miles, of course!"

I say, "It is not that simple."

People who are having fun will spend money freely. Making money is a fringe benefit. Rip people off, con them, try to take their money, and you will not make a profit. I think this is something very basic about doing business—any business. It's all about satisfied customers. The fair no longer satisfies attendees. It's all about making money! The public and the vendors know it. The parking lot has holes in it big enough to hide a car—if you can find a parking spot. Parking fees are now as high as fair entry fees used to be. No more family pass, horrible bathrooms that never get fixed year after year. Places that flood when it rains, and have for over thirty years. The fair got into a money argument with the ride people who left so they brought in an outside carnival from Canada. The fair got into a contract money argument with the people who run the beer tent and they quit. Front page news a week before the fair, the people who collect the cans and plastic got in an argument with the fair over $200 owed! Over a $200 problem the fair makes front page news about being cheapskates and does not appear to care. I think the public does, I know I do. I feel the greed and lack of caring.

"Remember Iris, when our booth fee doubled with no explanation?" She nods. I was puzzled and politely asked with concern if everything is ok? I thought at first there is some major issue the fair has to cover the cost, maybe things that need fixing. Like rewire the place, or fill in the low spots finally, so we all need to chip in and help. "No problem, glad to be part of a better event!" The reply was, 'None of your business; get lost! If you do not like it, get out!' And, "So why should I rent the space to you for $700 when I can get $3,000 from a food vendor?" I think, the fair is not just about food.

I was at a point of needing to invest in a new tent. I was reaching the age of feeling the work load of setting up. I no longer needed the fair for a social life as I once did. My good friends, Don and Vision at the Patty Wagon just got an award for being vendors for forty years. Just two years longer than me.

"Miles, we have always heard doom and gloom, you know that. The fair goes on anyhow. With or without disgruntled vendors."

Yes, we have had similar conversations. But my outlook on life has changed. At some point nothing but good cheer can be wearing rose colored glasses, or burying our head in the sand. There is also something called reality. The answer in life is not just to always press forward with good news, fair sky, and good weather. No matter what happens. That doesn't work in the middle of a typhoon. We can slip and fall in the do do and concentrate on the smell of the roses. Isn't survival at least acknowledging the do do exists, and is effecting my life? We smell of it, and no one wants to be around us. No matter how much we explain the beauty that surrounds us. We are only fools. Smart successful people know where to put their energy and do not randomly give of it to every cause.

If I were younger and dedicated to the fair's success, I would try to get on the board. I had been asked once to represent the vendors, but I am in Nenana and do not drive, so said no at the time. Now I have legal issues and can't sell the usual wolf claws and Indian type stuff I am known for. I see no future in the fair for me without making major changes I am not interested in making, with the attitude of the fair board as it is.

Iris and I attend, and I am very glad I did not set up. It rains as usual. The new vendors are shocked there is water a foot deep in the booth. Naturally this affects who wants to walk in to buy something. Wet inventory is a disaster and financial loss. I'm not part of it this year. I nod, smile, walk along. Don and Vision are not here this year. The place is getting sold to one of the long time workers.

"Yes, sales are half what they should be, Miles. Attendance is half." There is no craft area. Food vendors and commercial people dominate. This is not a fair, it's a business scam. I do find our potter friends and get something for my collection. Iris is upset, saying we do not need anything more! We have tons of pottery! That's ok, I'm helping out friends.

"Think of it as a donation. Instead of paying taxes, I prefer to hand out money to worthy causes I believe in." There is a granddaughter now, just getting into pottery. I say to the mother, "I recall when you were this size, making your first pottery, and it was your father and mother sitting here selling."

"Yes, and you were set up across from us, and us kids would come over and work for you untangling chains, and you'd give us ride tickets! We'd crawl under your table looking for dropped pennies and playing hide and seek." We both have fond memories. I ask the little six year old girl how much she wants for this little pot? I'd like to buy it.

"It's beautiful!" She is so ecstatic! Her first sale. I am honored to be her first customer! She turns to her mother for guidance. She is learning about money, wages, work. Again, I am so excited to be part of this education. In fifty years she will still remember her first sale. I can tell by the look in her eyes. The lights come on. She has earned money and can go buy something! *Welcome little girl to the wonderful world of independence!* I give her five dollars for a lopsided finger bowl I might be able to put salad dressing in when I want to eat a carrot for a snack.

"Perfect!" I say with sincerity. "I will have fond memories when I use it!"

Iris mumbles afterwards, "The last thing you need is another salad dressing bowl, Honey!"

"It is not the bowl I need. I agree. I need memories. I need friends. I need to support my tribe. It's about forming alliances, bonds, trust. These are lifelong friends, Iris." The next generation is about all of us. How all the children turn out effects our old age and retirement. It is they who will run things. The children need us, as one day we will need them. I stop, Iris has heard enough of my lectures. I hold her hand as we walk and enjoy the fair. I want us to have a good time. Let me be a foolish old man and waste my money on children.

Everywhere we go, people holler and know me, inquire of my health, tell me it is good to see me. I know just about everyone. A third of everyone here knows me. I estimated once, a good 20,000 people in Fairbanks know me. Iris is constantly commenting how many people greet me everywhere we go. Bank clerks, taxi drivers, store managers, people on the street. Not once in a while, everywhere we go. More oddly, when we travel, this happens at airports across the country.

I was told, "I was at a meeting in the Netherlands, Miles, and the lady across from me was wearing one of your art pieces. I mention I know you and she wanted to know all about you." I have arrived at a good place in life, a respected elder. Honored for my art and contributions to society. Not because I demanded it, but because I earned it. I do not need to worry about people like Foil or the fair managers. *I just have to remember that!* I squeeze Iris's hand as we walk. Instead of the pressure of manning a booth I can relax and enjoy.

We visit the wildlife photographer I have known for forty years. The fur sewing lady is here and the cartoonist. We get the latest cartoon book in his collection. Most say they do not expect to come back to the fair. There are only four craft vendors in the big craft tent that once held forty. I imagine this will be used as an excuse not to have the tent, do away with it, make room for more food vendors. Many sellers I know are not here. The guy who paints the tee shirts as you wait is gone. The wood sign maker is not coming back. I often had him make signs for my business. Some I needed, some not.

"Did he make the one on the shop that says Mammoth Hunter?" I smile that yes, this is one of this guy's signs.

"Also, 'We don't dial 911.'" My business card holder he made. This has my web address carved in the wood with a card holder under it, and 'visit my web store'. I painted flowers and animals on it. Oh yes, everywhere I go I promote the web store, even now!

"Not set up this year, Miles? How do I get hold of you? Where is your work these days?" I hand out a card. "Cool, I'll go on line!" I did in fact, bring a few books and some art in a briefcase. I sell to some exclusive customers, and make $400.

"Beats working for a living!"

"Yes, Miles, your favorite line!" We stop to read poetry written by children, and look at children's drawings. Often it is the children who have more imagination than the adults, so I prefer looking at their art. Just want to keep up with what the next generation is doing.

"Iris, I have to stop to see the turkeys and ducks!" She knows by now, I imitate them and get them to answer. I insult one big turkey. He huffs and fluffs up and stands straight, "gobble gobble!" I wait the appropriate time as required to digest what he just said, and think up a suitable insult reply.

"Ah, your mother wears bloomers!" I say in turkey language.

"Why I never!" he huffs back. He follows me to the end of his cage as I walk by, and spits at me as I leave.

"And good riddance too!" he gobbles. I get to the ducks, who have been following the conversation. Ducks do not respond to insults. They think it's funny.

"What a sour puss, huh!" I say in duck talk.

"Wack, wack, ft, ft, ft." One replies.

I go, "Quack, quack, quack," no takers.

One looks at me, "That's not a very good imitation you know!"

I have to translate for Iris who can't follow the conversation and subtleties of animal communication. "Because these are domestic ducks. They do not care for my wild accent. It's all about manners and protocol with a duck you know. They are very sensitive.

One old looking duck makes one sound. "Awk?"

It is a question. I am not sure what he is asking though. I have to guess or make that up, but I know a question when I hear it. Every mammal has language things in common. Questions always go up at the end. The end is the loudest part of the communication. Because they want an answer. They want to make sure you understand when it is your turn to talk. Frogs, songbirds, rabbits, eagles, tigers, and man. We all do it.

To explain what I mean I tell Iris, "Ok, see that mallard way up the line we will be coming to in fifty feet?" She does not know a mallard from a wood duck. "The one by himself with the sun shining on his wings with the blue showing and the green head."

"Oh yes."

"He's asleep now. I will give one question quack. He will open his eyes and wiggle his tail, to let me know he heard me, and is thinking. The other ducks will ignore me. It's our conversation or game. Game because I will ask if he wants to follow me. He knows he is in a cage. I am out, and I am human, so this is a ridiculous question. The real question is, if he is bored and wants to play a game of imitation. I'm guessing he'll play. If so he will stand up, stretch his neck, open his mouth, and not say anything, but walk towards me. I will try to convince him to play and he will imitate me. We will scream, "Follow me!" back and forth. It will mean nothing but a big joke. The others will laugh.

Ever since I was a kid, I imitated animals and sounds around me. We walk past a cash register and I go 'Ding' imitating the exact sound of a register ding. I imitate computers. I imitate the train, the sounds of traffic. I imitate the sound of a mother hollering at her children to come back here right now. My favorite though, is the ducks and geese at the fair.

"Weird, huh, Iris?"

She shrugs. "I suppose it has to do with being a story teller?"

Yes, story tellers must be born that way. God says at birth, "And you my child, will be a story teller." The male at the end does just as I said he would, proving I understand at least something.

"WILD MILES!" I turn around. I hardly get called that anymore. This must be someone who has known me a lot of years.

"Never see you at the Howling Dog any more, man! What it is Bro?"

I smile and nod. "It's all good, man, bogus, but you know, on top of my game." I bob my head as is the custom. I'm a good imitator. He bobs his head, much like the turkey did. I understand. "Iris, this is Scout." We met at the fair over thirty-five years ago. Scout is wearing a top hat and Dracula coat. He's a dumpster diver, a drug addict. I'm impressed he's still alive.

"Hear ya a felon, Wild Man." After speaking he closes his eyes and looks like he is falling asleep.

I nod that indeed he has heard correctly. His social status is now higher than mine. I thought Will told me Scout had died. He gets tossed in jail quite a lot to sober up, but is not a felon. He's a petty thief, nickel and dime stuff. I'm big time. I can tell Iris is not impressed with Scout. I need to cut this short as she tugs my arm to get out of here.

"Scout, you want to come watch the pigs get judged at the barn?"

"I show ya pig judging, and it ain't in no barn!" We both laugh; he, of course, is not interested in anything in the barn. His attention span is not long, and I know that. My invite was a good way to politely get rid of him.

"What was that all about, Miles, I could not follow the conversation. Was it English?"

It's true. Some tribes have their own language. Like the blacks in prison I met. "One of the guys in my first book, when the leather coats were stolen, remember? Back in about 1975 or so." He is among the ones who introduced me to the notion, goods of the world are about musical chairs. Round and round they go, where they stop no one knows, and no one owns them. The guy who stole the leather jackets got them from a guy who smuggled them through customs without duty and did not want to press charges. I got laughed at because I was so non-survival in his world, being an educated idiot as it was called.

Yes, language experts can tell by your speech where you're born, how you were raised, maybe what you do for a living. Mostly what tribe you belong to. I'm guessing most people's tribes are only about 100 people. The size of the groups Genghis allowed, back when he owned the world. The number of people capable of getting along without killing each other. Tribes get along with related tribes, like when we travel, and have to sit on a bus. We know who to sit next to, or at least who to say hello to. When we walk on the crowded sidewalk we know who to walk near, and who to cross the street to get away from. "That's all tribal stuff." We recognize like minded people by how we dress, walk, act, and talk. Much is so unconscious we are not aware we do it. But never mind.

"I decided not to do the fair, Iris. I do not need the money that bad, with the aggravation as a vendor. Let the fair find out how long they last with nothing but high paying food vendors. I'm glad not to be between a rock and a hard place here, stuck because I need the money." They really do not want craft people. So ends my love affair with the fair. Very little in life is forever.

Back in Nenana, I run into my accountant friend, Bean. In the past I had given him fair tickets I used to get for my helpers. I mention why I am not handing out tickets this year. This gets us in a discussion of why, making a living, and in general control. There can be control without fighting or war! We are on the subject of my being a felon.

"The art of gifting is a war tactic the Chinese use, Miles." He gives as an example. "China imports tea kettles to us for almost nothing. We all end up with one. We all need one. When it is time to negotiate, there is the possibility we can't get tea pots." This method of control is cheaper than war. We are discussing various 'controls' put on us. Ways to win wars, or gain control. Maybe sneaky ways, or ways without fighting, through dependence. Creating felons is one example. Bean says, "Instead of simply offing people, as in the old days, enemies of the government are simply made ineffective. As a felon, you can't get a good job, make any money that is unknown, vote, or arm yourself."

"Disguised as doing society a favor by identifying a problem. We associate certain people with the problem. Government solves the problem by incapacitating individuals associated with the invented problem." I add, "Yes, invented, because there is some other hidden problem we do not want to address. So we give it another name that offers a simple solution." Least a felon does not understand, a felon has far fewer rights than others. A second offense gets a great deal more punishment, and a third gets you life. I understand, as Bean does, the average citizen is not interested. It doesn't affect them. In fact, 'Keep all that riff-raff out of my neighborhood, and away from my children and environment, I want to be safe!'

Bean chuckles. "Safe is about your neighborhood, like Nenana. What a mess, huh. I could get Nenana out of its financial paperwork mix up in about three days. It is not that complicated!" True, any serious accountant can manage such a small community's business.

"Miles, I have managed a dozen currencies at one time. One currency is easy!" He has not taken the job because it does not pay much, and it so thankless.

Speaking of truths. I leave a note on the table for Iris.

# CHAPTER TWELVE

## CITY MONEY, POLITICS, SHADY DEALINGS

**Past Flash**

In the 1970s. I know State Senator Charlie Parr, who owns Alaska House art gallery where I sell my art and do shows. He and I chat, and sometimes discuss politics. I have an interest in how our system works.

"Miles, once I am voted in I have no obligation to listen to those who voted me in."

I strongly disagree. "You represent the people, how can you say you should not listen to them?"

"Before I am elected, I listen, state my case and the public votes. Once I am involved and hearing a variety of sides to situations as a full time job, I make decisions based on what I feel is in the best interest of those I represent. They are not privy to the knowledge and events as I am, so are not in a position to make intelligent decisions." I guess then he informs the public to some extent as best he can, often after he votes on our behalf. "The public voted for me and is supposed to trust me enough to represent them."

I thought we were supposed to keep tabs on those we vote for; lobby, keep them informed of our wishes. Then our elected officials try to keep a pulse on what it is we the people want. This is when I understand the difference between a democracy and a republic. In a democracy all the people vote on everything. In a republic, we vote for a representative. This representative should represent us. But this is not a legal obligation. There are lobbyists who can sway a representative, Or we wrongly understood our representative, who lied to us when he was campaigning. He has professionals hired who tell a politician what can be said and promised, that will get the votes.

"What about issues like gun control, abortion, minority rights?"

A politician can repeat what gets votes, not how he feels, or will act. It is possible to go back and look over records concerning how this person behaved in the past. However modern technology, news, information disposal methods can be controlled, made hard to access, hushed, altered, not made public, so very difficult to sort out. Long ago when our county was smaller we all knew people, who knew other people, who knew the candidate firsthand.' I know his family.' 'Went to school with his sister!' 'Worked with his Dad in the factory, 'Go to his church.' It would have been hard to make up a background lie about what you did, or how you feel. After getting to know Charlie, I understand some of his true feelings on a variety of subjects he would never tell the public. I like and admire Charlie, yet he is very rigid in his views of lifestyles. He is very suit and tie, feels everyone should be.

**Past flash ends**

I am not as sure now as I once was, and wonder if Charlie Parr was right. There can be people in the community who are adamant their way is right! Convinced they represent a majority of the people and occupy many hours of time trying to convince the leaders of the error of their ways. If these citizens had their way, nothing would get done. Totally disruptive people, to the extent one wonders if this is their game plan, to destroy the system by dogging it down with trivial drivel, while arguing their opinion matters. Some are simply bonkers, too many drugs in their brain. Others are making decisions on emotions, unwilling to digest the facts. I understand the long ago argument, when only land owners were qualified to vote.

I have heard Nenana city meetings disrupted with, 'But what about the frogs?' 'There are eggs in a bird nest,' 'The poor family of otters in front of my house.' Or 'There is a pothole in front of my house!' 'I saw Sasquatch footprints.'

These people are allowed to occupy an hour of the council's time while citizens want answers or a vote taken on a subject. The topic at hand being, our entire water plant is about to quit, or the airport is about to get shut down. I understand there are citizens who can barely repeat their name who have no clue where water comes from. A lot of such people. Should there be some level you need to come to vote, or disrupt a city meeting? If we say, 'Put it in writing; submit this for approval on the agenda.' The reply would be, 'What about the poor people who do not know how to write?' Or in some areas, 'Do not know English!' By law we'd have to hire a Spanish and Athabascan interpreter when our entire community budget is under $1,000.

I am close enough to have some understanding of what goes on behind the scenes; sometimes I hear insider information. Mayor Johnson wrote a letter of reference stating I am a valued citizen of good character in our community and handed it to the judge during my legal problems. Johnson and I agree on some major ways to view life and government; how things get done, ethics and such things. Unless he was stringing me along. I do not think so. Johnson is 'one of us'; a local citizen who lives like most of us with a normal income. He goes out, as we do, to cut firewood for his home. His home looks like ours. He wears jeans, plaid shirt, hunts, fishes, has a hobby racing junk cars. Mingles with the rest of us. He is of our tribe.

There are rumors money is missing from city funds; many feel, 'stolen.' I wonder, if this is so, who is spending it? No one on the council or city office goes on vacations, has material goods that reflects living beyond their means. Johnson volunteers to plow roads, does city work off hours to help out. I believe he truly cares about our community, partly based on his volunteer work. Others tell me a smart thief could save the money for later. That is possible, yes.

"Miles, he has not been the same since he lost his son!"

I agree. He lost a lot of energy and got apathetic perhaps. Lazy is not the word. The drive to get things done was gone. I did not talk about personal matters with him. His son was killed crossing the highway on his snow machine. Known for speeding, not looking where he was going. Perhaps a somewhat typical teen. So Johnson may not run this election. I am not allowed to vote, being a felon. Or no, I went to vote earlier. My name is still on the list of registered voters. One of the hired ballot watchers who knows I am a felon but also knows my views, would not let me vote.

Mrs. Probation told me I could legally run for city council. "I just do not recommend it because your first priority is to get your own life to get together. Stop taking on projects involving others… for now at least."

Ollie decides to run against Johnson in the upcoming election, as the only other candidate. He put up fliers promising the community a new swimming pool and Jacuzzi as his only campaign promise. A high percent of the community is thrilled. I am puzzled. I thought a foolish offer. The community had discussed this very subject ten years ago when we did a ten year plan. An investigation into the reality revealed the huge upkeep cost. If such a pool was given to us free, we could not afford to run it. Lifeguard, heated treated water, insurance, was overwhelming. Imagine fifty below zero.

That idea was dismissed. The community should know we are in financial straits. Federal funding cuts, state budget cuts, costs of gas and equipment and repairs going up. Much of our equipment is in need of repairs and is so outdated we have problems even getting parts. Our sewer water system is in trouble. A new community swimming pool seems like an odd priority.

Ollie was not in town during the election, nor did he show up after he won. Johnson told me Ollie asked how much time he had before he has to show up and take over. He's busy. That does not sound like someone very interested. A week after being elected, Ollie resigns, quits; declines the position. The community now has no one at the helm. The official reason should be brought up at this city meeting we are waiting for. Rumor has it, he was shocked at how low the pay is, and decided after a day's review of the books, that the city bookwork is so messed up he does not want to deal with it.

My feelings on the matter are, he should have investigated these issues before raising his hand saying, "I'm your man!" It's nice to say, "I'm going to fix what ails you." But let those words have substance. My respect is when actions back up words. Talk is cheap. *Show us,* I think. I kept my mouth shut until I see what the actions will be.

"You are not among the voters, Miles, so what is your opinion worth? Huh?"

I know that when a mayor quits, it can be expected to be a long and unprecedented process to get new leadership. Months. Meanwhile, one of the main reasons, as I understand why we have little money, is paperwork has not been turned in on time, an audit has to be approved before we can accept a huge amount of state revenue sharing. There is a time limit, or this state money will be withdrawn, or greatly reduced. There have been financial appropriations for projects like the sewer treatment plant with time limits. Major decisions must be made soon. Each week delay costs the community thousands of dollars. In fact our daily interest on what is owed is thousands of dollars.

The bottom line, however, is the revenue sharing is promised, owed, and secure. We borrowed from it to cover costs we can't afford. We wish we did not have to spend money we do not have yet, but life is like that sometimes. It's like using credit. Like spending some of next month's pay check to make a house payment when times get rough. This promised money is half a million dollars. Plenty to pay off what is owed, and have enough to press forward and cover upcoming bills. Two new council members who have never attended a city meeting before, come unglued.

"What do you mean we are in debt! How can you call the budget balanced! We can't pass this budget!" Followed by, "So where is all the city money? Stolen?" Those of us who have a better handle on what is going on groan, and cover our eyes. Those already distrustful of government on all levels jump on the charges with a doom and gloom outlook. There is a personality type, that if you trip and fall, they will kick you and steal your wallet.

"Obviously, our money is stolen! That's what governments do!" It is easy to join this commonly shared mass hysteria. It is easy to add my own evil government story and get attention, be part of a tribe. 'Us against them'.

At one city meeting: "And the city cannot even afford the interest on the loan for the student living center! Our homes are up as collateral! We can lose our homes!" People listening want to believe this. No amount of facts will change their mind. It's all lies, cover ups, because again, that's what all governments do. Steal, lie, and cheat.

However. The head of the school was at a previous council meeting I attended.

There was not a big community turn out because nothing exciting was on the agenda. The superintendent is asked by the mayor, "What is the city's financial situation with the school and living center?"

The superintendent says, "Everything is fine. The city and the school have worked out trades that help us both. You are paid up." *If the school is not complaining, and feels we have worked everything out to its satisfaction, why should anyone else object?*

There is more to the student living center debt, and I know most of the details. Possibly we owe not just the school. However we are the bank, and we owe ourselves. Long and involved. The bottom line is what the superintendent is saying. The state is not complaining. Ultimately they will likely take over the living center as it is more a state issue than a city one anyhow! Many debts brought up have a story behind them. The bottom line would be, those involved have things under control.

"City fuel bill?" The local fuel company is not complaining. We owe, but it gets paid with interest when the matching state funds clear, as has happened for the past twenty years. We are a couple of months behind on most bills. Not exciting to hear, but not criminal. This would be more of a problem if the fuel company was in the mood to sue.

Much of our community is about trades. It's about lifestyle. How subsistence people live. We are classified a subsistence community. Subsistence, even off grid, means something different than other communities expected to be money-based communities. Cash does not define the only way to pay people, or our bills! When money is tight, we exchange favors, services, etc. The city lends its equipment, like graders, loaders, fork lift. We trade services like plowing private parking lots and roads, or school property. The city can give deals on leasing city property to those we do business with, and those the city owes. Those who owe the city are having financial problems which puts the city in a cash bind. Out of necessity we get creative.

I'm in business. I say to those who are broke, "What have you got to trade?" I give them a list of what I need. A small community can operate the same in hard times. I talk to the mayor. The city trades for advertising, signs, grant sharing, surplus building materials, fuel, fire equipment, police protection, and these favors and trades get traded again and passed around like IOU's. This gets done between smaller communities up and down the highway. Much is hard to properly record with a dollar value. Much like how it is in my own personal business. I get it! If we are forced to pay hard cash for everything we need, we are all in trouble! Why can't the community get that! *Do these complaining drunks buy every beer they drink? Isn't, "I owe you one!" the word of the day?*

The truth of the matter is, if no one has money to spare, business comes to a halt. Everyone hunkers down. It does the city no good if homes are foreclosed, property confiscated, and a citizen lost. The solution might this home owner is out of work but happens to own a boat which is just what the community rescue emergency response team needs. Or such a person is capable of mowing the city park, shoveling snow off city office steps, the library and the senior center. They are not employees; we do not pay them and they do not have workman's comp. *Do our children or wife? No! It's family! This is what a small community is, family.*

What is a used, outdated, no longer up to code section of sewer pipe worth? As long as all involved are happy with the trade, why does it have to get converted to a dollar value? It is a fact, we got such a used piece of pipe, put it in ourselves, and got sewer back to an entire block. Going through proper channels, we were told, would be $200,000. The question becomes, what is more important? That we follow proper procedure and leave the block without septic service for a year while we raise the money? Or do it ourselves, get septic back in a few days, and cross our fingers it keeps working correctly? The community is divided on this basic concept. Divided between, "Get it done!" and "Do it right!" While there are pros and cons to each side, I feel neither side is necessarily criminal in concept. It's a lifestyle choice. In my own view, if you do not like a subsistence community, do not live in one.

Eventually, we need to write it out proper for tax purposes. For no other reason than it has to look neat, tidy and balanced. So another government agency far away can look at the numbers and they all add up. These far off people stamp it with official seals, and file it someplace. On a small scale, this is like my own life.

I learned long ago it is not so important what one knife sells for. What matters, is how my world looks at the end of the year when all is reckoned and balanced. What matters is I eat and everyone I owe is satisfied. What does not work is having lots of inventory at the end of the year because I held out for what I consider top dollar. I may not get what I want. What I need to know is what can I accept and make a profit! I can afford sometimes to make a little profit here and there, and make up for it someplace else with higher profit. In other words, sometimes I work for a dollar an hour. Other times I earn $100 an hour. I can't live on that dollar an hour, but I also can't hold out and expect to always make $100 an hour!

Put another way, look at a family - husband and wife. What is housework worth? Do we write it all down? 'Cooked two and a half meals, did ten pounds of laundry.' Does the one doing this submit a bill, get a receipt, collect cash? Someone else in the family takes trash out, mows the lawn, rakes leaves. Someone else earns cash. We can add it all up however we wish, and the numbers are going to tell us what? Will it define a happy marriage, that each submitted their bills and collected? Do all pay into and get workman's compensation, insurance, a W2 form? The bottom line is, we are either happy with the arrangement, or not.

A small community we call a family. If we are not getting along, then yes, suddenly we are not appreciated and we begin to add up what is owed us! All we do for each other that we are owed for! What is it all worth? It's divorce time! Time to call a sit down strike. Time to bring in the lawyers and witnesses! Who will win? The lawyers! So stop screaming and let's figure this out! This is my view of a community of 300 people. Family. Let's keep the divorce lawyers out of this! Ollie wants a divorce.

The 'pro tem'—whatever that means—is one of the assembly members - Mrs. Assembly. *The 'tem' part of her title must have something to do with temporary but does pro mean professional?* I wonder why we need a fancy Latin name for such a crappy job. I find out this position is voluntary. She's our temporary leader. Mrs. Assembly has to quit her paying job to take a position with little thanks, and a lot of criticism about how it all could be done so much better if you would only listen to me. How perhaps all of you on the assembly need to go to jail, for being such screw ups!

"They should know what is going on! That is part of their job! They all get a packet before the meeting and should study it and be prepared, Miles!"

I reply, "These are the people we elected. The only ones who will show up for meetings. Who else would come to meetings? They all work and have jobs like us. They do not have time to volunteer to spend hours going over paperwork."

The truth is we are a community of people who hate politics; do not want to get involved. 'Just do it, take care of the details, leave me out! I want to do my thing and be left alone!' How many citizens anywhere show up at city council or Borough meetings so they may be informed to vote? It's advertised as a big deal, to show up to vote! Much less stay informed! Or heaven forbid, participate, volunteer on a committee. If one in a hundred people step forward in a community of 300, that's three people. Ra, ra.

I was—even am like this! "Who needs politics! You can have it!" No stress out on the river fishing, feeding sled dogs. That's the life. Who needs endless meetings, facing unhappy neighbors! Geez, you'd have to be nuts! It's like volunteering for jury duty! Mayor Johnson and I speak of this often.

I know a little about this. I was the head of our Chamber of Commerce for two terms. Just getting a quorum was difficult, much less get anyone to study anything, be responsible, actually do something. I find in many groups, there are a few who do 90% of the work. There often needs to be one dynamic person who leads, one the rest rally behind.

"What will motivate these step forward people, Mayor?" He chuckles because we both know. Power, money. "Does the job pay well?"

"Nope." Mayor gets $35,000 a year.

There are other ways to get power and money by being in charge. I refer to this as perks that come with the job. Understood. "Within certain acceptable boundaries. That can get creative, fine, take half the pie, not all of it." I do not like it but consider it reality when 1% of the population is motivated enough to show up. Without perks the percent might be one in ten thousand. Among the local perks for being on the city council? The city plow may make a pass up your driveway when it goes by. In any issue involves a 911 call - fire or police - there will be a tad faster response.

"Legal smeagle. You are nice to me, I know you, you help others, give of your time, I thank you with more than words, its that simple. I'll mow your lawn, watch your dog, give you a deal on your Christmas presents." Is that fair? Absolutely! Are we all equal? Absolutely not!

So, they—we—all left it up to our trusted mayor to make it all happen! Why is it now all his fault?

I say, "We, the voters are just as responsible! It is we who need to come to meetings, know what is going on so we can at least vote intelligently! Know the issues!" Anyone who had attended even two meetings would know the last thing we need is a swimming pool!

I recall Johnson trying to inform us at community meetings, "There is no money. We are going broke."

The directive we give him as a group is not, "Oh my gosh, pay our bills, let's cut spending and get out of debt!" No, the mayor heard from the public, "Fix the lights, plow the roads, give me more! But do not tax me! Find a grant! My hand is out, I'm owed!"

We show up at community meetings for the food. No foody, no showy uppy. As long as our personal lives were fine, who cares.

"Just do not raise our taxes!" "Just do not ask me to get involved, I'm busy!" So the mayor pressed on for fifteen years. We all smiled and nodded.

One of the new city council members hates the librarian for reasons no one is sure of. "He might be uneducated. Hardly knows how to read. Was in the military. Has an axe to grind against education and educated people?" Maybe. Mrs. Librarian lives outside city limits and was one of the main forces behind stopping a fact finding mission of the borough investigative committee. Feelings were hot enough lives were threatened. I believe it has to do with why I am not connected to the library anymore. I was in favor of getting information. Mrs. Librarian was in favor of using any method necessary to stop the inquiry. Yet, this assembly member should have been on the librarian's side on this issue, knowing how he feels!

Mrs. Librarian says she is dead set against paying any fees or taxes of any kind, for anything. Many feel she benefits from those of us who pay, by using plowed roads, having a city job, having fire service, rescue service. All for free. Mrs. Librarian tells me, "I do contribute! I pay sales tax when I shop in Nenana!" However, she had told me many times in the past, she does all her shopping in Fairbanks.

"The heck with Nenana!" What she pays in sales tax is minimal. Four percent on $100 worth of local groceries a year is not paying for an emergency rescue. Our assembly member might not like the librarian's outlook. He hates welfare types, living off other people's hard work.

BIG NEWS in the paper based on interviews with Ollie. "Obvious misappropriation; incompetency. Those folks have a problem!" I noticed not 'us and we'. He goes back up North where his big bucks oil company job is. I'm curious how statements can be legally said that discredits us without evidence. Appearing like, 'With malicious intent.'

No official is saying there has been money stolen, or misappropriated. Yet, it looks like no one knows how to do the books, and the system itself is a mess. No one knows for sure if we are arriving or leaving. Ollie is saying the previous mayor kept it all to himself and told no one. Yet, the clerk says Ollie was not there when the reins were turned over to be shown the ropes. At another time, Johnson spent time trying to show the new mayor around, offered more time. The new mayor declined. Furthermore, the new mayor brought in his own clerk, without city council approval. Word is, she showed up drunk and combative.

The impression is, the new mayor assumed everyone in the old administration is crooked and up to no good, so will not work with them. Wants to bring in all his own people. Ollie heard what he knows at the bar, not by attending meetings. The new mayor was going to fix everything wrong, by firing everyone. Bring in his own accountant, go over the records, find evidence of wrong doing, and heads will fly. Arriving distrustful of everyone. His own accountant was unable to figure it out. Apparently no better a bookkeeper than the old one. Or, she had been bookkeeper for our previous drunk mayor. Johnson fired her when he took office ten years ago, for being drunk on the job.

Miss Bookkeeper is present at this city meeting, and often interrupts the council with points of order. "That's not legal! Excuse me!" She is ignored. This is a city council meeting. We can speak during public comment. Limited to three minutes. Comment does not mean ask questions and be guaranteed an answer. Or interrupt without being called on. There is a specific time on the agenda for public comment on agenda items. Otherwise, disruptive people could sabotage meetings. We, the public, are here to listen. Miss Bookkeeper appears to have an axe to grind. She in fact seems too often to be, wrong in her opinion of how it ought to be done, or even what is legal.

Bookkeeper lost her last job as burger flipper at the local café, and is now unemployed.

There were a few more 'events,' issues, scenes, political maneuvers, but this hits the highlights. Neither Johnson or Ollie attended the meeting. The pro tem is in charge. Oh, guy assigned by the state is here helping us stay legal. So far, he says no wrong doing found.

"There are other communities in a bad way as well. This is not the only one; nor the worst."

Iris points out another article in the News Miner. "Nenana mayor details reasons for resigning." She reads the article. "Dismal record keeping and potential conflicts of interest by Nenana's former longtime mayor. Things are a mess, the only one who knew where files and fund figures are is the former mayor, which he kept to himself. I feel you'll need professional help to fix these issues."

I support our previous mayor Johnson, as having had good dealings with him. The new mayor I have had dubious dealings with.

Others say, "The previous mayor lied to me!" I'm puzzled, having not had this experience. I was not there, so do not know what the question was, or situation the mayor might have lied about or hedged. It's possible I am naïve, getting told a line of bull, and believing it.

On the subject of Doyon and the gas oil exploration. I see evidence Johnson is correct, and I agree with his stand. Doyon wants control. It is not about being part of, or cooperating with, our community. Ollie works for the same oil company as Doyon. A notice is up on the public bulletin boards.

"Doyon will be doing work across the river. There will be limited, restricted access. Alternate routes will be provided." There had been talk in the past of' authorized personnel' having a gate key. I had asked if I would be authorized to have a key, since it was the only access to my Kantishna homestead. I was told, "We have good lawyers and always win." Not the sound of working with and caring about others. This is the same mentality I would expect to gate any bridge that they are in control of. The community may well say, "Who cares! Just a handful of stupid subsistence people going over there anyhow!"

I know my community, and this is what I'd expect. Nenana has been changing over the decades. I wonder how many would be effected by how Nenana is run? Who among us depends on Nenana money or commerce? Indian dividends, welfare, school, government jobs, is possibly a majority.

Front page headlines…

**"Hunting investigations hike fees"**
Subheading: "Guide licensing program increased price to cover cost of state inquires."
"If we have a guide who has done some fairly erroneous acts, he'll lawyer up and then we'll have to get our own lawyers involved. We can easily run up a $30,000 bill on just one case."
"They were hitting every transgression with a mallet. Some of our guys just forgot

to fill out a form right, or they were late registering for one of their guide areas. They were treated like they were sneaking around breaking into liquor stores. Guides will now pay $1,700 a year, an increase of $400."

Who in their right mind would read this article and want to be a guide? In what other business do you not only pay for your defense if you get arrested, but an annual punishment fee for your occupation so the prosecutor has enough money to take you to court? Who wants to be a guide now? Not smart Nenana kids! They are out of here! Headed to greener pastures, encouraged by the school to move to the big city! Guiding is one of the few jobs in the wilds. This means big changes in a subsistence village. As a community, we no longer depend on the river, berry picking, firewood hauling, or fishing. That is all the past; heritage to feel nostalgic about. We feel lost. What is it now that holds us together as a tribal family? The bonds are gone.

While I am looking at the newspaper, another headline in the same issue!

**First burn ban issued in North Pole**

There has been an ongoing issue the nearby Fairbanks Borough has had with not meeting federal air quality standards for many years. The Feds are coming down on the city, saying federal funds will get cut if air quality is not met. There is what is called a temperature inversion in the valley where cold air gets trapped down low. This happens about a week out of each winter. The rest of the year the air is pure and pristine. I wonder, how much money we spend to fix a week's worth of air? It is costing millions, even a billion to fix. That is a lot of funds for a community of 70,000 people.

"You told me before, Miles!" I forgot. We were part of the proposed pollution solution. Iris and I were given a brand new $6,000 catalytic stove in order to be more efficient, and not pollute with wood smoke!

I repeat, "I breathe that fog in Fairbanks. I know what wood smoke smells like. I am not smelling wood smoke. I smell car exhaust and coal power plant fumes!" Iris is not listening because I have said this many times. "I bet after everyone is stopped from burning wood, the smog problem will not change by a measurable amount!" Already it was admitted, that there was no change after spending millions on the wood stove exchange program. "So why not spend that same several million and subsidize public transportation and cab drivers and encourage people not to drive on bad days!" The problem is car exhaust not wood smoke. "Is this all just politics of no interest to us? Off the grid, subsistence people use wood for heat and do not wish to depend on oil; may not have access to it, or the money for it." How is it when those not involved have the police at their door arresting them for using wood. At that point it will matter.

The article points out some people are exempt if you apply for a permit, if wood or pellets is your only source of heat. 'To get the rules accepted and passed, make it reasonable.' Get everyone used to it, then the permit costs increase, more people fail to qualify for exemptions. Until eventually, the exemption permit is no longer issued, impossible, or not available, even when it is supposed to be. Big fines and a crime to not have a permit that is impossible to get. No one wants to hear what I say.

In the future my neighbor went to the biggest wood stove shop in Fairbanks to get a new wood stove. She cannot buy a wood stove without proving she lives in an exempted area. The proof permit requires an inspection. In short, trappers, homesteaders, off grid people may not be able to buy wood stoves. Few have normal kinds of proof of address. Few can afford someone to come out and do an inspection, and few would pass inspection because they built their own home, not up to anyone's code. No woodstove, no can keep warm. No can keep warm, no live in pucker brush. It's a big deal if you want to be off the grid, or not dependent on oil.

The power plant was shown by a study to be the single biggest polluter. The reply from the power plant, "We can't afford to make the legal changes!" No more word about it; suddenly the wood stove people are the target. Do they get to say they do not have the money to make the changes? Yes, for now they can be part of weatherization and get a new stove if they qualify or get an exemption. Meanwhile, it is a $1,000 fine for the first offense.

"We are not pressing it now." Yes, that's how it begins, or the public would be outraged. In a year, "Citizens were warned, informed, should know, we have been nice; now we need to start enforcing." Followed by, "We need to make it a felony; it's really a federal issue." Already I have seen another article where concerned citizens are taking note of who burns wood, and politely going over and having a talk with them to help educate them on the evils of wood burning.

"It affects the planet, everyone's health and is quite selfish. You really need to stop. Think of my poor child!"

Iris and I wonder what happens when the power goes off, when you depend on an oil furnace. At fifty below zero it does not take long for water pipes to start to freeze, along with home dwellers. Power outages are common. Oil furnaces depend on electric. We have already seen in the TV news, what happens in the lower states when a record cold spell hits, takes the power grid out, and thousands are without adequate heat. Some burning their furniture, but where? No woodstove to burn in. Iris points out, "One woman and children went in the garage and ran the car to keep warm, died of carbon monoxide."

I visit my friend, Witty. She made some glass beads that went flat! I told her not to toss them out! I can get creative with them. I make metal pendant caps and think they came out nice. They look almost like exotic rocks or opal.

"Need any more yogurt, Miles? I just made a new batch." She still owes me on a deal where she acquired a $200 strand of opal beads. I already got a lot of her cut pork worth $15 a pound. Range fed, as good as you get meat. Equal to our moose. Only more fat! We talk about the city meeting and exchange ideas. She and I are both going to the WIN meetings and care about the community. She is on the city council. We talk about Witty's neighbor. "Yes, now she is on the assembly, too. She did a drive by, and shot Mad Jay's house full of bullets."

I ask, "Mrs. Problem? Is it her son who is going on trial for raping all those under age girls?"

"Yes, her. Anyhow, related, Mrs. Problem threatened the girls who turned her son in. The girls went to the living center in tears and the cops were called. Now Mrs. Problem is banned from going to the school."

Iris told me Problem has been angrily saying the girls were willing, wanted it, and it's not fair her son is in trouble. The girls were thirteen. Now Mrs. Problem represents us on the council. [1] Interestingly, Mrs. Problem won by one vote! I was not allowed to vote. The school superintendent's husband ran against her. The choice was pro education, or pro drugs and crime. Drugs and crime won by one vote.

We no longer have someone from the tribe on the council, which I think would help our community since we are half Native. Mrs. Assembly, the pro tem, has worked for the tribe a lot of years, is respected, and understands tribal issues that she can look out for as a city council member.

Bean tells me the state could take over, considering Nenana too incompetent to run itself. All that potential oil money under us, and we are so broke we can't function. Is that interesting or what?

"Bean, the city clerk told me more damage was done by the weeklong wonder Ollie during his reign, than by Johnson in fifteen years."

"Ollie is retiring from a federal and big oil company job."

"I don't think he got paid to help destroy Nenana, do you?"

"Probably not." *Only probably?* There is talk someone Ollie wanted as city clerk was behind manipulating him into running for office, egged him on. Thinking maybe she could run things while all the mayor would have to do is sign checks and relax.

"Yes, heard from a reliable source."

"Makes sense to anyone who has been observing over the past decade and attending meetings. It is difficult to separate rumor and speculation from fact."

"It also looks like it is possible to win an election by going to the bar and buying drinks for voters. There is apparent apathy among the sober population. Thinking maybe their vote is not going to matter. Those who want no police, or law and order, may not be the majority population, but have been the majority voters." History shows that.

"I tend to agree, Miles. Most of us do not truly support Nenana like we once did. We shop in and show our allegiance to Fairbanks. It is easier to get there now than in the past, roads have been improved. Fairbanks is where we haul our garbage, do our shopping, and look for services.

Nenana is a place to get mail, store our stuff, and commute from, paying low costs. We want minimum taxes, minimum services. Minimum government." *Or the most services for the least money, whatever we can get.*

"But, the priority is not raising taxes or having any costs here."

"As the last head of our Chamber of Commerce, I agree with you."

I give an example: "We had a Chamber board meeting in which we discussed supporting local business and how to promote that." Someone suggested we make signs encouraging buying local. Another board member says, 'Good idea, I'll go to Fairbanks and get some paint!' Without thinking, and realizing, one of our strongest businesses is the local hardware store that sells paint for just fifty cents more than Fairbanks, saving a 100 mile round trip and day's time. Many locals drive to Fairbanks almost every day. We get our car worked on there, get gifts, food, and entertain ourselves. The bottom line is, what is Nenana to us? What do we need Nenana for? There is no use forcing something that does not want to happen. It might be best to take an honest look, and provide what the people want. No taxes, no services.

"No services can mean no water, school, mail, sewer, or electric."

"That wouldn't be legal, Miles." *So what do we owe people for free?*

"Over time, change the kind of people who settle here; those who would like utilities, plowed roads, fire, and police service. People who understand these things cost." Bean nods. Yet, I see the wisdom in wanting and expecting nothing! I prefer to take care of myself. I do not care if there are lights, plowed roads, or police. If I have a fire, I am in trouble. I accept that. I can't afford insurance, or maintaining our own fire department. I see the budget at the city meetings.

"Oh, well." No taxes, no services, works for me. I know how to use an outhouse and haul water from the river.

Those who want service have many cities to go to, but places like Nenana, with low tax and no service are few! I have enjoyed building how I want without a permit. No one tells me I have to mow my lawn, put up a fence, or maintain standards others put on me. I can store whatever I want on my land; dig holes, ditches, cut trees, plant trees, build sheds, store abandoned cars. No permits, no permission. We are family here and take care of each other without being instructed or made to. It's not a law.

We spread surplus food around that has not been inspected. We have built homes without charge for those who lost homes in fires. We do fund raisers for people with medical issues. We all show up to look for missing people in the wilds. We donate time, boats, gas, everything needed. For all our faults, it's a great place. One issue is, "Will the government allow a community like we want, to exist?" And, "Is this truly what the majority want?" It is hard to picture the biggest complainers - Mr. Assembly, Dalia, Mad Jay, and the like - using an outhouse and hauling water from the river in buckets. In short, living subsistence. What I do not want, is for my community to be in debt supporting a lifestyle we cannot, or are unwilling to pay for. We cannot cry for help when we have a need, but did not pay in.

"This agenda may also involve having citizens accountable for damages to the community. Criminal activity should not be forgiven and swept under the rug as acceptable behavior. We almost have a dysfunctional community at the moment. Ninety percent of the trouble comes from five percent of the population." We forgive crime, say we understand, and it's ok, and like parents, we cover for the child who robs the family piggy bank.

"Well, Miles, an interesting point of view, spoken by a felon!" We both laugh.

"I have morals, Bean!"

"So we all do, Miles!"

We laugh again. The dynamics of the community may be more complicated than can be easily stated by one view. A reporter for the Fairbanks News Miner is determined to write a story about Nenana, but can't find anyone who will talk. As a community, we are unified in the belief the news media gives a negatively slanted view on most of its stories; that whatever we say, we can count on the news media not getting it right, misquoting us, giving any story a predetermined slant, in order to sell the paper.

I admit that I badmouth the news for giving a slanted negative view when that view goes against what I prefer to hear. I quote the news as factual when the negative news suits my own agenda beliefs. I'm not always conscious of doing so at the time, just notice after the fact.

Much is up to interpretation, much in conflict. Sometimes you do what you have to do. Not everyone understands or agrees. It may take a court to sort it out. The question could be, 'How bad do you want to sort this out?' *Good luck getting proof.* My view is, if the deed is not selfish; is for the community, and it is your job to look out for the community, then I believe in some leeway. "What would my peers say?" is the key question. I may not want to know. It's all about trust. Sometimes in failing systems, to survive one needs to make things happen. The bigger system is not working. It's time to break up into smaller groups and put food in our mouths, or die. If the Federal government has as its agenda, the disbandment of all small communities and small business, then what? How does one answer?

Bean and I hear a complaint, sounds like Mad Jay, "A city vehicle was used to do personal shopping! This employee needs to be fired! It's an outrage!" *Ya, ya, ya. Cool your jets. I expect a few perks go on here and there.* I am not excited. Why am I not excited? I happen to know the fire truck was donated by another community to us as a favor owed. Because our volunteers haul Healy medical emergencies to Fairbanks to save Healy huge travel costs. Being gone from the community, puts their community at risk for many hours while making such a trip. Nenana has a bulk fuel plant with deals on gas. Healy does not.

"You got an extra truck and we have gas." *You have a pair of roller skates and I have a key*, or however that song goes.

Somewhere in that mix, someone takes the head guy who got the fire truck, out to dinner in the fire truck he donated. Is it legal? I really do not care. Shut up. Fires get put out, people get rescued, we have a truck that runs, our neighbor community is happy, we are happy. Where is the victim? Who suffers? Whose business is this?

No! You can't go explaining such matters to the IRS, auditors, inspectors, city lawyers. I can imagine there needs to be a proper paper trail and some money written down someplace - 'To look good.' I get it. An outraged public would occupy several city meetings trying to get to the bottom of how we got the fire truck. Headlines: "City kickbacks an outrage in Nenana!" Investigations, lawyers, court, hundreds of thousands of dollars to get to the bottom of why the fire truck was in front of Fred Meyers on Tuesday.

Our fire chief speaks to me sometimes about department issues. "By law we have to turn tires in for new ones every two years to meet Federal standards. We do not have the twenty-eight thousand to do it, not in such a small community."

The choice would be to refuse to drive a firetruck with tires not up to code, and let homes burn instead. Similar issues involve fire suits that are out of code after five years, all equipment. Keeping up makes more sense in a big city. We often have to repeat, "'A small subsistence community can not operate by big city standards. The standards are not lower, just different.' Well... maybe lower... on some issues, but this is a choice anyone makes in deciding where and how to live. Does our form of government require everything is exactly the same everywhere, concerning everything? Houses all have to match, firetrucks, streets, with no community standing out for any reason as different?

"This is more the concept behind communism. Yet, Nenana, as it is, is also not a democracy."

I reply to Bean, "Yeah, democracy is two wolves and a sheep voting on what to have for dinner." We both laugh. When I was young I was told how our form of government is about protecting personal freedoms. However I see that goes against the basic concept of democracy, so am puzzled how you protect the individual's rights to personal freedom when the majority rules."Or the rights of a small community to remain subsistence and not depend on government hand-outs." An individual is allowed to dumpster dive, live on second hand stuff, collect antiques, keep outdated stuff running, and enjoy a way of life a hundred years outdated. Why can't an entire community?

Bean and I agree, we see how this helps society and mankind from a biological standpoint. "This allows diversity; keeps past knowledge active in case it is ever needed again by civilization. Like how to grow heirloom food crops without chemical fertilizers." Yes good food is one of the advantages to a small Nenana. We all own a share in the cows, and get fresh milk and such. We are able to exist on wild game, offer a garden plot.

"Or how to protect people and put out fires without modern equipment or funding. How to keep those who need drugs happy; communicate without high speed internet, and distribute books and information - all on a low budget." I could see as well, how anyone who wishes to study the old ways can come here to observe and learn. They may wish to do a life expectancy study or comparison. In our minds, it is not just some useless way to live with no purpose and nothing to gain.

"If we are not huge consumers, there is a smaller carbon print. We do not maintain winter roads, we walk. We do not get new cars, new buildings, and this helps the environment."

"Maybe. Usually upgraded equipment is more efficient, Miles. Newer houses need less heat, newer cars pollute less." So who knows, but studies could be done, and here is an entire community to study.

I GET enough details over thirty years of attending meetings to understand enough to believe that when local people are in charge, they care about my community, and are not ripping us off.

I say, "Nice fire truck!" Big grin. "It's not stolen? Ok, that's all I want to know. You want to go shopping in it? Have at it." The city sure as heck can't afford a fire truck through proper channels, that is for sure. I saw the bill at the city meeting for what one costs. Dream on! Is it safe, up to code? All I care as a citizen is, "Do our medics and volunteers trust it? Will they go out in it with confidence?" That's all I want to know. Has it ever failed to work when they got to a fire? Then I'll cover for you. Do I want my home to burn down or my neighbors, or even have us die in a house fire because the headlights on a fire truck are not up to code, and, or, the tires are three years old now? It's hard times. We use baling wire and duct tape it together until it quits. I assume we take care of the safety issues, more than cosmetic.

This outlook is not shared by everyone, possibly not even many. The consensus as I understand it is expressed by my friend Valerie at the senior center. "The laws need to be followed, Miles! We can't make them up!"

Up to a point I agree. She has more to say, but already my mind has blocked out what comes next. I do not want to hear it. We get into a heated discussion. Views are strong on the subject. Our prison system has said to me, 'No, we could not operate if we had to do so legally.' To be legal then is to not survive. That's the message. More than just this. From many fronts I have heard it; seen it with my own eyes. It's not possible to get ahead and be legal. It is possible to only survive as a slave. If there is other knowledge out there I have not seen it. I do not know anyone for example, who has a garage sale and tells the IRS about it.

If I do not survive, I can do nothing, not even be a good slave. Spreading outward, my next priority is family, then friends, then community, then ever outward, my tribe, my state and near the top, my country, and higher up humans, and on outward to the world and the universe. It all begins at the center, me. It all begins at your center, you. The right for me and you to do what it takes to ensure our own personal survival. After that is taken care of, look outward. I reach the level of my community. I will look out for my community before I look out for higher levels.

I believe if our community did everything by the book, had all the permits required, and followed all the proper procedures, we would not exist as a community. I do not believe highest level of government has as its priority, our survival, except as slaves. They would prefer to see us all in one place where it is easier to control us and keep an eye on us, within drone and cell phone tracking reach. Ideally, big companies, huge governments, do not want smaller entities near the resources. Those high up do not want interferences they are not in control of as an unknown.

This is not Valerie's belief. "Miles, you have been sucked in by the mayor. He lies! He has lied to me, to the city assembly and the entire community!" She goes further as she talks louder in anger. "I doubt very much that sewer line would have cost 200 grand to fix! The entire sewer line is band aid and chewing gum, and needs replacing. It's a disaster, and someone putting diapers down the sewer line was just a small part of a bigger problem!"

I have been following along with the sewer problems for many years. I believe the mayor. As a surveyor I know what just the survey would cost. I know what union labor gets paid. I know something about pipe work.

Mayor explains, "It is easier to get money to replace the entire system, than fix the old one. If this one breaks and cannot be fixed, the government will step forward and a new one will get put in."

I agree. Did we deliberately ruin it so we could get a new one? No. It is forty years old, twenty years past its replacement date. Who could fault us if it simply fails completely. Then - "We need a new one." Under the term of 'emergency aid'. We can't come out and make a public statement to the news media that we are just waiting until it fails and becomes an emergency.

Diplomacy calls for, 'We are doing our best, master! See? We fixed it, we struggle; look, we are doing our best!' We all nod with sincerity, and look at each other with somber sad faces. What would Valarie expect? That we have fundraisers and try to collect several million dollars? When a fund raiser that generates $1,000 is a big deal? Will this kind of money come from the taxes eighty people pay? This is the number of people out of 300, qualified to pay. The rest are exempt for one reason or another.

To be honest, my personal answer is, we can't afford either a sewer system, or city water. I'd vote for holding tanks, a truck that brings water, another that hauls sewage. We might afford that. Even each of us buys our own tanks. The destitute we might help. That idea would never fly, so I keep quiet.

I DO NOT AGREE small communities need to operate by the same rules as big cities. People who do not like living like this should move someplace where protocol and strict rules are the rage. Valerie came from a big city where she was in charge of a bigger organization with many employees under her. With a much bigger budget. It might be a discouraging step downward to be in Nenana. People she worked with and hired where she is from went to college and were certified. Here, everyone appears to be an idiot by comparison. Here, when a Postmaster was needed, Josh's wife was grabbed off the street.

"Hey, you want a job? We need a Postmaster."

As she tells it. "And there I was with a job as Postmaster." Had the job for twenty years and retired. No test, no security clearance.' We want you; you're in, done deal.'

I am very much in favor us being in control of ourselves and what we want. I strongly dislike Nenana getting sent some certified postal mucky muck we do not know, who shows up in suit and tie, and tells us the rules. "No key, no picky up your maily" "No, your wife can't pick up the mail, it says right here under rule number sixty-nine!" My concern is, our entire community could end up like this - all about protocol. Sound nuts? Can't happen? Another post office story.

I go in to get my mail and notice a screw loose on the metal strip on the threshold where the door closes. I inform the Postmaster I am about to screw it back down with my Leatherman tool. The door cannot close due to this screw. Therefore, the post office cannot be locked up tonight.

"Miles, by law I have to call the mail office in Fairbanks and have them send a certified person to perform this task correctly and legally. If I do it, or have knowledge an unauthorized person performed this task, I can be fired."

Is that nuttso or what? *We wonder why the postal system is going broke?* I fix the problem. One tiny loose screw and two minutes saved the post office at least $500. Likewise, the Postmaster is not authorized to change a light bulb. We, the community, can't paint the building. We can't cut our costs and save money. It would be illegal, we could be arrested and go to jail if we did. The postal system does not have the money to do these things, so it doesn't get done. I do not agree this makes sense.

"Valerie, I understand your view. I agree even 'if'; if the system is functional." I believe in the principals our system was set up to operate under. I like the idea of the police stepping in to settle disputes between people when there is trouble. Before people get hurt, and to protect the weak. "I like 'innocent until proven guilty by a court of law,' to stop lynch mobs from hanging the wrong person."

I agree there should be some workable rules we all agree on, so we are all on the same page and know what to expect, and is expected of us. I say, "If small communities take care of themselves because the government is busy and poor, the same as us, maybe we can hang in there until things get fixed." If small communities take care of themselves so the bigger government can deal with bigger problems, and the small communities still pay tribute, what is the harm? Big government can't get blood from a turnip. To pay tribute, we must first survive. If we are all to be treated like outlaws and sent to jail, who is paying for that in a collapsing economy?

Mayor once told me Nenana was offered Nenana a new computerized water treatment plant, run from Washington. He tells me that we all prefer a system we can fix ourselves if something goes wrong. "Under this agreement, the system is monitored and run from out of state. If something goes wrong, someone from far away may or may not arrive to fix it. We are at the mercy of big government far away. Is that what we want? Right now we have a system Ricky can go over and fix and make work. We can baby it, run it part time, have control over our own communities water." Some community members fear control from far away. Again, not everyone agrees. Nenana does not come together on what kind of community we wish to be!

"We are just forty miles from Denali Park. We could be a tourist attraction if we were run right. We could all work for Princess at slave wages."

Freedom is work and takes effort; I agree. It might well be easier to be a slave.

Issued food, given a roof over head. It is true, some locals do not have this, and being a slave would be a blessing and a step up.

I write a letter of support to the city council.

**Written comment submitted by Miles Martin**

I trust the majority of you on the city council we the citizens elected. I stand by your decisions as a group. My biggest concern is that the atmosphere created in the news and public notices may discourage good qualified people from wanting to step up to serve our community.

I believe it is a punishable crime to deliberately disseminate opinions disguised as facts, and disinformation from vague sources for the purpose of discrediting, dismantling, our city officials, government and community.

I recall a sewer lift pump going out, and frozen line caused by a citizen's negligence. $200,000 bill to fix. Our mayor scrounged up old unapproved used pipe, fixed it without union workers, surveyor, inspection, environmental impact study, or cleanup crew in Zuit suits. What he did was probably illegal. I only heard words of gratitude. I did not hear, "You should have gotten a permit first, and gone through proper channels!"

We are the hub of 300 citizens, 80 who pay taxes, who serve about 800 total who depend on Nenana, and use our services. This sounds like a formula for financial issues, no matter who runs things.

This is my home. I thank my city assembly for volunteering to do the hard work ahead. I thank all our city workers for their dedication. We have an outstanding volunteer fire and medical group! Ok, there is room for improvement! Our representatives are only as good as our community. I'd like to be part of a solution. Whatever you decide, I will abide by. Let's roll our sleeves up together! What can I do to help, as a citizen of Nenana?

I'm concerned I am sticking my neck out. I ask my friend Witty. Her comment is, "The Chinese have a saying, 'The nail that sticks up gets hammered.'"

The city clerk adds, "Leave it to you to make how you feel known to all. Well, someone needs to stand up and be counted. Can I make copies and pass them around?"

Hopefully there will be no serious consequences. Meaning, if bigger government represented by gas and oil interests are trying to dismantle the community and take over, my words clearly interfere with this objective. Will I be silenced? In fact, has the effort already been made, does it have something to do with why I am now a felon and cannot vote? *I'm just paranoid! Do not mind me ha ha.*

I had thought of writing an article for the Fairbanks paper, since all they publish about Nenana seems like negative gossip. But no, the truth will not set us free. If civilization realizes there is an entire community trying to avoid big government, or prefers not to be like you, will it only attract trouble? From the position of being a felon, is it my place to step forward representing my community? I think not. What would I accomplish? Nothing. Would, "Stop badmouthing my community!" Help? No.

My shop could not be run legally in most places. Nenana has few regulations.

# CHAPTER THIRTEEN

## RIVER TRIP MAMMOTH TUSKS, GREENPEACE ISSUES, CORRUPTION

The whole summer is record wet and cool. The boat is loaded for a long trip that is never taken. When the weather finally breaks and warms to sixty without freezing at night, I take off. There is over eighty gallons of gas on board - enough to potentially go 1,000 miles. I am not sure where I am going. 'Out hunting' allows for flexibility. I will look here, I will look there. I have in mind some places to check out. Various factors affect details. If I encounter wind, I will head for small twisty creeks in the trees where wind does not create waves. If the water has dropped too much for the smaller creeks to be navigated, or I find to many moose hunters, the plan can change to go out further on the bigger rivers, like the Yukon.

I bring this up, because I am amazed how many people are puzzled, confused, displeased, curious, or disbelieving when I answer with, "I'm not sure, just out. Out hunting. I will come back when I have something worth coming back with." That is what 'subsistence, hunter gather' means. Dah! It seems odd this is so hard to comprehend. Considering it is how mankind lived for 50,000 years; considering Nenana is called a subsistence community.

This means coming back with something that pays for the trip; pays for gas; gives meaning to the trip. 'Meaning' can be merely an adventure; learning something; having a new experience. Mostly I wish to be satisfied with the trip, and call it a success. This can happen in a day or two, or three, or a week. In the past, I'd mean gone - "For a month or a year." The various things I am looking for are a moose, interesting sellable rocks, good pictures for my web site or book, wood burls, chaga, or just interesting wood, catching fish, finding fossils like mammoth ivory, country previously unexplored, useful to me, finding an old cabin or artifacts, discovering something going on, like a change in my environment, useful to know. I do not bring a watch. It takes about two days to forget what day it is. I smile at the fact I can drop everything any time I want, and simply disappear for as long as I wish.

The weather cooperates. I try a faster boat speed, burning more gas per hour to see if this is more economical than slower, with less gas per hour burned. Nothing will be certain until the entire trip is figured out, how far, and how much gas I used.

I stop at Fish Creek to fish and camp for the night. I catch a twenty pound pike! The biggest I ever got using a fishing pole! There is a lot of strength in such a fish, so it takes a while to land him. A nice picture is taken with it before it is cleaned and put it in my electric cooler. I learned something about what conditions bring big pike here, and that my expensive spider wire fish line works well. I got good pictures that help me market my product, illustrate my books, promote my way of life.

I pull my sleeping gear out of its waterproof bag, and discover the bag was not waterproof. Everything is soaking wet! The wet tent is set up in the bow of the boat as there is no place level and dry to set up on shore. I often prefer setting up on the boat so nothing has to be carried in and out of the boat and potentially left behind. I cook a meal and live off the boat. At sunset I go to bed—about 10:00 pm. A dry set of coveralls is put under the wet sleeping bag, and I crawl in fully clothed. A propane heater in the small tent is turned on and off all night to keep me warm. This helps only a little to dry the wetness all around me because heating with propane produces moisture along with the heat. I sleep fitfully. In the night I hear rustling, something hitting the tent. Half asleep, I think a tree branch hanging over the boat hanging is brushing the tent as the boat swings in the current, or a breeze moves it.

In the morning, I discover two tent poles are broken! *How odd!* At first I do not think much of it. Later the fact that two poles broke in the same spot has me thinking this is strange; not an accident, and would take substantial force - more than wind moving some leaves and branches across the tent. Upon inspection, there are no branches overhead that could potentially hit the tent. *So what was it I heard, and what broke the poles?*

There are two new tears near the top of the tent. I look for animal tracks on shore, but see none. My best guess is that a large animal tried to get in the boat to steal the fish and ended up stepping off the river bank on to the top of my tent breaking the poles. The animal gave up trying to get past a soft tent that cannot be walked on. Maybe the animal heard me move inside and got scared. I'm thinking an otter, wolf, possibly a small bear, or wolverine. I will never know, but best guess is large otter. All I know for sure is two broken tent poles, and a claw torn tent. Oh, well, just another oddity; wondering at the sort of things that can happen. Wishing I could carry a gun in case it was a bear.

The only people I run into on the river are Moonshine with Wren and Cider. "Looking for good spots to set a fish wheel, Miles." They still have sled dogs. Cider speaks of someday racing the sled dogs.

I ask Wren, "You growing your crooked neck squash? I use those heirloom seeds you gave me, they do really well in the Nenana environment." She is pleased I remember and get good use out of saved seeds. Moonshine is not as interested. He'll eat whatever he is served. Mostly he is a big meat eater!

"Miles, can you swing through this eddy with your boat and tell me the depth?" He knows I have a depth sounder on my boat. I read off the depths as I swing through the eddy.

"Eighteen, twenty-one, eighteen. Looks like twenty-one is the deepest. No reading of any logs below." We both know it might be a good place for a net, not as good for a wheel. Nets are not legal this year, but maybe next year. If you bought nets because they were legal last year, tough.

"Not a huge, big deal, Miles, I still have the contract and the government pays me to catch fish, and supplies me with whatever I need to be legal." We both say, "Sweet!" Moonshine rolls his eyes. I know what he means is, he'd rather have his freedom. He likes his new engine. Moonshine built a wood shelter on his boat. His fishing side-job makes enough money he can afford the needed extra gas. "And I got a child with me." Cider frowns. She does not mind the wind and rain. I wonder if this is more about Moonshine getting older and preferring to be dry and warm. I do not say anything about it. I notice some grayling in the boat.

"Where you getting these, Moonshine?" We know they are usually found way up fast moving water with gravel on the bottom. Nothing like this near here. We both also know grayling migrate down to deeper water. How predictable is this to know when?

"It's just a week time period at Rock Creek." I did not know. I never got grayling there. He smiles, "The secret is to guess, and try a light line with a fly as the only way to know. They will not go after the usual big pike lure."

"I got whitefish this way in early spring, right there at the mouth."

"Yes, but if you catch a lot of whitefish you need even smaller lures for grayling, and lighter line—they can see the line." I can see Moonshine wants to get back to work. He is not big on socializing.

I address Cider, "You got any more fossils for your collection?"

"I found a dinosaur bone, but dad thinks it is just a rock!"

I nod, "Well if I find anything interesting, I will let you know!"

Moonshine says, "We should be here at camp for the next month." This lets me know he should be around on my return trip, without asking me where I go, or when I'll be back. They are still living nomadic subsistence, following the game and fish through the seasons, with a variety of places to stay.

I HEAD up the Kantishna River to a more unfamiliar section up some back sloughs and side creeks. Local rain has raised the water level up more than normal. Several interesting wood burls are found, with one very odd huge alder burl. These will slice and stain to make exceptional knife scales this winter! A mammoth tusk is spotted! It looks like two, side by side! However, not so exciting news. They are way up a cliff, with no easy access from the top, no easy way up from the bottom, and no place to tie up the boat. *Dang! Now what?* I decide to hang around to look over the area and make a decision later. I can decide if I want to work hard at great risk to try to retrieve what is probably $20,000 worth of mammoth ivory. *The tusks are pointed into the cliff, which is frozen, so even if I get to them, it may not be possible to get them out of the ice.* Another view is taken through binoculars. It appears someone saw the first tusk. There was more of this one exposed, and they crudely cut it off, or shot the tusk in half from below as I once had to do. *What rotten luck, dang!*

Such things are on my mind as I look up at $20,000 I shall not have, but might have if Foil was here to climb, help dig, be at the top while I am at the bottom. I tell myself once again, *There is no use counting the fish we saw, but did not catch. We can look at diamond rings in the store under glass all we want. That spendy diamond is not ours till we buy it. Likewise, the tusks are not mine unless I can get them.* Just that, gosh darn it! Is there a way to get these? I leave and look elsewhere. No valuable tusks, but some intriguing fossil bones. There is a musk ox jaw bone with teeth. I have a lower mammoth jaw with a missing tooth, but showing how the tooth fits in. In the mud under a log I find a musk ox horn and partial skull, probably a match to the nearby jaw. In a creek bottom running through the mine claim I am on, are three matching mammoth vertebrae still connected. There is an assortment of scrap bones. A few specimen bones. The scraps sell wholesale by the pound for ten dollars a pound. It takes a lot to make any money. I'd like to find enough to sell, to make enough to pay for my trip. Fossil hunting as I do it is interesting from the standpoint of availability.

The water level rises and falls by the day. Fossils get buried, uncovered, recovered, and uncovered again almost hourly. What I find is not likely available tomorrow. What disappears is often gone forever downriver, buried in the mud randomly, never to be exposed to the air again. I can only speculate how much disappears, and what percent I salvage.

It is doubtful I can get over $500 for everything I have so far. I have walked away from plenty of tusks over the years. Money is not my God. I have said this many times. In this case it means I am not willing to drastically alter the land to get my fossils. No bulldozers, blasting, major excavating of any kind. I try to be satisfied with what falls in the water on its own, or is about to, and easy to get.

My tent and sleeping bag get well dried out in perfect, late season hot weather. I feel so glad to be outdoors now. Fall colors are pretty, with yellow poplar, dark red willows, and bright green spruce. A lot of pictures are taken that have money value as well as beauty to me. Two more nice wood burls are found. I see a good twenty eagles and thirty swans. How beautiful. I'm thinking of a time frame, and how long I want to stay. I have looked at the edge of the dropping water several times. This is the third time I am covering this same ground, looking at a slightly lower water level each time, 'just in case.' In case a fossil fell from the cliff in the water and has been under water most of the summer, just now being exposed as the water drops!

A section of tusk is spotted! I am elated! *Yes, the trip is paid for!* I know right away this is ivory, by the shape and color. Right at the water line. All I have to do is lift it into the boat. A nice dark fifty pound section. This will have the coveted blue the buyers want. Fossils in this area have been carbon dated between 40,000 and 60,000 years old. This looks like a fossil on the older side. Around the tusk are spruce cones, ferns, a prehistoric mouse nest. These items speak of the times the mammoth lived in. A bog with spruce trees, the edge of a swamp with ferns. Mice stored seeds under tree roots. Sometimes there is a hint as to how the animal died. In this case, there is only a partial tusk that fell from someplace up higher. I look up the cliff for evidence of more of this animal, but it has all fallen in the river and washed away. The sun shines through bent over trees on top of the cliff. Swallows fly in and out of mud holes. A hawk watches to see if one bird makes a mistake that he can take advantage of. Bird feathers at the water's edge show the hawk has his meals.

This is $2,000 worth of ivory. I can go home with at least $2,500 worth of raw fossils, and forget the two tusks in the cliff. I am tired after just a few miles of travel. I'll take a nap for a while. The boat is pulled in and tied up. I set the tent up on shore in a nice sunny flat spot of clean sand. The bright sun warms the inside of the tent as I pass out for a few hours.

On my hands and knees I doggie shuffle out of the tent, look up, and my boat is gone! My heart stops in my throat. In a panic I look around. No rope left behind. Nothing I can see to indicate a problem. However, the wind has picked up. I surmise I had not tied my boat well enough. Wind raised waves moved the boat which jerked on the rope pulling it off the tree I had it tied to. Looking downstream, I do not see my boat. Gone. It could be miles away. Could be blown to the other side of the river a mile away and I'd never see it, or I'd have no way to get at it. No other boaters have been seen, and none are expected. My camp spot is out of the main channel on the other side of the river from where boaters would normally come. Any travelers would be a mile away on the other side. I am on my own and must solve this, or perish.

All my goods and supplies are on the boat. Maybe most important, my blood pressure, diabetic pills, and food. All I can really do is start walking this side of the river and hope my boat stayed on this side, and hung up where I can find it. This however is not very likely. The only good news is, I am in a five mile slow bend that is like the letter C. There is a small chance the boat could get hung up on the upper part of the C, five miles from here. All I can do is hope. I'm already having sugar imbalance problems because this is why I had to take a nap in the first place. This might be why I was forgetful, and did not tie my boat better. I am normally not this careless.

I begin a walk that could be my forever walk. I am calm and collected, not running or in a panic. I crawl and slash up and down hard ravines filled with heavy brush. One birch on top of a bluff has a perfect exotic burl I have been hoping to find! I of course leave it behind. I come across fresh bear tracks. If the bear is in the area he will know for sure I am here, due to all the crashing. I am going through heavy alder growth. If the bear hears me and listens, he will not overlook the fact I am in trouble. I see more bear tracks of a different size. More than one bear. The fall salmon run has attracted them to the river. I am not armed, so feel very vulnerable. Uncertain if I could bluff my way out of trouble. Predators know when you are injured. If the bears are after salmon, there is at least a chance they are not hungry and not interested in me and my issues.

Good news is, I feel alert, strong, not overly tired or weak. I stop for a rest after two hours of walking. I will be ok for the day. I can make it through a night. I can make it through another day. I am sure. I am also sure this good feeling will not last more than a few days without food or pills. Freezing at night will not be good for me when trying to sleep. Though I have my tent set up, I had not needed my sleeping bag in the heat of the day. The sleeping bag is with the boat. On one of my rests, I take inventory of what I have for survival supplies. I have a few pills in a tin in my pocket, a knife, and some matches. I used to keep a fishing line and hook sewed in my jacket in the old days. I have been lax, figuring I am not likely to get separated from my boat. Still, these items I do have can be enough to help me out a lot.

I have to walk close enough to the river to be able to glance at it and see if my boat is hung up below me when I am up on a bluff. It would be easier walking further back in the taller trees with less underbrush. Brush grows low and thick near the river's edge, due to lots of water, and branches being able to reach out over the water for sunlight. Taller trees do not survive the bank erosion and wind.

Here are some Eskimo potato plants in the silt on the river cut-bank. I dig up enough for a meal with my knife. I cut a piece of birch bark peeled off the tree, folding it into the shape of a cup and lace it closed with spruce root. I get a fire going. While the fire is burning down to large hot embers, I hunt for more food. I spot a dried mushroom, some rosehips, a few cranberries. A fist size round smooth rock is set in the fire embers to get hot. I know not to choose a porous rock that might explode.

The red hot rock is set in the birch cup with creek water which comes to a boil in only seconds. The rock is fished out and the Eskimo potato is added, along with herbs and greenery. I do not add the rosehips because I want to make tea later, to ensure I am drinking lots of liquids. I have to heat the rock a second time and hold it in the cup to get the water boiling again until the potato is done. I have about half a quart of hot soup. This mix has starch, vitamins, and flavor, but no protein or calories. I could eat like this a few days, but know I would need fish or red meat sometime if I am out for many days.

I have the knowledge to make either a fish hook, or a wood fish trap if needed. I make tea, but decide it is too hard to carry and drink it all, so can now abandon the rock and cup. Another cup can be made easily at my next meal time. Now I feel full and rested. I go only another few hundred yards and see my boat! I am not sure how close to shore it is until I can get closer. Too much brush blocks my view. In a few minutes I come closer, and see it better. Through the thick alder leaves and willow branches, I see the boat is out of the strong current not far from shore, hung up on a sweeper barely at the river's edge where the bank fell down. Another birch tree with leaves still on it leans way out over the water at the height bow. The boat is gently resting up against this tree, nose into the current. Any other direction and the boat would roll over. My boat is not known for being safe and stable.

I get to the river edge and jump from one dead tree over to the live birch sweeper, then walk out along the tree trunk and step into the boat. It has gone about five miles into the top part of the 'C' as I had hoped would happen. It has been five hours including my stops since I started walking. No other boat has come by. I feel lucky, but at the same time afraid for the future if I am getting this forgetful about the boat rope when out on my own. Next time I might not be so lucky! What starts out being routine, can turn deadly very fast!

This is the very reason I want to do things slow, think about each thing I do. Load my boat carefully. Pick good weather as best I can. Not a lot of elders my age venture out alone for a week in the wilds as I do. No one knows where I am. It would be at least another week before anyone would think something has gone wrong. I feel there are more disadvantages in letting people know where I am, than advantages.

I pack up and head home! The weather stays perfect. I take many pictures of the scenery and an ocean craft stuck on a sandbar. Some gold prospectors took off from Nenana in hopes of getting to the ocean and Nome over 1,000 miles away. They went eighty miles, got stuck, and had to abandon the ship. Locals have been hearing news as the story progresses all summer. They had advised these prospectors to launch on the Yukon River where there would be deeper water! There is a road to the Yukon now. This is an ocean boat drawing four feet of water! The local barge stops and tries to help, but the boat is old and the barge captain believes his tow strap will yank the boat apart if he pulls. He does not want the liability mostly because the boat owners are adamant they can continue on their journey, do not want the boat damaged, and have a 'sue you' attitude if the boat is damaged!

The owners live on this stranded boat, digging by hand for weeks, as the water drops faster than they can dig. The boat is eventually abandoned and locals assume, written off as an insurance loss. I vaguely wonder if it is worth towing any place if I can get it free. Use it as a river home. The boat is now high and dry. I believe a car jack and some log rollers is all I would need to salvage it. A day's work could move it maybe. I decide no. I do not have any place to put it. With a round hull it would be difficult to make a stand for it so it sits upright. Or more, how would I pull it ashore if it rests on its side? I see the engine has been removed. There is now a big hole in the stern where the outdrive went. If I got it back in the river it would fill with water. There are ways to plug the hole, but the easy is getting complicated. A nice thirty-five foot, $100,000 ship is boated away from. Partly, I am not sure if I could keep it if I salvaged it.

I get a good picture of a black bear on the side hill near Manley Hot Springs. Near the Manley slough is a tent camp the size of Minto! *What is going on?* On the other side of the river is the rocky Bean Ridge. Along the shore are randomly spaced numbered signs - not like survey markers I have seen. Later I wonder if this is the university archeological sight that has been in the news. I read about the finding of dinosaur footprints in rocks at the river's edge. The village of Tanana was mentioned, but I cannot think of any rock formation along the water anywhere in this area. Bean Ridge, one of the oldest rock formations in the interior of Alaska, would make more sense. I may check this place out later. Pictures of dinosaur tracks would be cool! *If there are tracks, maybe there are bones.*

The rest of the trip is uneventful. Perfect travel weather. There is work to do as soon as I get home. The ivory must get wrapped in plastic, put in a cool place, so it dries slow. There is a lot of cleaning, sorting all the gear. I tend to forget it takes two days to get ready for a trip, then two days after getting back to clean and sort everything!

There is a routine for fossils. First, I lay them all out in the grass and spray all the mud off with the water hose. My lawn is rich green, a foot tall. While still damp, I coat the fossils with a special Elmer's glue mixture, to seal and stabilize the outside of both ivory and bone. The damp, coated fossils are placed into plastic bags and sealed. After a week of being in a cool place I turn the bags over to redistribute moisture, and cut a few holes in the bag to let some moisture out. I have to decide when each fossil gets taken out of the bag and sorted, left to dry for many months on a shelf in the storage room. I may not know the value until the item is fully dry and I see if it cracked. Then determine what shape it is in, what part of what animal, and come up with a value estimate.

A year or more may go by before items sell. A few items might sell if a buyer comes all the way to Nenana to look over what I have. Some fossils work well with the general tourist market, while others are collector items - museum type pieces. If I locate a specialty market I can get more money. Some fossils, I cut up and make knife scales. To make any serious money takes some level of skill. I have to know where to go and have some credibility as to what fossils are and what they are worth. I started out in the business selling to the local buyer, Tusk, like most of us did, for ten cents on the dollar. Many fossil hunters were, and still are, happy with this. Not many go into business for themselves.

For now, Mrs. Probation says I can have them, look at them, but not sell them. That is what I am doing. Once again, I am glad I am not financially between a rock and a hard place, desperate for money, being seriously hurt by restrictions. Many people in the system want to see me hurting. My yard has a nice hedge all around it, making it hard to see into my property. I still keep an eye out for Mad Jay doing his drive by. I am a little concerned the sky is so bright and blue. Satellites could see in and take pictures. I'd prefer a cloudy day. While Mrs. Probation tentatively says I can have fossils. I am not sure how pleased she'd be if I went out of my way to actually find and collect them. It would not surprise me if she confiscated the fossils to sell herself, or give them to someone who owes her a favor. I believe it is common to confiscate goods and not make an official report to make some side money, like the officer in Nome with the bear claws, or the eagle feathers confiscated at the homestead. I recall getting told, 'You will never see these again!' No write up, ticket, report. So it is best to not even take a chance with these fossils, and keep this to myself.

I do not let anyone know I am back for several days. Hopefully, even better, few know I was gone. Iris tells me Foil left a note on my truck down at the river, saying, "I know who you are. I know where you are, and what you are doing!" I snort in disgust. Iris removed the note. This is further evidence this guy is not a friend. He thinks I am paranoid, that such a note might freak me out, cause me to go off the deep end. It just shows me why it is good not to let on to others where your weakness might be. I assume Foil is upset I was gone, he did not know about it, nor take him with me. *Going with me is a privilege, not a right.* I lock up part of my shop so Foil does not know if I found fossils or not. He might be capable of seeing I go to jail so he can have my land. Somewhat like happened to Woman who I met in prison. Neighbors wanted and got his farm. Set him up to sell them unpasteurized milk. While he was gone he could not take care of his farm.

Foil now and then tries to talk me into selling something I am not allowed to sell. "I need a whale bone, Miles, it's a fossil! Come on, no big deal, I just want to put it up in my cabin!" Almost the same exact words the undercover agent used when wanting the dead raven. I recall having some old whale bones, but am unsure if the word fossil really applies. Old bones wash up on the beach in Nome where Dodger lives. Ages ago we traded for some. I had a market for them with Native carvers. Some bones may only be a decade or two old. Old enough no one killed the whale to sell the parts. I preferred the less expensive broken ones that collectors were not looking for that could be used in artwork or ceremonial situations by other Natives. I know whale is a button, a key in, unspeakable word from a legal standpoint. 'Save the whale' is more than a slogan. Guaranteed to get me in trouble. What is Foil thinking! He doesn't need the aggravation either.

"F%$^& the Feds, Miles!"

I explain to Foil what I explain to some customers. I had to give this some thought. "I am motivated by three factors when deciding what to do with my time, now that I am semi-retired. One: Joy, Two: Reward, and Three: Money.

"But, Miles, I need your help and you owe me. Look at all the times I helped you!"

"Obligation is not one of my motivators. Sometimes obligation fits under one of the other categories. My suggestion is that if you want work done at your convenience, when you want, how you want, then pay me." In reference to hauling supplies for him, not the whale bone.

While pay is on my mind, Iris and I collect a pile of money from Mr. Glitter in Denali Park. The culture center has a last large check for me. The local Farmers Market has gone well, and has brought me some good money on the weekends. Much end-of-the-summer income is cash, and the total is whatever I say it is.

Iris and I hang out in the morning at the senior center to read the paper and socialize. Iris gets a job there answering the phone and simple office work. It's a few hours a day, basically getting paid to do what she does most days anyhow, hang out at the seniors. It helps her be more financially independent so she keeps her own bank account. I'm happier if we are together because we want to be. Not for financial reasons. We have had some ups and downs, but the relationship seems secure and stable now. Foil had tried to split us up, making fun of me for, 'checking in' with my woman, instead of telling her how it is, not asking, as he says he treats his wife. I smile, imagining what would happen if anyone tried to tell Iris what to do! Or how it would be!

I think couples who get along should keep each other informed where they are and what they are doing. If you are gone all day or more at least! When I come home, it is nice if there is a note on the table, "Gone on a walk with Sharon, back in an hour." So I know everything is ok.

"Foil, because I like it when Iris leaves a note, it is only right to offer it in return. It's not a demand and I do not have to. This is something I want to do."

"I wouldn't put up with that, Miles. I have a good woman I do not have to answer to! I'm just trying to look out for you, Miles. You were happier out in the woods. That's where you belong!"

Maybe yes, maybe no. It's up to me to decide. Foil has an ulterior motive wanting me to be available in the wilds to help him and be a partner he depends on. Yet, appears to me to not have learned the social skills required to get what he wants. I tell Iris, "All he has to do is pay me. I think he has the money. He sees it as the principal of the matter, to not have to pay a friend."

"Maybe if you two were friends? But he's a user, friendship can't be just one way. He was supposed to help us in Tucson." Iris is still mad about that.

I told Iris, Foil said I do not need a place in Tucson, that I have my mother's. But even now, mom and I have an issue.

Iris asks me, "Miles, what are you going to do with all your stuff stored under mom's trailer?"

Mom is concerned because it is not legal to store anything under the trailer - park rules. I have nowhere to put all the totes, tables, displays and inventory we used at the shows. Mom does not have room for it. She has a shed that would hold it all, but she uses the shed to store empty cardboard boxes. It's her shed, so no use suggesting the boxes are useless, compared to my show stuff. I want her to be happy, otherwise what is the use of saying we arrive to help?

"As you say, I am now in a bind as we thought we could move our things over to Foil's trailer he says he never uses or into a shack of our own, on our own piece of land Foil helps us get." I had told mom not to worry, we are taking care of it. We had spent a little time looking around various areas for cheap land. It's a little more difficult without my regular job.

"Iris, I hate to pay for storage in Tucson!" I was in hopes there are situations in Tucson, as here in Nenana. Like the deal I got Foil. A log cabin with the land for under four grand. It is common to find trailers good enough for storage for a few hundred dollars, even free if you move them. This might require buying tires. I already got two trailers like this on my land in Nenana. Likewise, there are empty parcels of land all over, cheap enough. Normal price for a lot is $2,000. No water or power. So we keep hoping somewhere out in the desert in a more remote community with depressed economy, no work around, land might be this cheap near Tucson. A worn out camper, not road legal, that we could stay in for a month a year and store some stuff out of the weather. Basically camping for a month. Rent a car, head out most days to run around.

"Yeah, Iris, battery power, some solar panels to run my laptop computer and work on my writing. You can sew or read." We envision doing some swap meets, local shows to pay the bills, supplement our retirement. I tell her about seniors I met who own a mobile home and live in it. Travel, do craft shows along the way to pay for gas and food; a yearly circuit of shows. Each year I see them set up at the same shows. Park in a selling place, set up a table out front like at Quartzite, Arizona. It looked like a good life.

I have toyed with different lifestyle ideas. I have been with women that wanted to travel. I believed at one time I could travel anywhere I wanted in the world, and pay my way with my art work. Later, I thought, as a trader, importing/exporting. Maybe gather things from all over the world and bring them to the Tucson show to turn into cash.

I went to Germany, Kodiak, Alaska, Olympia, Washington, and other places, all paid for by selling my art in those places. I have been invited to many countries. I wanted to go to Africa for a while, to visit an African I met in Tucson who told me I could be welcome and do good business in his village with animal parts. I met a guy I still admire, who owns an opal mine in Australia. He cuts and polishes his own stones. He fit several hundred thousand dollars worth of opals in a shoebox and paid for his travels around the world selling and trading these opals. I do some business with him every year. He looked for things he could take back to Australia and sell in his area for add on value. There is a customer in New Zealand who lives on a sailboat and sells her art at docks she pulls into and supports herself. It was a brief idea to bring her raw materials she needs. She pays by putting me up for a while and I stay with her, sell my own art and raw materials in her area. Write the trip off as a business expense.

She sends pictures of a big sailboat with mountains all around. Clear calm, water. Eating lobster, scallops. Laying on a boat deck watching the sunset. Without a care in the world. Seagulls calling as I fall asleep. She sells her crafts off her thirty-six foot sailboat at a tourist dock. I had done similar off my houseboat in Fairbanks.

One version of the idea was similar to the 'stay with this gal in New Zealand.' To partner up with a smart pretty young intelligent woman as a travel companion. I bring to the table what? Adventure, opportunity. I may offer her a chance to travel, learn a trade as an apprentice, meet other people from all over. Some money, not a lot, but basic expenses paid for. She brings to the table? Her youth. Cash in on it while you can. Possibly women in other countries, in poverty areas anyplace, with little chance to get away. No money or knowledge to do so. I've met such couples at shows who are together in an 'arrangement.'

There was one young pretty Russian gal dealing in Siberian ivory interested in becoming an American. If I had been interested enough. Another young gal whose family owned an opal mine in Mexico was looking for 'a situation' in the USA with a sense of adventure. Another young woman contacted me after reading my book who dreamed of a life like mine, doing crafts, and wants to learn the trade from me. *And you are offering?* I did not really want any of this enough to do anything about it. Just choices and ideas. Thinking, *I could do this if I wanted. I have options and choices.* In truth, travel is not the most exciting thing to me.

I moved a lot growing up, so staying put appeals to me. Traveling only a month a year has more appeal. I could envision being a snowbird; having two homes. This is common enough. As for fanciful 'what if' with young women, I never actually did this when I had a chance. It may have been best to leave this notion as a fantasy! Now I have Iris and am content. She is not an outdoor companion, but I am used to being alone in the wilds, so that works for me.

Winter in Alaska has lost a lot of its appeal, since I no longer trap and spend the time outdoors as I once did. Now winter is a lot about trying to keep the shop warm enough so I can work. It's a huge expense of either time or money to heat the home and shop. Of course, winter is what keeps property cheap here. Just like summer is what keeps property cheaper in Tucson. Though I assume snowbird's nice homes sell high. Homes for the poor would be of little interest for the rich snowbirds.

This line of thought has me wondering about my own community of Nenana.

"Iris, I notice more junk yards, and storage units as well as mobile homes on properties in Nenana. People may be using cheap land and low taxes as a good place simply to store stuff, visit when weather is nice, hunt and fish, but do not live here. Much like Foil found. Such people may not care about the community, services, road conditions, police, fire, etc. The bottom line being, the cheapest taxes, minimum services. What if this represents a majority of the community?"

Iris notices there are a lot of people not dependent on Nenana for an income, or anything at all! The best of both worlds. All the niceties Fairbanks has to offer without paying taxes. Like we almost all haul and dump our garbage in Fairbanks transfer stations. There is no state tax. We all enjoy museums, plowed roads, libraries, the sorts of things taxes usually pay for. We may not care very much if these things are available in Nenana. Or we care, if it's free. Heaven forbid we are asked to pay for it!

Nenana then, may attract the poor, and those who need storage space. Our community is also known for taking care of the poor and elderly, as a village tradition. We find people jobs, take them in as 'one of us'. We put out the fire at their home, haul them to the hospital, and do not charge. If you do not pay your water, sewage bill, we forgive you, and stop trying to collect. We do not have the heart to evict you. Our clinic is free to all. Our library offers many services such as free email and computer use. Our elders get a free ride to Fairbanks once a week. We are asked to donate if we can, but that is a loose request.

We have no police, so few get arrested for things like being drunk, or normal petty incidents that are huge issues in large communities. We have few rules, laws, permits. You can build a junk shack, haul in a junk trailer, have an outhouse, no running water, and there are no laws we enforce against these things. There is no vehicle inspection, so we legally drive condemned cars with cracked windshields, spouting blue smoke. You can burn garbage, fill in wetlands, leave junk, discharge firearms, abandon cars, any number of activities forbidden in civilization. There is no borough, so not much government. You can be wanted by the law. Who checks? Who cares? You can find work. Maybe word gets around, "Come to Nenana and get taken care of, live how you want, pay nothing!" Who does that attract?

I confess this is how I arrived, as a user. I parked my houseboat, paid no taxes, or fees, and enjoyed the amenities a community offers. Showed up for free food, liked the library. Some folks who know me say I did contribute. I donated art for fund raisers, took people out on my boat for free, fed sled dogs for people, shared moose meat and fish, and such things as is called services or favors, not noticed when counting dollars.

"Miles, how did you get mixed up with the likes of Foil! You should know better! How come these kinds of people find you!" My friend, Witty wants to know. She works in mental health, so has an interest in why things happen to us.

"Witty, I think we get what we deserve. I do not put the blame on others." I think over what I feel happens and explain. It seems to me, good people who like me, understand I am a loner and value my privacy, do not impose on me. I like to be with people on my terms, with no obligations. Those who like me, accept that. Good people who do not like me simply go away. The more selfish types may not care what I think, or what I want. It is all about them and what they want. I've said before, sadly, flattery works on me. Schmooze me; sometimes I do not spot it, and fall for it. Or, I spot an ulterior motive, but do not know what to do about it. I've spotted it too late and do not know how to extricate myself from a situation. I want to give the person the benefit of the doubt. Understand their view. Think the best. Do not want to believe a person I once liked, set me up and betrayed me. I feel I get misunderstood, so I want to give others a chance.

"Miles, sometimes people end up in dysfunctional, even abusive situations because it is what they learned, know and feel comfortable with."

I'm not convinced this applies. I would not define my past as abused. "Witty, I like to think that only so much damage can be done. I manage to get free when there is absolute certainty this person is out to use me; hurt me, and does not care about me. I usually consider it more their loss than mine. What is it Foil will end up with for all his effort to use me? I think he will end up spending a lot of money and effort and never end up with the land he says he wants." He does not have enough money or time to make up for his lack of knowledge. He will need a new boat; other items he buys will not work as advertised. He will essentially go through what I did, only I had time on my side. Foil cannot accomplish in a few years what took me over twenty years. A person can make up for knowledge by tossing money at it. In my opinion, we are talking a few hundred grand. "I do not think Foil will be willing to put that kind of money into his project."

"Just wondering, Miles. You so often have people disaster stories, is all I mean."

Yes, I understand not everyone has such stories. Therefore, at least part of the problem is me! I think I am nice right up until I am not. There is not much gradient. One day you are my friend. The next day you are not, and never will be again. This might be a perceived slight you did not intend. Usually from a specific personality type - people who do not have a lot of friends—underdogs; problem people I feel sorry for. Or, who I think I can help. I, at first, think they will appreciate it. It could be I look down on them in some way. I'm happier, better in some way; offering my generosity not as an equal, but with a helping hand offered from above. That is not their perception. In their eyes we are equals, offering as much as they get. Helping me in some way. That is not my perception. There is usually nothing they have that I want. They try to convince me there is. My mistake is pretending to go along with that. Ideally, I should spell out from the beginning where we are. Yet the explanation is not that simple.

Such as with Foil. I could have said, "I do not mind offering my homestead so you can have your lifelong Alaska dream." Followed by what? "It doesn't mean we are friends?" From the get go the implication is we are not equals. Foil has a want he cannot afford. I am not in that situation. It is not me expressing a wish to do something, followed by regrets. It is not me who does not have enough money to live my dreams. I feel sorry for Foil. That may imply, 'Superior.'

In my defense, he seemed to play into that role. I am his mentor. He desires my knowledge. He admires and looks up to me. This is what he expresses when he wants something. The truth might be, he feels superior to me, and I am a sucker. I deserve to be conned for having the nerve to act superior to him. It's hard to know what is going on. Witty would not have an opinion without more information. She just wants me to think about it, so I learn something and move towards 'recovery', get away from a possible addiction to being a victim.

"I'm only saying, Miles, not everyone has these issues with relationships."

I have noticed, those people who are my true friends have never said we are friends! They simply 'are.' I am usually suspicious when someone tells me they are my friend, or tells me they love me. I prefer showing me, with less talk.

I can blame Iris! Why not! It is she who accepted Foil's favors. Visited, stayed at his house, accepted firewood from him. Created obligations. I repeated several times I would be happier if Iris burned fuel oil while I was in prison. We got a bunch of free fuel on some kind of senior program or whatever. Our friend Valerie explained and signed us up. The firewood that Foil cut turned out to be wet, rotten birch that did not burn and created problems. Worth about nothing. Not Foil's fault. We did not blame him. He simply does not know our kinds of wood. He lives in a desert.

Foil asked me what he could do for me. There is nothing I want or need. I pointed to dead trees in the back yard. I suggested he cut these for Iris's firewood and clean up the back yard in doing so. He did not want to. He preferred going out exploring in the woods, and indirectly haul wood, saying that was his primary goal, helping us. Using my four wheeler, saw, and gas. I'm pretty sure he used the four wheeler to go exploring and entertained himself exploring the country. In my view, bringing back some wood was payment for the use of my equipment. So what does one do when it comes out, "You owe me big time, Miles, I cut wood for your wife!" In most cases I smile kindly, agree, make it right, and have nothing to do with that person again. I do not like the other options I see.

"YOU HAVE A BAD LIVER. Do you drink?" I'm surprised, I never drank. The VA doctor, "You have the liver of an alcoholic." She reviews my records.

I say, "I have had a physically hard life. The liver cleans out poisons? I work with a lot of toxic chemicals in my work. Acetone, fiberglass resin, nitric acid, welding fumes, just off the top of my head."

"That'll do it!"

I just add, "Hmmm."

"Your diabetes is much worse, Miles, what's going on?"

I'm discouraged. "I eat good foods. We grow it ourselves and eat fish, wild game. Hardly anything from a can."

"It is also about balancing sugars, carbs, and proteins, Miles."

"Yes, I'm on top of that."

"So, what changed in the past couple of years?"

"Prison."

"Ah, yes, that explains it. We see a lot of this. Not good food or care in prison." I explain how I worked it out so I was in the garden and able to steal garden foods when I could.

"Probably saved your life, Miles, but even so, a lot of damage was done."

"Yes, I knew it at the time. I'd get dizzy, not able to feel my feet, almost pass out. Be without medicine for days and weeks at a time."

"That can kill you, Miles."

"Yes, I guessed that."

"Well, all we can do is work forward with what we have!"

I'm guessing ten years was taken off my life because of six months in prison. The quality of my life will never be the same. "I'd rather stay away from a life on insulin for as long as I can. I want to manage diet and use pills if possible." I'm sixty-four years old.

She wants to know more before agreeing. "Do you get depressed? Stay away from people, need naps, feel disoriented?" I look away and do not want to answer. Shrug my shoulders. I've always been such an optimist throughout my life. People expect it of me; depend on me. It's what I give. Without hope and optimism what is there? Well. I am not a quitter.

Iris and I see a diabetic diet expert as part of the VA program. "I want Iris in on this, since she is the cook and takes care of most of the food."

The dietician says, "I agree, you can't do this alone."

Iris has been frustrated. "You can't eat this, you can't eat that, geez!" Angry. As if I make this up. I get sugar counts up over 300 when under 100 is normal and desired. I'm aware that levels over 300 will kill me. It's a matter of what organ will fail first. Liver it looks like. Usually that, or pancreas, kidneys. But the biggest concern is losing my feet, or my eyes. That'd be a bummer. None of it is pretty. Already living in a world of pills. That's for old people. I do not really feel old, just sick. The sort of sick where I should be able to get over this. The doctor puts me on another medicine as long as I watch my sugar numbers. If I take this medicine when I shouldn't, it will kill me. The only reason she allows it at all is because I obviously am conscientious, take my sugar numbers regularly and seem responsible enough not to kill myself with these pills.

I take one, and my sugar drops 100 points in fifteen minutes, as advertised. As in "dang!"

"It tells your pancreas to give insulin."

I'm guessing the good news is, my pancreas still works. The other simpler medicine tells my liver to do something. My liver is not responding. But if things work out, it is possible for the liver to heal. *Yeah, right.* After talking to the diet expert, I have a better idea what went wrong, and why.

"It's partly genetic. My dad died of this and mom has issues." I tell Iris it might have to do with my wilderness diet! Supposedly so healthy! What can be better than natural foods right off the land! Well it is rarely balanced. For an eight month winter there is no fresh greenery. Lots of moose meat! I recall eating an entire 1,000 pound moose in a winter - up to five pounds a day. High animal protein diet. Over a long period of time.

Vegetarians say, "No meat at all! Bad, bad, bad for the body!" I do not believe it. But I do believe in moderation and balance. High animal protein is harder to digest, harder on the body than vegetables. I bragged I lived on a food budget of $300 a year! Proud of it! But common sense tells me $300 does not buy good quality food to mix with my moose. I did not buy junk food, but bulk flour, rice, corn meal, whole grain rice. A lot of carbs; extremely few vegetables in winter. A dozen cans of corn. Maybe a few bags of frozen vegetables.

Later in life when I had good gardens, I could put up squash, dry celery, carrot tops, pickle beets, turnips, and such. Possibly a bit late in life. There was at least a decade or two of no vegetables or greenery. Nor vitamin supplements. I was healthy and sort of diet conscious.

"Like my walk out where I had to live on sugar and berries for five days and almost died. I bet a lot of damage was done then!" I learned not to depend on Crisco, lard, or white rice! Luckily early on or I might be dead now! My thinking at the time is, "I eat wild game from the land, how wrong can I be with this?" Primitive people do not have degrees nor are they experts in diet! I followed the good food rules!

"If it's advertised on TV do not eat it! Eat what your grandmother ate."

I recall a simple quote, "Eat it if it is from a plant. Don't eat it if it is made in a plant!"

I lacked the vitamins, vegetables, greenery. When young I said, "Oh well! Nothing is perfect! I'm healthy. So what's all the fuss!"

Possibly nothing especially wrong was done. When we get older, things begin to fail. It's called getting old. I have a recollection of the last time I saw my father. My son Mitch noticed, too, and commented. We were all at the dinner table and it was desert time - homemade apple pie and ice cream. Dad's wife tells him he can't have any because of his diet. I ate mine and did not pay attention to anyone else. Dad quietly got up from the table without excusing himself. I saw him as he went up the stairs. Slow, depressed, discouraged, with an expression of, "If I can't eat homemade apple pie what good is life?" He was dead not long after. I suspect he killed himself. Or, simply stopped taking his pills. Same thing. I understand. I'm puzzled his wife did not happily offer him a desert substitute, like the pie made with a sugar substitute, diet ice cream, ice milk. There are foods that can be eaten that taste good. Why didn't she serve him any? I do not think she liked him.

I am determined to be stronger. Unlike my father, I have reasons to live, things to live for! It is hard mentally to be stronger than my father. He was a god difficult to live up to! It has always been me who was the idiot, the weak one, the one the family is embarrassed to be related to. That's a lot to overcome. So, not abused as Witty suggests, but a self worth issue, but only when around people. Alone, without family, works much better when we are young! I smile. When we get older, slow down, get more needy, it is harder to face it all alone.

Well, I was not totally without compassion for others in my life. I have the memory of the church lady in Galena. I thoughtlessly ran thorough the wild roses in her yard. She burst out in tears. I was puzzled.

"When we are young, we trample the roses. When we get older, we stop to smell them. They smell better after being trampled."

She threw her hands up and cried harder. But then laughed. "So true," she said. "You dear boy."

I had not meant to upset her. It never occurred to me until then, anyone would mind running through the roses. Good grief, isn't that why God put roses along the path? For children to run through? I was forever more careful after this. I liked this old nun. I would not hurt her on purpose for the world! But yes, civilization is all about guilt. God would say, "Yes, my child, that is why I put roses along the path, for children to run through." You'd think a nun would know that. Anyhow, here I am, I have arrived. I am now that nun. Cussing kids for making too much noise and running!

"Running of all things! Can't their parents teach them to mind! Where have manners gone!" Actually, this sounds more like Iris than me. It is me who says, "Now now dear, we were all young once, can't you remember?"

"These silly new fads! What nonsense!"

I smile. "Hey, Honey, do you recall when the Beatles came along? Our parents thought it was the end of the world! That horrible long hair! Those bell bottoms! What a disgrace! That horrible music without a beat, just loud!" Today, that would be like insulting Beethoven. *Roll over Beethoven, by the Beatles, remember?* So I smile.

When my parents were little, the world was coming to an end when saddle shoes came out. That horrible jazz! It gave them the shivers, what the world was coming to! Yes, all parents I think. All the way back to, "That disgraceful leopard skin loincloth Thor is encouraging us to wear! That ugly flint object on the end of his wood spear! I tell you, the Gods are not pleased and there will be a reckoning!" When the flood came it was proof all right! Caused by the wickedness of others! All about eating that silly cloven hoofed beast!

I nod with understanding and say to the young, "I'm not convinced so much has changed in the past 10,000 years." Or, "The older I get the less I know."

My son Mitch was disgusted with how stupid adults are. I agreed! Smiled and nodded! My father would have slapped me and put my head through the wall for talking back to him, or questioning him. Well... maybe not. It would depend what mood he was in. I say to my own Mitch, "Enjoy this time son, it only comes once in your life. You will never be smarter than you are now. Right now, you know everything! I did too when I was your age. It's a great time in life! When you are my age, you will be certain of nothing." Very little is an absolute fact set in concrete. I laugh and my son looks at me like I'm an idiot. *Adults are so stupid!* It's true. I enjoyed life a lot more when I knew everything. Picasso said the day before he died, "I think I'm beginning to get the hang of this art thing.'

Another winter begins. They all seem the same. A late freeze though.

"Miles, did those National Geographic guys ever get hold of you?"

"No, I do not expect them to." I can see what they are after. I can't provide it. Let the young kid, Jade, deal with it. *When you know how to do things, you don't have adventure anymore.* Like Jade and the film crew not having to be breaking down and floating like they did! But it was exciting! What good footage! Yes, I imagine. I do not float anymore. I get to where I want to go. Who wants to hear about that?

I tell Iris the latest. "Jade tells me they are filming him out on the river ice with the dog team."

"Is there ice, Miles, I thought the river is still open?"

Yes, the river is still open. But there is some thin shelf ice along the shore. If one of the dogs decides it needs a drink of water and heads just one foot over, they all die. Likewise, the river is dropping, leaving no water under the ice to support it. There is a good chance this thin ice will break. If it does, no one can save Jade. Due to the current, if the ice breaks and he goes down, he will be under the ice in about two seconds.

"That would make great film footage!" The end of Jade. He'd be a hero! If he makes it or not, this is where the high Jesus factor comes in. Like with me. I did stuff like Jade as well.

A WEEK GOES BY.

I am out at a back slough on the river with the snow machine. Sort of frozen. I head out on the slough, but see some wet patches, some freshly frozen spots. I decide to come back. What is out there at the end of the line I need to get to, that is worth the risk? There are other days. But yes. When I was Jade's age I would have smiled, "Because it is there!" *God protects the young and foolish. But at some point God expects us to smarten up and take care of ourselves so He has more time for the foolish. At some point it is time to pay God back for all the jams He got us out of when we were young. Time to do God's work.*

Next day I go down to 10$^{th}$ Street to look at the river. Maybe cross to see what firewood is available over there. I have been crossing the Nenana River here for forty years. Doyon is running water on the ice to get it thicker so they can take heavy equipment across to drill for oil. I see the bridge pilings in the river and wonder now if the bridge will get finished, and who will own it. The water being pumped on the ice looks deep. My opinion is, there is too much water being pumped for the temperature conditions. The weight of the water on the ice will push the ice down into the river and the water under this ice will erode the ice and make it thinner rather than thicker.

I was going to cross, but I stare a long time and decide I will not cross; not safe. It is very rare I do not go when I come down to cross! In a thousand crossings, I can think of only three times I decided not to cross. I run into Jade at the café.

"Miles, I came across the Nenana this morning. I heard the ice crack and looked behind me, and there was a huge open hole! Turbulent current gushed up! Just two weeks ago the ice was measured three feet thick there!" I may have made it across as Jade did. But if so, coming back would be an issue with a hole to negotiate around.

Also, pulling a load of wood in a sled, and being so much heavier than the dog team, might have created an even bigger hole, even a hole that gobbled me up. This is an odd year for river ice. The swamps are all soft. There are open leads in the ice in main Tanana River channel. I ask Jade about the National Geographic film. I think a series called, "Life Below Zero."

"Well, they did not leave me with a snow machine as promised. I'm a little upset. They said they did not want the liability. Yet, the entire crew got their own snow machines. I have not been paid all I was promised. The film guy told me I need to boycott and refuse to do the next episode without a pay increase." Jade and I agree this kind of world is not what we understand, nor believe in. He went ahead with filming because it needed to get done, and lost his ability to negotiate. Jade is not getting paid much, and thinks he is being played for a sucker. Another Indian family who was filmed got screwed even worse, the film guy tells Jade, 'anytime they can save a little money, the company person that saves the money gets a pat on the back." I tell Jade of my own similar experiences long ago.

"Yeah, Jade, I had to bring the film crew out to my homestead once by snow machine. They did not even pay for my gas. I had to feed them at my expense."

I recall their reply, "We do not pay the subjects of our stories! It should be enough that they get the advertising!" At the time I am looking at a well paid pilot, film crew, all making top dollar. Would they be happy with just the advertising? I was young. Life was not about money. I did not care so much. Money comes and goes when you are young. I was a star, and that was enough.

"They flattered me instead of paying me." Jade thinks he needs a lawyer. We both wonder what kind of life that is! He's a film star, and getting paid chump change. *I heard this is similar to musicians and rock stars.*

"I feel like a lower class person." It seems as if much of this issue is about class discrimination. "No, Miles, I have not even seen the episodes. I do not have electricity or TV. I get feedback on Facebook. It sounds like it is all edited to suit what they think will sell. It's not the reality we are filming, and that I want to show. There are a lot of negative comments from the public apparently. I'm not sure if it is Alaskans who understand what a farce it is. I'm not sure who is complaining!" Jade is vague, as he is not sure why or what the problem is. Just angry people, who do not leave their real name."One comment had to do with me looking like a bum with long hair."

I am puzzled. The story is about a lifestyle, not a beauty contest. "If you had a suit and tie on, Jade, there would be those who would complain you do not look like a wilderness type."

National Geographic admits Jade and the episodes are worth millions. The film crew even says, "It's not real money, we just spend it. It's limitless." So yeah, why can't they keep the hero happy? What's another few thousand to them? Nothing. It's the principal of the matter. That would never do, to set a precedence and actually pay the subjects of the films. Jade tells me how much this dedication to the film is costing him in terms of affecting his life.

"I have to live for this show alone. I cannot get into my foot races. I have to give up my old boat. I had to acquire ten more sled dogs. I had to cut trails open we need to use for filming." Jade had to build a smokehouse to make it all look good. It's a full time job. He should not be broke. "It is costing me $100 a day to feed the sled dogs." He wants the best food so he can win the race coming up that will be filmed. "The good news is, I am writing to four fine chicks who think we are soul mates, and are in love with me!" Yes, that's what happens when you are a celebrity. I tell him some of my adventures and encounters. *All just pleasant memories now.* Yes, it's all about youth! We talk about the city mayor. It's the talk everywhere. Who is running, who is a write in. There is an upcoming debate of candidates.

"Alley wants to turn Nenana into a Native only village."

"I heard that. No way can he win anyhow."

"Well, if he gets all the Native vote?"

"Tripod runs against him, he'll win."

I say I agree and add, "He does well with the Ice Classic, really smart. My main concern is he has never showed up at a city meeting. Why? I like the idea of getting the Natives and Whites together in our community. He is Native, but seems to get along with everyone. It could help unite us!"

"I agree Miles, except for one thing. I think Tripod is lazy. Not good considering the situation the city is in!"

"For sure I would not want Books to win! What a nut case!" We agree she has a hidden agenda that is not good for the community.

"An axe to grind."

"If she is as good an good accountant as she says, how come she does not have a job, and got fired as a waitress at the Mondo?" I'm not sure the average voter will know, ask, or care. "The last idiot promised us a swimming pool and we voted him in! Geez!"

"Why didn't you run, Miles?"

"Can't, I'm a felon" This is not totally true, but works as a short simple answer. I think I would not be good for the job. I'm not good with numbers. I'm a bit of a maverick, not a good rule follower. I forget names, dates, times, places. Those are not habits good for a mayor! I get along with the various groups of our community. I know what is going on for the most part. I even understand politics better than most in our community. I'd care, be honest, work hard. I know how to delegate and could surround myself with those who make up for my faults. If I wanted the job bad enough. Not sure I want a regular job with regular hours. I'd rather glide into retirement doing the things I enjoy, and live within my means. Being Mayor does not pay a lot. Well thirty-five grand a year. I think I can make that doing things I enjoy.

"How is business anyhow, Miles?"

"Well, we were talking about the river ice, the global warming issue. I notice the river is changing without the permafrost to hold it in place. This helps the fossil business. Provided I can get back into that one day. For now, work is slower than I'd wish, but I'm not hurting." Getting a lot of visits on my web site, but no sales. Bean thinks my hits are just robots not people customers. I might discover if this is so or not. There are statistics that show how long the visits are, if they are new or repeat, and if they went to other pages. I think even where they arrived from, like a google search, or typed in, which might indicate they see it printed someplace like my business card. I just haven't studied on it much.

Part of the reason is, I do not favor all the information gathering. I go to buy something on Ebay. I do not like the fact buyers can know who I am, where I live, what search words I used, how long I visited, on what pages, what I looked at and did not buy, how long I looked. Put all this in an analyzing program and profile me, so I may be targeted later. If I do not like it done to me, I am reluctant to do this to others. This is a new concept.

When I walk into a physical store I hand over cash. It would be rude to even ask my name. Much less, "How long were you in the store? What did you look at and not buy? Who sent you to this store? What is your income? What ethnic race are you?"

"I just came in for a candy bar, geez!"

I REALLY PREFER to make stuff, then sell it. Most artists would prefer someone else sell it. Most of us never get the right situation. Those in a position to sell for us, like an agent, want a 60% fee. The shop wants 50%, so that means I owe 10% out of my pocket! Ha! Anyhow, it usually works out I get 10%. That could work if I import from China at ten cents on the dollar. It's tough on those who do handcraft locally. There are fewer of us.

"The issue is similar to what you face, Jade, a class issue. I am not convinced the issue is racial as some feel."

"Partly, Miles. Indians, Blacks, Mexicans, any minority will not be treated equally. However whites who choose to live like a minority will be treated even worse!"

Maybe. I see something else when I speak of art sales. "Long ago there were no malls in the area." If someone needed a knife, they came to the local knife maker; we all did. He could make a living. Now we mostly go to Walmart. 'Look at this cool knife I got for $3.99!' With a free sheath. It's difficult to know how that is done. The blank steel I get wholesale is at least five dollars. An unfinished sheath is $15. Does the price really come down so much when you can buy a million of something? Commerce is interesting all right. The Walmart knife is not horrible. It's ok, it does the job.

"Miles, I notice a lot has to do with what we get used to as a standard. Who really needs a good knife anymore? If it is no better than a butter knife, who would know? It cuts string and looks cool!"

One solution to keep my costs down on lower end knives, is to look for worn out knives selling for under three dollars at thrift stores and garage sales. I bust the handle off with a hammer, refurbish the blade on the grinder, then sander. I acid etch something cool on the blade after sanding off the maker's name. I etch my own name on, put a new handle on from local materials. Total time two hours, selling price $50.

"Why are you telling me this, Miles. Why are you getting into the details?" I suppose not many people get into the details of their lives. 'Who cares!'

"Many people have a dream of living a life as we do." I begin. First, we have this in common, living the Alaska dream. Jade nods. I go on. "'How do you do it! Tell me!' Said with envy that I have no boss, spent most of my life doing as I wish out in the wilds, hunting, fishing, building cabins, and such. There are those like Foil who have ideas on how it is done and set out to do so! There are young ones like you, Jade, with a dream setting out in life to make your mark. All of us have certain things that are a must in order to make it work! One of the biggest issues is, how to make money to buy the basics! There are few jobs in the wilds. People like Foil are older and have a secure job that makes them enough money to live two lives. Not everyone is so lucky. There are disadvantages to taking this on when past mid life, as it is a physically hard, dangerous learning process best suited for the young, strong and healthy. You are getting paid at least a little to record this life."

However Jade is not in charge; he has to dance to some else's tune to get paid. Jade is not offering the true product he wants to offer. "It is similar to being the artist, Jade. My customers or the shops who sell my work have to be pleased. How will I sell a knife that cost me $15 in parts, for under $5?"

"What you do, that's cheating, Miles!"

Hmm. "Life is cruel don't you agree? I'm cheating who? Myself? I can stay afloat without asking for a hand out. Am I cheating my customer?" For those who want cheap, cheap, and even cheaper, I have a deal for them! I do not call it cheating. If anything, the customer thinks they are cheating me, thinking I am working for ten cents an hour, and how they got a slave to work for them! I rework a blade so it is worth more. I may reshape it, add art work, get rid of the plastic handle, and add value with a good handle. It's worth what you pay.

"For those who want better than cheap, I have all levels." I explain and show, "Here is a hand forged blade, custom edge hardened, triple tempered, cryo cold treated. This is a one of a kind, hand drawn design, never to be repeated." The final product is about five times as good as the cheap. The ordinary person has never seen a blade as good as my best custom. It costs. Good steel costs more as a raw material than the cheap finished knife. It takes time to build. For you, a special deal, $500. It's all about telling me what it is you want. I am here to fill that need. "What's the problem? Why should anyone feel cheated?"

An artist, maker, or company tends to get known for a certain product of a certain quality. We associate that product and quality with the name brand. We do not expect the guy who sells us our diamond wedding ring to also sell glass diamonds and brass metal to our children. It is unusual to see three dollar blades, on the same table as $3,000 blades. It's something to think about, being adaptable, able to sell to whomever shows up in a remote area. The audience is not as big as we expect in civilization. My role can be much like that of the traveling salesman of long ago. A sucker for the child, a cure for rheumatism for the elderly, washing machine for the wife, new rifle for the father. The concept seems normal to me.

"So Jade, what about these women?"

He brightens up. "One - from Italy, tall, short dark hair, skinny but good looking, cheerful, likes to work hard. She wants to take care of the sled dogs for me while I train. She will be here in two weeks, stay a month and then Gretchen from Germany is coming." Jade has three women lined up for this winter. "To see how it goes, if anything works out they can come back next winter. How many did you try out, Miles?"

I'm not sure I'd word it that way, but not going to debate the wording. "Well, into the dozens anyhow."

"Did any work out?"

"They all worked out, Jade. Or mostly we parted on good terms, and each got out of it what we put into it." *For the most part.* "Some were fans, arrived with ideas about what life would be like with a real Mountain Man. I had my own ideas of what life might be like with someone who worships you."

"Yeah, I know what you mean. These women would do anything for me!" *Sometimes the reality is better than the dream, but more often there is a reason something has been just a dream up until now.* I do not tell Jade my thoughts, he looks so happy in his fantasy.

**Past Flash**

My memories back to the land ideas begin in the late 1950s. A whole generation began to tune in and drop out. Donovan's 'Sunshine Superman' song is the inspiration for the name of my business, 'Sunshine Jewelry'. Previously the rage was industry and high tech. Babies are getting fed new space age formula, better than breast milk. Electric toasters, TV, refrigerators are all the rage. Man headed for the moon, and got there. Even the sky is not the limit! Women do not have to be mothers, so can compete in the work force for the first time since fighting for these rights beginning in the late roaring 1920s and prohibition days, the depression.

I talked to my grandmother who lived those days… and remembers. There were no public lavatories for women back then; if she had to go potty she had to go home. Women did not shop. They went to the store with a list and picked up what was on the list. Women were not out by themselves unescorted. My mother was born into an age where women begin to work and be free! Have money not handed to them by the husband who earns it and doles it out. The industrial age became filled with gadgets. Mostly for women to ease the drudgery. Gadgets men had to pay for. In time, the woman of the house had to help pay for a new way of life as a jet setter. Women wanted to have fun! No more drudgery, let the machines do that!

The beginnings of serious pollution begin to surface - the price for industry and free enterprise. Civilization used the ocean as a dump. I lived in upstate New York when the Love Canal caught fire in the late 60s. A generation of babies not breast fed did not bond to their mothers, bonded to sucking drugs instead. Capitalism and fast paced industry has a price. This is a major wake up call.

Hippies speak of going back to the land, our roots, the basics, before all the problems. Perhaps unaware there were problems being left behind and is why there was an industrial revolution! Hippies are hopeless dreamers. Fox Fire books and the Whole Earth catalog came out, along with the Mother Earth magazine. *Before it became a yuppie magazine.* There was serious information on sources for hand tools, basic life without industry. How to build log cabins, fireplaces, bow and arrows, and where to get the parts, tools, knowledge. A whole young generation began to protest against capitalism, industry, progress. We were just radical hippies. Supposedly just a small troublesome minority. So the news media said.

There were some serious protests that got things changed! The Black Panthers were a serious group to contend with. Environmental groups like Greenpeace got started in the early 70s. There was Martin Luther King. I remember. I was just arriving in Alaska when 'Save the whale and the seal' was in the limelight. Ramming whale ships, spray painting seals so the fur had no value, putting spikes in trees to stop tree cutting; stuff like that became news worthy as the actions of a new age.

Deforestation of the Amazon forest made news in the 80s. Along with a newly discovered hole in the ozone. I never heard any success stories about these drop out teens and the communes they formed. All I heard in the news was the bad stories. How one leader got his group to drink drug laced cool aid and all died. Other such happenings. Charles Manson and his group started as a tune in, drop out, down with capitalism, waving peace symbols, playing Bob Dylan, back to basics group.

It was not until 2014, I began hearing in the news some success stories of these drop out hippie groups! Some went to Patagonia, and created their own society, still in existence today! Another place out west got started by some hippie glass blowers doing it as something cool while tripping on acid. Now a world famous glass blowing college. One of the best in the world. It's all on Nova now; not when it was happening! Glass blowing was part of a 'back to nature life,' where they grew their own food, had their own money system, and form of local government.

If I had known the truth, I might have been interested in joining some commune. As it was, all I heard was horror stories while at the same time embracing the basic concepts of conservation. I assumed if I am going to do anything about it, I will be on my own. I am not interested in being someone violent or radical the government would want to kill. I love my country and support my government. In 1988, the world passed the 350 parts per million carbon dioxide limit in air worldwide that the scientists said was the tipping point to being unhealthy. Ordinary people became concerned, not just hippie radicals. Problems could no longer be ignored. Problems that big companies and the government had been trying to hush up and downplay since the 60s. Back when police water cannoned protesting crowds, beat protesters up, and put them in jail. Called the facts lies. Covered up things like cigarettes kill you but make a lot of money.

Big companies got sued, lost cases. My guess is, did not give up and did not accept defeat. But learned an important lesson. They began profiling. Predicting who was likely to end up a problem. Nip it at the bud. Quietly auditing people of interest who suddenly found themselves in trouble with the IRS, or some other issue. The bottom line being, dealt with or silenced, before they could form groups, gain support, lead mobs. Before they could become martyrs.

Climate change became real, when a 1985 record heat wave hit and killed people. Events like Hurricane Katrina became yearly events. Yet, there has still been little meaningful legislation, even with public understanding we need to do something. Pollution and waste is big money.

Flower children of the 60s saw this all along; saw this coming. We talked about it; what could we do about it? As I say, some got violent. Some left the country in groups to form their own lifestyle closer to nature and less wasteful with farms using horses and heirloom seeds and such. My answer was to leave civilization. Live a life I thought would not be such a big part of the problem. Thinking, I cannot make others do anything, nor should I. All I can do is take care of myself and do what I think is right. Be right with myself. At best, set an example. I am not responsible for what the rest of the world decides. Basically the same idea as the communes, only I did it alone. Again, I did not know any successful communes existed. The mountain-man became my symbol, for a while, of being in tune with the land, as a nomadic subsistence individual. Indians were ok too, but they did not do it alone, they had entire tribal and family support. Indians have nothing in their culture about holding those who live alone in reverence. Life on the reservation did not seem to me to be getting back to the land and life of freedom. I was not hearing about free Indians off on their own.

Anyhow, *I am the wrong race, I cannot be an Indian.* Living in the old way, of the Mountain Men through a list of TV programs like Daniel Boone, Davy Crocket, Jeremiah Johnson, Grizzly Adams and more. I was not trusting anyone. I suspected I was being fed lies from every angle. Who to trust? Myself.

It took until 1992 for a first world wide climate change summit meeting. Most of us knew there were serious problems when the Love Canal caught on fire! Big health investigation. A third of the children born in the area had birth defects. Horrible smelling chemicals seeping up into basements. A government study showed no direct link. Just a random bunch of sick people. I never drank or smoked. I ate off the land. For decades, the only food from a can or package amounted to about a can a month. I bragged that garbage I accumulated for an entire year filled one garbage bag. I recycled, looked for everything used, made it myself. 'New' is not even a positive word. It says to me 'bummer. Too bad I had to get it new.' For decades, no electric, no phone, no credit, no bank account, no ID.

Until forced to have these things. Forced out of a lifestyle. Trying to look at the bright side. See the good in it, trying to adjust, Seeking the merit in civilization since there is now no choice. Jokingly ask you to picture Tarzan in modern society getting arrested for everything he stands for. No permit for the monkey, etc. So! I am in civilization. I give it a try! That or perish.

I see the attraction and advantages. I still believe it is not worth the price! But, I have no choice. I am in my ending years. My decisions might be different if I were twenty. If civilization goes off the cliff like the lemming, what's it to me at my age? My personal belief is it is now too late. There is no recovery for mankind. Global warming, the hole in the ozone, the polluted oceans and air, is now irreversible. Human life cannot be supported by what cannot be stopped.

It was May who said to me when she was eleven years old, "Why bother? Your generation ruined the planet. By the time I am old enough to do anything about it, it will be too late!"

This helps explain, in my mind, why elders say today's younger generation does not appear to be highly motivated. Motivated to do what? What is it we'd have them do? Besides bend over and kiss their behind good bye? Go hide where? Go where to 'get back to nature?' We have managed to pollute every ocean and all the atmosphere. Even in the far arctic, caribou eat radioactive lichen. Some animals are doing ok in high radiation in the Chernobyl area at ground zero of nuclear activity.

Certain realities ended up not being as I dreamed! Many rewards not as rewarding, but many fears not as scary once I got here.

**Past Flash ends**

As the revolutionary personalities get quieted and dealt with before they could sway others, compared to the 60s, the overall dissatisfaction of an entire civilization seems higher. It's not just a few disgruntled hotheads. It is not just gullible college kids who riot, or a few hoodlum drug addict minorities. The government appears to be scared in a different way than it used to be. It would not take a lot for a revolution. We are being disarmed, crowds dispersed, systematically moved into larger areas where we can all be watched. Police are getting twitchy fingers everywhere they go. Fear and anger is palatable in the air. Interesting. I envision sitting in my rocking chair overlooking my garden, and watch it all out there in the street with interest. I've already been carted off in chains and returned as a warning I would not be treated so nice next time. I smile, "Josh! Remember when the motorcycle gang tried to take over Healy down the road?"

Josh is riding a bike now for health reasons, and shows up to visit Jade at the river. He recalls, "The old miners and trappers sitting in their rocking chairs pulled out shotguns and said, 'I don't think so!' Ran them off! Remember?" Josh chuckles. He does not believe in gardens and putting food by.

There was the kid in Manley, named Joe. Same conversation so many years go, who told me, "Nope, not gonna put anything up or stockpile. When it's all in the fan, I'm going to take it from people like you, Miles!" Dead now, didn't live a year after that. Killed by someone just like him. Life is like that.

Josh thinks he can retreat to his remote homestead. He has a new generator. I think one of the first supplies to fail us will be fuel. Though it may not be individuals who survive, but groups of like minded people working together. But breathing and drinking what? Under what kind of weather conditions? Tune in and drop out in the 60s like I and others did will no longer work. The entire planet is polluted now.

"It's possible, Josh, ending times have already begun. It starts with few jobs, unreliable and expensive necessities not all of us can afford. Those that have, skimming off the top, and those that do not have, restless and resisting."

Josh thinks it is a bible prophesy, and tries to look for the predicted signs. "So Miles, who will rise from the East?"

I assume it's a prophesy. "What will the mark of the beast be Josh? Have we already accepted it?" I think it's our Social Security number, but Josh says it has not been tattooed on our forehead. *Yet.* "Chips are coming, Josh!"

Bean thinks cash and money are almost over. "Too much counterfeiting going on to keep up with, Miles." He's a banker, accountant, money advisor, so he should know more than I do. Certainly the technology to implant credit and identifier chips in us is here. Fingerprint scans; eyeball scans, both here. Facial recognition computer programs are already here, and being used. I believe there is a file on everyone. I'm not sure how the information is used. I'm guessing cautiously, *for now.* I believe information is gathered even if not admissible in court. Decisions are based on our profile. Ninety percent we do ourselves on Facebook, twitter, social media on the web. That's where the police and government goes when it wants information. The government is the spider that built the web in the first place.

If there was the threat of a revolution, I think it would take only a matter of hours to compile a very accurate list of everyone in the country who does not like our president. The list may already exist. Word recognition. Associate the presidents name with a negative word. Look at every past email and every past phone call. The capability is there and being used already. A program searches, not human eyes.

Our local trooper got on the computer while I was in the office in answer to a question. "Did Kelly come back to Nenana? Has anyone found her yet?"

A warrant is out for her arrest. Facebook has her friends listed; where they live, as well as their comments as to what she is doing, who she has visited. I see it on the screen along with the police. Friends who do not know there is a warrant out speak openly about all of her activities. Parties they saw her at. Who her latest boyfriend is, and where he lives. What kind of car she is driving - with pictures. It occurs to me, most of us have that kind of information out there in the web. It is easy to find out about most people - what your income is, where you work, where you vacation and when. What your home and car look like. What clothes you usually wear, where you hang out, who your friends are. What you care about. If you own a gun, where you keep it, how to hurt you, how to con you, gain your trust.

"You like Buddy Holly, too?! Wow! That is so weird! And you surf in Hawaii! Geez! then I bet you know Tammy?" Like that. *Now we have your confidence.*

If I was on top of my game and into it, I could look up all kinds of people in Fairbanks. "Hmm, looks like citizen X loves to cook. Wow, look at that crummy knife in her hand at the kitchen table in that one picture! Obviously, she could use a custom chef knife. She likes flowers?" Find out who her husband is and where he works. Accidentally bump into him. Come up with a reason to bring up the subject. "Hey, I ran into someone who knows your wife! Birthday coming up right? Loves to cook?" The hook and reel, "I happen to be a custom knife maker." *What are the odds, huh!? Talk about karma!* Have you thank me for a deal on a chef knife the wife will appreciate. For the bargain price of $495.

Do that about... oh... I could pull that off twenty-five times a day. Even hire other people to do it. Not guessing it's illegal. Guessing in fact it's already being done.

My concept includes really getting the wife something she wants and needs, doing all of you a favor. I can picture the same methods used to con people out of stuff they have no use for, or much worse. Ways to blackmail, control, steer people in political directions.

If I was a professional thief, I'd google your street, check where your windows are, what kind of car you have; go to Facebook, find out what hours you work, when you go on vacation. I'd scope out an escape route. I could determine if you have a coin collection, a safe. A pretty daughter. Learn enough about the neighbors to help me out, like who your enemies are. Who I could set up to be blamed, or show me any defects in my plan. You'd blame the thieving busy body bitch down the block. *Sweet!*

What would be even more cool and lucrative! *Get this!* Cruise the entire country looking for situations. Even have a computer program that brings various facts together. It's not rocket science anymore. Just google earth.

"Wow! Check it out! Jim in Atlanta had his secretary with him in Iowa at the hotel at midnight on December 1st. The car was parked there all night! I wonder if the wife, Gloria, in New York knows this? Hmm, wonder what ole buddy Jim might pay to hush that up?"

A computer program could spend 24 hours sorting data, comparing notes, finding links, connecting dots. License plate numbers, facial recognition, matched to what should be going on and seen, with anomalies that need looking into. Who is pregnant, who is attending a church not acceptable to the family.

So and so went to the synagogue instead of a church my oh my! Ooooh! It does not look to me like Buster in Hawaii can afford the car he just got. I'm guessing a guy with a computer and time on his hands could make a living in the information business. Just charge $100 a pop. I see an easy grand a day here. *If money was my God, if ethics goes out the window. It would not be difficult to get rich. Probably not illegal.*

I could picture, "Hi, Miles, I live in New York. I was on google earth and see you in Nenana, Alaska, population 300 and see you have an unregistered boat parked in front of your house. Could you explain that to me?"

It's not illegal, rocket science, or expensive. Some bum sitting on a park bench with a laptop. Would I like to donate to his 'go fund me'? Vote for Grumpy? Contribute to the Humane society?"

There are lifestyle choices to think about, in the light of changing times. I have fully explored life alone in the wilds off the grid with no rules but God's. I have explored civilization, trusting and being part of the legal process that runs our lives, working from within to help bring about changes we vote on in an acceptable, approved, accepted manner within the system. In terms of survival, are there other ways yet to explore?

**THE END OF BOOK 7**

Iris and I having fun in Denali Park.

**A personal note—**

Reviews help! If you enjoyed this book, please leave a review where you purchased it—it would be greatly appreciated!

Sign up for my newsletter, "Keeping Up With Miles," @ www.milesofalaska.com Deals, new books, comments, links to YouTube. Stay updated!

## The Alaska Off Grid Survival Series Summary

**Book 1 - Going Wild**

In 1973, I am 22 years old, and a city kid. I enlisted in the Navy and got out after the Vietnam War.

I travel to interior Alaska, a 'Cheechako' (Greenhorn) by Alaskan standards. I have been raised on Walt Disney and feel qualified to be a mountain man!

I arranged with a pilot to drop me off in the wilds of Alaska. I do not have everything I need and have things I do not need. I learn about guns, trapping, and the loneliness of living in the vast wilderness with no other humans around.

I do not see anyone for many months, then walk out of the wilds to civilization in the spring. After working odd jobs to make supply money, I return to the wilds in the fall and have a hard time my second winter. I almost die, and need to be rescued.

I decide to build a houseboat so I can travel around without having to build another cabin. I have to accept summer work in Fairbanks to pay for boat materials and work under a builder. The boat takes much longer to build than expected.

I live as a street person much of the time to keep expenses down.

**Book 2 - Gone Wild**

I have many adventures on the houseboat and acquire a dog team. There are issues with the police, a bear on my boat, and a trip to see my family who live a civilized life.

My houseboat sinks. I get lost and learn other hard lessons. I start doing artwork and end up on TV. I win a land lottery and start my first homestead.

There are mail order women, and I live with a woman and her kids. Ten people are murdered in a village we visit, and myself and the family are almost among them. Family life is more difficult than I imagined.

Fish and Game becomes a concern.

I head back into the wilderness, which leads into book 3.

**Book 3 - Still Wild**

I acquire a couple more homesteads and cut more trapline.

I give up sled dogs and enter the world of snow machine adventures.

I winter in Galena and visit many native villages. There are bear encounters, and many survival situations to learn about.

I become a serious mammoth hunter and find fossils as part of my living. I work with a land surveyor specializing in homesteads and wilderness surveys, getting paid to use my boat.

My art sells well, so I do some big shows. I become more social and understand

## ABOUT THE ALASKA OFF GRID SURVIVAL SERIES

civilization better. I see the wisdom of being accepted by others. I learn. I grow. I try to change, as the world does.

The economy changes. It is less acceptable to be a trapper. I never become totally civilized as a city person defines it, but maybe I do, relative to the life I had in book one.

### Book 4 - Beyond Wild

I am getting past just survival and doing well, even prospering. I own more than the houseboat can easily haul. Gas gets expensive. I need a new houseboat engine.

There is a homestead and trapline that keeps me in one place now. There are more bear stories and adventures into the wilds, including a 300-mile boat trip looking for mammoth tusks, which has disastrous consequences.

I find where I want to live on the Kantishna River. A river 300 miles long with about five people on it. I hang out in the native village of Nenana, spending a lot of time here.

I get my first computer and learn to build a website. People are looking at the pictures and buying my raw materials and art. This is a chance to make a difference.

Life is beautiful. Life is precious. I Dare to live it.

### Book 5 - Back To Wild

I acquire a home in Nenana and start a web store. I am forced out of my subsistence lifestyle, partly because of changes in the laws. I do some serious mammoth hunting.

Unstable power causes a lot of computer data loss. I learn by punching keys to see what happens. It takes a long time to get good enough to create a book.

I continue the Mammoth hunts. The Tucson fossil gem show and State fair do well for me.

This period of 'being civilized' that I am trying out, has advantages, but also a price to pay—a big change from the wilderness life and being alone!

I am a suspect in a murder investigation. Another trapper tries to move in on my territory. There are neighbors and infringements on my property.

I fear I cannot change who I am. There is difficulty blending the two lives and ways of thinking. There are mail-order women coming and going, as well as the usual adventures and situations I manage to get myself into.

### Book 6 - Surviving Wild

Iris is my partner. Business grows, with money coming in, but causes 'complications.' I understand why I left for the wilds in the first place.

I get better at fossil hunting and have some exciting trips getting mammoth tusks and other ancient treasures. I am viewed as an expert on a few subjects and Discovery TV and reality shows contact me several times.

The new life in town causes legal issues that have been nipping at my heels off

## ABOUT THE ALASKA OFF GRID SURVIVAL SERIES

and on throughout my time in Alaska. Fish and Wildlife ask, "Why are you alone out here where we cannot keep an eye on you? We know you are up to something. What is it you have to hide? We will find out!" This mentality is that different is bad and of concern. I end up being investigated. A SWAT team shows up at my property with a dozen cars and 20 cops.

My arrest makes headlines. I'm sentenced to Federal Prison for six months as a felon. This is a stark contrast to 'Book 1-Going Wild,' where I have as much freedom as it is possible to have.

*How did I get from there to here?*

### Book 7 - Secretly Wild (This Book)

I am a convicted felon, describing life in prison from the viewpoint of someone used to freedom and the wilderness life. The same feather in the hat I wore on the cover of Ruralite magazine in 1979 is now worth five years in prison.

What do I need to do to survive here? There are classes to take, books to read, farm work to do, and people to help. There are interesting felon stories.

I observe more crime within the prison system by the system than I am accused of committing. "The prison could not survive if we operated legally," I am told by officials. I do my time. Now what? Am I a better person? I see the error of my ways. I am saved. Society is safer now.

### Book 8 - Retiring Wild

I talk about news relevant to living off the grid as an individual in the wilderness that few citizens are aware of. I adapt my business, and still have adventures, depending as much as I can on the subsistence life I love and understand that is now becoming illegal as a white man.

I ponder whether the end of my life is in agreement with the views I held dear from the beginning. I have hope that even in times of control and suppression, I can still focus on the plus side, and continue to find ways to enjoy personal freedoms and individuality.

I continue to explore choices, how to have better control of my destiny, happiness, and success. I refer to this as 'Survival.' I have few regrets, and hope my life's path as written can provide entertainment and insight.

As someone who is interested in being different, not one of the sheep, I look realistically at the rewards that choice offers, but also the price that has to be paid.

---

Please visit www.alaskadp.com for links to the books.

Visit www.milesofalaska.com to find a bio of Miles, additional photos, stories, how-to videos, handmade artwork, and raw materials for sale.

## Magazine and News Stories

*Alaska Magazine*

Alaska Magazine July 77—Survive by Miles Martin two pages, Photos. By Miles about my rescue, walk out on the Yukon River, five days at 50 below zero.

**Nomadic House Boater Have Cabin Will Travel** January 81—by Miles. Three pages, four color photos, a map. About life living on a houseboat, trapping and selling art (photo of my art), and all the adventures I have had on the river.

**Would You Make A Good Bush Homesteader?** June 86—by Miles four pages, six color pictures (One shows my custom knives.) A story I wrote about what it takes to be a homesteader.

**Surviving The Big Lonesome**— March 98—by Jim Rearden five pages, two color photos, one double page photo of Miles. Photos by world-famous photographer Jean Erick Pasquier. Describes life in the wilderness.

*GEO Magazine*

GEO in Germany is like "National Geographic" in the US.

**Life in The Wilderness Alaska Special**—87 by Miles Martin ten pages, sixteen color photos, a map

Photos by Jean Erick, one of the best photographers in the world, I Wrote it myself, winter life in the wilderness.

**Alaska Special - 95** Einer gegen den Rest der Welt

Eight pages, seven color photos, three are double page. A follow up story to the first, written by New York Times reporter Ted Morgan, with Brigitte Helbing, photos by New York Times photographer Rex Rystedt. My fight for a lifestyle.

*The New York Times*

**New York Times Magazine** an insert to the paper, April 17, 1994, section six, The Vexing Adventures of the Last Alaskan Bushrat.

Six pages, four color photos, one is a double page Written by New York Times writer and bestselling author Ted Morgan. Photos by Rex Rystedt (World-renowned photographer). Facing twenty years in jail and a $10,000 fine for putting artwork on a bear claw and selling it.

**Book-- A Shovel Full of Stars** 95—Published by Simon and Schuster — New York

By Ted Morgan about ten pages with Miles. About one of the last homesteaders, and the lifestyle I live, of a Subsistence person.

*Ruralite Magazine*

Put out by Golden Valley 180,000 circulation
   **Wild Miles August 79**, two pages, four black and white photos, Full cover page photo of Miles doing artwork. Story and photos by Margaret Van Cleve — Mostly about my artwork, some about my lifestyle on a houseboat

*Newspaper, Daily Newsminer, Fairbanks Alaska*

Associated Press, date unreadable, think a Thursday, and think spring of circa 74 **'Trapper rescued by Chopper**; Vows to Return to the Bush' headline, one column, National news, about my rescue after five days walking at 50 below.

*Alaska Trapper Magazine*

Put out by Alaska Trappers Association, a cover photo of me with Wolf. Five-page story by Miles comparing snowmachine and snowshoe trapping Nov. 99—four pages. Over the years, another six-seven articles on various trapping and related issues. Contact organization for exact issues.

Me in 1975.

# OTHER TITLES AVAILABLE FROM ALASKA DREAMS PUBLISHING

Visit www.alaskadp.com to see these titles.

**Books by Miles Martin:**

- Going Wild
- Gone Wild
- Still Wild
- Beyond Wild
- Back To Wild
- Surviving Wild
- Secretly Wild
- Retiring Wild

**Titles by other ADP authors:**

- Rookie
- Alaska Freedom Brigade
- Apache Snow
- In Search of Honor
- A Coming Storm
- Arizona Rangers Series – Blake's War
- Legend of Silene
- Inspiring Special Needs Stories
- My Life In The Wilderness
- All Over The Road
- Ghost Cave Mountain
- Inside the Circle
- The Silver Horn of Robin Hood
- Alaskan Troll Eggs
- Through My Eyes
- The Professional Ghost Investigator
- The Adventures of Jason and Bo
- Seeds Of The Pirate Rebels

# NOTES

## CHAPTER 1

1. If it were not for a diary and record keeping I would not recall. Few of us do. Prison, like war, becomes a blank space filled with nightmares after it is over.
2. Two years from now I have a heart attack, directly related to high blood pressure and poor care. The problem took a while to develop.
3. Several years from now in the news are a series of unexplained unusual deaths that make the Fairbanks news. Cover ups, inquires, film footages, new evidence, more inquires , a series of indignations, getting to the bottom of, needing to change things, prison reform. Talk, little action, and then silence again.
4. I am adaptable. If there is a workable law and order I participate and fit in. If there is no law and order, I grasp this, and fit into that situation as well. Sanity is preferred, but survival is the objective
5. Studies I read show 90% of drug users do so responsibly. Drug health problems tend to have more to do with contaminants due to no regulations. 'The war on drugs' has proven to make the situation worse. I believe the government is the biggest drug dealer in the country. There are sheep who wish, even need to be lead. Many need, or enjoy an escape.

## CHAPTER 2

1. In all my time here I never once felt intimidated, threatened, scared, unsafe, due to other prisoners. We seem to all try to make the best of a situation we find ourselves in. This is not so of the general population or the state institution I was in.
2. "Do you feel like you are getting your money's worth at $80,000 for each one of us to be here?" I'd ask taxpayers.
3. My locker was never inspected. Maybe there are snitches pointing out 'problem people.' "Miles is ok," is hopefully the word getting put out.

## CHAPTER 3

1. Two years from now I get an email from him! he survived prison! Says I'm the only one he has contacted, and appreciated the help and friendship I showed him. He'd like his boys to come to Alaska and meet me.
2. Doyon, the local Nenana Native Corporation, is partnered up with British Petroleum exploring for and finding, gas and oil in the Nenana area.

## CHAPTER 4

1. Later in life I see a documentary. A bunch of hippies in the 60's started a commune in a remote wilderness. They decided to take up 'glass blowing.' At the time, a trippy far out fun thing. That caught on, attracted some of the best glass blowers in the world. Today is a college, based on the same principals established in the beginning. Learning is fun.
2. Covered well in my early books in the series, book one 'Going Wild.'
3. Fairbanks News Miner Nov. 5th 2015. Survey: Half of Black populations are familiar with police abuse. 54% of minorities surveyed report having personal experience with police abuse. "Victimized by violence or harassment from law enforcement."

# NOTES

4. Many including myself, do not believe President Obama got a majority of votes. The voting computers were hacked into. The subject at hand is trust.

## CHAPTER 5

1. I talk to a politician friend later in life who says, "If we keep former inmates poor and disarmed it is less likely they will ever become a government threat again. It's also easier and workable to buy competitive citizens off, rather than have them as rivals or complainers. It is hard to be rebellious when you depend on government hand outs. We have a chain to yank. The choice is to get bought off or go to jail. The outcome is the same for us."
2. In a previous book I mention a beginning internet business with a first customer. I sell him a moose leg bone five inches long for $30! I took it from a wild dog in the street. The joke was on me. This customer added $100 more value to his custom knife saying, "Wolf chewed bone from an Alaskan wilderness moose."

## CHAPTER 6

1. Covered well in the previous book.
2. The programs and help vary. It comes and goes, have different requirements. We decided the details need to remain our private business.

## CHAPTER 7

1. I assume he can't do his job and ends up making up names, numbers, interviews, that never took place. I get a long distance call almost a year from now, asking me if someone from the census interviewed me. Did I indeed take him to remote cabins. I didn't, but do not want either some flunky person low on the totem pole to get fired over it, or have someone else come out to do the job right. Nor do I wish to get caught in a lie. I get asked," Exactly what cabins and who was there?" I said, "You'll have to talk to my lawyer." And hung up.
2. As I edit, yesterday a teen at the student living center hung herself. It might have been good if she had an adult around she trusted, like a local elder mentor who could offer sober advice, from someone who cared and has her best interest in mind. She did not wish to be civilized. She missed her village life. Her village does not have a high school. She'd rather be dead, then made White.
3. Those days on the houseboat, small engines, no money, are covered well in the previous books in this series.

## CHAPTER 8

1. Most civilized people I know have many friends and relationships. They do not agree good fences make good neighbors as I do. "What's the big deal Miles? Geez!" So this is the 'Geez big deal.' I spend time to go into the details.
2. In truth I graduated from high school with a B+ average. Having the set back of moving a lot, not enjoying school and not trying very hard. When my father passed away and I saw his records, I discover my grades were the same as his.

## CHAPTER 10

1. I had this discussion with a registered hunting guide in 2015. He tells me he has to get a special permit if his clients take a photograph of scenery on federal land, because he is in business. If you take a picture of Mt. Denali, wildlife, lakes, water in the park, or any federal land, you need a permit to sell

## NOTES

the pictures. He assumes, the same as if you were on someone else's property, or in someone's store taking pictures.
2. Well told in previous books in this series.
3. As previously mentioned I think, a year from now I have a heart attack. Problems are developing and I know it. The doctors did not agree, but I knew something was very wrong.
4. A year from now I trade the needed weld work for a custom knife.

## CHAPTER 11

1. Several long discussions in my early books in this series when I worked with a fur dealer and hunting guide, as a fire fighter when I was 23.

## CHAPTER 12

1. I'm not sure how many layers and how deep to go here with all the names. Who is related to, friends with, has an issue with, who. In truth I am impacted by thousands of people. Surely I cannot name them all. How much will it take to scrape the surface of the dynamics of any small community? All our stories intertwine.

www.ingramcontent.com/pod-product-compliance
Lightning Source LLC
Chambersburg PA
CBHW061603110426
42742CB00039B/2621